The Complete Handbook of
Profitable Trade Show Exhibiting

The Complete Handbook
of Profitable
Trade Show Exhibiting

by

Christine Christman

PRENTICE HALL
Englewood Cliffs, New Jersey 07632

Prentice-Hall International (UK) Limited, *London*
Prentice-Hall of Australia Pty. Limited, *Sydney*
Prentice-Hall Canada, Inc., *Toronto*
Prentice-Hall Hispanoamericana, S.A., *Mexico*
Prentice-Hall of India Private Limited, *New Delhi*
Prentice-Hall of Japan, Inc., *Tokyo*
Simon & Schuster Asia Pte. Ltd., *Singapore*
Editora Prentice-Hall do Brasil, Ltda., *Rio de Janeiro*

© 1991 *by*
Christine Christman

All rights reserved. No part of this
book may be reproduced in any form or
by any means, without permission in
writing from the publisher.

10   9   8   7   6   5   4   3   2   1

Library of Congress Cataloging-in-Publication Data

Christman, Christine.
    The complete handbook of profitable trade show exhibiting / by
Christine Christman.
       p.   cm.
    Includes bibliographical references (p.   ) and index.
    ISBN 0-13-155722-X
    1. Exhibitions. 2. Marketing. I. Title.
T396.C49 1991
659.1′52—dc20
                                      90-23919
                                          CIP

ISBN 0-13-155722-X

PRENTICE HALL
BUSINESS & PROFESSIONAL DIVISION
A division of Simon & Schuster
Englewood Cliffs, New Jersey 07632

Printed in the United States of America

This Book is Dedicated to
Robert F. Kuemmerle
and
Charlotte L. Kuemmerle

What This Book
Can Do for You

Trade shows as sales and marketing media provide unparalleled opportunities for making *face-to-face* contact with a great number of prospects in a short period of time. It is because of that face-to-face opportunity that trade shows are being accepted as a unique and vital component of the corporate marketing communications mix.

Yet, this sophisticated media has been underestimated and misunderstood by so many marketing experts, that few companies truly use it most effectively. Trade shows are a demanding media. Using them correctly goes far beyond getting the exhibit set up and finding someone to do booth duty. In this book you will find everything you need to manage trade shows for optimal results, from how to select the right shows to setting up and managing a corporate exhibits department.

And, this book is designed the way trade show planning functions: on a time line. Whether you have participated in one trade show or one hundred, you know that in the trade show world more than anywhere else, time is money. In this time-driven activity, missed deadlines not only cause frustration, they also cost money. This book will help you avoid those costs by helping you organize your time.

If trade shows are your only responsibility, time management is critical or you are likely to be overrun with details. If trade shows are just one of many responsibilities for you, time management is even more important. And if you are a sales manager, marketing communications manager, or administrator, this book will help you organize the trade show function as a systematic part of your job.

This book is divided into two sections. The first section is about planning for show participation. Starting 18 months in advance of the show, it takes you through each step of preparation, along with post-show evaluations. It includes a planning time line, calendar, and checklists to help you quickly and directly apply the schedule here to your own program. The second section is about program management. It provides guidelines and tools for managing the corporate exhibits department.

Organize Show Participation. Section I is organized on a timeline with a calendar to help you plan the time-driven logistics of your own program, even as you are reading. The calendar is designed so you can plot the date of each show you plan to attend, and, working back from that date, plot the date by which each of the essential planning tasks will need to be accomplished. If you use the calendar as you are reading the book, by the time you finish Part I you will have your planning timeframe plotted out. Section I will:

- **Guide You in Your Planning.** This is the only book that *walks you, step-by-step*, through the process of trade show planning. It begins with a guide for writing a trade show plan which becomes the tool you will use in planning every other component of your trade show strategy. The plan will walk you through goal-setting for all aspects of your show participation.

- **Show You How to Purchase Exhibits That Work for You.** This book shows you how to *buy smart* when purchasing a new exhibit. Will the new exhibit meet your objectives for the next three years, not just this year? This book will help you assure that it will.

- **Take You from Plans to Actions.** This book shows you how to *make key decisions* to put a trade show plan into action. It shows you how to evaluate promotional opportunities, select show services and prepare budgets, and more.

- **Help You Create Strategies That Work.** This book helps you *operationalize* your show strategy—getting the exhibit design approved, creating the selling action plan, creating the best promotions strategy, planning for inquiry processing and selecting the exhibit staffing team that will work for you, not against you.

- **Get You Organized, Keep You Organized.** This book prompts you to *remember the important details* and keep them organized. You will learn how to conduct an exhibit preview, create a checklist for exhibit set-up, manage your new exhibit construction project, and implement your promotions strategy.

- **Trouble-Shoot.** This book will help you *trouble-shoot* on the show floor. It shows you what to do when crates are missing, workers aren't working, or graphics don't arrive. It gives you a list of help points for trouble spots.

- **After the Show.** This book walks you through *post-show procedures* such as auditing invoices, finalizing show budgets, tracking leads to sales, and using staffer evaluations.

Program Management. This is the focus of Section II. It is designed to help you organize your long-range thinking about your trade show program and evaluate programs you might wish to put into place. It will include a checklist for evaluating the effectiveness of your programs and areas you wish to improve. It includes instruction and tools on managing: budgets, personnel, exhibit staffers, leads, exhibit properties, and communicating your show program to upper management.

It then takes you beyond the day-to-day operations of your program to thinking about how it contributes to your company's overall objectives. It includes an evaluation tool to measure the contribution this program makes to your corporate goals, and case study examples to help you see future possibilities for the program. It also includes tools and checklists to help you set long-range goals that will significantly contribute to your company's growth. Section II will show you how to:

- **Organize the Exhibits Department.** This book also helps you *manage growth* in your exhibits department. Is a separate department necessary? Where does it fit in the overall company structure? How are budget allocations determined? Who should be hired to staff the department?

- **Create a Complete Lead Tracking Program.** This book will help you *analyze your lead processing* function. What works and what doesn't? Should you computerize trade show leads? What else can the lead tracking system do? How you can get salespeople to participate more in lead tracking.

- **Build the Exhibit Staff Team.** This book will help you *gain more control in the staffing function* of your exhibits program. You will learn how to work with sales managers to get the best staffers, how to determine the number of staffers you need, how to build a strong staffer team, and how to evaluate their performance.

- **Manage Exhibit Properties.** This book examines the *management of exhibit properties*. It will help you evaluate how much you should be doing in-house and how much to safely turn over to your supplier.

- **Work with Management.** This book shows you how to *get upper management involved* in successful trade show participation. It tells you how to listen to them, get them to contribute, and get them to listen to you.

- **Evaluate New Opportunities.** This book looks beyond the day-to-day details of trade show logistics to *examine growth opportunities* for your company's trade show program. It will show you how to evaluate new opportunities, reach new markets, and find new ways to make trade shows a revenue-generating activity for your company.

Christine Christman

Acknowledgments

I would like to thank the scores of exhibits managers and industry suppliers who have taken time through the years to share their ideas, tips, insights, and expertise with me. It is from those many conversations and interviews that this book is created.

Special thanks must go to four people who made significant contributions to this book. To Lee Knight, publisher of the *Exhibitor Magazine*, who pioneered the ideas for much of the high quality information available in the industry today. To Diane K. Weintraub, president of Communique Exhibitor Education, Inc., for her role in my own education as well as that of many of today's trade show industry leaders. And finally, to Dick Swandby and Skip Cox of Exhibit Surveys, Inc. for countless hours spent shedding light on the statistical perspective on trade show marketing.

And, of course, thank you Roy and Kate.

Table of Contents

SECTION I: PLANNING AND IMPLEMENTING SHOW PARTICIPATION

SECTION II: MANAGING THE EXHIBITS DEPARTMENT

I

PLANNING
AND IMPLEMENTING
SHOW PARTICIPATION

THE SCHEDULING CALENDAR

Use the calendar to organize the seemingly infinite tasks and details that make a show successful. It is designed to interpret the timeline format of the book to your show schedule.

Ideally, you should plan for show activities 12 to 18 months in advance and the calendar is designed to allow you to do that in rolling quarters. It is set up with one quarter (three months) on each page. At the end of one quarter simply remove that page and add a clean page to the end of your calendar to schedule for the new quarter. If you work on an 18-month rolling quarter schedule you will have six pages in your calendar at any given time. If you work on a 12-month rolling quarter schedule you will use four pages at any given time.

Invest an hour here, and you will have the time management plan for your show. You will be able to see at a glance what needs to be accomplished each month prior to the show.

And it is easy to use. Just follow these six steps.

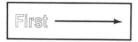

1. Use the Timeframe Checklist on page 5 to determine activities you will need to accomplish for this particular show. (You won't be doing all of the activities discussed in the book for every show you attend. For example, if you are planning for a new exhibit structure, you will probably schedule the related activities just for the first show in which it will be used.) Also add activities that are not included on the standard checklist, but are specific to your show program.

2. After you have checked off the activities, pencil them into the appropriate timeframe sections on your calendar (sample calendar is on page 8). Put the show dates on the calendar first, and then work backward to schedule each activity.

3. Adjust your calendar to accommodate dates you have already missed.

4. Repeat the process for each show for which you are planning.

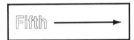

5. Add new shows to the schedule as they are selected. The calendar can be updated on a show-by-show basis.

6. When the schedule is completed fill out the Monthly "To Do" Checklist: Work down the schedule vertically to list the items that will be completed for each month. This will give you a month-by-month checklist of tasks to complete (which you can organize by week if you care to get more specific).

The schedule is designed to be flexible. The timeframes recommended here allow the optimum amount of time to complete tasks. Trade show activities being what they are, you will undoubtedly find that some tasks will have to be accomplished in shorter timeframes. If your timeframe for a project doesn't match that outlined here, simply adjust the calendar to meet your requirements.

| First ——→ | For information on using this checklist see the show Scheduling Calendar instructions. |

TIMEFRAME CHECKLIST

SHOW: _____

	YES	NO	TIME
1. SELECT SPACE	☐	☐	12 Months
2. PREPARE OPERATIONAL PLANS	☐	☐	12 Months
3. NEW EXHIBIT GOAL-SETTING	☐	☐	9 Months
4. NEW EXHIBIT BUDGET	☐	☐	9 Months
5. SELECT EXHIBIT SUPPLIER	☐	☐	9 Months
6. FINALIZE EXHIBIT SUPPLIER	☐	☐	6 Months
7. EVALUATE PROMOTION OPPORTUNITIES	☐	☐	6 Months
8. SELECT SHOW SERVICES	☐	☐	6 Months
9. PREPARE SHOW BUDGET	☐	☐	6 Months
10. PLAN STAFFER MEETING	☐	☐	6 Months
11. PLAN DESIGN PRESENTATION	☐	☐	5 Months
12. PLAN PROMOTIONS STRATEGY	☐	☐	5 Months
13. PLAN INQUIRY PROCESSING	☐	☐	5 Months
14. SELECT TRANSPORTATION & INSTALLATION FIRMS	☐	☐	5 Months
15. FINALIZE EXHIBIT DESIGN	☐	☐	4 Months

	YES	NO	TIME
16. PLAN DIRECT MAIL PROMO	☐	☐	4 Months
17. IMPLEMENT LEAD PROCESSING	☐	☐	4 Months
18. PLAN THE SITE VISIT	☐	☐	4 Months
19. SELECT EXHIBIT STAFFERS	☐	☐	4 Months
20. MANAGE EXHIBIT PRODUCTION	☐	☐	3 Months
21. IMPLEMENT PROMO STRATEGY	☐	☐	3 Months
22. PREPARE PRE-SHOW MEMO	☐	☐	3 Months
23. SELECT PORTABLE EXHIBIT SUPPLIER	☐	☐	3 Months
24. EXHIBIT PREVIEW	☐	☐	2 Months
25. PLAN DIRECT MAIL PACKAGE	☐	☐	2 Months
26. PLAN EXHIBIT SET-UP	☐	☐	2 Months
27. SELECT PORTABLE STRUCTURE	☐	☐	2 Months
28. NEW GRAPHICS (PORTABLE)	☐	☐	2 Months
29. CHECKLIST FOR SET-UP	☐	☐	1 Month
30. SEND D.M. PACKAGE	☐	☐	1 Month
31. PREPARE ORIENTATION MTG.	☐	☐	1 Month
32. PORTABLE PREVIEW	☐	☐	1 Month
33. AUDITING INVOICES	☐	☐	Post-show

	YES	NO	TIME
34. LEAD FULFILLMENT/ TRACKING	☐	☐	Post-show
35. FINALIZE SHOW BUDGET	☐	☐	Post-show
36. _____	☐	☐	
37. _____	☐	☐	
38. _____	☐	☐	

Second →	Third →	Fourth →	Fifth →

Qrtr. _____ 1 _____ FY __'91__

_____JAN._____ ___FEB___ __MARCH__

Show Name/Dates

SHOW # 1 JAN. 5-8 1992	SELECT SPACE	SET GOALS FOR EXHIBIT DESIGN	
SHOW # 2 JUNE 6-9 1992	COMPLETE SHOW PLAN		

Qrtr. _____2_____ FY _'91_

APRIL _MAY_ _JUNE_

Show Name/Dates

	APRIL	MAY	JUNE
SHOW # 2 JUNE 6-9 '92			SELECT SPACE

Qrtr. _____ 3 _____ FY '91

Show Name/Dates	JULY	AUGUST	SEPT.
SHOW #1 JAN. 5-8 1992	1. EVALUATE PROMOTION OPPORTUNITIES 2. SELECT SHOW SERVICES 3. PREPARE SHOW BUDGETS 4. SCHEDULE PRE-SHOW MEETING	1. EXHIBIT DESIGN APPROVAL 2. PLAN PROMOTIONAL STRATEGY 3. PLAN INQUIRY PROCESSING	1. PLAN DIRECT MAIL PROMOTION 2. GET LEAD PROCESSING IN PLACE 3. PLAN SET-UP 4. SELECT STAFFERS
SHOW #2 JUNE 6-9 1992			1. SET GOALS FOR NEW EXHIBIT 2. ESTABLISH BUDGET FOR NEW EXHIBIT 3. SELECT EXHIBIT BUILDER 4. REVIEW EXHIBITOR MANUAL

Qrtr. _____ 4 _____ FY '91

Show Name/Dates	OCTOBER	NOVEMBER	DECEMBER
SHOW #1 JAN. 5-8 1992	1. EXHIBIT PREVIEW 2. PREPARE PRE-SHOW MEMO 3. CHECK PORTABLE EXHIBIT	1. IMPLEMENT DIRECT MAIL PROGRAM 2. PLAN SET-UP 3. PLAN GRAPHICS FOR PORTABLE DISPLAY	1. PREPARE SET-UP CHECKLIST 2. SEND DIRECT MAIL PROMOTIONS 3. PREPARE PRE-SHOW MEETING
SHOW #2 JUNE 6-9 1992			1. SELECT EXHIBIT SUPPLIER 2. EVALUATE PROMOTIONAL OPPORTUNITIES 3. SELECT SHOW SERVICES 4. PREPARE SHOW BUDGET 5. PLAN PRE-SHOW MEETING

Qrtr. _____/_____   FY '92

	JANUARY	FEBRUARY	MARCH
Show Name/Dates			
SHOW #1 JAN. 5-8	SHOW DATES 5-8	1. FULFILL LEADS 2. SEND STAFF EVALUATION	1. AUDIT SHOW INVOICES 2. COMPLETE BUDGET SUMMARIES
SHOW #2 JUNE 6-9 1992	1. EXHIBIT DESIGN APPROVAL 2. CREATE PROMOTIONS STRATEGIES 3. PLAN INQUIRY PROCESSING	1. FINAL EXHIBIT DESIGN 2. PLAN DIRECT MAIL PROMOTION 3. GET LEAD PROCESSING IN PLACE 4. PLAN SET-UP 5. SELECT STAFF	1. EXHIBIT CHECK 2. SCHEDULE PROMOTIONS 3. CREATE/SEND PRE-SHOW MEMO 4. SELECT PORTABLE EXHIBIT SUPPLIER

Qrtr. _____ 2 _____ FY _'91_

APRIL	MAY	JUNE

Show Name/Dates

SHOW #2 JUNE 6-9	1. EXHIBIT PREVIEW	1. CONFIRM CHECKLIST	SHOW #2 JUNE 6-9
	2. CREATE DIRECT MAIL PROMOTION	2. SEND DIRECT MAIL PROMOTION	
	3. PREPARE SET-UP CHECKLIST	3. PREPARE PRE-SHOW MEETING	
	4. SELECT PORTABLE STRUCTURE	4. PORTABLE EXHIBIT PREVIEW	

Sixth ⟶

For information on how to use this form see the Scheduling Calendar instructions.

MONTHLY "TO DO" LIST

MONTH: _Dec. '91_

- ☐ Prepare set-up checklist for #1
- ☐ Prepare pre-show meeting for #1
- ☐ Send direct mail promotions for #1
- ☐ Select supplier for new exhibit
- ☐ Evaluate promotion opportunities for #2
- ☐ Select show services for #2
- ☐ Prepare show budget for #2
- ☐ Plan pre-show meeting for #2
- ☐ _____
- ☐ _____
- ☐ _____
- ☐ _____
- ☐ _____
- ☐ _____
- ☐ _____
- ☐ _____

Chapter 1: You are here:

	18 Mo.	12 Mo.	9 Mo.
Planning	Create strategic plan	Create Operational Plans	
Goal-Setting	Set long-range objectives	Set short-term, show-by-show goals	
Budgeting		Establish resource needs Create show budget estimates	
Promo-tions	Review current promotions mix	Plan promotion strategy	
Product Demos	Determine products exhibited	Decide on product demos	
Exhibits		Plan exhibit structure	Set goals and budget for new structure Select supplier
Install-ation			
Staffing		Plan staffing needs	
Inquiry Process-ing			
Measuring Results		Determine how results will be measured	

1

Strategic Planning: How to Set Long-Range Objectives and Identify Target Markets (18 Months in Advance)

Note: This section of the book is designed to step you through a timeline for show planning and therefore is divided, not by topic, but by timeframe. To use the content most efficiently, first read the introduction about scheduling show tasks.

Success with trade shows depends, to a large degree, on your perspective. The function of trade shows in a company can be viewed one of two ways. It can be viewed as a singular isolated event. Or it can be viewed as a key component of the company's marketing communications mix, implemented to contribute to specific goals in both the long- and short-term objectives of the company.

How does your company view shows? Most handle shows as though they were only isolated events. In that case the only planning required is strictly operational planning: which exhibit should you use, how will you get it to the show and get it set-up, etc.?

Companies with the hardest-working trade show dollars view shows the second way, as an integral part of the total sales and marketing strategy. And this requires a different type of planning altogether. It requires strategic planning that applies marketing principles to trade show participation.

For the second type of company, a basic strategic analysis provides the foundation to determine exactly how trade shows as a marketing communications medium can further the company's goals and objectives. In this type of planning an entirely different set of questions are asked. Questions about corporate image objectives, product positioning, and market penetration become steering elements that guide decisions about show participation.

Creating a *complete* Trade Show Plan requires answering both types of questions: strategic and operational. Determining how trade shows will contribute to long-range corporate objectives is accomplished in the Strategic Planning Process. The Strategic Plan then becomes the foundation that supports the Operational Plan. Making decisions about specific shows, setting goals for those shows, and measuring performance on a show-by-show basis is the Operational Planning Process.

What Is the Trade Show Plan? The Trade Show Plan is a document that puts all of the reasons for show participation, and the resulting strategy for each show, down on paper. It is frequently created in the trade show or marketing communications department, approved by upper management, and used as a tool to communicate with other divisions or departments within the company.

More specifically, a thorough show plan includes a Strategic Plan and a set of Operational Plans which are explained in detail in Chapters 1 and 2. Strategic planning is done once, and reviewed and updated each quarter for shows 18 months out. It covers participation in all shows. An Operational Plan is created for *each* show in which you participate. It includes specific goals for that show and plans for implementing those goals. The Operational Plan typically covers at least the following seven categories.

1. Show audience statistics and past performance reports.
2. Goals for show participation.
3. The Communications Message for this show.
4. The exhibit structure and graphics used to communicate this message.
5. Product displays, demonstrations, and presentations.
6. Promotional plan for this show.
7. Budget estimates.

You may also want to add a section on installation/dismantle, which would include preliminary details such as space size and location, space contract, official show contractor name, etc. However, many exhibitors prefer keeping installation/dismantle details in a separate notebook, a Site Book, which they take to the show.

Organizational Tip: Keep your Trade Show Plan in a large
looseleaf binder. The first tab or section will be the Strategic
Plan section. Behind that include a section for the Operational
Plan for each show, divided by the seven categories indicated
above (or more as your plan requires.) Your "Trade Show Plan
Notebook" will be dynamic and you will add Operational Plans
as they are completed for shows and take out sections to file
when the shows are over.

Chapter 1 will cover the Strategic Planning Process. Chapters 2
through 11 will cover Operational Planning and tactics for implementing
the Operational Plan. In this chapter you will see:

1. A DEFINITION: What is Strategic Planning for Trade Shows?
2. THE CORPORATE STRATEGIC PLAN: How it differs from, yet contributes to, the trade show plan.
3. MARKETING DIRECTION: How to interpret sales and marketing strategies for trade show objectives.
4. THE MISSION STATEMENT: How to prepare a mission statement for trade show participation.
5. THE STRATEGIC PLAN: A worksheet and outline for preparing the Strategic Plan.
6. TARGET MARKETS: How to find and evaluate target audiences in trade show opportunities.

INTRODUCTION TO STRATEGIC PLANNING FOR TRADE SHOW PARTICIPATION

Most simply put, the Strategic Plan defines the mission or purpose of
trade show efforts as they contribute to long-term objectives for corporate growth. The goal of strategic planning is to identify target markets
that can be reached through trade show marketing, long-range objectives
for reaching those markets, and define a communications message for
those markets.

Strategic planning by its very nature is long range and visionary. The
strategic plan is prepared for shows—not just in the following year—but
18 months down the road. It is reviewed and updated each quarter for
shows 18 months out. This is important because the Strategic Plan
becomes the road map for show participation planning, which most often
begins with space selections 12 months in advance of the show.

Eighteen months in advance might seem extremely early for preparing the Strategic Plan. Especially when Trade Show Bureau statistics say

that the majority of exhibitors begin planning for shows just three to four months in advance. But a few of the advantages that can be realized by early planning include:

1. Space selection is often held a year in advance of the show, and getting prior approval for show selection (which is an integral component of Strategic Planning) will make that selection more accurate, helping to avoid late changes and unnecessary expenses.

2. Getting necessary input for show participation from other departments is an ongoing struggle. The earlier people begin thinking about it, the better.

3. Getting necessary management approval for show selection early helps to avoid last-minute disagreements that can delay progress at critical points.

How You Will Use the Strategic Plan

This plan will be your reference guide for all of the remaining decisions you make about show participation. If you are a corporate trade show department with separate divisional departments, the Strategic Plan points everyone in the same direction. It sets the corporate direction for trade show functions which are often implemented on a divisional level. If you plan all shows, it becomes a guiding beacon for setting specific show goals and creating the Operational Plans.

Not for Executives Only

To identify the task of up-front planning for trade shows, the term strategic planning has been borrowed from the disciplines of executive management. But don't worry about having to make decisions or set directions that are typically handled by the executive team. What you will be doing is identifying the direction and strategies that have been set, and then interpreting them for the exhibits program.

But before you get started, it will be useful to review the concept of corporate strategic planning, and what executives consider when they create a strategic plan. In their book "The Executive Guide to Strategic Planning," Below, Morrisey, and Acomb list seven elements of the corporate strategic plan:(1)

1. Organization mission
2. Strategic analysis
3. Strategy
4. Long-term objectives
5. Integrated programs

(1)Chapter footnotes are at the back of the book, beginning page 461.

6. Financial projections

7. Executive summary.

There are some important differences between corporate strategic planning and the type of strategic planning you will do for trade shows. Corporate strategic planning typically considers five and ten years into the future. You will only be considering 18 months into the future. The goal for the corporate strategic plan is to set long-range objectives and directions for the company. By contrast, the goal for your strategic plan is to interpret those objectives as they relate to the trade show environment. Corporate strategic planning defines objectives for all functions of the company from R&D to human resources. Your Strategic Plan will focus primarily on sales- and marketing-related objectives.

As you embark on the research required to identify corporate long-range objectives, keep the variance in timeframes in mind. Be sure that you are interpreting the job requirements for the next 18 months that will contribute to long-range goals that are set for five or ten years into the future.

Four Steps to Creating the Strategic Plan

Creating the strategic plan is an exercise in getting to know your company and products. For example, do you know how different products within your company are perceived in their various markets? Do you know what market share they currently hold? Do you know the long-range plans for the corporation? Answering these, along with other questions, helps to clearly bring into view the role which trade shows play in the overall sales and marketing functions of the company.

Strategic planning will follow a four-step process. First you will take a step back to get an overview of the corporate direction by considering the nature of your business, corporate positioning, and corporate direction. Second, you will step in a bit closer to review the sales and marketing structure of your company and how it influences and directs the trade show function. Third, you will look specifically at how trade shows will work within and contribute to the corporate *and* sales and marketing objectives of the company, identifying target markets and related shows for participation. Fourth, you will organize the plan as a working document.

Step One: The Corporate Overview

Begin by answering the following questions:

1. **What business are we in?** Answer this question as succinctly, yet specifically, as possible. It is important because a company's view of its

own business will limit or encourage its growth. For example, a company that once sold cardboard file boxes saw its business take off when it determined it was not in the cardboard file business but in the records storage business. If your corporation has a "mission statement" it should clearly answer this question for you.

2. **What is our corporate position in the marketplace?** Where does the company image stand as compared with that of the competition? If you work for a small company with a single product line, product image and corporate image may be one and the same. But if you work for a larger company with multiple product lines, the corporate image is going to be distinct from that of any single product or product line. When there is a discrepancy between corporate and product image, focus here on the *corporate* image. Reviewing positions of specific products will be covered later.

   Reality is important here, so don't guess. This is part of the strategic analysis step in corporate strategic planning. For many companies, this type of analysis is a basic component of advertising planning. You probably have a department in your company, or at least a person, who has done some research here and given it some thought. Talk to them and review results of any research that is available to you.

3. **What are the long-range objectives of the company?** Just to emphasize the point, *you* won't be making these decisions, but knowing what they are is the only way you will be able to plan a trade show program that contributes to those objectives. The following are examples of corporate long-range objectives:

   - To be a $200 mm company in ten years.
   - To establish the company as a leading supplier of X products in X industry in five years.
   - Introduce X products to new markets with at least 30% of those products' revenues coming from newly defined markets.
   - To change perceptions of the company from technology supplier to service supplier in X markets in five years.
   - Move from product-based sales structure to market-based sales structure within five years.

Since many of the long-range objectives will not relate to the trade show function, part of your job is to identify those objectives to which the trade show function can contribute. Most of them will either be *sales* or *marketing* objectives. Any of those listed above are objectives to which trade shows could contribute.

After you have identified long-range corporate objectives, spend some time thinking about the long-range trade show objectives that would contribute. It's a matter of translating the objectives for the trade show function. The chart in Exhibit 1-1 offers a few examples of how to make that translation.

| **Exhibit 1-1** Translating Long-Range Objectives | |
Corporate Objectives	**Trade Show Objectives**
> Be a $200 mm company in ten years.	> Generate sales leads to contribute to revenue increases to $200 mm in ten years.
> Establish the company as a leading supplier of X products in X industry in five years.	> Identify trade show opportunities in X industry where leading supplier position will be established for X products.
> Introduce X products to new markets with at least 30% of those products' revenues generated from newly defined markets.	> Identify trade show opportunities in new markets selected. Generate sales leads for X products in those markets.
> Change perceptions of company from technology supplier to services supplier in X markets in five years.	> Commit communications message for X products at shows in X markets to build image of company as a service supplier.
> Move from product-based sales structure to market-based sales structure within five years.	> Move from product-based exhibits strategies to market-based exhibit strategies within five years.

Step Two: Review Four Components of the Sales and Marketing Strategies

Before launching into this section of the plan think for a moment about how trade shows are managed in your company. Are they perceived as a sales function and thus managed in the sales department? Or are they perceived as a marketing function and managed in the marketing or marketing communications department?

Actually trade shows are both sales and marketing functions. Trade shows are a microcosm of the sales and marketing functions of your business. Just as marketing prepares the way for sales to occur by providing direction and strategy, so too, taking a marketing approach to trade shows will lay the groundwork for shows to be used efficiently as a sales function to generate new business.

Just as defining audiences for a product, selecting target markets, and creating a promotional mix are marketing functions, so too, defining show audiences, selecting target markets at shows, and creating a promotional mix for show participation are also marketing functions.

And, once the marketing decisions and strategies have been established, the sales force takes over to sell the product. So, too, once the marketing strategies for a trade show have been put into place the sales team or exhibit staffers move in to make the strategy work.

Each component—sales and marketing—carries equal importance in using trade shows successfully. To emphasize one at the exclusion of the other leaves you with the cart and no horse.

At this point you will move in a bit closer and take a look at sales and marketing strategies in place to reach those long-range objectives. To organize your thinking, this section will be divided along the classic four components known in "Marketing 101" terminology as the Marketing Mix: product development, product position and pricing, sales and distribution, and promotion.

Component #1: Products and Product Development. At the pace companies move today it is difficult to identify product developments planned for ten years into the future. Fortunately, you won't have to worry about that. Begin by getting a fix on product plans that are *targeted* for introduction in your 18-month timeframe. Identify target markets for those products. As you will see, the target markets defined become the guidelines for identifying your potential audience at each trade show you plan to attend.

Once you have identified new products or product lines you will be working with, move on to the more familiar. Identify all existing products or product lines that will be marketed or sold through trade shows. (As the term product is used here it includes services.)

Next, determine where each product line is in its life cycle stage. A product's life cycle stage can influence everything from the amount of money allocated to its promotion at trade shows, to the amount of exhibit space used and its placement in the exhibit. The chart in Exhibit 1-2 illustrates a time line of product life cycle stages with related trade show marketing implications.

Component #2: Price and Position. The pricing and position of the product line will relate to trade shows primarily as they influence messages that are communicated through graphics, literature, and product displays. Pricing is important here, not in terms of how a product price is determined, but in terms of how the product price influences its perception in the marketplace. A variety of factors influence how a product is priced, but the end result is that the price determined will influence the marketing strategy for that product.

Exhibit 1-2   Life Cycle Stages and Trade Show Planning

Introduction	Growth	Maturity	Decline
The marketing strategy here is one of survival. The goal is to provide enough marketing support in the way of promotion so that the product will experience sales and profit growth. Therefore, trade shows may be selected just for the purpose of introducing this new product to markets. More dollars are invested in the product at this stage although the return on those dollars is yet unknown. Unfortunately many new products never get beyond the introduction stage.	As profits and sales on the product grow, there are new promotional factors to consider. Competition may be a factor now where it hadn't been in the past. As a result the entire promotional strategy, and the trade show strategy as part of it, will change. More emphasis will be placed on brand preference, thus focusing the marketing strategy on benefits over competing products rather than on the product's features alone. You may deal more with price and distribution issues. Healthy amounts of resources will still be invested in this product to see how high sales and profits will go.	At this point competition is becoming stronger and expenditures required to maintain sales continue to increase. Management may consider expanding the life cycle of this product by developing new uses for it (baking soda being a classic case). They may also choose to promote to more vertical markets. Either approach could affect your trade show strategy as you will either be presenting the product from a different vantage point or looking for new shows to meet identified vertical markets.	Here profit margins are extremely low, and competition is very intense. If products are not dropped from the line then management may choose to maintain sales and profits by reducing costs, among them promotion costs. They may not be considered at all in show strategies, or be entered in shows with a much more limited effort. Thus, if you have participated in shows where that product was the main focus, you might exclude that show from the list and allocate resources to products in different life cycle stages.

Factors that influence price/positioning strategies are market segmentations, competition's prices and positioning, and "not in kind" competitors. An example of a "not in kind competitor" would be paint companies viewing wall paper manufacturers as competitors. They are not selling the same product but they compete as a solution for the same applications.

In its simplest sense, when high costs force high prices, the product must be positioned in such a way that the higher prices are acceptable. For example, for one company higher costs are a factor of additional service provided with the product. The costs are passed on in the product price which is significantly higher than that of competing products. The company has justified that price by establishing its position as far and away superior in service to any other supplier.

Volumes have been written on the subject of product positioning, and the task identified here is certainly not to establish or define a positioning strategy. You simply need to know what strategy has been selected for various products or product lines. To determine price and positioning factors relative to specific product lines, ask the following questions:

Where Do These Products Fall in Price Range as Compared with Competing Products? The chart in Exhibit 1-3a will help you organize and categorize competing products' pricing and related positioning strategies as compared to yours. To answer this question you will only complete the left column. Write the names of each company or product on the boxes that fit their pricing (either high, medium, or low). To illustrate, the example here uses three well-known retailers. (See also Exhibit 1-3.)

What Are Our Products' Positions in the Marketplace? Based on the price established how has the product line been positioned? In the section labled "relative position," write a position statement for each product line identified (both yours and those of the competition) as clearly as you can. Their advertising and promotional messages should provide some clues. The example here illustrates how the retailers listed have positioned themselves relative to pricing strategies.

Once you have identified your pricing and positioning strategy relative to your competitors', determine future goals for that strategy. In the next 18 months will the goal be for your position to remain the same, or to be changed in some way? If changes are indicated, clearly identify the direction of those changes.

Component #3: Sales and Distribution Channels. In the sales and distribution component of the marketing mix, you are most concerned about the *channel of distribution* or how the product is sold, and will not deal with physical distribution (how it is shipped to customers). The sales and distribution strategy selected for a product can have a

Exhibit 1-3a Price and Position

	Price	Relative product positions
High $	Nieman Marcus	
Medium $	Sears	
Low $	K-Mart	

significant impact on your trade show goals and objectives, because it directly relates to how the exhibit will be staffed and how leads at trade shows will be followed up. If these two functions have not already been established, after defining the sales and distribution strategies, identify how that will affect staffing and follow-up.

For example, if you sell through third parties such as dealers or distributors, will they staff the exhibit? Will they receive leads for follow-up? Will they distribute post-show literature or will you?

The following list identifies common sales and distribution options. You may want to add your own. In the Strategic Plan worksheet you will identify sales and distribution channels for each product line.

Common Sales and Distribution Channels

1. Direct sales
2. Sales through distributors or wholesalers

Exhibit 1-3b Price and Position

Price		Relative product positions
High $	Nieman Marcus	Premium and exclusive merchandise
Medium $	Sears	The family store
Low $	K-Mart	The savings place

3. Sales through dealers and retailers
4. Sales through value-added resellers (VARs) or original equipment manufacturers (OEMs).
5. Other? _____

Component #4: Promotion. The final component of the classic
marketing mix, promotion, has perhaps the strongest implications for the
strategic trade show plan. With the value of repeat exposure strongly
established in the advertising industry, it is surprising to see that companies don't regularly integrate trade show messages with those used in
other promotional media. In fact the trade show strategy is often created
in complete isolation from other promotional strategies.

To assure that trade shows are working in concert with all promotional media and messages, take time to identify all promotional activities
for the product lines you will be exhibiting. Among them you may find:
newspaper, magazine, radio, television advertising, direct mail, store

signs, billboards, giveaways and novelties, and publicity efforts. List all media where advertising is placed, direction and key messages of that advertising, public relations efforts, and planned or scheduled press conferences for new product introductions. When applicable differentiate consumer or end-user advertising and promotional strategies from those directed at third-party vendors. Keep a file of tear sheets of ads that have been run, for reference.

This is not to say that advertisements should be exactly duplicated in exhibits. But consistency of product positioning messages throughout all promotional components will strengthen each effort.

Now that you have thought through the components of your marketing mix as they relate to trade shows, you are ready to answer two key questions that will guide your strategic plan. Then you can write the mission statement, the first step in preparing the Strategic Plan.

Will We Emphasize Individual Products in Our Show Communications, or Overall Corporate Image? This may vary from show to show, and you might in fact want to use a combination of the two with one objective being dominant over the other. Keep in mind that marketing experts recommend establishing product position first, as a basis for corporate image.

Caution: If you are a relatively young company, be sure that your product images are strong before attempting to gloss over them with a slick corporate image that has no basis in customer experience.

This is an important decision because it will influence exhibit graphics, product displays, booth size, sales presentations, even exhibit color.

One company successfully used a combination of both to boost its image as a supplier with worldwide resources and capabilities. It wanted to underscore a worldwide corporate image with a host of detailed product demonstrations. It told the corporate image story in a formal A-V presentation and the product demo stories through exhibit graphics and individual product demonstrations.

Who Do We Need to Reach in Order to Accomplish the Long-Range Objectives We've Set? Step back at this point and list all of the markets in which your products will be sold. Then consider the types of people within those markets you will need to reach to increase penetration there.

One company focused initial marketing efforts for their products on the manufacturers who installed them in their equipment. But after receiving a lukewarm response from the manufacturers, the company began educating the end user that they have a choice of products to specify when they order the equipment. Once the company began marketing to the end user it saw market share steadily increase. And trade shows turned out to be one of the most efficient vehicles for reaching that end-user market.

Is it just end users or need we be concerned about distribution channels, influencers in the industry, company influencers in the buying process? Are we targeting one market segment or several? Will we work at reaching a mass market with a general message (for example, all computer users with a new software program) or specific (niche) markets with a very customized message (for example, all accountants who use computers with a new tax program)? Do we need to target specific regions of the county or make our promotional efforts national in scope? For help here refer to Exhibit 1-4, a checklist of potential target audiences.

Exhibit 1-4   Potential Audience Checklist

Considering your potential audience at a show requires that you take into account more than just your direct customers. You may in fact have several audiences at a show that you are trying to reach. Use this checklist to determine those audiences that are important to your company.

Yes   No

1. End users
2. Retailers
3. Third-party resellers such as original equipment manufacturers (OEMs)
4. Press
5. Industry analysts
6. Consultants
7. Distributors
8. Dealers
9. Other exhibitors
10. Value added resellers
11. Specifiers
12. Purchasing agents
13. Other _____
14. Other _____
15. Other _____

By way of review, you will find a checklist in Exhibit 1-5 with a summary list of questions to answer before creating the strategic plan. If you have read through each section here of the marketing mix as it relates to trade shows, you will have begun to answer many of the questions.

Exhibit 1-5 Strategic Planning Questionnaire

STRATEGIC PLANNING
15 QUESTIONS TO ANSWER

1. What business are we in?
2. What are the long-range objectives and goals of our company?
3. What products or product lines will be displayed at trade shows?
4. Where is each product in its life cycle?
5. What is the perceived positioning image of each product in the marketplace?
6. Do we need to change those perceptions?
7. Who are our primary competitors for each product?
8. What are their product's perceived positions in the marketplace?
9. What features/benefits of their products will we need to work to overcome?
10. What are our target markets for each product?
11. Who within those target markets must we influence in order to reach our objectives?
12. Which trade shows will help us reach those target markets?
13. What types of *image* objectives can trade shows help us meet in light of our corporate goals and objectives?
14. What type of *sales* objectives can trade shows help us meet in light of our corporate goals and objectives?
15. What is our mission statement for trade show participation?

This analysis is really about using trade shows for product or corporate positioning. Companies spend millions to position their products for success in the marketplace. Taking time for this analysis provides the foundation for using trade shows to supplement carefully crafted positioning strategies.

The worksheet in Exhibit 1-6, Strategic Planning Worksheet, is designed to organize this analysis in one place. You will use it as a guide in creating the Strategic Plan.

Key Point. At trade shows you can find more exposure, more one-on-one interaction, get more feedback, and influence more people in a short period of time than with any other marketing communications medium available.

Step Three: How to Write a Mission Statement and Define Long-Range Objectives

The mission statement is a big picture statement and doesn't get into specifics. A mission statement is short; you should be able to fit it on the back of a business card. It is visionary and motivational. It summarizes how trade shows will contribute to long-range corporate objectives.

Sample Mission Statement: A quality glassware company's mission statement for the next 18 months could be as follows:

The long-term objectives of the trade show program are to support new product introductions and increase market penetration for existing products by promoting to targeted audiences and generating qualified sales leads.

With the mission statement completed, turn your attention to writing long-range objectives. Keep in mind that target markets for show participation will be identified based on the long-range objectives set. A few guidelines for writing long-range objectives:

Make Them Specific to Products or Product Lines. For example, "Introduce new unbreakable wine glasses to the pool and outdoor recreation market through dealers and retailers at targeted shows."

Make Them Specific to Industry or Target Markets. For example: "Maintain our image as an established supplier to the restaurant industry nationwide in targeted industry shows."

Make Them Specific to Tasks. For example: "Generate sales leads for increased market penetration in the following markets:

- Restaurant
- Hotel
- High-end retail"

If at this point you are having trouble defining your long-range objectives, go back to the chart in Section II that illustrates how to translate corporate long-range objectives into trade show objectives. You can create a chart of your own to organize your thoughts.

Step Four: How to Organize the Strategic Plan as a Working Document

Before writing the Strategic Plan complete the worksheet in Exhibit 1-6, keeping in mind your three goals for strategic planning: to identify target markets for product sales and promotion, to identify trade shows that provide that target market, and to identify the communications message that should be used at those shows.

Exhibit 1-6   Strategic Planning Worksheet

Trade Show Program Mission Statement:

_____

_____

_____

_____

Section I: Products and Product Developments

Complete one of these sections for each product line that will be included in trade shows.

Product Line:_____

Existing Products   New Products

_____   _____

_____   _____

_____   _____

_____   _____

Product Line's Lifecycle Stage:

Check all that apply and list products in appropriate category.
☐ Introduction: _____
☐ Growth: _____
☐ Maturity: _____
☐ Declining profits: _____

Section II: Pricing and Positioning

Competing Products

Company/Product	Price range	Position statement
_____	_____	_____
_____	_____	_____
_____	_____	_____
_____	_____	_____

Comments:_____
_____
_____

Section III: Sales/Distribution Channels
□ Direct sales
□ Distributors/wholesalers
□ Dealers/retailers
□ Third-party resellers (VARs, OEMs)
□ Other_____

How will this affect:
□ Exhibit staffing _____
□ Lead processing _____
□ Lead follow-up _____
□ Lead tracking _____

Notes:
_____
_____
_____

Section III: Existing Promotional Strategies

Advertising: Publicity:
□ Trade publications   □ Press events
□ Television   □ News releases
□ Radio   □ New product announcements
□ Billboards   □ Publications targeted for
□ Direct mail   publicity
□ Giveaways/novelties

□ Theme message for all promotional media:
_____
_____
_____

□ File of print media advertising and publicity clippings

Long-Range Objectives for Trade Show Participation

Objective #1

Objective #2

Objective #3

(Continue as necessary.)

Existing Target Markets:

_____

_____

_____

_____

New Target Markets:

_____

_____

_____

_____

Audiences Within Target Markets

Market #1	Market #2	Market #3	Market #4
_____	_____	_____	_____
_____	_____	_____	_____
_____	_____	_____	_____
_____	_____	_____	_____
_____	_____	_____	_____

At this point, most of the work required to write the Strategic Plan is complete. The only task remaining is to write in report format what you have identified on the planning worksheet. The following outline can serve as a guideline.

STRATEGIC PLAN OUTLINE

I. Introduction

Begin with a brief paragraph on the purpose of the strategic plan. Close with your mission statement for the exhibits department

II. Products

Include a section in this category for *each* product or product line. Under each product write a brief synopsis of the following.

A. Lifecycle stage

B. Competing products

C. Relative price and position

III. Sales and Distribution Channels

A. Restate here the sales and distribution channels for your products. If they vary according to product line, complete a section for each different type of channel identified and related product lines.

B. Include a brief paragraph to explain how this will influence:
    i. exhibit staffing
    ii. lead processing
    iii. lead follow-up
    iv. lead tracking

IV. Promotion Strategies

A. Include a brief paragraph for each product line describing promotional strategies currently used in other media. Indicate how you plan to build on or incorporate existing promotional strategies and themes into the exhibits program.

V. Long-Range Objectives

A. List long-range objectives for shows. If you are dealing with many product lines, you might organize objectives by product line.
B. Include a brief paragraph to describe how these objectives will contribute to corporate long-range objectives and growth.

VI. Target Markets

A. Summarize by identifying the target markets that you will attempt to reach through trade shows. You needn't identify the shows yet, just use a description of the market. For example:
    *restaurant owners
    *glassware wholesalers
    *glassware retailers
    *pool and spa dealers
B. Then review the audiences within those markets you are specifically targeting. Job titles, geographic breakdowns, or product applications provide useful guidelines here. For example:
    *owners
    *buyers
    *West coast region
    *New York City and vicinity

VII. Close

Indicate in the close that the scope of the strategic plan encompasses an 18-month timeframe and all shows in which the company participates. Indicate that operational plans will be drawn up for each show you will attend and outline some of the details they can expect to see in the operational plans. (You can include a timeframe for operational plans if you know when they will be completed.) Close with an optimistic story or comment on future contributions trade shows will make toward the company's growth.

HOW TO SELECT SHOWS TO REACH YOUR TARGET MARKETS

Now that you have identified your target markets, the next step is to evaluate shows based on how well they deliver those markets. Evaluating shows occurs at two different times. First there are the shows that you attend regularly that have become part of your ongoing show schedule. Those shows should each be evaluated shortly after you have attended them. At this time you can best determine whether you have reached show objectives and whether the show continues to provide the right audience.

Second are those new shows that you want to evaluate for potential participation. These are either new show opportunities that may come across your desk, or existing shows that you are anticipating using for the first time to reach new markets.

Show participation decisions should be made about a year in advance of the show date. For many shows this is when space reservations are made. Two types of tools are available to help you make decisions about show participation. The first is a statistical method for defining your target market at a show. The second is a list of additional judgment factors you will want to consider when determining the degree to which this particular show can contribute to your overall objectives.

How to Identify Your Target Market at Each Show

Advice from the Experts

Exhibit Surveys president Richard K. Swandby and vice president Jonathan "Skip" Cox have been advising companies on show selection for over 25 years. Here they will share with you their observations, and advice on selecting shows.

Q: What is the most common error you've seen exhibitors make when selecting shows to attend?

A: The most common error is not taking the time required to investigate the show thoroughly. This is compounded by a lack of detailed information about the audience for most shows. Companies look for a quick, easy way to make a decision about shows. But there is a lot of judgment involved because of the limited audience information available. And there is a distinct advantage to doing the investigation yourself. It allows you to understand the audience and market provided by that show which will guide many other decisions related to show participation.

Q: How do these errors affect a company's performance at a show?

A: We often hear the question "Is this the right show for us?" We've evaluated over 1,000 shows and we don't find many companies that are in the wrong shows. The challenge is reaching the people attending the show in the right way. You have to ask yourself: what are the right products to emphasize for this audience, what does the audience want? You may be going to the right show, but with the wrong products.

Q: How can a company begin to find the answers to these questions?

A: Through a fairly straightforward process that can be as simple or complex as you would care to make it. You have to begin by creating your laundry list of all shows you might attend. There are several sources of show information which will help you begin that research. Then narrow the list and contact the show managers, asking them for very specific information about the previous year's show attendance. Then examine each show individually to determine how the audience data fits with your own marketing objectives to determine whether it will be a good fit.

Techniques for Evaluating a Show Audience

Begin by going back to your long-range planning objectives to review the markets you have targeted to reach through trade shows. Select shows based on their ability to offer you the group most representing those target markets. First, simply find out which shows are available. A list of sources for show information is available in the appendix. Check your company's past trade show participation, and ask associates in other companies for more ideas.

This process is a bit like brainstorming in that you want to list as many potential shows as possible. You will narrow the list significantly as you begin doing statistical evaluation on the potential shows.

While researching shows, you can gather statistics that will help you determine their value. Unfortunately the information available on trade shows varies dramatically. The best shows offer complete statistical breakdowns of the attendees, often indicating the job titles, product interests, and geographic location of visitors. With the worst shows, you are lucky to get legitimate attendance figures. And be careful because frequently attendance figures quoted on a show may include, along with total attendees, exhibitor personnel, attendee spouses, students, press representatives, and no-show registrants.

The questionnaire in Exhibit 1-7 "Show Profile Questionnaire" will help you gather the appropriate information from a show manager or sponsor during the preliminary research. With some shows this might only require a letter requesting information on the show. For others it might require a phone call to ask the detailed questions in person. If show managers will not provide audience profiles . . . beware.

Exhibit 1-7   Show Profile Questionnaire

SHOW NAME: _____

TARGET MARKET: _____

   1. Last year's total attendance for the show: _____

   2. Last year's net attendance for the show: _____
     (Excluding exhibitor personnel, press, spouses,
     students)

   3. Last year's show site: _____

   4. Net paid square footage of space: _____

   5. Number of exhibiting companies: _____

   6. Price of exhibit space: _____

   7. Application deadline for signing up for space:_____

   Is the following information available?

	Yes	No
8. Product interest breakdown?	____	____
9. Geographic breakdown?	____	____
10. Job title breakdown?	____	____
11. Audience interest factor statistics?	____	____
12. Buying plans?	____	____
13. Directory of exhibitors?	____	____

Comments:

How to Get a True Picture from Statistics and Demographics

Your "potential audience" at a show is that percentage of the total show audience that will have a high level of interest in your products or services. There is a standard formula for calculating potential audience.(2) To calculate that figure you need at least the following information on the show. At this point you will have gathered this information from show management and can find it on your show profile questionnaire sheet.

Total Attendees: The total number of registrants for the most recent show.

Net Attendees: The total number of registrants excluding exhibitor personnel, press, spouses, students.

Product Interest: This figure represents the percentage of the total audience who had a high level of interest in your products. Custom research is available to determine product interest for your specific company and products. Industry averages are also available to use as a rule of thumb figure. For tips on calculating product interest see Exhibit 1-8, Three Ways to Determine Product Interest.

Audience Interest Factor (AIF): This is a figure calculated by Exhibit Surveys and available on the shows they survey. It indicates the percentage of show attendees who stop to talk or acquire literature at 2 out of 10 exhibits at the show. There are actually very few shows that will have AIF figures, but there are ways to calculate them which are accurate enough for your use in calculating potential audiences. For tips on discovering a show's AIF see Exhibit 1-9, Two Ways to Learn a Show's AIF.

With those numbers in hand, your two-step calculation will look like this.

Step 1: Net Attendees X Audience Interest Factor = High Interest Attendees

Step 2: High Interest Attendees × Product Interest = Potential Audience

The potential audience for each show you are considering becomes a primary factor on which you will base your attendance decision.

Calculating Potential Audience—Sample Calculation

Essential Information

Total Attendees - 20,000   Product Interest - 16%
Net attendees - 12,000   AIF - Vertical Buyer/Horizontal
                                             Seller show. Average AIF: 48%

Step One:	Net Attendees	12,000
	× AIF	× .48
	High Interest Attendees	5,760
Step Two:	High Interest Attendees	5,760
	× Product Interest	× .16
	Potential Audience	921

At this point the audience figures begin to resemble the *real* potential audience at a show. Out of a gross attendance of 20,000, the number of people with a high interest in the products or services you will display is about 900. Keep in mind that these are just estimates and not exact statistics, but they are close enough to help in making intelligent decisions about the show. Use that figure, not the 20,000, when evaluating shows for participation and planning a show strategy.

Exhibit 1-8   Three Ways to Determine Product Interest

Number One: Show Management's Audience Profile

When show management provides an audience profile, it often breaks total registration into categories such as job title, job function, and particularly product interest. When product interest breakouts are available, use those percentages. If they are not available you can use the more general job title, or industry representation breakouts, but keep in mind that your potential audience figure will probably be slightly inflated as a result.

Number Two: Use the Industry Average

As a result of making product interest calculations at thousands of shows Exhibit Surveys, Inc. has arrived at an average product interest of 16%. This means that on the average 16% of any given show audience will have a high level of interest in any single product displayed at this show. However, this statistic only represents a single product. If you display multiple products at a show, while you won't see doubling in product interest (because there is usually some overlap in interest among products), your product interest will be slightly higher.

Another factor that influences this average is whether your product is a mainline or fringe product in the industry. For example, a personal computer would be a mainline product at PC Expo and the interest in those products could be three to four times higher than the average 16%. Conversely, a personal computer used to make estimate applications for the construction industry would be a fringe product at the Homebuilders Show and the product interest might be lower than the average. You can see how the figure needs to be used with some judgment. Use this average as a ballpark figure only, since it covers a wide variety of shows and industries.

Number Three: Purchase Statistics

Professional surveys are the best way to get the most accurate information on the show audience as it relates to your market strategies. These surveys will identify audience interest levels and purchasing patterns based on your specific products. Survey prices start at $1,500 to $2,500 for syndicated studies and can run from $5,000 to $10,000 for custom studies.

Exhibit 1-9   Two Ways to Learn a Show's AIF

Number One: Show Management

Some shows contract with professional survey companies to conduct post-show surveys of their audiences. When a survey has been conducted, typically, an Audience Interest Factor has been calculated. Ask show management if they have those statistics available.

Number Two: Identify Show Type and Use Averages

When statistics aren't available on a show you can use average figures which are based on the type of exhibitors and types of audiences the show has. Shows can be broken down into four types based on whether the exhibitors and the attendees would comprise a horizontal or vertical group.

A horizontal group is one that encompasses a variety of industries or functions.

A vertical group is one that represents a single industry or function. As a result shows can be classified four ways. Each classification has its own average AIF. The following chart diagrams the four show types.

Exhibit 1-10

	Vertical Seller		Horizontal Seller	
	Vertical Buyer	Horizontal Buyer	Vertical Buyer	Horizontal Buyer
Average AIF	57%	48%	39%	35%

Help! Therefore to use averages to determine AIF for shows you are planning to attend, you have to determine whether the exhibiting companies as a group, and the audience as a group, are vertical or horizontal. Here are a few examples to help you as you think about your own shows.

Vertical Seller/Vertical Buyer—Association of Operating Room Nurses. All attendees represent one industry: operating room nurses. All exhibitors represent one industry: suppliers of medical products for the operating room.

Vertical Seller/Horizontal Buyer—ScanTech. All of the exhibitors sell products related to automated identification, bar coding being the primary example. But the attendees come from a variety of industries: retailers, manufacturers, warehouses, distribution companies, all use automated identification.

Horizontal Seller/Vertical Buyer—The Food Marketing Institute. Exhibitors represent a variety of industries trying to get their products onto grocers' shelves: food producers, automotive suppliers, greeting card companies, video rental companies. All attendees represent one industry, they are all supermarket management personnel.

Horizontal Seller/Horizontal Buyer—Plant Engineer and Maintenance. Exhibitors come from a variety of industries such as air conditioning, floor maintenance equipment, maintenance products such as cleaning products. Attendees also come from a variety of industries, because most any business in any industry deals with plant maintenance.

At this point in the evaluation process it is helpful to go back to your list of shows and calculate the potential audience for each show. The chart in Exhibit 1-11, "Show Evaluations," will help you to organize the information. The second column on the sheet is for potential audience. Evaluating the information is easier when shows are listed in order with the show providing the greatest potential audience first, and that providing the lowest potential audience last. The remaining columns will be explained in the following section.

A SECOND LOOK

This section is designed for those who are familiar with the basic concepts and are looking for new ways to apply them to their programs.

Using Attendee Statistics Creatively

Attendee profile statistics can be used in a variety of ways beyond determining potential audience at a show. The key here is to get good statistics on *Product Interest* of the show audience.

For example, if your company has multiple divisions, or multiple product lines, the product interest percentages will help you refine your show strategy by answering a few key questions.

1. Which divisions should participate or which products should be displayed? (Those with the highest interest among the audience.)
2. Should divisions participate together, or should they have separate exhibits? (Charts can be created using product interest percentages that

Exhibit 1-11 Show Evaluation Chart

Show Name	Potential Audience	Show Type			Market	Comments
		Attendees	Exhibitors	Geography		

indicate the overlap among divisions or products. Divisions or products with high overlap will benefit from exhibiting together.)

3. Where should products be located in the exhibit? (These overlap charts can even help to identify products that draw the same visitor and should be grouped together or exhibited side by side.)

These types of statistical breakouts are occasionally available from show management, but most often must be gathered through custom surveys conducted by independent research firms.

After the Statistics: Four Questions to Answer

Selecting shows based on statistics alone is sort of like using a computer service to select a mate. It only provides one dimension of the total picture. When reviewing how potential audiences at shows stack up one against another, to get the whole picture you will want to consider how a variety of nonstatistical factors affect the show's ability to contribute to show goals and long range objectives.

For example, one show may appear to offer a higher potential audience, but may be located in an area of the country which has not been targeted for new product distribution. Or show goals may include targeted penetration and certain shows would require more expense to reach that targeted percentage of a total show audience.

At this point review the long-term objectives for show participation from the Strategic Plan Worksheet and answer the following questions.

1. **What are our geographic goals for show participation?** (National, Regional, International?) The geographic distribution of show audiences varies quite a bit. There are standards by which shows are defined National, Regional, or International. However, just because a show is billed as a National show, doesn't mean it falls within those standards. This is why requesting a geographic break out of the show audience is important. The standards are as follows: (3)

    National Shows: To be considered National in scope, 60% or more of the show attendees must come from outside a 200-mile radius of the city in which the show is held.

    Regional Shows: To be considered Regional, 40% or more of the attendees will come from within a 200-mile radius of the city in which the show is held.

    International Shows: To be considered International, at least 10% of the show attendees must come from countries other than that within which the show is held.

    Keep in mind that a regional show held in Los Angeles one year and in New York the next will have significantly different groups of attendees each year. Look at each show on your Show Evaluation Chart and in the geographic column indicate whether the audience is National, Regional, or International in scope.

2. **Which distribution channels will be reached?** Review here the distribution channels identified in the strategic plan. At some shows you will be able to reach distribution channels which represent your primary market: those people to whom you sell directly. If, for example, you sell glassware to consumers, your distribution will probably be through retailers. Thus the retailers represent for you a primary market because you will sell directly to them.

Other show audiences will represent a secondary market for you, or end users of your products. In the glassware example here the consumers would represent a secondary market. (If your company sells directly to the end user, you will not have to be concerned about secondary markets.)

Reaching a primary market is typically the least expensive, most efficient way to launch distribution. However, to promote brand preference, and generate pull-through sales, it may be necessary to go to the secondary market.

Now go back to your Show Evaluation Chart and under the market column indicate whether the show offers you a primary or secondary market.

3. **Is mass exposure or vertical marketing more important?** Do we want shows that provide a broad industry representation (horizontal attendees) or a narrow, homogeneous group (vertical attendees)? Shows with horizontal audiences are good for testing new markets or new product applications. Vertical audiences are good for reaching a select group of attendees.

On the Show Evaluation Chart identify under "Attendees" whether the show provides a horizontal group, or a vertical group.

4. **Can we afford to be a small fish in a big pond?** Remember that at those shows with horizontal exhibitor groups, the percent interest in your products will probably be lower. Attendees come with very specific interest and with the variety of products on display, there will be a lower percent interest in any given product.

To succeed in the "big pond" you will have to spend more money on promotion and work harder at finding those visitors who will be interested in your products and services. At shows with vertical exhibitor groups, the percent interest in your products will probably be higher (unless you have a "fringe" product such as glassware in a swimming pool show). Therefore you will not need to promote as heavily to draw attention to your products.

On the Show Evaluation Chart evaluate each show under "Exhibitors" and indicate whether they represent a horizontal or a vertical group.

It is rare that you will have such a variety of shows from which to choose that you will be able to select one that meets all of your criteria. So before you review your chart to evaluate shows, prioritize your criteria based on the above four questions. Will finding a show that provides a primary market for you be the top priority? Or will finding a show that is national in scope be most important? After you've established those priorities review your list for those shows that provide the most qualities you need.

Key Ingredient: Friends and Neighbors

Input from people who have participated in a show, along with your own personal review of the show, most often provides quality information that statistics just don't reveal.

One of the best ways to evaluate a show is to participate as an attendee one year. Watch the traffic flow. Talk to exhibitors (all types: salespeople, marketing people, company owners) to get their feedback on the quality of the show. Consider their products, locations, and exhibit sizes and how that might influence their perceptions.

And talk to exhibitors at other companies who have attended in the past. Ask them about the type of audience they thought the show offered, whether or not they accomplished their goals for the show, quantity and quality of traffic.

If you want to gather these subjective comments on your evaluation sheet, use the column marked "Comments."

The complete chart is just a tool to collect all the thoughts and research on shows in one place. You now have the information you need to decide on the shows in which you will participate.

But, as Skip Cox said, companies don't usually participate in the wrong shows. They most often don't understand their audiences as well as they could to use the shows most effectively. They attend the right shows with the wrong products. Or they attend the right shows with the right products, but don't promote enough to reach their target audience. Even if participation in certain shows is a given at your company, this planning process provides the tools for refining the show strategy to make it most successful, as you will see in the next chapter.

Chapter 2: You are here:

	18 Mo.	12 Mo.	9 Mo.
Planning	Create strategic plan	Create Operational Plans	
Goal-Setting	Set long-range objectives	Set short-term, show-by-show goals	
Budgeting		Establish resource needs Create show budget estimates	
Promotions	Review current promotions mix	Plan promotion strategy	
Product Demos	Determine products exhibited	Decide on product demos	
Exhibits		Plan exhibit structure	Set goals and budget for new structure Select supplier
Installation			
Staffing		Plan staffing needs	
Inquiry Processing			
Measuring Results		Determine how results will be measured	

2

How to Prepare
Show-by-Show
Operational Plans
(12 Months in Advance)

INTRODUCTION TO OPERATIONAL PLANNING

Operational Plans are working documents which outline the tactics for each show you will attend. A separate plan is created for each show, since every plan will be different. The operational plan includes five parts. In this chapter you will cover each part and learn how to plan for:

1. BOOTH PLACEMENT: Finding the best booth location.
2. SHOW GOALS: How to make them realistic and measurable.
3. THE EXHIBIT PLAN: Planning exhibit objectives and product demonstrations or presentations.
4. PROMOTIONS: Planning the strategy
5. RESOURCES: How to establish budget and personnel needs.

The explanation you will find here for each section is fairly lengthy, but in your show plan each section will take just a few paragraphs to explain.

THREE STEPS TO SUCCESSFUL BOOTH PLACEMENT

Interestingly, unlike advertising placement, very little research exists to verify the best booth *locations* in any given show hall. In fact, quite to the contrary, the only research that does exist suggests that booth location, in and of itself, does not significantly affect a company's success at a show.

However, there are many factors that must be considered regarding exhibit location that *can* affect traffic flow to your booth. A variety of pet theories about where a booth should be placed crop up among exhibit managers and other experts, and it is difficult to discern fact from myth. Selecting the optimum *location* is the *art* of booth placement.

However, the *size* of the space you select for your booth will definitely affect your success. The two most common errors made in booth placement have to do with space size.

The first, the "Big Ego" theory, rests on the belief that more is more impressive. The reasoning typically goes something like this: "This show is our opportunity to knock our competitors dead and create an impressive image for our company. Let's get the largest space we can . . . that ought to be impressive." At a recent ski show, a major industry manufacturer who used the "Big Ego" theory suffered an empty looking exhibit even with fairly steady traffic. The result? An image exactly opposite to that which they hoped to create.

The second is the "Let's get by" theory. The reasoning typically goes like this: "Well, I suppose we have to be at the show, but let's keep our costs down. What's the least expensive space we can get?" If you buy that theory, while your exhibit may be packed, you could lose valuable opportunities to meet new prospects simply because there wasn't enough space or personnel in the exhibit to handle them.

Determining the optimum space *size* is the *science* of booth placement. And using the art and science of booth placement requires three steps.

Step One: How to Identify Your Options

Naturally, before making any selection you need to know your options. You can review them best by making sense of the exhibit floorplan provided by show management. (Typically, the floorplan is provided in the show prospectus, a kit of materials show management sends to companies interested in exhibiting.) Most exhibit floorplans are divided into four different types of booth spaces: aisle, cross-aisle, peninsula, and island spaces. The sample floorplan in Exhibit 2-1 identifies three of the four space types which are your options in selecting space.

The information in Exhibit 2-2 provides a quick overview of the advantages and disadvantages of each type of space. The type of space you select will be based on the amount of space required (which you will see how to calculate in the next section) and your own judgments about where you can receive the optimum traffic flow for the size space you select.

Exhibit 2-1 Booth Space Types

Aisle Space: Also called linear or in-line space, these are bordered on one side by an aisle and on three sides by other booths. They are typically 10' deep and from 10' to 60' long and longer.

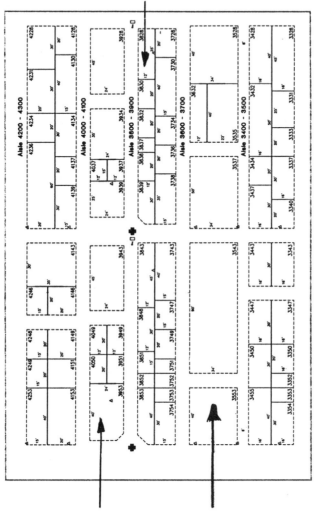

Peninsula Space: This space is bordered on one side by other booths and on three sides by aisles.

Island Space: Bordered on all four sides by aisles. Requires a minimum of 400 square feet.

Cross-Aisle Space: (Not pictured)—These spaces are made by selecting two aisle spaces directly across from one another. They require a minimum of 30 linear feet to be effective.

Exhibit 2-2   Booth Space Types

Pros	Cons
Aisle Spaces	
• Many choices • Minimum expense • Wide range of sizes	• Hard to stand out • Single aisle for visitor contact
Cross-Aisle Spaces	
• Reduce entry barrier • More space when aisle can be carpeted	• Often requires special permission • Limited choices
Peninsula Spaces	
• Three aisles for visitor contact • Can still use a backwall exhibit structure	• Limited choices • Minimum depth of 20′ for best sightline exposure • Possible height restrictions
Island Spaces	
• Four aisles for visitor contact • Accommodates wide variety of exhibit structures and designs	• Limited choices • Minimum size is 20′×20′

At this point you are just getting familiar with the floorplan. The checklist in Exhibit 2-3 will help you identify additional points to consider when evaluating traffic flow.

Exhibit 2-3   Floorplan Checklist

Highlight the following areas on your floorplan to determine traffic flow patterns and important location considerations.

1. Restrooms
2. Restaurants
3. Entrances and registration area
4. Exits

5. Escalator/elevators
6. Freight doors
7. Conference session locations
8. Windows
9. Columns
10. Association exhibit/lounge
11. Power sources
12. Plumbing/drainage

Step Two: Determining Size Requirements

Determining the size of the booth space you will need requires just a few simple calculations. (1) Use the potential audience figures you calculated in the Strategic Plan in Chapter 1. Along with potential audience, there are a few additional numbers you will need to use. The chart in Exhibit 2-4 organizes the information required for the calculation. Use the chart to gather the information. Use the blank box on the far right to fill in the figure you plan to use.

The four-step calculation looks like this:

1. Potential audience ÷ Total show hours = Visitors per hour.
2. Visitors per hour ÷ Staffer capacity = Staffers required.
3. Staffers required × Open working space = Total open space required.
4. Open space + Occupied space = Total space required.

While you will have to use a certain amount of judgment, such as the amount of occupied space you will need, deciding on the optimum amount of exhibit space to buy is fairly straightforward.

If one of your goals is to be among the top ten most remembered exhibits at the show, sheer volume of space will help get you there. There is a standard calculation for determining the correlation between space size and memorability. The equation, for shows greater than 40,000 square feet, is: $Y = .0075X + 720$, where Y is the size of the exhibit in square feet and X is the total paid square footage of all exhibits in the show. For shows under 40,000 square feet a 400-sq. ft. space should be sufficient.(2)

Step Three: Tips for Selecting and Reserving Space

Once you've made sense out of the floorplan and know the size of the exhibit space required, you can begin evaluating the floorplan to determine the best location. Trace traffic patterns starting at the entrance. First, go to the right and follow the aisles with your pencil to determine how traffic might flow through the hall. Watch for dead end aisles,

Exhibit 2-4

Information	Definition	Source	Average	Figure to Use
Potential Audience	The number of show visitors you can expect to reach	Calculations done during Big Picture Planning	No average exists	
Total Show Hours	Total number of hours the exhibit hall is open to visitors	Show prospectus	No average exists	
Staffer Capacity	Number of visitors a booth staffer can handle in an hour	Past history	12*	
Open Working Space	Square footage required per staffer	Industry standard	50 sq. ft. each	
Occupied Space	Space taken by exhibit structure and product displays	Actual size of products and exhibit	No average exists	

*12–15 is the average number of visitors a staffer can talk to in an hour. However, the types of products displayed can significantly affect this number. For technical products the average can be as low as 5–7 visitors per hour because explanations are more detailed and more questions are asked. For commodity type products the number could be much higher because interactions are shorter.

Exhibit 2-5 Sample Space Size Calculation

If our completed chart looks like this:

Information	Definition	Source	Average	Figure to Use
Potential Audience	The number of show visitors you can reasonably expect to reach	Calculations done during Big Picture Planning	No average exists	900 (From Chapter 1)
Total Show Hours	Total number of hours the exhibit hall is open to visitors	Show prospectus	No average exists	24 hours
Staffer Capacity	Number of visitors a booth staffer can handle in an hour	Past history or industry averages	12	12
Open Working Space	Square footage required per staffer	Past history or industry avg.	50 sq. ft.	50 sq. ft.
Occupied Space	Space taken by exhibit structure and product displays	Actual size of products and exhibit	No average exists	200 sq. ft.

Then the calculation will look like this:

1. Potential Audience 900 ÷ Total Show Hours 24 = 37.5 Visitors per hour.
2. Visitors per hour 37.5 ÷ Staffer Capacity 12 = 3 Staffers
3. Numbers of Staffers 3 × 50 sq. ft. per staffer = 150 square feet of open space.
4. Open Space 150 + Occupied Space 200 sq. ft. = 350 square feet.

Booth space is typically sold in 100-square foot increments. You could round your figure down to 300 square feet and purchase a 10'×30' linear space or up to 400 square feet to purchase a 20'×20' island space.

---

columns that redirect traffic, off-the-beaten-path rooms or corners. Then begin again going to the left after entering the hall. While traffic pattern studies in retail environments say that the majority of people turn to the right when entering a store, no studies exist to assure that is the case in exhibit halls.

Highlight the zones where the most traffic is likely to pass. If you still have trouble identifying those areas, you are in good company. Experts within the trade show industry still argue over whether certain areas of show halls are better than others. Lengthy articles have been written to explore a variety of theories about booth placement. Some experienced exhibitors like to be near their competitors, others swear by the center of the exhibit hall, still others will only be right inside the door. Actually all locations have their pros and cons. If you would like to read more on the subject, *Exhibitor Magazine* published a two-part article about booth placement theories. You will find their address and phone number in the resource appendix.

Once you've settled on a space size and a preferred zone within the hall, you can select the space type (aisle, peninsula, cross-aisle, or island) and highlight those spaces in your selected zone. Be sure to make at least a second and third choice . . . the premium spaces often go fast.

Learn the space selection procedures for each show you plan to attend, because they vary by show. Many shows require that you commit to a space a year in advance. Some hold selection meetings at the show with lottery type procedures for selection. Others give priority to companies based on their longevity with the show. Some shows operate on a mail-in request basis with a first come, first served policy.

Eight Points to Check Before Signing the Space Contract

Whether you sign up for booth space at a show selection meeting or by mail, you will be required to sign a contract to reserve that space. The contracts are of the small print variety and often look too imposing to take the time to read. Take the time. They (or inclusive materials attached to the space contract) specify not only what you are getting, but what you are agreeing to when you reserve that space by signing the contract. They also typically outline deposit and payment policies along with cancellation procedures.

Exhibit 2-6   Advice from the Experts

The following tips are taken from a speech given by Jed Mandel at the International Exhibitors' Association conference. Mandel is a partner with the Chicago law firm Neal Gerber Eisenberg & Lurie and is General Counsel for the International Exhibitors Association. He is an expert in trade show and meeting planning law and specializes in representing non-profit organizations.

This brief checklist outlines eight of the most important clauses commonly found in exhibit space contracts. It is impossible in this context to address all of the contractual concerns or ways to negotiate contract changes. Mandel suggests if you find clauses in a contract that are unclear or that your company cannot accept, show management should be asked to make the necessary changes. *And get it in writing.* If the contract cannot be modified in a manner that is acceptable, then don't sign it.

1. **Nuts and bolts.** Double-check the dates and hours of the show (specifically, those when the exhibit hall will be open, which can vary from the conference schedule). Check dismantle dates and times, watch for target move-in/move-out schedules. Look at the show floorplan, and check any special rules such as height restrictions, or promotional regulations, regarding your show participation.

2. **Eligibility requirements.** Some shows limit participation to only certain industry-related products, certain geographical locations, or association membership. Be sure that your company, and the products or services which you intend to display, will qualify.

3. **Costs for space.** Some shows charge by the square foot, some charge by 10-foot square spaces. Some space costs include drayage charges, some don't. Some shows charge extra for

"premium" spaces. Be sure you know exactly what you are getting (and not getting) for your money.

4. **Payment schedules.** These also vary dramatically from show to show. Some require a deposit and payment schedule. Others require 50% up front and 50% at a specified date before the show. Missing payment deadlines means risking losing your space . . . and sometimes your deposit. It is important to know, understand, and be willing to live with the deposit and payment schedule which each particular show requires. The International Exhibitors Association has published a position paper on deposit procedures. For more information you can contact the Association. The address and phone number are listed in the resource appendix.

5. **Cancellation policy.** Know in advance what the penalties will be if you should need to cancel your participation. Some shows keep your deposit, others have a refund schedule based on how far in advance of the show you cancel. Also see if the contract specifies show management's liability to you should they cancel the show or should the show be canceled as a result of an "Act of God."

6. **Hold harmless clause.** Some contracts ask you to indemnify many participating parties (show management, the hall, the city, etc.) from any and all damage or injury. Some contracts even state that the indemnified parties are held harmless even if they negligently or intentionally caused the damage. Be sure to understand the scope of any indemnification you are asked to provide and avoid indemnifying participants against their own improper acts. You can request some changes to make the contract more equitable, but remember, your only recourse should show management deny your request is to sign the contract or choose not to exhibit.

7. **Security provisions.** Show managements often hire security guards during shows, but still deny any responsibility for damage to or theft of any of the exhibitors' materials. It typically means you need to have your own insurance for your show properties.

8. **Insurance provisions.** Most show managers require that you carry liability insurance in order to participate in the show. Some even insist on being named as an additional insured on your policy. And they will request a certificate of that insurance before allowing you to participate. Check with your insurance carrier to determine the most cost-effective way to obtain the types of insurance that will be needed for the various shows in which you will be participating.

HOW TO SET REALISTIC, MEASURABLE SHOW GOALS

I once met a man on an airplane who laughed at me when I told him I did exhibit staff training. Trade shows were a joke at his company, he said. They were a lot of fun, but he was sure they never added up to much more. I asked him if they set goals for show participation. If they did, he wasn't aware of it. Any strategy? No. In fact he said they just stand around in the booth and tell jokes.

He echoed a popular myth that goes something like this: "We only attend shows because we would be conspicuous by our absence. We never really get very much out of them. It's impossible to determine whether shows are doing any good for us at all." The primary reason that myth is perpetuated is because many companies neglect to set measurable goals for show participation.

However, those companies that do set goals, and measure their performance at shows, also identify and quantify success. Setting goals will give your show program a number of advantages. You will be able to measure that show's value, compare one show against another more objectively, justify your show participation, and know which shows are dead-beats and should no longer be attended. The next part of the Show Plan is a statement of the goals for this specific show.

A Critical Step: Quantifying Goals

Establish one or more goal statements for the show and be sure they can be measured. For example, many companies say they attend shows to keep up their image in the industry. When the show is over, how could they tell whether or not they had succeeded? Companies also say that they attend shows to generate sales leads. But how many leads would it take to make the show worth the investment?

The following chart illustrates nine common show goals and ways to quantify the goals to make them measurable.

Generate sales leads.	Establish a number of leads that are realistic based on your potential audience at the show. Determine how much you will be willing to spend for each lead.
Write orders.	Establish a dollar volume expected based on the potential for your company.
Change or enhance your image.	Define a specific part of your image that you would want to change (i.e., from poor service to good service, from arrogant to friendly).

Sign new distributors/retailers/ or third-party vendors.	Define exactly the number you expect to sign, and target specific geographic regions, volumes, or specialties when appropriate. Decide what you plan to spend per contact.
Get press coverage.	Target specific magazines for the press coverage you would like to receive.
Introduce a new product.	Define what you want people to know about the product. Who will be your target audience for the introduction?
Gather competitive information.	Determine exactly which competitors will be evaluated and what you want to know about each.
Meet existing customers.	Why? And who? Determine in advance who can be met at the show and what can be accomplished that couldn't be done in the field. (Preview a new product, for example.)
Support the industry.	This indicates a desire to convey support to someone: The association president? Key customers within the industry? Think about what specifically would demonstrate that support and how you can determine whether you accomplished it. One way is to be a part of the conference schedule by teaching a session.

Making Goals Realistic

The number of goals you can expect to accomplish at the show is usually determined by the amount of resources available. It's best to begin by brainstorming about what you would like to accomplish, prioritizing your list, and then selecting the goals according to your time, budget, and personnel. For example, if one of your goals is to preview a new product for key customers, you will need personnel and space for those meetings along with the exhibit and staff.

How to Get from Goals to Plans

Each goal that you set will require resources and a strategy to accomplish it. For example, to introduce a new product to a pre-defined audience you might want to consider pre-show direct mail invitations to see the product, new graphics for the exhibit featuring the product, and product training for exhibit personnel. The chart in Exhibit 2-7 lists the above goals along with some considerations to make toward accomplishing each goal. The chart is meant to be adapted to fit your own situation.

If, for example, press coverage (#5) is one of your goals, you will need to consider some promotion to get the press interested, and you will need special personnel in the exhibit to handle press inquiries.

The chart is designed to get you thinking about the components of the strategy you will use to accomplish show goals. In the remaining chapters of the first section of this book you will see how to put these strategies into action. At this point you only need to know *what you plan to do.*

Techniques for Evaluating and Measuring Success

A variety of tools have been created by exhibitors to measure their success at accomplishing show goals. Most of these evaluations fall into two categories which can be defined as objective and subjective.

Objective forms of evaluation range from simple return on investment measures to sophisticated survey statistics. The simplest measures are the "cost per" measures of performance. For example, cost per lead, cost per sale closed, cost per contact made, cost per column inch of press coverage, or other equally creative variations can be calculated from show results. This is less than scientific, but very valuable for comparing show to show.

The most often used figure is *cost per lead.* Calculate cost per lead by adding your total show costs and dividing by the total number of leads generated at the show. (If my total show budget was $100,000 and we wrote 1,000 leads, the cost per lead would be $100.) Depending on how your exhibit personnel expenses are covered, you may or may not want to add them to the total. When using cost per lead figures to compare against others in your industry, or against industry averages, be sure you know whether or not those in the comparison include personnel costs.

A bit more sophisticated are the *return on investment* ratios. To calculate these determine the sales generated from leads gathered at a show and divide this by the total show costs. While there is no hard-and-fast rule, a minimum 10:1 return on investment is a loose industry standard. Calculating return on investment is more complicated because it requires that you have a process in place for tracking trade show leads.

Exhibit 2-7

	Graphics	Products	Personnel	Promote	Lead Processing	Sales Stations	Conference Areas
1. Generate leads			✓		✓	✓	
2. Write orders			✓			✓	
3. Change/ enhance image	✓	✓	✓	✓			
4. Sign third-party vendors		✓	✓			✓	
5. Get press coverage			✓	✓			
6. Introduce new product	✓	✓		✓			
7. Gather competitive info			✓				
8. Meet existing customers			✓				✓

For an explanation of the steps involved in calculating return on investment from a show see Exhibit 2-8.

Exhibit 2-8   Calculating Return on Investment

Calculating the return on a trade show investment requires two pieces of information: the total cost of the show, and the amount of sales generated from the show. The first is fairly easy to come by, the second is more difficult. Salespeople must report back to you the sales generated from trade show leads and a lead tracking system is required. The process follows these four basic steps, but for more detailed information on lead tracking see Chapters 5, 6, and 11.

1. Generate leads at the show with complete, accurate information.
2. Track and record all show expenses.
3. Distribute the leads for follow-up.
4. Sales reps report back to the trade show department on sales generated from those trade show leads with the amount of sale.
5. After a predetermined timeframe, depending on your typical sales cycles, divide the total sales generated by the total show costs.

Finally, and most sophisticated, are *audience survey measures* provided by research firms. Firms that specialize in trade show research conduct post-show surveys of the audience. The survey questions can be customized to your specific needs. Exhibit Surveys, for example, pioneers in trade show research, can measure pre- and post-show audience perceptions of your company or product, audience memorability for your company or specific products, audience evaluation of your booth personnel, and your efficiency at reaching your target audience at a show, to name a few.

Subjective Evaluations include external reactions to your program (customers, industry influencers, competitors) and internal reactions (upper management, exhibit personnel) as well as your own assessment of the show's success. Some exhibitors like to get this in informal conversations with people. Others prefer post-show evaluation forms because they get the comments in writing which can be valuable when planning for the next show.

In summary, the three keys to goal-setting for shows are:

1. Set realistic, measurable goals.
2. Have a strategy in mind for accomplishing those goals.
3. Have a tool in place for measuring whether the goals were met.

The following case study of a show program used by the John Deere Chassis group illustrates how generic goals were given a strategy in the exhibit program.

A Multiple-Goal Case Study: John Deere Chassis Division

The Chassis division of the John Deere company sold chassis to original equipment manufacturers (OEM) who installed their large vehicles on them, such as delivery trucks and recreational vehicles (RVs). For example, when Winnebago builds an RV, they order their chassis from another supplier, typically automobile manufacturers. In fact when Deere entered the chassis market, one auto company had locked up more than 90% of the chassis sales in the RV market. In just two years, Deere had gained approximately 25% of that market share.

Trade shows became an integral tool for promoting Deere's presence in that industry, and gaining accessibility to three of their key prospects: the OEM's (the Winnebagos of the world), the dealers who sold the RVs, and the end users. The show we will review here is the Annual National RV Trade Show, a gathering of RV dealers from all over the U.S. This show actually provided two target audiences for Deere, because the OEMs were the exhibitors and the dealers were the show audience.

Deere's overriding marketing objective for the show was to get the *dealers* to specify a John Deere chassis when they ordered an RV from the manufacturer. To meet that objective four goals were set for the RV show. The following chart illustrates the goals that were set, and the accompanying strategy for accomplishing those goals.

Goals	Strategy
1. Promote and enhance a positive image of John Deere, its chassis product and personnel.	1. Exhibit graphics, premiums, and literature were all designed to emphasize the new product name. Bullet points on vehicle displays called out key product benefits. Booth training reinforced positive image of sales force.

Goals	Strategy
2. Increase dealer inventories of RVs with Deere chassis.	2. Assign staffers to make daily contact with RV manufacturers exhibiting at the show with four objectives for each meeting. • Learn how many Deere chassis they had displayed. • Learn whether the OEM offers a choice of chassis on their vehicles. • Offer support. • Close with a thank you premium.
3. Increase the number of dealers that service Deere Chassis.	3. Write leads on dealers visiting the exhibit who are interested in being service dealers. Develop a lead form to accommodate those inquiries. Offer an incentive program for staffers who write the most leads.
4. Introduce two new products to: • the press • the RV dealers (attendees) • the RV manufacturers (exhibitors)	4. Create new literature for each product. Use a special premium in the exhibit. Hold a press reception to introduce the products. Create press releases to get press exposure for the products. Create special displays to showcase the new products in the exhibit. Discuss new products when contacting RV OEMs at their exhibits.

PLANNING THE EXHIBIT: FOUR CRITICAL DECISIONS

The third part of the operational plan considers the exhibit structure. If you need help in planning a new exhibit structure, look to Chapter 3, where that is covered in detail. In this part of the plan you are not putting all of the nuts and bolts of the exhibit in place. Instead, begin by thinking conceptually and considering these four key points:

1. What will the *exhibit concept* be? The exhibit could have a product, image, or customer concept or a combination.
2. What will the *communications message* for the exhibit be? This guides creation of exhibit graphics.
3. What type of *product displays and presentations* will be conducted in the exhibit?
4. What type of *structure* will be required?

How to Define the Exhibit Concept

Exhibit concepts fall into three categories and you can see from the descriptions here how different concepts work best with different goals. The concepts do not have to be mutually exclusive. You can combine concepts to achieve multiple goals, but be careful that your concepts are clearly defined.

Product Focus Concept. As the title suggests these exhibits focus on one or a group of products. For example, a company selling typewriters may use a supersize graphic of their typewriter as a backwall graphic for the exhibit. The focus is clearly on the product. This does not mean that the exhibit is filled with products, which is often a detriment to even product-focused goals. This concept is typically a good choice for a new company, since the product must be accepted by the marketplace before the company image statements ring true.

Corporate Image Concept. These exhibits, in contrast to those with a product focus, emphasize predominantly an image that the company is trying to portray about itself. It does not exclude products in the exhibit although exhibits with an image focus may not have products in them. Many companies today use a corporate image focus to position themselves as suppliers in the *global* marketplace, or to show commitment to servicing their customers' needs. Corporate image concepts are most useful when the primary goals are to enhance or change a company image in some way.

Customer or Marketplace Concept. In this concept the exhibit is designed to say "here's how you can benefit from using our products or services," rather than "here's what we do." For example, when computer technology was relatively new, hardware and software manufacturers often used their exhibit spaces as small classrooms and held on-site seminars for their dealer customers at major trade shows. Medical companies often do this at nursing shows as well.

But the marketplace concept exhibit need not be that sophisticated.

It can be as simple as dividing the exhibit and graphics by market categories instead of by product categories. If our glassware manufacturer from the previous chapter divided their exhibit by product category it might include display areas for unbreakables, formal glassware, informal glassware, etc.; whereas, if divided by market category, it would include display areas for pool retailers, high end retailers, catalog merchandisers, etc. Customer, or marketplace concept, exhibits are most useful when the show audience is horizontal. (Horizontal audiences represent a variety of industries or job functions.) This will help visitors target in on products of their interest more quickly.

Writing the Communications Message

Your next decision in setting goals for the exhibit is the communications message. Create a simple statement that sets the content and focus for exhibit graphics and supporting literature. If, for example, you are introducing a new product at the show, the communications message might be a slogan taken from existing promotional material. Be careful with the communications message so that it doesn't become a cliche. "Serving the world with state-of-the-art technology . . ." Have you heard that, or one of its simple sisters before?

Deciding What to Display and How to Demonstrate

In this section of the plan, list each product you will display at the show and define briefly how it will be demonstrated or presented. If, for example, you exhibit back-hoe haulers, your presentation will be very different than if you exhibit financial services. Your choices for product presentation generally fall within the following categories.

Graphic Displays. These include photomurals, silkscreened murals, and drawing diagrams. There are a variety of techniques for producing these graphics. (For more information on graphics see Chapter 3.) These displays are *least* interactive.

Static Displays. Static displays are simply products set on pedestals or tables for casual observation. The display draws attention based only on its visual merits, and static displays *can* be visually interesting enough to attract quite a bit of attention. For example, to illustrate how its add-on circuit boards installed easily into personal computers, one company painted the computers (inside and out) white and slipped the black board in place as a visual demonstration.

Informal Demonstrations. These are the most common types of product demonstrations used at shows. They can be facilitated two ways: with a "hands on" display where visitors are invited to try out the products themselves, or with small group demonstrations designed for staffer use as aides in the selling process.

Formal Demonstrations. These types of demonstrations are designed to run at regular intervals and present pre-defined product features to a mid-size audience (5–15 people). A bit of staging is required here, such as large visuals, a microphone for the presenter, and possibly scripted product demos.

Formal Presentations. These come in a variety of forms from multi-screen A-V productions to live stage shows. They require fairly elaborate investments and often a professional company to aid in such things as script creation, set design, and performances. (For more information on formal presentations see Chapter 7.)

At this point in the planning, you need not outline the details of your presentation, just the method(s) you will use.

Identifying Structural Needs

Finally, as part of the plan, determine the size and type of exhibit required. Your choices are: building a new structure, renting a structure, or adapting an existing structure to meet your needs. If you plan to build a new structure, at this point that is all you need to determine. You will work through the remaining details in Chapter 3.

If you are using an existing structure, this is the time to determine what is needed to make that structure function within your goals. A few points to consider:

Size: Will the structure adequately fill the space you have reserved? Is it right for the type of space you are using? (Exhibits designed for in-line spaces often include panels which are finished only on one side. Therefore they won't work in an island space without some refurbishing.)

Graphics: Do you need to change the graphics? Can you simply reskin existing graphic panels or do you need to create an entirely new set?

Display Pedestals: Are there enough to accommodate all of the products you plan to display? Are they the right size? Will they work with the wiring requirements of your products? An exhibit designer should be able to help you determine the proper height and size for ergonomically correct display stations.

Demonstration Areas: Do you have the properties to create the types of demonstration areas you have in mind?
  • Adequate seating
  • Proper height table pedestals
  • Microphones
  • Graphics
  • Accessory areas (tools, paper, etc.)
  • Lighting

Live Presentation Needs: Is there enough standing or sitting room for the crowds? Is there enough area for a stage? Will the stage location cause the presentation to interfere with ongoing sales conversations? Can the exhibit accommodate appropriate lighting and sound systems? A brief paragraph for each of the four considerations about your exhibit should provide sufficient direction for the operational plan.

FIRST STEP TO A SUCCESSFUL PROMOTIONS STRATEGY

Just as in advertising it is necessary to break through the maze of competing ads, at trade shows it is necessary to stand out from the maze of exhibits at the show. Promotion helps you do that at several points before and during the event. In this part of your plan, select the media you will use to promote your presence at the show. Media, here, includes a variety of promotional tools from publications advertising to contests and in-booth giveaways.

The success of different promotional media for shows varies dramatically. A study on the effects of pre-show advertising on booth traffic, for example, indicated it can have a significant impact. The study showed that companies which advertised in a leading industry publication with full page ads at a six-time rate "achieved an average stopped booth traffic that was 55% greater than non-advertisers."(3)

In contrast, a study done on the memorability resulting from booth contests and giveaways showed that, in a post-show survey, only 19% of the show audience remembered companies who used giveaways and only 12% remembered companies who used contests.(4)

Existing research on the effects of show promotion is fairly inconclusive because it is difficult to isolate all of the factors that make a particular trade show promotion work. The art of using promotional tools skillfully is selecting those tools that work best to meet your objectives. Second in importance is creating promotions designed specifically for your targeted audience at a show.

To help you select promotional media, the following list identifies a variety of those commonly used at shows. The accompanying chart in Exhibit 2-9 (page 72) identifies some advantages and disadvantages of each type of promotion and indicates which goals they would be most useful in working to achieve.

Two Considerations for Media Options

First: Location and Timing

Before the Show

Personal Invitations. One of the most commonly used promotion techniques is a personal invitation from sales reps to their clients. Show management firms frequently provide exhibitors with coupons for free entry to the exhibit hall which can be passed on to clients and prospects.

Trade Magazine Advertising. Prior to the show many companies advertise their presence at the show in leading industry publications. To succeed here, select the publications with a high readership among the show audience. Some show managers provide statistics on the percentage of their audience that reads a variety of industry-related publications.

Direct Mail. It is also common for companies to promote their presence at a show using direct mail. Success with this method varies dramatically based on the direct mail strategy and content.

Telemarketing. This is rare, but occasionally companies use telemarketing to set appointments with show visitors prior to the show.

Press Releases and Editor Contacts. Sending out press releases about your company's newsworthy events at the show, and contacting editors in advance to schedule interviews at the show, offers a more strategic approach to getting press coverage, rather than just banking on them picking up your kit in the press room.

In the Show City

Billboards. In several show cities such as Atlanta, Chicago, Las Vegas, and others, billboards are located on major thoroughfares between the airport, show hotels, and the show hall and are frequently used for exhibitor advertising.

Airport Advertising. Airports offer a variety of advertising display opportunities from static graphic displays along major concourses, to the large-screen video monitors at the baggage claim area at McCarran airport in Las Vegas.

Hotel TV Advertising. At some shows, a closed circuit TV program sponsored by show management is broadcast in the major show hotels. Advertising spots are usually sold on these programs. In addition, exhibitors frequently buy local advertising spots on popular morning news shows.

Mobile Ads. For lack of a better term, this is used to describe a variety of advertising opportunities seen on taxi cabs, hot air balloons, buses, and even sandwich boards and promoters dressed up like Santa Claus. Your imagination (and show and city restrictions) are the limit here.

Hotel Room Promotions. When blocks of rooms at specified hotels are reserved for show attendees, clever exhibitors distribute promotional items to each room. Here again your imagination and the hotel's restrictions are the only limits. Promotions range from complimentary newspapers to the show cities' top chocolate chip cookies, to splits of champagne.

When hotels are willing to cooperate in these efforts, they typically charge a fee for the service.

At the Show Hall

Show Issue Trade Publication Advertising. Most industry magazines publish special show issues, often with show directories, product listings, and floorplans. They are usually sent to subscribers just prior to the show, and handed out at the show site.

Show Daily Advertising. Show daily newspapers are published each day of the show and contain that day's news and photos. They vary greatly in size, quality, and readership from show to show.

Hall Advertising. Just recently at some larger shows, advertising kiosks and display areas within and outside of the show hall have been made available to exhibitors.

TV/Photo Opportunities. At many shows the local TV stations will bring camera crews to cover the highlights of the show. Larger shows occasionally receive national coverage. Keep your audience in mind here and be sure that any effort you expend to get this kind of coverage will result in your reaching your customers.

Press Kits/Briefings/Interviews. Many shows provide abundant opportunities to meet with industry press representatives through group briefings or individual interviews. It's best to stick with individual interviews unless your news is so dramatic as to warrant coverage by several publications. Remember the old adage "it's tough to get a scoop in a press conference." If press coverage is among your show goals be sure to plan on having press kits available in the press room or in your exhibit.

Show Directory Advertising. The listing of participating exhibitors provided by show management usually has room for advertising spots. When they include fold-out maps, the cover of the map is a favorite advertising spot . . . most visitors see it sooner or later.

In Your Exhibit

Contests and Drawings. These are most useful when you are working to draw a selected group from among the show audience to your exhibit, or need to work hard to stand out among the exhibiting crowd. These types of promotions have to be handled carefully so that they draw a targeted audience that will help you meet your show objectives. (Specifics on using promotions are covered in detail in Chapter 5.)

In-Booth Premiums (Giveaways). These little promotional tools are gems when used correctly (to break the ice or graciously close a conversation) but can be expensive losers when handed out indiscriminately.

Second: Show Goals

The chart in Exhibit 2-9 takes you a step further in selecting media options for your promotions by helping you to evaluate each option based on advantages, disadvantages, and goals they help to accomplish.

For this section of your plan, simply identify which promotion(s) you will use and why. Keep in mind that the number of tools you can use will be limited by your resources. Most companies use just one or two at each show.

Exhibit 2-9

Promotion	Advantages	Dis-advantages	Objectives
Before the Show			
Personal invitations	Personal contact	Limited reach	New product introduction Image awareness
Trade publication advertising	Wide reach	Not selective or targeted	Image awareness More effective for vertical audience shows
Direct mail	Targeted reach	Limited list availability	Generate leads New product introduction
Telemarketing	Direct contact/ direct feedback	Expensive and time-consuming	Generate leads Pre-set appointments
Press releases and editor contacts	Inexpensive Credible voice	Less control over type of exposure	Press exposure Image awareness
In the Show City			
Billboards	Wide reach	Limited locations	Image awareness
Airport advertising	Early exposure	Limited timeframe exposure	Image awareness

Promotion	Advantages	Dis-advantages	Objectives
In the Show City			
Hotel TV advertising	Less competition for visibility	Limited time exposure	Image awareness
Mobile ads	Repeat exposure	Restrictions in some cities or for some shows	Image awareness
Hotel room promotions	Less competition for visibility	Additional time and cost for on-site distribution	Image awareness
At the Hall			
Show issue trade publication advertising	Wide reach	Not targeted or selective	Image awareness New product introduction
Show daily advertising	Wide reach Show-related editorial	Vary in readership from show to show	Image awareness New product introduction Promote a show event or contest
Hall advertising	Additional on-site exposure Repeat exposure	Limited choices	Image awareness
TV/photo opportunities	Local or national exposure Inexpensive	Limited time exposure Little control Limited show audience exposure	Image awareness to a public audience
Press briefings/ interviews	Inexpensive press coverage Credible objective source exposure	Little control Requires special personnel to handle press	Image awareness New product introduction

Promotion	Advantages	Dis-advantages	Objectives
At the Hall			
Show directory advertising	Outer covers provide good exposure Selective reach	Limited availability	Image awareness New product introduction
In Your Exhibit			
Contests and drawings	Ability to draw targeted audience	Often time-consuming Can draw too generally	Generate qualified leads
In-booth premiums (Giveaways)	Relatively inexpensive	Frequently misused by exhibit personnel	Generate leads (When premium is used to open a sales conversation)

ESTABLISHING RESOURCE NEEDS

Finally, the operational plan should include an estimate of the resources required. This includes both budgets and personnel.

Four Quick Methods for Estimating Budgets

At this point you don't yet have the information required to make an accurate line-item budget estimate for the show, but a few techniques exist to get a ballpark idea of anticipated costs.

There are two ways to approach budgeting for a show. You can either establish a budget based on resources available (we only have $20,000 to spend on this show) and the budget dictates most show decisions. Or you can establish your show program and determine the budget required to accomplish your objectives. In most cases exhibitors use a combination of the two, knowing that their resources are not unlimited but basing costs on the show strategy.

Your methods for estimating budgets at this point will depend on the information available to you.

1. If you know what you are willing to spend to reach each contact you make at a show, you can multiply that number by your potential audience. (The formula for calculating potential audience is explained in Chapter 1.)

The best source for determining what you are willing to spend is past history, and comparison to costs of other media used by your company. A few examples include:

- Average cost per contact at past shows.
- Average cost per advertising lead. You may want to establish that as a minimum.

This will give you a rough total budget estimate. If you do not have points of comparison established, there are a few industry standards which provide a useful benchmark.(5)

Cost per Visitor Reached (CVR). This industry average is calculated with several different factors. (Most recent figures are 1985.)

- Average CVR excluding personnel costs: $79.57
- Average CVR including personnel costs: $106.80
- CVR for top performing exhibits: $58.97

To use the CVR in estimating a budget, multiply the CVR that most reflects your situation by your potential audience for the show. If my potential audience is 500 and I am willing to spend the average cost per visitor reached including personnel costs of $106.80, then my budget will be approximately $53,400. (500 × $106.80 = $53,400.)

Cost to Make a Field Sales Call. If you attend trade shows primarily to generate sales leads and want to keep trade show costs in line with field sales costs, you can establish your budgets based on comparative costs to make that number of contacts in the field. The most recent McGraw Hill research (1987) established the cost of a field sales call at $251.63. You might want to establish that as your upward limit. If your company calculates its own figure, that would keep your show costs even more in line with your field sales costs.

2. If you have been given a total budget figure you can estimate expenses for various budget items. The Trade Show Bureau regularly reports on average expenditures for a variety of typical trade show budget items. The average percentage allocations can provide a guideline for estimating your expenses. (Most current figures are 1987.)(6)

Exhibit construction   23%
(Costs to build a new exhibit, amortized over the number
of shows at which it is expected to be used.)

Booth space rental	27%
Refurbishing	8%
(Cost to refurbish the exhibit for a single show.)	
Transportation	14%
Show services	21%
(Installation/dismantle labor, drayage, electrical, etc.)	
Special Personnel	1%
(Hosts, hostesses, presenters.)	
Specialty advertising	2%
(Pre-show promotions, at-show promotions, giveaways, etc.)	
Miscellaneous	4%
TOTAL	100%
Exhibit personnel costs	34%

(These are not calculated into the 100% total, and average an additional 34% beyond that total.)

A word of warning about using these percent allocation averages. They are calculated based on surveys of larger companies and tend to be skewed toward larger exhibit programs. The best allocation percentages are those based on your own past history.

3. If you have a record of past expenditures on the same show you can adjust for inflation and add new items you will be using this year to calculate a current budget estimate. The International Exhibitors Association publishes a budget guide that walks you through the steps of calculating budget estimates this way. The guide can be purchased from the IEA whose number is listed in the resource appendix.

4. If you know how much you will spend on your space, you can use the 27% average to calculate a ballpark estimate. In other words, knowing that space costs are approximately ¼ of the total budget, multiply that cost by four to get a very rough ballpark figure. Since space reservations are typically made a year in advance of the show, that budget figure is one of the first you will know for certain, and can be useful for these early estimates. Keep in mind that these statistics are skewed toward larger shows with custom displays. If you use a portable exhibit, space costs often represent a larger percentage (from 30–50%) of the total budget.

How to Identify Personnel Requirements

Along with budget resources, special personnel are needed for the show. First and foremost are the people who will staff the exhibit. You have already calculated the number of personnel you will need in the exhibit at any given time. If you want to split shifts you will need roughly twice that many. Depending on your goals and strategy for the show PR, personnel, engineering personnel, upper management people might also be needed at the show. Outline briefly the types of people that will contribute to the show's success as the first step to recruiting those personnel to work the show.

CONCLUSION: HOW TO STRUCTURE AND USE THE OPERATIONAL PLAN

It is rare that the Operational Plan you prepare a year in advance of the show will reflect exactly what actually happens at the show. The watchword in business today is change and flexibility and this plan should be considered flexible. It will probably be constantly changed and updated as the actual strategy takes shape.

But the plan will be useful. It will be a benchmark for decision-making now on every step of action taken. It will also provide a guideline for communicating within the company. Getting management to sign off on the plan will provide the authority you might need to get cooperation from other departments (sales for exhibit staffing, advertising for support on promotional ideas, public relations for help with press objectives, etc.). And when distributed among the appropriate departments it will remind them of the participation you will need from them when the time comes (engineering or manufacturing for that new product, for example).

You will see, as you work through the other chapters in this section, how the operational plan becomes the foundation on which the rest of your show program will be built.

Exhibit 2-10   Operational Plan Outline

This outline provides the structure for writing out the operational plan. The plan should be brief and allow room for changes as it takes shape. Each section should be just a paragraph or two.

Show Name _____ Show Dates _____

Show Location _____ Potential Audience _____

I. Booth Placement
   A. Personnel and booth size requirements
   B. Booth location (include a photocopy of the floorplan with your
      space highlighted)

II. Show Goals (One paragraph for each goal explaining the following)
   A. Goal
   B. Strategy
   C. Measure of success

III. The Exhibit Plan
   A. The exhibit concept
   B. The communications message
   C. Product demonstrations and/or presentations
   D. The exhibit structure

IV. The Promotions Plan
   Include here a paragraph listing the promotions that have been selected for this show and why they were selected.

V. Establishing Resource Needs
   A. Budget estimate
   B. Personnel requirements

Chapter 3: You are here: ↓

	12 Mo.	9 Mo.	6 Mo.
Planning	Create Operational Plans		
Goal-Setting	Set short-term, show-by-show goals		
Budgeting	Establish resource needs Create show budget estimates		Prepare zero-based show budget
Promo-tions	Plan promotion strategy		Evaluate promotion options
Product Demos	Decide on product demos		
Exhibits	Plan exhibit structure	Set goals and budget for new structure Select supplier	Finalize supplier selection
Install-ation			Select show services
Staffing	Plan staffing needs		Plan pre-show staff meeting
Inquiry Process-ing			
Measuring Results	Determine how results will be measured		

3

Planning the New Exhibit Purchase— Getting Your Money's Worth (9 Months in Advance)

When buying a new exhibit, regardless of size, you have two creative dynamics to consider. The first is: What do you want the exhibit to say? The second is: How do you want the exhibit to function? The answers to both questions are rooted in the long-range objectives and show-by-show goals you established in the Show Plan. What you want the exhibit to say is essentially an image consideration. How you want the exhibit to function is essentially a logistical consideration. Both considerations require that you take a good, hard look at your company and products. This chapter takes you through that process.

The materials in this chapter focuses on design planning for the *custom-built exhibit.* Considerations for portable exhibits are covered in Chapters 7 and 8. In this chapter you will learn about:

1. GOAL-SETTING: How to set goals for the new exhibit.
2. BUDGETING: How to plan budgets for the new exhibit.
3. SELECTING A SUPPLIER: Five steps to assure a good working relationship.

GOAL-SETTING FOR THE NEW EXHIBIT

Think for a moment about the last exhibit purchase your company made. Do you know on what basis they made the decision? If yours is like most companies they likely selected either the low bid or the best looking design.

The visual aspect of the exhibit is important, but, as the saying goes, try to think of it as more than just a pretty face. Think of the exhibit as a sales and marketing tool. The exhibit should be designed to meet very specific sales and marketing goals and objectives.

Thus the first step in the new exhibit purchase process is goal-setting. When goals are established for the exhibit, the primary selection criteria will be how well the proposed structure will *accomplish your goals.* This chapter will show you how to draw on the goals and objectives you have already set to guide you in the design of a new exhibit.

Vital Background Information

McDonald's (the hamburger people) is a master at designing market-specific advertising. When ethnic shows are on television, their advertising caters to that culture, during children's shows the ads are of tap-dancing, giant red Ronald McDonald shoes, for the young teenage audience, an ad about "my most embarrassing moment." While exhibits needn't cater to markets with as much variety as McDonald's, an exhibit that works well will be designed specifically for the audience and the market you plan to reach.

That takes research. The pre-design research for a new exhibit falls into three categories: audience, product, and company research. Understanding your markets, and specifically your audiences at different shows, will affect your exhibit structure, graphics messages, and presentations. For example, you would create one story about your product for technical people, and quite another for financial decision-makers. Our glassware company would create a very different exhibit for the Pool & Spa show than they would for the National Restaurant Association show. For more specific information on how research can guide design decisions see Exhibit 3-2 on using custom research.

The chart in Exhibit 3-1 lists a variety of information to collect that will guide your goal-setting for the new exhibit.

How can you find the research information? Check your corporate research department to see what type of research exists. You might find most of what you need on markets and customers right there. Or check with show managers about audience statistics. Several of the larger shows contract for audience surveys and provide statistical data to their exhibitors.

If no research exists, your company's research department can gather a great deal of information through an informal, but structured, telephone survey. You can also purchase custom surveys of show audiences, but they are fairly expensive. For more information on using custom research, see Exhibit 3-2.

Exhibit 3-1 Research Information

About Your Audience	About Your Products	About Your Company
☐ Existing survey data	☐ Product names	☐ Corporate image
☐ Custom survey data	☐ Product weights	☐ Corporate culture
☐ Attendee job functions	☐ Product dimensions	☐ Image changes
☐ Potential audience	☐ Electrical requirements	☐ Logo requirements
☐ Attendee psychographics	☐ Plumbing requirements	☐ Past history of exhibits
☐ Attendee demographics	☐ Demonstrations	☐ Management preferences
☐ Markets	☐ Lighting needs	☐ Divisions involved
	☐ Colors	☐ Advertising programs
	☐ Technical specifications	☐ Public relations programs
	☐ Features/ benefits	☐ Show schedule
	☐ Literature	☐ Additional uses of the structure

Exhibit 3-2 Using Custom Research for Exhibit Design Planning

Custom research can provide a variety of show audience statistics, based on your specific need. Some of the most commonly used are listed here.

Level of Awareness. Statistics show that a primary reason people attend trade shows is to see products. If your products have a high level of awareness among the show audience, then you have a natural drawing card. However, if they don't you will have to focus new exhibit goals on building that awareness.

Potential Audience. In Chapter 1 you learned how to determine the potential audience for each show you plan to attend. This figure is the key to determining the size exhibit you will need.

Product Interest. A tabulation of the percentage of the audience that is interested in specific products should influence decisions you make on which products to display more prominently than others. It guides your choice of graphics messages and product placements.

Job Function. Knowing your audience is the key to success. Case in point: One company focused their exhibit strategy on applications of their product for many years until they discovered, through research, that the audience was more interested in technical information. They changed their entire exhibit strategy and saw a significant improvement in their show results.(1)

Types of Business. It may seem apparent what types of business a show audience represents, but it can be deceiving. Comdex, a computer dealer show, is known by many exhibitors as a reseller show. In fact only about half of the show audience is actually resellers. Knowing *all* of the types of businesses represented will help you to succeed with a greater percentage of your potential audiences.

Two Types of Goals That Drive the New Exhibit Design

Setting specific goals for your new exhibit is important because they will be the criteria by which you will judge the design solutions that are presented to you. Therefore you will want the goals to be as specific as possible.

How to Set Image Goals

The first type of goals to define are *image goals.* This is tougher than defining logistical goals because image is not a tangible commodity. You can certainly tell whether or not the exhibit is flexible to meet the variety of configurations you will need, but it is more difficult to tell whether or not it communicates the correct image.

Draw on the goals you set in both the strategic and operational plans for direction. Here are a few tips for communicating image goals as succinctly as possible. First, if you want to create a new or different image for the company create two lists of adjectives, one defining the old image and one defining the new image. Second, attend trade shows and collect photographs of exhibits that reflect the image you would like your exhibit to convey. Finally, if your goal is to simply reflect a strong existing image, collect as much information as possible that will define that image for the designer (product brochures, annual reports, advertisements, etc.)

Functional Goals to Consider

The second type of goals, functional goals, allow you to be much more specific. In fact, you have been thinking about functional goals throughout this chapter. Refer back to the list of research information you collected about your product, and the considerations you made in the first part of this chapter. The Design Guidelines sheet at the end of the chapter will provide a format for collecting this information.

As important as it is to establish goals, it's equally important to remain flexible. Goals that are too rigid can inhibit the design solution. Let your designer know that the goals are guidelines, and that you are open to his or her input.

Who Should Participate in Goal-Setting?

A general guideline: At the beginning of the process involve as many people as you can; at the end involve only those you must. In other words, the exhibit will be most successful if, during your initial research, you get input from a variety of people within the company: engineering, advertising, public relations, and sales managers, for example. But when it comes to decision-making, keep the group as small as possible. Define early on *exactly* who will be the final decision-maker(s) on the design and once design is in progress restrict input opportunities to only those people.

The exhibit manager's role is to coordinate the input from all groups within the company. You will also locate an exhibit house to work with and solicit the initial exhibit design concepts.

The advertising manager's role, is simply to provide input about ongoing and future advertising plans that will affect and be affected by the company's trade show participation.

The product manager's role is to provide as much specific input about the products that will be exhibited as possible. This includes promoted features and benefits, and demonstration recommendations, along with technical specifications.

Management's role is usually to approve the final exhibit design. You as the exhibit manager will see a variety of design options before the final option goes to management for approval. Be sure to leave enough time after that final design review before the show so that input from management can be accommodated.

After you've done some research and set goals, there is one more step you can take before calling in the designer. Take time to review some primary design considerations about your structure. What follows is a list of seven considerations that are frequently overlooked.

Seven Common Design Oversites

Goal-setting for exhibit design requires a host of considerations— from the size of the structure to the color and graphics. Most exhibit buyers leave some of the most important considerations to an exhibit designer, as they should. But taking time to think through some of these considerations before meeting with the designer can help you to provide more input on your wants and needs for the structure. Plan to consider some of these areas that are typically overlooked, and bring some guidelines to the design process.

Oversight #1: Color.

Effects on your program: Influences image and communications message.

Consideration: Should we use our corporate colors? It makes sense, of course, to select the corporate color as a primary or secondary color for the exhibit, and many companies do. But this can create a message in your exhibit exactly contrary to that which you would want to convey. Red, for example is considered an uncomfortable color and is commonly associated with "stop." While it would catch the eye if used sparingly as an accent, it would be overwhelming as the primary color for an exhibit, and may even keep visitors out.

Consideration: What does the color communicate? When exploring colors for the exhibit think about what the color communicates and how it will affect the attendees' impressions of your company. Keep in mind that colors communicate different messages in different countries. In some Middle Eastern countries for example white, not black, is associated with death.

Consideration: Will the color date the structure? Colors that are popular in contemporary designs can give your exhibit a leading edge look, but will also date the structure in a few years when the colors are no longer in vogue. For example in the early 1980s, pastel colors were used in many leading edge designs. Just a few years later white became popular and the pastels began to look old. Then bright colors began to dominate design trends and the white structures went by the wayside. Keep this in mind when planning for a new structure. Will the colors selected date the exhibit while you still plan to use it? Can the colors be changed easily to keep the look current?

Question: What are our color guidelines?

Oversight #2: Traffic Flow.

Effects on your program: Significantly influences visitor participation in your exhibit.

Consideration: Is the exhibit easy to enter? Good fences may make good neighbors but they rarely make good exhibits. Consider how you want traffic to flow into (and out of) your exhibit. Barriers to entering an exhibit (walls, products, elevation) are used only to selectively attract and prequalify target groups from among the show audience. Do you want to use the exhibit structure itself to qualify visitors (they would have to be very interested to want to enter the space), or do you want it to attract as many show visitors as possible?

Consideration: How will traffic flow within the exhibit? How would you like traffic to flow through the exhibit? Do you want the visitor's experience to be controlled (a staffer greets them and guides them through the exhibit) or exploratory (visitors browse through the space and guide themselves to product areas of interest)? Do you want traffic to flow freely to each product area, or are there areas that should be set apart from the main traffic flow?

It's always surprising to see companies purchase prime island exhibit space with four open traffic aisles and enclose the exhibit with walls or panels on every aisle. There is only one good reason to use a space this way, and that is when you need to *plan* to keep visitors out of your exhibit. This may sound ludicrous, but for large companies at horizontal industry shows, this is a strategy they employ to pre-qualify their audience. Visitors will have to have a high interest in their products to go to the effort of entering their space. If you are considering this option, think carefully about it. Enclosed exhibits must be planned to carefully attract their audience.

Traffic flow is important even in the smallest spaces. If you have a 10' linear exhibit, consider whether you want to work primarily on the aisles, or will you be drawing traffic into the space to demonstrate products? Or would you prefer to use a two-phase selling process to open the interaction on the aisle, and invite visitors in only when you've established their interest?

Consideration: Trace traffic flow. When a design is proposed, trace the traffic flow on a plan view or model of the exhibit to insure that it meets your requirements.

Question: What are our traffic flow guidelines?

Oversight #3: Lighting.

Effects on your program: Lighting can affect each step of the exhibit selling process from attracting visitors to your exhibit, to assuring they can see product demonstrations and graphics clearly.

Consideration: Is the lighting functional? Lighting the exhibit and products properly, avoiding potential glare that makes graphics hard to read, considering the ambient light in the hall and its affects on the exhibit structure, are all as important as the size or color of the structure.

Consideration: Will dramatic lighting techniques further our objectives? This is a creative consideration and most of the possibilities will be presented by a designer. But if you think about lighting applications that you like, and have examples of exhibits to show your designer, the direction will provide him or her with more possibilities for your design solution. A few examples of dramatic lighting follow.

Consideration: Using lighting to identify product areas. At one Consumer Electronics Show a major exhibitor rented a large room instead of an exhibit space in the show hall. The room was divided by color-coded product categories and special colored spot lights created a glow of color that tied to that product category. The lights reflected onto gray carpet, flooding that section of the room in the appropriate color.

Consideration: Using lighting to attract attention. The Computer Graphics show typically keeps the ambient light in the hall very low so that the exhibitors' computer-generated images appear brighter on the screens. Knowing that, designer Mitchell Mauk created an exhibit that Sun Microsystems would use at that show with a white overhead canopy lit from within. The effect was a warm glow over the exhibit that could be seen throughout the show hall.

Consideration: Using lighting to dramatize exhibit graphics. Designer Charlie McMillan used colored spots in a 10′ linear exhibit designed for Communique, Exhibitor Education Inc. (Photo #3-1). The light reflected off the graphics and created an eye-catching, warm glow in the small space. For ICI he used lighting to create interesting shapes and shadows on the structure and draw attention up high, while spotlighting and emphasizing products at eye level (Photo #3-2). Another company used edge-lit plexiglass for signs and conference room walls in their exhibit. When the plexiglass is lit, all edges and any images etched in the material glow.

Question: What are our lighting preferences/guidelines?

Oversight #4: Exhibit Installation and Dismantling.

Effect on program: Additional and often unnecessary expense.

Consideration: Estimate budgets for exhibit I&D. One exhibitor had a beautiful, large custom display built for his company and planned to

Photo 3-1.

Photo courtesy the McMillan Group and Communique Exhibitor
Education, Inc.

use it for five years. After just two years he scrapped the structure because
it was so heavy he could no longer afford storage, shipping, drayage, and
installation/dismantle costs. Dramatic, yes, but variations on this theme
are not uncommon. When setting goals for an exhibit consider the ongoing
expenses incurred *for each use.*

To do that, estimate what you can spend on transportation, drayage,
and installation/dismantle for each show. The percent allocation figures
from Chapter 2 can be used as guidelines here. According to the averages,

Photo 3-2.

Photo courtesy ICI Americas Inc. and the McMillan Group.

approximately 14% of the total show budget is spent on transportation, and 21% is spent on show services (installation/dismantle labor, drayage, electrical, etc.).

Consideration: Get cost estimates for each design considered. When you review the design, inquire about the approximate shipping weight and get estimates for transportation costs to a variety of show cities on your schedule. Ask the exhibit supplier for an estimate of time to install and dismantle the structure and estimate labor costs. The exhibitors manual or the official contractor for each show can provide per hour labor rates.

Consideration: Show regulations. Be sure to check your show manuals for restrictions on exhibit heights, hanging signs, and depth of the exhibit structures. Incorporate those restrictions into your goals for the exhibit.

Question: What are the budget guidelines and show regulations?

Oversight #5: The Life of the Structure.

Effect on program: Structural adequacy over the planned life of the structure, and expense.

Consideration: Length of time. If you are planning on using the structure for several years it will be important that finishes are durable, and that the colors and graphics can be changed with minimal expense. If you only need the structure for short-term use (one or two shows), the materials will not have to be as sturdy and you may be able to use a less expensive structure.

Consideration: Number of shows. Will the structure be used for just one or two shows a year with the same audiences in the same markets, or for a variety of shows to reach different markets? This will affect the types of graphics you use, how the structure will be shipped and stored, and also how flexible it will need to be for handling and installation.

Consideration: What configurations will be needed? If you exhibit in many shows or plan to within the life of the exhibit, you might need a structure to work in space sizes from 100 square feet up to 2,000 square feet or more. Is the structure easily adjusted to fit different spaces? Is it expandable?

Questions: How long will we use the exhibit? What configurations will we need?

Oversight #6: Graphics Options.

Effect on the program: Graphics have a significant effect on the communications impact of your structure.

Consideration: Explore a variety of graphics solutions. Traditionally, exhibit designers are the keepers of knowledge on graphics solutions available for exhibit structures. There are a variety of techniques for producing exhibit graphics, but the key is creativity. The chart in Exhibit 3-3, prepared by Charlie McMillan of the McMillan Group will help you explore graphic options that you can use to make your structure best meet your goals.(2)

Exhibit 3-3 Graphics Techniques

Graphic	Technique	Possibilities	Limitations	Price Range
Hand-painted signs	Hand-lettered with brush and paint or airbrush.	Unlimited possibilities of size, color, and lettering styles.	Not practical for multiples. Limited by skills of painter.	Low to medium (Multiples are higher)
Scenic painting	Hand-painted with brush, airbrush, indian cans, sponges, etc.	Create scenes and effects that don't exist in reality: forced perspectives for example.	Vulnerable surface. Must use fireproof canvas. Limited by artist's skill.	Low to medium based on subject
Frisket	Spray paint over a stencil onto a finished surface leaving stencil image. (Varied materials are used in stencils.)	Very precise color and image matching.	Requires very specialized skills and labor. The graphics can be fragile and must be protected from scratching.	Medium to high
Silk-screen	A stencil of the image is adhered to fabric stretched across a frame. Ink is pulled across the fabric with a squeegee to produce the image on a panel.	Good for large (12″×12″ and larger) images where multiples are needed.	Requires special equipment and skills. Can reproduce detailed images with special fine mesh and screens, but this is typically not done for trade shows. Silkscreen for exhibits is usually limited to 10 pt. type or larger.	Medium to high Cost drops as multiples increase

	Description	Advantages	Limitations	Rating
Photo prints (reflective)	Original art is photographed and prints are produced from either a negative or a positive, depending on the process.	Offers a great variety of sizes and true-to-life enlargements of nearly any subject that can be photographed.	Original art must be clean. Enlargements can be grainy. Lengths are limited to length of the roll, 25' +. With a few exceptions, Ektacolor Professional 72" can be printed wider.	Medium to high
Photo prints (backlit)	Negative images are printed on a translucent film which is mounted on a light box.	Backlighting dramatizes images and visually lifts them off the surface to attract attention. Any size can be used but the substrate plastic material comes at a maximum width of 48", with a few exceptions.	Require the added cost of lightbox, electrical, ventilation, shipping cases for protection.	High
Megaprints Rosco-murals Scana-murals	The image is reproduced by paint jets onto a substrate (typically fabric) on a rotating drum.	Good for large scenic images, backdrops, full-scale product reproductions.	Images smaller than 4×3' may be very grainy due to a smaller piece needing a closer viewing range. They work best when viewed from 21' or more away from audience to allow the eye to mix the colors.	Medium to high

Exhibit 3-3 Graphics Techniques

Graphic	Technique	Possibilities	Limitations	Price Range
Bowers prints	Similar to Scanamural type prints but a different process is used	Finer grain allows closer viewing range. Great color reproduction. Because a translucent paper is used as the substrate, a bowers print can be used as front- or back-lit art.	Durability and longevity are not as good as Scanamurals or typical photo prints due to paper substrate. Overlam helps this situation and still allows a low price.	Low
Vinyl letters	Typefaces reproduced from digital fonts. The vinyl cutting machine uses a rotating drum with razor point to physically cut the letters into colored sticky-back vinyl material.	Quickly creates large letters, logos, and images. Use expanding in exhibit industry and most exhibit houses use them to expand applications and reduce reliance on silk screen.	Silkscreen can be more economical when more than about 3 prints are needed depending on complexity and number of colors produced. Type smaller than ½" doesn't work well.	Low to medium

| Dimensional letters | Stock letters cut from plastic and custom-cut lettering, artwork or logos from almost any material (or made to look like any material if custom-finished). | Add drama and dimension to nearly any image. Good lighting can enhance the dimension of the image. Materials can be simulated, such as solid stone or metal made from light-weight cores of wood or foam with epoxy coating, painted or laminated to look like a substantial finish. Actual stone and/or metals can also be used but weight and cost factors limit the exhibit applications. | The nature of a small object projecting out from a flat panel makes them susceptible to getting dented or knocked off the panels. | Medium to high |

95

The following photopages illustrate several types of graphics described above.

Photo 3-3. Scenic paintings are used for backgrounds in this theme exhibit.

Photo courtesy of The McMillan Group.

Consideration: What is the function of the graphics? Exhibit graphics serve three basic functions: to *attract*, to *direct*, and to *inform*. It follows that the graphics designed to attract should be large and arresting. Dramatic images work best here. Graphics designed to direct are typically words (but don't have to be) and are large enough for people to read once they are near or inside the exhibit space. Graphics designed to inform can be small, include type and pictures, but type should be limited. People rarely read volumes of type on an exhibit panel. (3)

Important point: graphics must tell the visitor who you are and what your company does.

Question: What are our graphics messages? Do we have graphics preferences?

Photo 3-4. Scanamurals work best with large images.

Photo courtesy of Scanamural.

Photos 3-5 and 3-6. Dimensional letters and graphics create
these corporate logos.

Photo courtesy of The McMillan Group and Reebok, Int'l. Ltd.

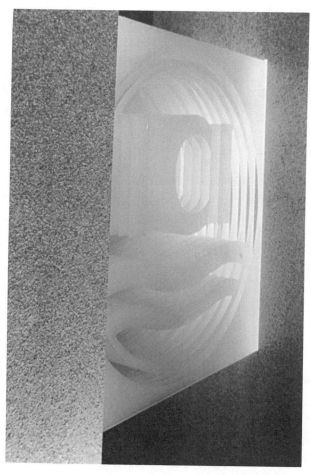

Photo courtesy of ICI Americas Inc. and The McMillan Group.

Photo 3-7. Here composite art (photos and graphics) are backlit using a lightbox.

Photo courtesy of The McMillan Group and Kreepy Krauly Inc.

Oversight #7: Considering All Structural Options.

Effect on program: Can dramatically affect flexibility, budgets, and image.

Consideration: Expense and Portability. Structural options for exhibits fall into five basic categories. The categories, which are defined below, provide you with the options of less expensive and more portable, to more expensive and less portable, in varying degrees. The chart in Exhibit 3-4 illustrates this. The direction of the arrows represents lowest to highest. For example, pipe and drape is least expensive and most portable.

Exhibit 3-4 Structural Options

		⟶ Expense ⟶		
Pipe & drape	Portable exhibits	System exhibits	Custom Systems	Custom Exhibits
		⟵ Portability ⟵		

These are basic guidelines, and in your search for an exhibit you will find some aberrations to this norm. For example, I have seen cases where portable displays are just as expensive as some custom displays of the same size. And custom systems can be as expensive as custom exhibits. But this range can be used as a general guideline.

Pipe and drape. Show managements use pipe and drape to divide exhibit spaces, so it usually is included in the price of your space rental. Custom drapes with your corporate logo can also be ordered through independent suppliers.

Portable exhibits. These structures have taken the exhibit industry by storm in the past five years. Research by the *Exhibitor Magazine* showed a 531% increase in sales of 10′ portable exhibits from 1981 to 1987.(4) Several companies now manufacture variations of the portable display which consists of a frame and panels that are packaged so that they can be checked as airline baggage. The graphics are customized, and, when searching for a portable display, ask for samples of graphics they have produced. Watch for input and direction in designing and producing your graphics.

System Exhibits. These exhibits are constructed of pre-fabricated components. The services of a designer are usually required to create a structure from the components that will serve your needs.

Custom Systems. These are system exhibits in which the components are created on a custom basis to your (or your designer's) specifications. They are most appropriate when you have a great need for flexibility and attend many shows.

Custom Exhibits. Buying a custom exhibit is like having your house designed and built. Based on your input a custom design solution is created and built.

Question: What are our structural preferences?

A source for detailed information on exhibit structures, from pipe and drape to custom builders, is *Exhibitor Magazine's Annual Buyer's Guide to Exhibits.*(5)

Three Guidelines for Budgeting for the New Structure

Determining how much you should spend for a new exhibit is like deciding how much you should spend on a house. There are rough guidelines but the best way to make that determination is to consider what you want, and then see what it typically sells for. For starters, here are a few guidelines offered in the trade show industry.

- **Industry Research.**(6) Research on what exhibitors spend to build a new exhibit indicates that the average is $963 per lineal foot for a backwall exhibit. That means a 10' linear exhibit costs $9,630. The cost for island and peninsula exhibits averages $37 per square foot, which means a 20' × 20' display costs approximately $14,800 (400 sq. ft. × $37). Unfortunately the most recent figures available are 1985, so you would have to adjust for inflation in setting your own guidelines.

  The same research identified that exhibitors spend, on the average, 21% of their total budget for a single show on exhibit construction. To calculate this percentage the price of the exhibit was amortized over its life. Therefore, it's a bit tricky to figure out guidelines here. But you could say that if you purchase an exhibit and plan to use it for three years, going to five shows each year, the amortized portion of the exhibit expensed in any single show budget would be ⅟₁₅th of the total exhibit cost. That ⅟₁₅th should represent about 21% of the show budget.

- **Industry Publications.** *Exhibitor Magazine* publishes the cost of exhibits featured in many of their articles. Reviewing a variety of articles and recording costs for varying size exhibits will give you an idea of what you can expect to pay. The magazine also publishes a monthly list of new exhibit projects on which various exhibit producers are bidding. This listing includes the budget and a description of the project which provides some current guidelines. For portable or system exhibits, check *Exhibitor's Annual Buyer's Guide to Exhibits.*(4) This guide lists several features of prefabricated exhibit structures along with their prices.

- **Other Exhibitors.** Asking someone how much they paid for their exhibit is sort of like asking how much they paid for their car. Some people will be offended, some like to brag about it, and you will most likely be more comfortable asking your friends. But getting this inside information will also provide some useful guidelines for your own budgeting decisions.

How to Get Accurate Price Estimates

Before you agree to an exhibit project, get a *detailed* estimate from your builder. Even if you are just ordering a portable or pre-fabricated display be sure to get estimates for costs such as graphics, or carpet. Estimate formats vary among exhibit builders, but generally fall under these categories.

- **The Lump Sum Estimate.** Here the exhibit firm, when presenting a concept or sketch, provides a flat price for the cost of the structure. Common business sense would raise some concerns here. First, interpretations of a drawing, sketch, or even a model can vary so dramatically that it might look like a Mercedes and turn out like a school bus. Also, it is difficult to determine exactly what is included. What, exactly, is the structure made of? Does the lump sum include storage and handling? Does it include crates for the structure? This type of bid allows for the least control over and knowledge about your purchase.

- **The Line Item Estimate.** Here everything is spelled out. In fact at some exhibit houses the line item estimate is so detailed it doubles as the invoice. This gives you a greater knowledge of and therefore control over what you get . . . right from the start. The only shortcoming of the line item bid is that it does not allow you to consider variable options.

- **The Alternate Option Estimate.** Some exhibit suppliers are using computers to generate estimates and a few provide some pretty fancy bids. The most sophisticated are those that provide variable prices for different solutions. For example an exhibit graphic illustrated in a sketch could be created in the exhibit either in neon (very expensive), or silkscreened onto a panel (less expensive), or applied with adhesive-backed striping (least expensive). This bid will indicate the cost for each option, allowing you to pick and choose where you want to indulge and where you want to economize. These bids tend to be most thorough and allow you the most input and control in the process.

- **Create Your Own Estimate.** If you receive estimates from more than one exhibit house, it will be difficult to make direct comparisons because their solutions differ. To make more of an apples to apples comparison when soliciting bids on a project, you can create a custom estimate sheet based on the basics of the proposals. Then complete the sheets as estimates come in.

Key Point: Know exactly what you are getting. Does this price include the shipping crates? Does it include storage and handling? Does it include a preview of the exhibit with it fully set up prior to the first show at which it will be used? Although it is not comprehensive, the following checklist provides most of the basic expenses you will want to assure have been included on your estimate. Add any additional expenses that you determine might be included.

Exhibit 3-5   Checklist of Estimate Items

☐ A description of all structural parts (for example two columns, three arches, two light boxes) should be listed. This description may include a single price estimate for all of the components or a line item for each component. Assure that all parts you expected to see from the rendering are included here in this description. This should include dimensions and materials used.

☐ Finishes. What types of finishes will be used on the various components of the display?

☐ Carpet. Be sure that the charge includes cutting the carpet and preparing it for the show. Will you need a special shipping container for the carpet?

☐ Lighting. Request a description of lights that will be used. Will any necessary wiring be included here?

☐ Crates. Decide whether or not you will need crates to ship the exhibit. Are they included in the price?

☐ Storage space. Be sure that your estimate indicates which components will provide storage space in the booth.

☐ Graphics. Look for a description of the type of graphics that will be used and a per-item estimate.

☐ Exhibit storage. If you decide to store the exhibit at the builder's facility, that may require an additional charge. Has that been considered in your estimate? What type of insurance coverage is included?

☐ Pre-show preview. Setting up an exhibit for your review prior to the first show is essential, and expensive. Be sure that the cost of that has been considered in your estimate.

☐ Handling. Your exhibit house may charge a handling fee to get the structure prepared for shipping.

Rarely do people decide on an exhibit structure based on cost alone. Before you compare the prices on various estimates, review your list of goals for the exhibit and look for the solution that best meets those goals.

The estimates then allow you to know more precisely what you are getting (and not getting) with each proposed solution.

Options for Managing the New Exhibit Expense

Companies typically manage the exhibit expense one of three ways. However, after reviewing the options here it would be beneficial to talk with your company's accountant to explore the best solution.

- **Amortize by show.** For those of you who break out in a cold sweat when you hear the word accounting, I'll define *amortize.* "To put money aside at intervals for gradual payment." (*Webster's New World Dictionary*). For our purposes here, it means the price of the exhibit is divided by the number of shows in which it will be used during it's projected life. That cost is then taken from the budget for each show.
- **Amortize by year.** Or you can amortize the price of the exhibit over the number of years it will be used. If the exhibit will be used for three years, one-third of the total price is taken out of the annual budget of the trade show department for each of the three years of its life.
- **Consider it a capital expense.** Or the price of the structure can be considered a piece of capital equipment purchased by your company and expensed as a budget item in the year it was purchased.

Different options will have advantages and disadvantages for your company based on your accounting and budgeting procedures.

SELECTING THE BEST SUPPLIER

Five Steps to Assure a Successful Working Relationship

People like to say that your relationship with an exhibit supplier is like a marriage. Well, it is and it isn't. It is like a marriage in that (hopefully) it will be a long-term relationship and it requires communication and contributions by both parties.

However, it is not like a marriage in one major way: you pay the exhibit supplier a lot of money for their expertise and for the product. So you can expect a *lot* from them in return. Your exhibit supplier should be willing to take the lead and introduce to you new concepts and ideas not only for your exhibit but also for your entire trade show program. As you select a supplier for the new exhibit, these five steps taken *in advance* help to make that working relationship a productive one.

Step One: Ten Questions to Ask Potential Suppliers

Start by listing the potential candidates. You can find exhibit firms through a variety of resources. Your yellow pages listings will be a good source for local firms. But you needn't restrict yourself to that. Some companies are finding it economical to go out of state for their exhibit firms because of competitive prices in various areas of the country. Another good source is trade shows. Find out who built the exhibits you liked best. If you don't get out to shows a lot, industry trade publications such as *Exhibitor Magazine* and *Trade Show and Exhibit Manager* feature photos of exhibits and their builders.

Narrow that initial list down to a handful, say five or six, then get to know more about them through phone interviews. The ten questions here are designed to get you started, and be supplemented by your own information requirements.

1. **What services do they offer?** "Full service" is an adjective that exhibit houses frequently use to describe themselves. That typically means that they offer some sort of marketing direction for your trade show program, exhibit design, construction, storage, shipping, and they will act as a resource for other needs you might have such as a lead processing system or exhibit staff training. Exhibit firms at the other end of the spectrum simply build exhibits, their shops tend to be smaller and prices are often lower. Identify what you are paying for early (overhead costs are built into the price of your structure), to determine whether or not you need it.

Exhibit 3-6   Exhibit Firm Size and Services

Exhibit Suppliers vary in size and resources		
Smaller firms	**Mid-size firms**	**Larger firms**
Less overhead	More services	More overhead
Fewer services	Personal attention	More services
Personal attention	More resources	More clients
		Greatest resources

2. **How do account executives and designers interface with clients?** Typically when you work with an exhibit supplier your relationship will begin with an account executive. In many cases you never meet with the person who designs your exhibit. The account executive translates all

of your needs for the designer who then creates your exhibit concept and gives it to the account executive to present to you. However, there are alternatives to this arrangement, as the diagram in Exhibit 3-7 illustrates. If you want a closer working relationship with your exhibit designer, assure ahead of time that the firm's employees are used to, and comfortable with, that arrangement.

Exhibit 3-7   Client/Account Executive/Designer Relationships

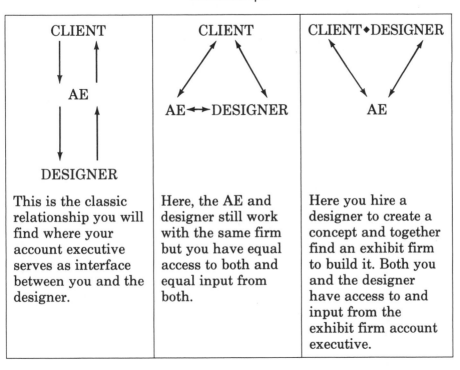

CLIENT	CLIENT	CLIENT◆DESIGNER
AE		
DESIGNER	AE◄─►DESIGNER	AE
This is the classic relationship you will find where your account executive serves as interface between you and the designer.	Here, the AE and designer still work with the same firm but you have equal access to both and equal input from both.	Here you hire a designer to create a concept and together find an exhibit firm to build it. Both you and the designer have access to and input from the exhibit firm account executive.

3. **Who are their major clients?** This helps to determine if they favor one industry or type of product. When an exhibit firm has experience in your industry, they are familiar with the shows, your competitors, and some of the quirks of the industry's events. This can only benefit you. If, however, they have little or no experience in your industry, it is not necessarily a reason to count them out. Just be aware that you will be learning together on some of the details.

4. **Do they have offices around the country?** The larger exhibit firms in the United States have offices in many of the country's major show cities. This can be a great advantage if you exhibit in many shows spread throughout the U.S.

5. **How many designers do they have on their staff?** Some firms will have a team of designers inside, others will job out their designs to freelancers. If they work with freelancers (which is not necessarily bad), you will want to be even more sure that you clarify expectations for your relationship with that designer.

6. **How is their business distributed among clients?** If a large percentage of their business comes from one or two clients, and your contribution is small by comparison, you might find your needs taking a back seat to theirs when time is short.

7. **How do they inventory exhibit properties?** Many houses are now going to computerized inventory of exhibit properties in their warehouse. This can reduce the hassle significantly if you need to keep track of several properties in use at the same time.

8. **Do they make competitive bids?** Competitive bidding is a hot issue in the exhibit industry. The typical purchasing scenario is to invite two or three exhibit houses to create a concept and bid on the project. They should all get the same information and guidelines up front and the same chance for a presentation of their solution. Unfortunately, at times, the level of energy and resources the exhibit firm commits to that solution is in direct proportion to the chance they think they have of getting the job. But, more importantly, some suppliers reject this process because it doesn't establish the climate of give-and-take between the client and the exhibit firm essential to a good working solution. A few exhibit firms will not participate in competitive bidding at all. They instead prefer to take a great deal of time up front getting to know you, the client, and your needs, and allowing you to get to know them before you make a decision to hire them. Then based on trust you work together to create the best design solution.

9. **On average, how many clients does each account executive handle?** There is no rule-of-thumb here, but comparing firm to firm will provide you with some guidelines as to the kind of personal service you will receive.

10. **What types of bids do they provide?** If the firm will only supply you with a lump sum bid . . . be careful.

After interviews, narrow down the list to two or three exhibit firms. Invite the firms to your facilities to make a presentation. Ask them to present a few specific problems their clients had and their solutions. Watch at this point for their problem-solving capabilities.

Next, check the firms' references. Request two or three references for each exhibit firm, and call them. The problem with checking references is that, of course, the firms provide names of those clients who will offer a rather glowing report. And human nature is such that most of us don't like to say bad things about people anyway. So to get a balanced picture of the references' relationships with their exhibit firm, ask specific questions, such as those following.

Step Two: Checking References: A Guide for Beginners

Exhibit 3-8

Of course you will not want to make the casual reference check call feel like an interrogation. But a list of questions prepared in advance will assure your conversation isn't filled with fluffy superlatives. After reviewing these questions you will probably want to come up with a few of your own.

1. Have you ever had to change account executives? If so, why?
2. Has the exhibit firm missed any deadlines? If so, how did they handle the situation?
3. Do they tend to stay within your budget parameters or go over?
4. Are their invoices clear and accurate?
5. What do you like best about their services?
6. What would you like to change if you could?
7. Do you have access to all of the people within the firm who are involved in your projects, or only the account executive?
8. How do they keep track of your exhibit properties?
9. Did your exhibit structure meet your expectations? If not, what were the shortcomings?
10. Is your account executive available at all times when you need him/her?

Step Three: Touring the Exhibit Firm—Seven Telling Observations

Representatives from exhibit houses will be anxious to have you visit their facilities. In fact the result of your first call to them might be an invitation for a tour. Try to hold off on this until you have narrowed your list of potential firms to two or three. Otherwise it becomes a waste of your time and that of the exhibit house, since many of the factors that will narrow your options can be discovered over the phone.

However once you narrow the list, it is worth the time to make a visit to the remaining firms. Their facilities can tell you a lot about the quality of their services.

Advice from the Experts

Gerry Howard served as Chief Executive Officer of Greyhound Exhibit Group Inc., the largest exhibit firm in the country. His experience at ExhibitGroup, along with his work as an exhibit designer at several firms, gives him a broad base from which to offer direction on what to look for during your tour of the exhibit firm.

Most importantly, he says, don't focus on structures so much as concepts. The exhibit structure is a tool used to accomplish marketing objectives. Therefore you want to try to discover how people are thinking, rather than how pieces of plywood are nailed together. How do they envision the exhibit functioning for their clients' purposes? The best thing you can do is *talk*—to a wide variety of their people—and *listen* to their attitudes about the *function* of an exhibit.

What does the firm and its employees think about themselves? When you walk into an advertising agency or an architectural firm you expect to see eager, bright, refreshing people. You should expect the same when you walk into an exhibit firm.

How is the facility designed and how does it function? The concern they have for their own workspace and its efficiency can tell you a lot about the approach they will take toward your exhibit and how it will work for you—selling *your* clients.

Look at work in progress. Do the craftsmen seem particularly attentive to details? Are they proud of what they are doing?

Are workspaces intentionally laid out? Is there a lot of clutter around, or does it look organized?

What are they doing besides construction? Are there areas for lighting applications, animation, demonstrations? This will give you an idea of the types of services they can offer besides just the construction of the exhibit.

What is in their library? Are there just product books, like laminate samples and fabric swatches, or are there also books on marketing and communications? This will give you an idea whether they approach exhibits as marketing tools or just as structures. It will also give you an idea of the resources they have available to you.

Is the warehouse organized? This is a good indicator of how your properties will be treated in storage.

Step Four: Matching Their Services with Your Needs

The challenge in finding the right exhibit firm is matching their services with your needs. A quick way to make that evaluation is to create a services/needs chart similar to the one in Exhibit 3-9. This chart is only a representative example and you will have to design your own, based on the services you find. That way you can compare, in one place, all of the services that the firms you interview have to offer, with those that you need.

In the previous example, our company might be focusing clearly on marketing strategies and be looking for marketing help. They already work with an independent installation and dismantle company so they won't need help there, and their exhibit can be shipped through the company's traffic department so no help is needed there.

Exhibit 3-9   Services/Needs Chart

Services	Firm #1	Firm #2	Firm #3	Our Needs
Resource library	√		√	√
Installation/ dismantle supervision	√	√	√	
Installation/ dismantle labor		√		
Marketing expertise	√		√	√
Transportation	√	√		
Storage	√	√	√	√
Computerized inventory		√	√	√
Alternate option bids			√	
Staff training			√	√

The idea here is for you to determine what your needs are (you may want to include a column for a wish list . . . things that aren't essential but would be nice to have). Then you can make a good comparison among the last two or three companies you are considering.

Step Five: How to Prepare Clear, Useful Design Guidelines

This is where you tie all of the thinking you have done in this chapter, along with goals you established in the previous chapters, together. The Design Guidelines consist of a document that outlines your goals and needs for the exhibit structure, and also established the timeframe in which you expect the work to be completed. If you are asking two or three exhibit firms to bid on a project, provide a set of Design Guidelines for each bidder. If you are working exclusively with one firm, provide the Guidelines for them as a starting point in the design process.

You can use your own copy of the design guidelines as an aid to evaluating proposed solutions. Create a copy for each solution and add a "Yes, No" column to indicate whether that criterion has been met.

An outline for the Design Guidelines follows:

I. Company Background. (For most of this information you can refer to your strategic plan for trade show participation.)

   A. Company, business, and product line.
   B. Markets
   C. Distribution channels
   D. Attendee profiles or market profiles
   E. Illustrative photos

II. Show Participation Objectives. (For this information, refer back to your strategic plan, and your operational plans for show participation.)

   A. Number of shows participated in annually
   B. Variety of markets reached at those shows
   C. Objectives for show participation (From the strategic plan)
   D. Goals for show participation (From the operational plans)

III. Image Goals.

	Yes	No
A. Image to present	____	____
B. Logo requirements	____	____
C. Then/now guidelines for image changes	____	____

IV. Functional Goals. (From your operational plans for show participation and material in this chapter)

	Yes	No
A. Variety of configurations required	____	____
B. Electrical and plumbing requirements	____	____

C. Height and weight restrictions   _____ _____
D. Demonstration and presentations used _____ _____
E. Lighting needs   _____ _____
F. Color preferences   _____ _____
G. Traffic flow preferences   _____ _____
H. Graphics preferences   _____ _____
I. I&D Budget guidelines   _____ _____
J. Show regulations   _____ _____
K. Structural preferences   _____ _____

Helpful input from the exhibit firm:

_____

_____

_____

_____

_____

A seminar participant once told me that she had spent a great deal of time reviewing exhibit designs to get just the look she had wanted. And she did, but a year later she discovered she had to spend half again as much to adapt the structure to meet all of their logistical requirements. Buying an exhibit on looks alone is like purchasing a car from a catalog.

Establishing goals contributes a great deal toward avoiding that situation. And design guidelines established early in the process provide a foundation on which to decide among proposed solutions. The guidelines can be flexible and maybe even change completely during the design process, but you will still have established what you need as a basis for selection.

Chapter 4: You are here:

↓

	9 Mo.	6 Mo.	5 Mo.
Planning			
Goal-Setting			
Budgeting		Prepare zero-based show budget	
Promotions		Evaluate promotion options	Create promotion strategy
Product Demos			
Exhibits	Set goals and budget for new structure Select supplier	Finalize supplier selection	Begin design process for new structure
Installation		Select show services	Plan transportation Select contractor
Staffing		Plan pre-show staff meeting	Create sales action plan for staffers
Inquiry Processing			Plan inquiry processing procedures
Measuring Results			

4

Putting
the Plan into Action
(6 Months in Advance)

*To succeed, planning alone is not enough. One must improve
as well.*

—Isaac Asimov

Improving, in this case, requires putting your plan into action. If you
have taken the time to create a strong plan, the rest of your show program
will begin to fall into place in this next six months as you see the plan take
shape. Much of what you will see in this chapter are the first steps toward
accomplishing the operational show plans.

The content may feel a bit choppy, because you will be working on
only part of several components of your show strategy. The following
chapters in Part I of this book will guide you through all of the steps
required to actualize those plans and as you work through the chapters
you will see your strategy come to life. In this chapter you will cover:

1. EXHIBIT DESIGN: Finalizing the supplier selection process.
2. PROMOTIONS: Evaluating promotional opportunities.
3. SHOW SERVICES: Selecting only the ones you need.
4. BUDGETING: Preparing zero-based, show-by-show budgets.
5. STAFFING: Tips for arranging the pre-show staffer meeting.

If your Show Plan (described in detail in Chapters 1 and 2) is divided
by show, and then by categories (exhibit, promotions, staff, etc.), you can
begin to file worksheets completed in these chapters and notes you make
under each category.

THE EXHIBIT SUPPLIER RELATIONSHIP: GETTING ACQUAINTED

In the process of creating a custom exhibit, communication between you and your exhibit supplier can make the difference between just an adequate working structure and an exceptional selling environment.

As the high-tech saying goes, "Garbage in, garbage out." This is as true for exhibit suppliers as it is for computers. If you only provide them with basic information, and keep them guessing about your company and products, their solution to you will be limited. However, if you provide them with a clear picture of your company, products, and markets, their recommended solutions should be of a much higher quality.

Assuming now that you have decided on one exhibit firm with which you will be working, it is time to become better acquainted. A good supplier will begin requesting a variety of information. You can be prepared, and even supplement, their inquiries with the following details about your company and the exhibit project. Remember, this is in addition to the information you provided in the Design Guidelines, earlier.

Ten Things Your Exhibit Supplier Must Know

1. **The Skeletons.** You needn't pull all of your corporate skeletons out of the closet when creating your Design Requirements, but as you develop a working relationship with your exhibit supplier, some of that information will be useful.

   A few examples are a disastrous product introduction at the previous show, or dealing with negative press, or problems with credibility in an industry. Admittedly, you are building a level of trust here and will need to begin where you feel comfortable to test the waters. See how your account executive handles the information and build from there.

2. **The Resistors.** When you and your account executive go to present a concept to the decision-makers in your company you are a team. Let the account executive know what to expect in the way of support and resistance from the participating parties. Clue him in as to where the mines are in the field, and where he will be able to look for support.

3. **The Products and Services.** Now is the time to allow your account executive, and perhaps your exhibit designer, to become painfully familiar with your products or services. They should see the products in action whenever possible, and understand exactly how they work, along with key benefits and features. If you sell services (insurance, for example), be sure they understand the distinctions between your offerings and those of your competitors.

4. **Your Competition.** Let them know who your chief competitors are along with their strengths and weaknesses in your markets. If you know who will be at the show, let them know that as well.

5. **Your Payment Procedures.** Ouch. This can often cause headaches,

and it will be helpful up front to let your account executive know how your invoices are processed and what to expect.

6. **Your Team.** If there are other people within your department with whom the account executive will be working, make introductions up front. Let them know each person's role in the exhibit department and how they might contribute to the process of the new exhibit construction.

7. **Past History.** If you worked with another exhibit firm in the past, let the account executive know this. Let him or her know why you left that firm and what work they had done for you.

8. **Outside Agencies.** Oftentimes advertising agencies and/or public relations agencies are asked to contribute during the exhibit design process. If your agencies will be involved, let the account executive know this as early as possible, and also exactly what their role will be. It is also important that the agency representatives understand that you and the account executive will take the lead on their project and will be requesting support input only.

9. **Sales and Distribution.** Outline for the account executive how sales and distribution functions within the company. Working with an inside sales team is very different than working with distributors. It can affect your exhibit and how it will function. It will also impact lead processing and follow-up which can be made much easier with a few accommodations in the exhibit design.

10. **Company Expectations.** Let the account executive know up front what type of expectations you, and others within your company, have for the working relationship. Do you expect day-to-day telephone communication as the project gets underway, or is a weekly memo more suited to your style? Do you want to be notified of each problem that comes up or would you rather he or she solve it and then let you know about it?

This information will probably be discussed in one or more meetings as your project gets underway. Telling the account executive is one way in which you can familiarize him or her with your company. But some of the most productive exhibit designs are the result of the client arranging a variety of ways for the account executive and designer to become familiar with your company.

Exhibit 4-1 Five Tips for Familiarizing Your Account Executive with Your Company

1. **Arrange for product demonstrations.** Set aside a morning when the account executive can meet with an engineer or product manager to learn about and use the product themselves, hands on.

2. **Let them meet with your salespeople.** Especially if salespeople will be staffing the exhibit, let the account executive talk with one or two of them about their jobs, the products, how they like to present them, and what they need as sales tools in the exhibit.

3. **Let them meet with your customers.** Ask a few of your key customers if they would be willing to take a little time to talk with your account executive about how they are using your products.

4. **The Company Tour.** Invite the account executive to tour a plant or manufacturing facility. One account executive says he learns a lot about a company's corporate culture by what the employees have hanging on their walls and doors, and what they wear to work.

5. **Films, Literature, Etc.** Provide the account executive with a variety of your promotional and sales tools. If you use videos to explain products, give the account executive a chance to see those. If you are in a rather remote industry, say wastewater management, let the account executive see a few issues of the industry trade publications.

The range and depth of involvement on the part of your account executive will depend, to a degree, on the size of your project. If you are purchasing a 10′ portable display, the relationship with your supplier won't be nearly as in depth as if you are creating a custom modular structure to use in a variety of shows and industries over five years. Consider the depth you think will be appropriate for your project and then plan to get the account executive, or representative, involved at that level.

FOUR CONSIDERATIONS FOR SELECTING THE BEST PROMOTIONAL TOOLS

Consider for a moment the comparative value to the exhibiting companies of the following two trade show promotions. One company holds a drawing for a free portable television. Entering is easy, a sign on the fish bowl says "just drop your business card in." No need to talk to or feel trapped by any sales representatives in the exhibit. No need to return to win the prize, they will notify the winner.

Another company is giving away t-shirts. They aren't even designer t-shirts, instead they sport the company logo. To receive a t-shirt you must tour the exhibit searching graphics and displays for answers to questions listed on a small card, along with a few inquiries about yourself and your job. The company's sales representatives are available both to help you uncover all of the answers, and to award your t-shirt.

In the first promotion, success means walking away with a handful of business cards. There is little opportunity for sales representatives to interact with the entrants. Of what value will those business cards be? What will be done with them after the show? How much do they tell you about the people who visited your exhibit, and your success at the show?

In the second promotion success meant walking away with a handful of contacts for people who had taken the time to learn something new about the company and its products. It also provided an icebreaker for sales representatives to open conversations with exhibit visitors about new products.

Which accomplished most for the company? Obviously the second. For promotions to be successful for you they must begin with five key considerations. And overlooking those five key considerations are the common mistakes made in planning promotions.

1. **Not Considering Show Goals.** Perhaps you have found yourself on a show planning team where someone suggests the need to increase traffic to your exhibit. "Let's have a drawing, that should bring them in," is a typical response. Then the operative goal is to build traffic, period. As people in the trade show industry like to say, if your only goal is to build traffic, stand on the edge of your booth and hand out $20 bills.

   Of course you can see that the thinking has to go beyond just building traffic. Why do you want to build traffic? What do you want them to do once they get to the exhibit? What do you want them to remember after having been there?

   The solution here is to tie the promotion to show goals. Take the folks who gave away t-shirts, for example. Their goal was to inform visitors about a new product and generate inquiries on it. By asking them to answer questions about the product the company incorporated a technique by which they taught themselves first. Then they had contact with a sales representative who inquired about their interests, and provided detailed information and an offer for follow-up after the show.

   Therefore the first step in planning a promotion is to go back to your show plans and review *your goals for the show.*

2. **Promotional Goals Aren't Clearly Defined.** If you are getting a bit inundated with goals here—remember, goals provide a purpose for the spending. Here state in simple, concise sentences exactly what you want the promotion to accomplish. Consider the audience you want to attract, what you want them to do and why, how the promotion will attract them to your product or service message, and what you would like them to remember as a result of the promotion. Try to state your objectives in numbers so that you have a measure for success at the end of the show.

3. **The Audience Is Not Clearly Defined.** If you find it difficult to state your promotional goals in numbers, it is probably because you haven't targeted the audience for your promotion. You can do this by referring to the Potential Audience figures in your Strategic Show Plan. This will let you know how many people at that show will be interested in the

products you have on display. Use that to determine how many people you can realistically expect to participate in the promotion.

Numbers, however, are not the only definition here. It is also useful to define your audience by job function, or the business they represent. For example, if you are planning a direct mail promotion you might purchase a show attendee list from the previous year. You will be wasting a lot of money if you mail to all of the people on that list. Try to clean the list by mailing only to those in a geographic territory close to the next year's show, or by the titles and job functions that you know purchase your products.

4. **No Response Mechanism.** If you set specific number goals for a promotion you will want to measure its performance. You can best do this by including a response mechanism in the promotion. Include something that inspires the visitor to act in a way that you can measure the results. In a direct mail campaign or pre-show ad, ask people to return a card to enter in a drawing or exchange for a gift.

Response mechanisms can be used with almost any type of promotion, even with billboards. Include copy on the billboard letting visitors know that if they come to your exhibit and inquire about a specific product they will receive a sample, or gift. The best awards are samples of products because they selectively draw people who are interested in those products.

Typically if you conduct a promotion, people will hear about it through word of mouth and come by for your "goodie" even if they didn't receive or see the promotion. There are two ways to look at that. You can keep your results pure by limiting giveaways only to those folks who bring in their cards, for example. Or you can provide entry cards for anyone who inquires about the exhibit, considering word of mouth a legitimate extension of your promotion and attributing all entries to your goals.

Use the contest or drawing entry card as a qualifier. Include a few specific questions about the entrant's business and use of yours or similar products. Or you can go a step further and request that a sales representative in the exhibit stamp the card before it can be entered into the drawing. That provides an opportunity for salespeople to connect with the visitors.

Some companies go so far as to require that visitors see a number of product demonstrations before their drawing entries can be validated. For this to work, though, your products must have a very high interest level among the show attendees, or they simply won't take the time. A high percentage of the show audience must also be prospects for your services, or your sales representatives waste quite a bit of time demonstrating to visitors who have no need for your products or services.

5. **Wrong Timing.** Timing is particularly important when you use a pre-show direct mail campaign for promotion. It is also critical for billboards, airport promotions, press releases, and press events. If you initiate the

promotion too early, show attendees will have forgotten about it before they even get to the show. If you initiate it too late they might not see the promotion until after the show is over.

Pre-show direct mail campaigns should be sent out (first class mail) about two weeks prior to the event, assuring that that the recipient sees it about a week in advance. Billboards should be in place at least a day prior to the show's opening. Press releases vary because of publications' deadlines. Check with individual publications to assure your press release is early enough to make it into their show issue. Publication deadlines can be set months in advance of printing.

The chart in Exhibit 4-2 offers general guidelines on timing for promotion. In many cases you need to check with sponsors to assure the correct timetables.

Exhibit 4-2 Promotions Timeframes

Promotion	Timeframe
Trade publication advertising	Check with publication for *show issue* deadlines.
Direct mail	Plan to mail two weeks in advance of the show for First Class mail.
Press releases and editor contact	Check with publication for editorial deadlines. Contact editors one week before the show to arrange interviews
Billboards	Space reservations can be required up to one year in advance. Timing varies from city to city. (Reservation three months in advance is typical)
Airport advertising	Begin advertising one day prior to show opening.
Hotel TV advertising	Plan for early morning or late evening airtime. Air during first two or three days of the show.
Mobile ads	Begin opening day of show.
Hotel room promotions	Distribute first two days of the show especially if response is required. Plan for early morning distribution. May require material supplied evening before show opens.

Show issue trade publications advertising	Check publication deadlines.
Show daily advertising	Check publication deadlines.
Hall advertising	Plan to put advertising in place for first set-up day through the end of the show.
TV/photo opportunities	Inform media at least one week prior to the show. Plan in-booth photo sessions either before or after show hours.
Show directory advertising	Check publication deadlines.
Contests and Drawings	All preparations completed prior to leaving for the show.
In-booth premiums	Plan for production completion two weeks prior to show set-up. Delivery to the booth on first set-up day.

How to Evaluate Media by Show Goals

You have a variety of promotional media from which to choose at a trade show. The challenge is selecting the media that best meets objectives you have set for the show. Some media work better to accomplish certain goals. For example, if your goal is press coverage, holding a contest in your exhibit is not as direct a route to accomplishing your goals as sending out press releases or holding a press briefing.

When considering promotional media's appropriateness, you also need to consider how actively it involves the attendees or your target audience. Almost any promotional media can be *made* to be interactive. But some are more naturally active and some more passive. Contests and drawings, for example, are inherently active because they require action by the participant. Press releases are inherently passive, because you have little control over how they will influence your target audience.

The chart in Exhibit 4-3 identifies a variety of promotional media and which goals they can help you accomplish. The media are listed in a range of active to passive. This range considers that media that require a response on the part of the attendee in order to participate are most active. Media that can be made active have the most chance of getting a response when it occurs at the show or on the show site. (A banner in the show hall, for example, offering a gift upon visiting an exhibit and viewing a demonstration will probably get more response than a similar ad at the airport.) Media that is further removed from the actual show by time or distance is more in the passive range because soliciting a response becomes more difficult.

To use the chart in Exhibit 4-3, first review your goals for the show and for the promotions. Second, determine how active you want the promotion to be. Third, start in the range of activity you prefer, and select media appropriate to your goals.

When You Can't Afford a Full-Scale Promotion: Using Advertising Specialty Items to Build Traffic

Not everyone can afford a full-scale promotion to draw traffic to the exhibit. Believe it or not there is a viable alternative in advertising specialties—those little key chains, embossed pens, product miniatures, coffee mugs work. When used correctly, they are one of the most powerful tools for building traffic in your exhibit. Unfortunately, they are also one of the most abused.

You have probably seen the scantily clad model at the edge of the booth approaching you to stick a little fuzzie on your shoulder. Weren't you embarrassed? Well, variations on that theme are how those trinkets and doo-dads are typically used. But that's not how they should be used. Use the following guidelines to put power into these promotional tools yourself.

Connect the giveaway to your products or services. Yes, everyone can use a pen, but unless you sell office supplies, how will giving away a pen help a visitor remember your products and help a sales representative open a *productive* conversation with show attendees?

Link the giveaways to your products or services. A bank that wanted to use a small giveaway as an icebreaker in their exhibit selected a small puzzle with the theme "We Help You Solve the Financial Services Puzzle." Exhibit personnel offered to help visitors put together the puzzle as a conversation starter. Or you can link it to a theme that runs through trade shows and advertising. To promote a new line of axles, a division of John Deere put a new twist on an old theme "It's hard to remember you came to clear the swamp when you are up to your *axles* in alligators." Alligators became the theme and they used little metal alligator clickers as giveaways.

Make the giveaways a bit extraordinary. Both the puzzle and alligator example above are a unique departure from the standard keychain and plastic bag giveaways we've come to expect at shows. A yeast producer from Holland offered miniature wooden shoes at a Baking show. A computer company offered mini-chocolate disks. *Exhibitor Magazine* gave out but-

Exhibit 4-3

	Image Awareness
Promotion Media	
Active Contests/Drawings	
Telemarketing	
Direct Mail	●
Giveaways	
Hotel promotions	●
Hall advertising (Signs/banners)	●
Show issue ads	●
Show daily ads	●
Show directory ads	●
Billboards	●
Airport ads	●
Hotel/TV Ads	●
Mobile advertising	●
Trade publication ad	●
National or local press ads	●
Press briefings	●
Press releases	●
Passive Photo opportunities	●

GOALS

Generate Leads	Appointments	Book Sales	Product Intro.	Press Exposure
●			●	
	●	●		
●	●		●	
●			●	
			●	
●			●	
●		●	●	
●		●	●	
●		●	●	
			●	
			●	
			●	
			●	
		●	●	
			●	
			●	●
			●	●
			●	●

tons, but instead of creating their own phrases for the buttons, asked readers to send in ideas. You get the idea.

Don't cater to the goodie-grabbers. Goodie-grabbers, as they are affectionately termed in the industry, are those people who seem to go to trade shows to pick up freebies. If you leave your giveaways in a basket on a counter they will be inviting goodie-grabbers. Instead, ask staffers to carry them in their pocket and hand them out to get the conversation started.

Clue-in the sales staff. You may have a brilliant idea for a giveaway, but unless the people staffing the exhibit are clued-in as to how it is intended to work it won't do the job you intended. Be sure the staff sees them before the show, and suggest some non-threatening openers they could use to get show attendees involved. The staffers in *Exhibitor Magazine's* exhibit would ask people as they passed by the booth "Did you get your button?" while showing them a button with a funny phrase. Then while handing it to the visitor or pinning it on their lapel they asked, "Do you read *Exhibitor Magazine?*" and transitioned right into a conversation about the product.

The best incentive to use those giveaways wisely is to ask yourself "What am I getting for the money I'm spending on these things?" By incorporating these simple techniques you can make them far more useful.

Four Methods for Measuring a Promotion's Effectiveness

To determine whether a promotion worked, you need to ask two questions. First is, what do we want show visitors to do as a result of the promotion? And the second question is whether or not they did it.

The first question will be determined by the goals you set for the promotion. The following list shows a few goals you might establish:

*Change attitudes or perceptions

*Inquire about products or services

*Request literature

*Request a sales call

*Just come to the exhibit

*Watch a product presentation

The key to answering the second question is that response mechanism. If you just want to draw traffic to the exhibit, include a card or coupon in your promotion that visitors can redeem for an award upon visiting the exhibit. If you want to use the promotion to encourage visitors to talk with your salespeople, ask that the card be stamped by a sales rep before the award is received, or before it is entered into a drawing.

Once you have incorporated a response mechanism you have to

create a technique for measuring this response. Counting entry cards to a drawing, or coupons exchanged for an award is the simplest measure. But that only tells you gross numbers, it doesn't give you an idea of how many qualified participants you drew.

To determine changes in attitudes or impressions. This is more difficult but can be done through pre- and post-show surveys. It is difficult to isolate the promotion from all of the other show activities, but the survey will show the success of your overall effort.

To determine the number of inquiries, literature, and sales call requests. To do this, don't use contest entries as lead forms. Keep them separate. Create a space on your lead card where staffers can indicate whether the contact in the exhibit was initiated by the promotion. Then you can measure the number of qualified inquiries that resulted from the promotion.

To determine whether the promotion drew traffic. If your only goal is to draw traffic, a count of the responses will tell you whether or not you succeeded.

To determine whether it promoted presentation attendance. Getting a pure reading can be done one of two ways. You can ask visitors to bring a coupon to the exhibit, view the presentation, and then exchange the coupon for a gift after the presentation. Or you can send them tickets and require the tickets for entry. Sending them tickets is much riskier because the attendees must be highly motivated to see the presentation. Using a gift can be done with a great deal of success. One industry consultant tested this system at several shows with gifts ranging from telephones to coin banks. He determined that the value of the gift needn't be high, but the level of interest in the product must be high, and the *perceived* value of the gift must be high. (2)

Measuring effectiveness of a promotion will provide you with proven results, not just a gut feel about whether it worked or not. Doing so on an ongoing basis and keeping records will help you determine types of promotions that work best for different shows and audiences.

Guidelines for Arranging a Press Event They'll Attend

At this point in your planning review your show goals. If you have any press goals for the show, think about whether you would like to hold a press event. Press events range from informal conferences to large-scale galas. But they are a bit tricky to pull off. The following guidelines will help you to determine if a press event will further your goals, and how to assure attendance.

Is it news? Be painfully critical in deciding whether your information is newsworthy enough to warrant a press event. Use the old journalism scale of newsworthiness: If a dog bites a man, that's not news. If a man bites a dog, that's news. How will your new product influence the industry? How will it help their readers? These are things editors are looking for.

Send invitations. Do this well in advance of the show. Follow up those invitations with phone calls to get commitments for attendance. And remember, those commitments are flexible.

Don't bribe them. Most journalists are insulted by "incentives" to attend events such as giveaways or contests. In fact they probably will wonder why that's necessary if your news is important.

Do feed them. Editors are very busy at shows. Arranging a press breakfast or luncheon may increase attendance.

Offer photo opportunities. Plan to have your product available for photographs during the event. And let the editors know about it so they can send a photographer.

Combine forces. One of the most successful press events I have seen was held at a major computer show. A small company knew they didn't have the clout in the industry to draw editors from major publications to their press event. So they invited a few non-competing companies to join them in sponsoring a press event that assured editors they could cover several stories in one night, and allowed the companies to afford an impressive event. They drew editors from not only the big-name computer publications, but also the *Wall Street Journal, The New York Times,* and several major business publications.

SELECTING ONLY THE SHOW SERVICES YOU NEED

The Exhibitor's Manual, sometimes called the Exhibitor's Kit, is a package containing all of the information you need to know in order to participate in the show. You usually receive it within six months of the show and it's best to review it *right away.* It contains show rules and regulations, order forms for show services, installation and dismantle dates, fire marshall requirements . . . in short, the kind of information that would be very expensive to overlook.

The chart in Exhibit 4-4 offers a checklist of information to review at this point in your planning process. Many exhibitors like to use a highlighter pen as they go through the manual to call out regulations and expenses that are pertinent to their program.

Chances are you won't need all of the services offered in the Exhibitor's Manual. And for some you can decide whether you would like to use the show contractor's services or manage the task on your own, floral services for example. In most cases you are not required to use the show florist and exhibitors like to pick up plant arrangements at local florists, or ship silk plants with the exhibit to save money. Unless you are serving

---

Exhibit 4-4   Exhibitor's Manual Review Checklist

☐ Key contact for exhibitors

☐ Display regulations

☐ Promotion rules

☐ Fire marshall regulations

☐ Building regulations

☐ Advance notice required for independent set-up firms?

☐ Housing policies

☐ Unions required for set-up

☐ Straight time and overtime rates

☐ Move-in/out dates & times

☐ Drayage charges

☐ Service order forms

☐ Late payment fees

☐ Advance payment discount

☐ A-V Services

☐ Registration procedures

☐ Is a booth sketch required?

☐ Insurance requirements

☐ Security procedures/svs

☐ Shipping instructions

☐ Show dates and hours

☐ Hospitality policies

Notes: _____

_____

_____

_____

_____

_____

_____

_____

_____

---

popcorn or peanuts in your exhibit, you probably don't need to have the carpet vacuumed each day. For a smaller booth, once on the morning the show opens is usually enough.

You don't have to use the designated labor contractor at most shows either. You can bring in your own independent contractor but in most show halls you must use union labor for installation, electrical, plumbing, and in some cities sign hanging. In any state that is not a "right to work state," unions have jurisdiction over much of the work done during exhibit installations in convention halls and hotels. For more information on union guidelines and exhibit set-up see Chapter 10, "How to Succeed with On-Site Set-Up."

Three People Who Can Help

Unfortunately at times selecting these services is confusing. If your eyes blurred the first time you looked at an electrical services order form, you understand. It is difficult to know exactly what you will need. When you order labor they often ask how many people you will need and for how long. If you have no experience with your exhibit, it's tough to determine.

There are at least three people who can help you straighten this out.

Your exhibit supplier should be able to help you determine what you will need in the way of set-up and dismantle labor for the exhibit. They can also guide you in selecting services such as floral, photography, furniture, etc.

The *labor contractor* whether appointed by the show or an independent contractor can help you determine which union services you will need in order to get your exhibit set up.

And finally *product experts* within your company can often help with the electrical guidelines if you need special wiring for products in the exhibit. A note about electrical services. If your wiring is complex, you can save money by having as much of the exhibit pre-wired as possible. Keep in mind, though, that the wiring must follow standards set for the exhibit halls. Standards for Chicago's McCormick Place are said to be toughest and best to follow. But check with the halls you will be using for guidelines.

A STEP-BY-STEP GUIDE TO PREPARING ZERO-BASED SHOW BUDGETS

If you have had any experience at all planning budgets, the system here will be fairly simple. But the details are important. To prepare *accurate* show budgets all details must be included. The budget worksheet in Exhibits 4-5 and 4-6 will provide prompts to remind you of the information you need to gather, and help you organize that information.

Zero-based budgeting is a method for establishing a budget based on the estimated price of each component of the project. You start with nothing, and for each item you bring to the project, you have a line-item in the zero-based budget. This type of budget estimate is the most accurate, and, as you would guess, the most time-consuming to complete.

It is started at this stage in your show planning because you have considered the major components of your budget (the exhibit structure, the show services, and promotions strategies.) You may not actually

Exhibit 4-5 Budget Checklist

Exhibit	Set-Up Services	Promotions	Staff	Hospitality	Product Demonstrations/ Presentations
☐ Structure	☐ Labor	☐ Ads/creative	☐ Travel	☐ Invitations	☐ Scripting
☐ Graphics	☐ Electrical	☐ Ads/media	☐ Hotel	☐ Room	☐ Staging
☐ Refurbish	☐ Plumbing	☐ Direct mail list	☐ Per diem	☐ Food/bvg.	☐ Actors
☐ Carpet	☐ Cleaning	☐ Direct mail creative	☐ Training	☐ Presentation	☐ Sound
☐ Shipping	☐ Rentals	☐ Direct mail postage	☐ Badges	☐ Entertainment	☐ Lighting
☐ Drayage	☐ Floral	☐ Premiums	☐ Special talent	☐ A-V rental	
☐ Special product demonstrations or presentations	☐ Phone			☐ Gifts	
	☐ Photography				
	☐ Security				
	☐ A-V Rental				

Exhibit 4-6   Budget Worksheet

	Budget Item	Cost/per	Needed	Estimate	Actual

Charge
Back   Exhibit Structure

☐ _____ _____ _____ _____ _____
☐ _____ _____ _____ _____ _____
☐ _____ _____ _____ _____ _____
☐ _____ _____ _____ _____ _____
☐ _____ _____ _____ _____ _____
☐ _____ _____ _____ _____ _____

Set-Up Services

☐ _____ _____ _____ _____ _____
☐ _____ _____ _____ _____ _____
☐ _____ _____ _____ _____ _____
☐ _____ _____ _____ _____ _____
☐ _____ _____ _____ _____ _____
☐ _____ _____ _____ _____ _____
☐ _____ _____ _____ _____ _____
☐ _____ _____ _____ _____ _____
☐ _____ _____ _____ _____ _____
☐ _____ _____ _____ _____ _____

Promotions

☐ _____ _____ _____ _____ _____
☐ _____ _____ _____ _____ _____
☐ _____ _____ _____ _____ _____
☐ _____ _____ _____ _____ _____
☐ _____ _____ _____ _____ _____
☐ _____ _____ _____ _____ _____

Staff

☐ _____ _____ _____ _____ _____
☐ _____ _____ _____ _____ _____
☐ _____ _____ _____ _____ _____
☐ _____ _____ _____ _____ _____
☐ _____ _____ _____ _____ _____
☐ _____ _____ _____ _____ _____

Charge
Back   Hospitality

☐ _____ _____ _____ _____ _____
☐ _____ _____ _____ _____ _____
☐ _____ _____ _____ _____ _____

Budget Item	Cost/per	Needed	Estimate	Actual

Charge
Back   Product demonstrations/presentations

☐ _____ _____ _____ _____ _____
☐ _____ _____ _____ _____ _____
☐ _____ _____ _____ _____ _____

Miscellaneous (Use for post-show final budget)

_____ _____ _____ _____ _____
_____ _____ _____ _____ _____
_____ _____ _____ _____ _____
_____ _____ _____ _____ _____
_____ _____ _____ _____ _____
_____ _____ _____ _____ _____
_____ _____ _____ _____ _____

TOTALS   _____ _____

Percent
change (+/−)   _____

Notes on special circumstances (Use for post-show final budget)

_____
_____
_____
_____
_____

Budget Summary (Use for post-show final budget)

_____
_____
_____
_____
_____
_____
_____

complete the zero-based budget until just a few months before the show, but now is the time to begin the process. Creating an accurate zero-based budget estimate takes a bit of research and calculating. The following steps will guide you through the process.

Step #1: Using the Budget Checklist

First, identify all budget items that must be included. The chart in Exhibit 4-5 is a list of items that are typically required for show participation. Since you probably won't use every item, the chart is designed so that you can check off only those services you need.

Then transfer those items selected onto your budget worksheet in Exhibit 4-6. On the budget worksheet where "Use for post-show final budget" is written in parentheses, this item is only completed after the show. It is explained in Chapter 11.

Step #2: Using the Budget Worksheet

Now you are ready to begin the research. Some items will be easier to estimate than others. Here's how the Budget Worksheet is designed to help you. The boxes on the left are to indicate which items will be charged back to other divisions when you are splitting show costs. You will most likely not use this until you calculate the actual post-show budget, and it is explained in Chapter 11. But if you are splitting costs among divisions and can identify those items at this point, go ahead and check the appropriate boxes.

In the first column you have listed the services needed, organized topically. In the second column list the price per item. For example, to estimate labor costs, under the "price per" column list the labor rate, say $35 per hour, for your set-up labor. Next, list how much or how many you will need under the "Needed" column. You might require 20 hours for set-up and 10 for tear-down. Then under the estimate column list your total estimate ($35 × 30 = $1,050). The "Actual" column isn't used until the show is over, to list the actual cost for that item.

Some entries will be easy. If you are having a new exhibit built you simply enter the bid price under that "Estimate" column because no math is required.

Most of the information you need to know for your exhibit, transportation, and show services can be gotten from the Exhibitor's Manual or from your exhibit supplier. Estimates for promotions, staff, hospitality and special demonstrations or presentations will require quotes from your suppliers.

Step #3: Calculate Totals

Next, calculate your total budget and compare it to the budget estimate in your show plan. Now you can see whether you will need to cut back in certain areas, campaign for more resources, or whether you have a few additional dollars to play with.

Now, a few tips to help you get accurate estimates. As with any budget, one of the barriers to getting accurate estimates are the oversights. The things that you just hadn't considered that somehow creep into the picture. The following list identifies ten common oversights that, when considered, will contribute to more accurate estimates.

Ten Oversights That Can Add Thousands to Your Budget

1. **Understanding union jurisdictions.** In most show cities unions have jurisdiction over much of the work involved in setting up the exhibits. The problem here is that jurisdictions vary from city to city. Therefore you might think you only need to hire carpenters and electricians when you will also need riggers for a hanging sign, or decorators to hang your graphics. The Exhibitor's Manual should identify union jurisdictions for you. However, if you would like more information, the National Association of Exposition Managers has published a guide of union jurisdiction. (3)

2. **Overtime labor rates.** Chances are part of your set-up will be done during hours that are considered overtime for the unions. These rates can be up to double the standard time rates.

3. **Overtime policies.** Knowing when overtime goes into effect can help you not only estimate budgets accurately, but plan your set-up to avoid those hours.

4. **Drayage charges and policies.** If your exhibit is wrapped in pads rather than packaged in crates, there is a surcharge for drayage services. Unions responsible for drayage also have strict overtime policies that can affect your costs. There are also minimum charges for drayage, and if you have one or two extra boxes coming in later, you will be charged the minimum for each separate drayage request.

5. **Late payment charges.** Many show services, from electrical to booth space reservations, charge fees for late payments. Conversely, however, they often offer discounts for advance payment.

6. **Set-up supervision.** If you are not available to supervise the set-up of your exhibit, the contractor often provides a supervisor and marks up your labor rates by about 30%.

7. **Late shipments.** When the literature isn't printed until the last minute, or graphic copy wasn't submitted in time to get the graphics shipped with the exhibit structure, those overnight shipments are expensive. You might want to plan a few into your budget.

8. **Phone calls.** If you have outgoing long distance service on your booth telephone, budget for those long distance calls.

9. **Rush jobs.** If you make last minute requests or changes that require a rush job by your exhibit supplier to get the structure finished on time, you might incur rush charges.

10. **Supplies.** Anything from extension cords, to lightbulbs, to touch-up paint can be required both during set-up and throughout the show.

Consider those additional supplies in your budget and plan for them. In most cases, purchasing them before the show will be significantly less expensive than purchasing them on the show floor.

Finally, to help still more with the budgeting process, a list of commonly asked questions, along with the source for the answers, is listed in Exhibit 4-7.

Exhibit 4-7 Sources for Answers to Budgeting Questions

Question	Source
1. How long will we need union workers?	Exhibit supplier or installation/dismantle contractor
2. What are our electrical requirements?	Exhibit supplier and engineering or product development people
3. How do we determine the exhibit's shipping weight for drayage estimates?	Transportation supplier and exhibit supplier
4. What is drayage?	Exhibit supplier and I&D contractor
5. What unions will we need to hire?	Show labor contractor
6. How many people will we need in the exhibit?	Your show plan
7. Do we have to use the "official" suppliers for furniture, photography, floral?	Show management
8. When will we need security in the booth?	Show management
9. How are drayage charges calculated?	Exhibit supplier or show contractor
10. What is included in space rental costs?	Show management or space contract

FOUR POINTERS FOR ARRANGING THE PRE-SHOW STAFFER MEETING

Although six months is a bit early to actually select your exhibit staff (that is covered in a later chapter), it is a good time to begin planning for your pre-show staffer meeting.

Imagine bringing someone in to build a new house for you. You found some people who would be willing to do it, told them when and where, and then set them loose to build. Do you suppose you would end up with the house of your dreams? Probably not. Yet many people do the equivalent with exhibit staffers. They get all who are willing, tell them when and where, and expect a stellar performance. To truly make trade show participation successful the exhibit staff needs to know what to accomplish, and how to do that. Those guidelines can be covered in the pre-show meeting.

Two Types of Pre-Show Meetings—How to Select the Right One for Each Show

The Orientation Meeting. The orientation meeting is the simplest to conduct and does just as the title suggests—orients all of the staffers as to the details of the show. Plan to cover your objectives for show participation and specific goals for this show. Review the booth duty schedule, any sales tools available for the staffers to use, special promotions or presentations that you'll be using, and how they will be conducted. The orientation meeting is typically conducted by the person in charge of shows (the exhibits coordinator or manager) and/or the person in charge of the exhibit staff (typically a sales manager).

Whether you have a large exhibit at a major show or a 10' booth at the local Holiday Inn, it is necessary to conduct an orientation meeting. This meeting often runs from 30-90 minutes depending on the amount of information to be covered.

The Staff Training Meeting. This meeting typically includes all of the orientation material, but is expanded to provide staffers with skills training for the unique type of selling they will encounter at trade shows. There are a variety of organizations that specialize in training for exhibit staffers and typically a staff training meeting is conducted by an expert in the field. It is structured so that a company representative (exhibits manager, or sales manager) presents the orientation information, and a subject matter expert conducts the training. The training meeting can take three to four hours depending on the content.

Selecting the right type of meeting requires evaluating a number of factors, most important being whether or not staffers *need* exhibit sales training. To determine that, take the following checklist along to your next show, and play the casual observer. Use the checklist as a guideline and make notes on behaviors that you observe. If you are not generating the leads you expect, if staffers are sloppy in their interactions and demonstrations, exhibit sales training may be appropriate.

Checklist for Evaluating Exhibit Staffers (4)

☐ ATTITUDE

    1. Do they show up on time?

    2. What is their attitude? Excited? Bored? Rather be somewhere else?

☐ ABILITY TO ENGAGE VISITORS

    3. Are they quick with all engaging comments and avoid using "Can I help you?"

    4. Do they respond quickly to visitors who show a high level of interest by coming into the exhibit and looking at products?

☐ ABILITY TO QUALIFY

    5. Do they qualify quickly and efficiently?

    6. Do they probe without being too aggressive?

    7. Do they use qualifying probes such as who, what, when, why?

☐ ABILITY TO PRESENT SOLUTION

    8. Do they qualify before demonstrating?

    9. Is the presentation balanced and benefits-oriented?

    10. Do they solicit feedback from the visitor?

☐ ABILITY TO CLOSE THE INTERACTION EFFICIENTLY

    11. Do they get a commitment for follow-up?

    12. Are lead forms complete and neat?

☐ NONVERBAL SKILLS

    13. Do staffers cluster together to chat?

    14. Do they smoke, eat, drink, sit down in the exhibit?

    15. Do they project a professional image?

☐ GENERAL OBSERVATIONS

    16. Does everyone in the exhibit know and execute their role properly? Executives too?

    17. Is attire correct?

    18. Do they use selling tools in the exhibit correctly?

Scheduling the Pre-Show Meeting

The closer the meeting is to the actual show, the better retention you will see on the part of exhibitors. The best time for the meeting is in the morning or afternoon, the day before the show opens. If the show opens later in the day (no earlier than 11:00 a.m.) the meeting can be held efficiently the morning of the show.

Think about where you would like to hold the meeting, and what type of refreshments to serve. This is also a good time to consider speakers, content, and support materials required. You can organize this information on the Pre-Show Meeting Checklist in Exhibit 4-8. The following chart will also give you a few basic do's and don'ts guidelines for the meeting.

This book is designed to guide you along a timetable, with step-by-step instructions for facilitating show plans. You've now covered most of the initial steps. In Chapter 5 you will move a step further by making final decisions in some of the areas you've explored in these chapters. Don't be confused by the fact that the same *topics* are being covered (for example Exhibit Design, Promotions) because each chapter takes you a *step further* in facilitating that component of your show program.

Exhibit 4-8
The Successful Pre-Show Meeting

What Works	What Doesn't
Light refreshments	Alcohol before/during the meeting
Opener by senior level manager	No management presence
Agenda	Informal structure
Handouts restating key details	Expecting staff to remember
High expectations	Apologies for taking their time
Visual aids	Discussion only
Making it mandatory	Making it optional
Booth tour or review	Expecting them to remember the exhibit
A bit of humor	Boredom

Chapter 5: You are here:
↓

	6 Mo.	5 Mo.	4 Mo.
Planning			
Goal-Setting			
Budgeting	Prepare zero-based show budget		
Promotions	Evaluate promotion options	Create promotion strategy	Create pre-show direct mail package
Product Demos			
Exhibits	Finalize supplier selection	Begin design process for new structure	Final decisions on new exhibit design
Installation	Select show services	Plan transportation Select contractor	Plan installation
Staffing	Plan pre-show staff meeting	Create sales action plan for staffers	Select staffers
Inquiry Processing		Plan inquiry processing procedures	Set up inquiry processing system
Measuring Results			

5

Critical Decisions
(5 Months in Advance)

If this were a race, you'd be heading into the mid-stretch about now. If you have been keeping up, you have set a good pace for getting tasks accomplished, and now we are going to cover a lot of ground. In this chapter you will reach some key decision points in six categories.

1. EXHIBIT DESIGN: Getting exhibit design approval.
2. STAFFING: Creating a sales action plan for the exhibit staffers.
3. EXHIBIT AND PRODUCT TRANSPORTATION: Deciding on the best mode of transportation.
4. INSTALLATION/DISMANTLE: Deciding whether to use the "official" contractor or an independent contractor.
5. PROMOTIONS: Creating your promotions strategy.
6. INQUIRY PROCESSING: Deciding how to manage inquiry processing.

FOUR STEPS TO EXHIBIT DESIGN APPROVAL

If you are the sole decision-maker on your new exhibit design, you only need to be concerned with the first section here on how to evaluate presentation drawings or sketches. If, however, you must present these ideas to a committee or manager for approval, the second section on presenting tips will help you get the best design approved.

How to Evaluate Presentation Drawings

At this point the exhibit firm(s) you have selected to bid on exhibit design should present their solutions. The presentations typically come in one of two forms, either a set of drawings or a model. There are three basic types of drawings you might see during the presentation.

An isometric drawing (Figure 5-1) is drawn at an angle that allows you to view the entire exhibit from three dimensions and is typically used for

141

Figure 5-1

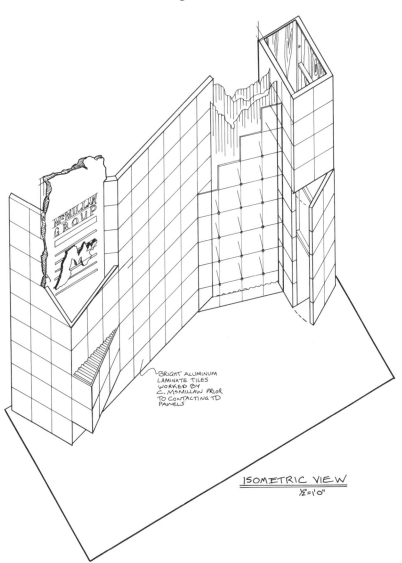

BRIGHT ALUMINUM
LAMINATE TILES
WORKED BY
C. MCMILLAN PRIOR
TO CONTACTING TD
PANELS

ISOMETRIC VIEW
½"=1'0"

Drawing courtesy of the McMillan Group

peninsula or island type displays. It provides an overall concept for the structure giving you a general idea of color, size, and components.

A floorplan or plan view (Figure 5-2) is drawn as if you are looking down at the floor from the ceiling. It is very useful for tracing traffic flow and evaluating placement of display stands, etc. However, it will not provide an idea of dimension or color.

Figure 5-2

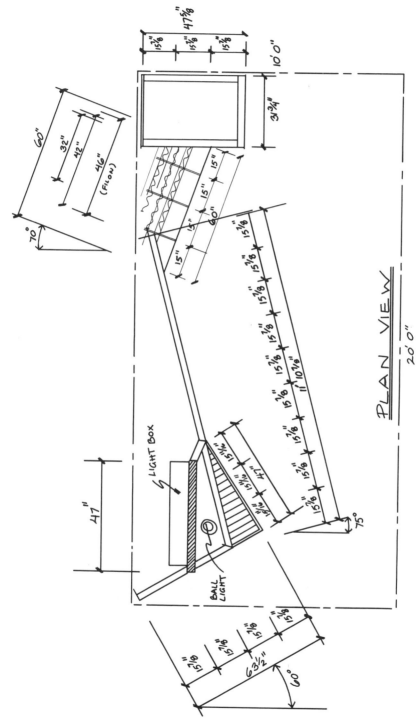

PLAN VIEW
20' 0"

Drawing courtesy of the McMillan Group

143

Figure 5-3

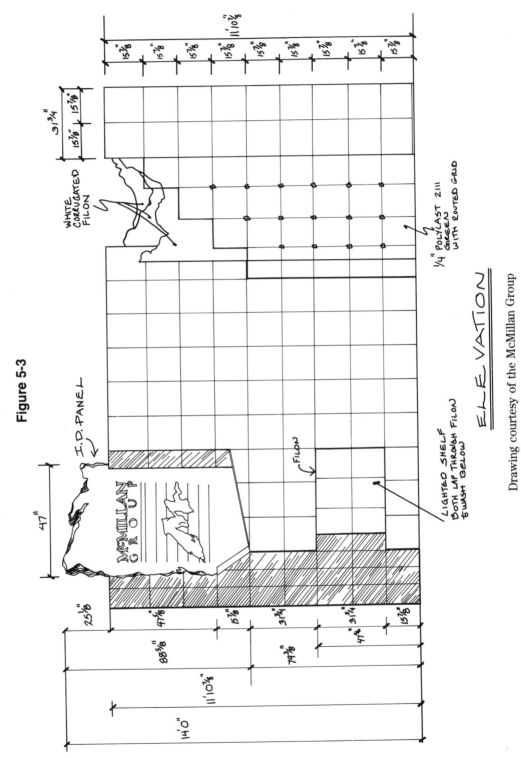

ELEVATION

Drawing courtesy of the McMillan Group

144

An elevation view (Figure 5-3) is drawn as if you are looking at one side of the structure, standing opposite it. Most linear exhibit plans are presented in elevation drawings because only one dimension needs to be represented. Here again, elevation views provide a good concept for the general color and size of the structure, but less so for traffic flow and floorplan.

Get out that list of goals for the exhibit and ask the account executive to walk through them, demonstrating how the design will accomplish those goals. A few extra details to watch for:

Materials. The account executive should provide a sample board with swatches of any fabric and carpet that will be used, along with tiles of the paint or laminate colors that will be used. Check these colors under a variety of lights. Many colors look entirely different under fluorescent lighting than they do under incandescent lighting, and types of lighting vary among show halls.

If you are told that there will be marble or other natural materials used in the exhibit, be sure you know whether it will be actual material or a look-alike laminate. One is not necessarily better than the other, but they do affect some other considerations. The stone looks, such as granite and marble, add an incredible amount of weight to the structure. Be sure whether you want to use the real thing or a more economical laminate. The same goes for wood finishes such as paneling and tambour and metallic finishes.

Specify Graphics. Most exhibit firms will outline for you the types of graphics that are represented in the presentation drawings. Be sure you are clear on what you are getting.

Traffic Flow. If you are shown a model or a plan view of the exhibit in your presentation, you can trace the traffic flow to be sure entrances, exits, and product demonstrations are in spots that provide smooth movement through the space.

Storage Space. If you have requested storage space in the exhibit, know for certain where it will be, especially in relation to hanging graphics. One company I know ended up with a graphic panel installed over the storage door, and they couldn't use the closet without removing the panel. While all of the information here has downplayed aesthetics, how the exhibit looks to you and how it will represent your company is *very* important. This content is weighted toward objectives, because human nature is such that we will be naturally drawn to the design solution that looks best to us and that attraction needs to be tempered to assure that not just the look, but the structure you need, is all there.

12 Points for a Strong Presentation

Depending on the type of managers you work for, their level of involvement in the decision-making process can range from signing off after a quick look, to in-depth critique of a proposal. One exhibit manager watched as the president of his company kicked and battered sample panels proposed for their new system exhibit to assure their durability. Sometimes you can't even anticipate the level of involvement they will take.

Whatever the decision-making process, it's best to be aware of it, and anticipate and plan for it. The following pointers represent typical considerations you'll want to make in planning your presentation for design approval.

1. *Review input* that you received from key decision-makers during the planning process. Be ready to explain how the design meets their objectives.

2. *Anticipate objections* to your proposed solution. Will the decision-makers balk at the cost, be concerned that the color selection doesn't reflect your corporate colors, feel that there is not enough product representation? Try to anticipate their concerns and prepare your explanations in advance to reduce the chance of being blindsided.

3. *Limit attendance* to key decision-makers. It seems that everyone in the company has an opinion about the exhibit, and the more input you get at this stage, the more bogged down the process will get. You will recall from Chapter 3 that the rule-of-thumb is ask everyone for input in the pre-design stage (covered in that chapter) and ask as few as possible to the review meetings.

4. *Strategize the presentation* with your account executive, designer, or any other representative invited to participate in the presentation. Review points to cover, anticipated objections, and responses.

5. *Use visual aids* as much as possible. If your exhibit firm has provided renderings, drawings, a model, or even a video tape, include any that will help the decision-makers to clearly visualize the overall concept of the exhibit.

6. *Record concerns and objections* during the meeting. Identify those that will require changes to your plan, and those that were overcome.

7. *Walk through an exhibit action plan.* Rather than just unveil a drawing or model, use it as a visual aid to describe exactly how the exhibit is designed to function. In the next section of this chapter you will learn how to create your action plan.

8. *Consider all costs involved* before the meeting. If you have determined exactly how much the project will cost to build, but not how much will

be required to ship it from show to show, you will be stuck when the inquiry is raised. Consider transportation, storage, and rough installation/dismantle costs. Many managers are not familiar enough with the trade show function to raise all of these questions, but should one come up, it will be worthwhile to be prepared. In your presentation, leave budget/cost issues until the end.

9. *Prepare a brief dossier* about the exhibit, summarizing the goals of the exhibit, the budget, and other key considerations. Use it as a handout for decision-makers to review. Hand it out near the end of the meeting, just about the time budget questions are raised.

10. *Speak their language.* If your boss signs off on the exhibit, think for a moment about what *his or her* conerns will be. Is money the most important factor or image? Is she more concerned about productivity or longevity? Speak to the decision-makers' hot buttons, in their language, as much as possible.

11. *Provide review time* for the decision-makers to evaluate the visual material, especially if you are presenting more than one option from which they can choose. One exhibit manager placed renderings of the three designs they would be evaluating on presentation easels in a large conference room. He created tags on which he wrote the designer, the builder, the bid for that project, and unique features. He then invited key decision-makers to review the proposals prior to their meeting, to become more familiar with the options they would be discussing.

12. *Get approval* in writing. Once the choice has been made and you are sure the decision-makers understand what they are getting, ask for approval in writing. Unfortunately, once a design concept or plan is approved for the exhibit firm, changes to that plan begin to cost money. If the decision-makers are requesting those changes, they need to understand how it affects the budget.

Timing is important here. If the design is approved, as is, then you have plenty of time to go ahead with construction. However, the more changes and revisions required, the further back it pushes your construction date. Taking the time up front to prepare your presentation well should minimize unimportant changes and allow you to focus only on those changes that are completely necessary.

WRITING THE EXHIBIT SELLING ACTION PLAN

The exhibit selling action plan mentioned previously, is a written plan for how the staff and visitors will function in the exhibit. It should be very detailed, even though some of the points may appear obvious. This plan becomes a foundation for understanding how the exhibit is designed to function for all staffers. Add it to your show plan and pre-show memo to staffers.

Step #1: Identify All Components

First, identify all of the components in your exhibit that will be part of the visitor's experience. The following list can help you to identify those that apply to your program.

☐ Overhead graphics   ☐ Introductory graphics

☐ Directive graphics   ☐ Entry points

☐ Product displays   ☐ Formal presentation area

☐ Presentation graphics   ☐ Lead-gathering points

☐ Handouts/premiums   ☐ Literature

☐ Other_____   ☐ Other_____

Step #2: Plan the Process

Now, think for a moment about exactly how you expect that a visitor would experience your exhibit, on a step-by-step basis. For example, if I had a 20′ in-line exhibit with oversized product graphics designed to capture attention, introductory graphics designed to describe our company and what it does, product displays toward the backwall, a lead-generating and literature counter toward the front, I might think through it this way: *Upon approaching the exhibit the visitor's attention will be drawn by the product graphics and raise their curiosity enough to see the introductory graphics. As they walk past the space, a staffer will stand on the edge of the exhibit to open the conversation and begin to qualify the visitor. Qualified visitors will then be invited into the exhibit for product demonstrations and then escorted to the edge to receive literature and complete a lead form.*

Once you've thought it through, assign numbers to your components in order of the steps that will be followed. In the example above, the product graphics would be #1, the introductory graphics #2, and so on.

Step #3: Plot the Points

Use a small floorplan drawing (or elevated drawing for in-line exhibits) to plot the numbers. Use a pencil to follow the process to assure that it will function as you have anticipated. Make any necessary changes and then write out your selling action plan in detail.

If you use a 10′ or 20′ in-line exhibit, your action plan will be very simple and take just a few minutes to construct. If your exhibit is a large one with many entry points, multiple product displays, and other components, it will require a more in-depth plan. Regardless of the size of the exhibit, the selling action plan is an important tool for understanding and communicating exactly how the structure and its components will be used.

SELECTING THE BEST TRANSPORTATION OPTION

A transportation expert in the trade show industry says he sees one problem common to exhibitors that always ends up costing them money. Too often they come to him at the last minute and need their exhibit in Chicago the day after tomorrow. If they only had more lead time, he says, they could save quite a bit of money. Still more could be saved by reviewing their show schedule well in advance to plan for transportation needs.

Admittedly, with all of those tariffs, CWTs, drop dates, charges, and other intimidating vernacular, planning for shipping falls right in there between having our teeth cleaned and filing our tax returns on the "things we like to do" list. But getting an early start on planning transportation can not only save money, it can also eliminate a bit of the uncertainty in your show program. Actually, there are just a few choices that need to be made. If you have a large exhibit, often your exhibit firm will handle transportation for you and if your show schedule is hectic it might be worth the price of their mark-up to save you the hassle.

Aside from driving the exhibit to the show in your own pickup truck, you have three options for shipping your exhibit structure and equipment. Generally, speaking, less time means more money, as is illustrated in Exhibit 5-1. This will vary based on your specific situation, but provides a guideline for planning.

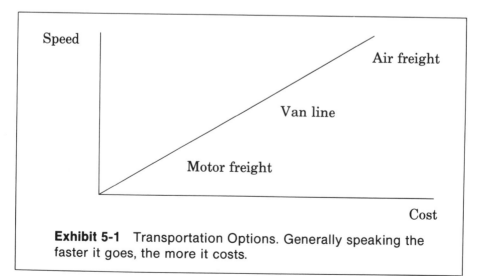

Exhibit 5-1   Transportation Options. Generally speaking the faster it goes, the more it costs.

The chart in Exhibit 5-2 lists the three most common transportation options, along with a definition of each, followed by descriptions of key areas for concern. This list is not exhaustive and there may be additional factors that you want to include in making the transportation decision.(1)

Exhibit 5-2   Transportation Options

	Van Line	**Motor Freight**	**Air Freight**
Definition	Custom shipping service that travels irregular and unscheduled routes.	Shipping service that travels regularly scheduled routes.	Custom shipping service by airline or air freight company.
Cost	Mid to high range.	Mid to low range (50–90% of van line costs).	High range.
Timeframes	Flexible to your needs. Shorter lead time required.	You accommodate to their schedule. Long lead required.	Shortest lead time required.
Service	You work with one contact. Often have reps on-site at shows.	No single contact. No reps at the show.	High level of service especially from companies who specialize in show freight.
Packaging	Contents can be crated or blanket-wrapped.	Contents must be crated.	Contents must be crated.
Handling	Least handling from pick-up to drop off point. Often just one load/unload.	Can be multiple load/unload at consolidation points.	Multiple load/unloading because of combination air and ground transport.

Methods for Evaluating Transportation Costs

As with any major purchase, the best way to assure that you are getting a fair price for the service is to compare bids from several suppliers. You needn't settle on a mode of transportation prior to soliciting these bids. In fact you might want to compare the price for a motor freight shipment with that of a van line shipment. Getting accurate costs can be difficult, not because the shipping agent isn't quoting correctly, but because exhibitors frequently omit variables that influence the bid.

Before soliciting bids from transportation suppliers, take the time to assure that you have considered all variables. The following list should get you started.

Three Key Factors in the Transportation Bid

Packaging. Whether your shipment is crated or blanket-wrapped will affect the shipping costs. The charge by weight or volume is typically more for blanket-wrapped shipments than for crated shipments. However, crates add weight to your shipment which may offset any savings. The amount the shipment will be handled can also influence this decision. If the exhibit will be used frequently, consider protecting it from damage not only during shipping, but also during drayage at the show site. Calculating cost variables that determine whether to use crates or blanket-wrap your shipment is outlined in detail in an *Exhibitor Magazine* article. (2)

Distance Traveled. This is a key variable on which shipping rates are based. Before going out for bid know your pickup and destination point(s).

Chargeable Weight. Shipping charges are based on a term the van line uses called chargeable weight. In many cases this is not usually the actual weight of the exhibit, but a figure based on the amount of space the shipment will take in a truck. The calculations for determining chargeable weight are a bit complex and handled by your shipping representative. *Exhibitor Magazine* has published an article outlining these procedures in detail, if you would like to do more research on the subject. (3)

Variables That Affect the Transportation Bid

Timing. Rush shipments and targeted arrival dates usually cost more money. The further in advance of the show date that you can ship your materials, the more flexibility you will find in transportation charges.

Extra Pickups. Keep in mind that if you request that the exhibit be picked up at the display house and the equipment be picked up at your facility this requires two pick-ups and may influence your charges.

Split deliveries. At times exhibitors hosting hospitality suites in satellite hotels need parts of a shipment delivered at the show hall and parts delivered at the hotel. This may also add a premium to your shipping rates.

Split outbound pick-ups and/or deliveries. If after a show you want a shipment to be split and sent to different destinations (sending part on to the next show and part back to the exhibit warehouse for example) it will influence your costs.

The worksheet in Exhibit 5-3 will help you organize this information when soliciting bids for transportation.

Exhibit 5-3 Transportation Bid Worksheet

Show: _____ Location: _____

Pre-Show Shipping Property	Pick-Up	Delivery
_____	_____	_____
_____	_____	_____
_____	_____	_____

Post-Show Shipping Property	Pick-Up	Delivery
_____	_____	_____
_____	_____	_____
_____	_____	

Charges	Bid #1	Bid #2	Bid #3
Standard point-to-point			
Crated	_____	_____	_____
Blanket-wrapped	_____	_____	_____
Options			
☐ Split pick-up/inbound	_____	_____	_____
☐ Split del./inbound	_____	_____	_____
☐ Split pick-up/outbound	_____	_____	_____
☐ Split del./outbound	_____	_____	_____
☐ Rush charges	_____	_____	_____
☐ On-site supervision	_____	_____	_____
TOTAL	_____	_____	_____

PROS AND CONS OF USING AN INDEPENDENT
SERVICE CONTRACTOR

A bit of history is important here to set the stage for what is happening with independent contractors in the trade show industry. At one time when companies needed special labor to set up their exhibits at trade shows, their only choice was to use the same contractor that show management used as a source for labor. This contractor is typically known as the "Official Contractor" for the show. Along with providing labor for exhibit set-up they also provided the labor and services to set up the show hall and conference areas for show management.

As the story goes, service among these official contractors began to slide as business grew, and many exhibitors wanted more personalized services than the official contractors offered. Thus companies were formed that offered the exhibitors the same services as the official contractor. Since they were not hired by show managements, but by the exhibitors, they gained the title "independent contractors."

Independent contractors earned the reputation as the source for set-up labor that went the extra mile for exhibitors. And they did. Now, in *Exhibitor Magazine's* resource directly alone, more than 20 companies are listed under installation/dismantle services. Independent contractors will handle all of the coordinating details of your exhibit set-up, from hand selecting the workers, to supervising on-site. But as you might guess, as the business grew, quality varied.

Also, independent service contractors began taking substantial amounts of work away from the official show contractors, thus leading to conflicts and restrictions surrounding the practice. Many show managers require that you give them 30 days advance notice if you plan to use an independent contractor. It has only been recently that independent contractors have been allowed to have work counters on the show floor during set-up and dismantle.

If you have an exhibit that requires union labor for any part of its set-up, you will need to make the decision between using the official show contractor or an independent contractor of your choice. The chart in Exhibit 5-4, listing the pros and cons of using independent contractors, can help you weigh the key factors that will affect your decision.

Selecting the best independent contractor can be tricky business, because those exhibitors who use them regularly claim the quality of one firm can vary from city to city. One exhibitor hires different firms in each city where she exhibits in order to get the people with whom she feels

Exhibit 5-4   Pros and Cons of Using an Independent
Service Contractor

Pros	Cons

Labor

Good independents have representatives who are very familiar with union workers in show cities. They can hand-pick the best workers for your crew, thus reducing the time and cost of your set-up.	The independent contractors get their workers from the same labor pool as anyone else, in most show cities. Know that when you use an independent contractor, you are not paying for different workers, you are paying for the expertise of the contractor to select the best workers for you.

Service

Good contractors anticipate problems and help you to trouble-shoot on the show floor. They can also make your set-up more efficient by determining the best strategy for your structure.	Exhibit managers who use independent contractors around the country report that quality of service can vary considerably. Be sure to check references when selecting a contractor.

Cost

If a contractor is doing a good job for you, they can save you money on set-up and tear-down by making the process more efficient.	These companies base their fees on the labor rates in the show city. Typically they charge 25–30% mark-up for supervision services.

Control

If you can't give set-up your full attention, your contractor will supervise the process for you and reduce the hassles.	As you give your contractor more responsibility you also give up more control over the process. Be sure they discuss decisions with you and keep you informed throughout the process.

most comfortable and works best. Other exhibitors develop fierce loyalties to their set-up companies and use the same firm wherever they go. The best approach is to avoid getting locked in with one firm until you have used them at several shows and feel they provide the quality of service you expect.

The following pointers can serve as a guideline when you interview prospective firms.

- □ How long have they been in business?
- □ How many offices do they have around the United States?
- □ In which convention halls do they do the majority of their work?
- □ Do they have "counters" on the show floor during set-up when it is allowed by show management?
- □ Do they offer 24-hour availability during set-up?
- □ How do they charge for their services?
- □ Request references.
- □ Other_____
- □ Other_____

HOW TO CREATE A COMPREHENSIVE PROMOTIONS STRATEGY

In Chapter 4 you considered show promotion opportunities in light of your show goals. At this point it is time to determine exactly how you will use the media selected.

The danger here is to create isolated promotions strategies that only work part time for you. Case in point: At a recent financial show, one bank exhibiting used a very clever strategy to draw visitors to their exhibit. They used small brass hour-glass timers as icebreakers to open the conversation. They connected them to their services by asking visitors who came by if their bankers were saving them time or using their time efficiently. Once they got visitors interested, they played a group game similar to a TV game show.

Here's where they went wrong. The visitors got very involved in the game, spent most of their time in the exhibit playing it, and then left when the game was over. Exhibit staffers got little to no time to actually talk with these high-level corporate finance people. A good opening strategy, but the promotion did not work full-time for them.

This raises the subject of a theme. Time savings was a good theme for this group. The giveaway was also a high-value giveaway. But the theme was not used to further the objectives of the bank at the show (or it didn't appear to).

Choosing and Using a Theme Successfully

A good theme gives your promotion life. It becomes the thread tied through every component that sets your efforts apart from every other exhibitor's. A few guidelines will help to assure that your promotion theme is on the right track.

1. Decide how the theme will be used in every component of your promotions strategy (direct mail, billboards, trade advertising, etc.)

2. Avoid cliched gimmicks. Do some brainstorming to come up with your theme and then eliminate all of the ideas that have been overused.

3. Consider contemporary trends. When the "We are the World" campaign was popular in the United States, one company used it for a promotions theme and held a drawing for "We Are the World" t-shirts.

4. Consider your audience. Do think about what will be appealing to your audience, but don't oversimplify your analysis. Who would think that small, stuffed teddy bears would be a high draw at a physicians conference? It was a hit since most physicians have children!

5. Create a "tie-in" to your show objectives. Use the promotion theme to reinforce your communications message for the show.

Selecting a good theme can be the most challenging part of creating a successful promotion. The following list of ideas that have been used can help to get the wheels turning.

Theme	Giveaway	Tie-In
Olympics	Olympic t-shirt and medals.	Technical products had been given sports theme names.
Holland	Miniature wooden shoes and drawing for wooden shoes carved on site.	Introducing a product produced in Holland
Magic	Magic Kit	"Use the Magic of Computing" as a theme for product introduction.
"Fire" prevention	Fire extinguisher kit	"Prevent departmental resource fires" with new computer system.

Theme	Giveaway	Tie-In
Harmony	Beethoven tape and conductor's wand.	Promote networking products to allow computing resource to work together.
Quality	Self-study module of quality assurance program used by the company.	Trying to promote image of quality for products.
Horse races	Visitors advanced along a track as they saw product demos that qualified them to enter the winner's circle and spin for prizes.	Two-horce race to create an image of edging out competitors.
Schoolhouse	Diplomas for course completion.	Teaching simple new technology to attendees in hands-on demos.
Environmental concerns	Custom posters by specially commissioned wildlife artist.	To promote new environmentally safe products in a high risk industry.
Nautical	Invitations printed on parchment maps and mailed in miniature Cutty Sark bottles.	New product "launch."
Growth	Packets of seeds in a pre-show mailer and a drawing for a free trip to famous English gardens.	To appeal to small businesses who would use their services.

Three Proven Advertising Options

Once you have chosen the theme, plan to use it in every component of your promotions strategy. If there is a typical weak link in a themed promotions strategy it is publications advertising. Due to cost constraints, exhibitors tend to put a lot of energy and resources in direct mail promotions, billboards, and anything that needs to be created originally for the show, but then just throw a tag line on the ad they've been running for months.

The alternatives to the standard tag line vary in cost and complexity, but in most cases there's a solution that will extend a promotions theme

Exhibit 5-5 Advertising Options

Least Expensive			**Most Expensive**
Invitation Ad	*Incentive Ad*	*Goal-Specific Ad*	*Audience Specific*
This ad simply lets the reader know what s/he will experience when they visit the exhibit, along with location. The invitation ad must always give the reader a reason to visit the exhibit, but it can be done very reasonably.	This ad usually includes a response mechanism, such as a coupon or contest entry form. This type can actually be very moderate or very expensive in cost depending on the creativity used, but can be done successfully at a moderate expense.	This type of ad is designed to address one or two specific show goals, such as recruiting personnel or new dealers. Copy and graphics are very customized and will require a creative investment.	These ads are used when you want to create separate messages for different audiences at a show. One ad might appeal to end users while another to resellers. Copy and graphics may need to be customized to each audience.

into this print medium. For those of you concerned with the value of repeat exposure in your advertising, consider creating the theme in advance to use it in both pre- and post-show issues of the publications.

Putting It All Together: Using the Promotions Strategy Planner

Up to this point you have been making a variety of decisions about your promotions strategy such as goals, media choices, theme, and content choices. They probably feel a bit disjointed. It will be useful now that some of the strategy is taking shape, to begin recording some of these decisions and plans in a single place. The worksheet in Exhibit 5-6 is designed to guide you in doing that. Complete the information you know and add that worksheet to the promotions section of your show plan. You can continue to fill in the details as new considerations arise.

The information at the top of the page is fairly straightforward. Complete a separate promotions planner for each show. The section

---

Exhibit 5-6   Promotions Strategy Planner

Show: _____ Dates: _____

Show Goals: _____

Promotion Goals: _____

Media Selected:

_____   _____

_____   _____

_____   _____

_____   _____

Theme: _____

_____

Giveaway/Incentive: _____

Media Contacts:
Name   Phone #

_____   _____

_____   _____

_____   _____

Suppliers Needed

_____

_____

_____

marked "media" is for you to list the promotional media you have selected, such as billboards, hotel TV advertising, or show directory advertising. Under the section title "Media Contacts," list the people you will need to reach to arrange those media (ad placement for example) and their phone numbers. In the section marked "Suppliers Needed" list any suppliers you will need to facilitate the promotions (a list broker for pre-show direct mail, an incentives supplier for your giveaways, etc.).

The Promotions Strategy Planner is designed to serve as a guideline for you. Plan to adapt it to work for your specific shows and promotion needs.

INQUIRY PROCESSING TO LEAD TRACKING: PLANNING A WORKABLE SYSTEM

There are two groups of exhibitors who need not be concerned with inquiry processing: those who sell products right at the show, and those who do not generate any type of inquiries at shows. For the rest, the questions are: 1. How valuable are those leads that are generated at shows? 2. How are you going to tell if they have paid off?

If you currently have shows in progress, take a minute to think about where the leads from your last show are right now:

- ☐ In a cabinet in the exhibit
- ☐ In the trade show department waiting to be fulfilled
- ☐ On a salesperson's desk somewhere
- ☐ At your fulfillment house
- ☐ Don't know
- ☐ What leads? (You don't use lead cards at all)

If they are still in the exhibit or you don't know where they are, chances are good they are not being used to their full potential. Aside from generating new business for your company (which is the primary purpose of show leads) they also provide you with an important measure of how trade shows are contributing to your company's goals and objectives. But they have to be taken seriously.

Typical Path of Trade Show Inquiries

The diagram in Exhibit 5-7 illustrates the typical life of a trade show lead at many companies.

The problem here is that once trade show leads are distributed to the sales department, all responsibility for them is relinquished by the trade show manager. The critical loop that provides the information required to

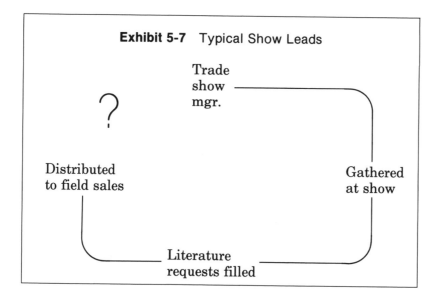

Exhibit 5-7   Typical Show Leads

evaluate shows most efficiently is not closed; salespeople do not report back on the status of leads generated from shows.

Lead Tracking: Standards and Variations

This process of following leads through to sales is called *lead tracking*. If you don't currently have a lead tracking system in place, or you are not satisfied with the one you are using, now is the time in the planning process to make those decisions about how leads will be handled. The chart in Exhibit 5-8 describes the typical flow of a lead

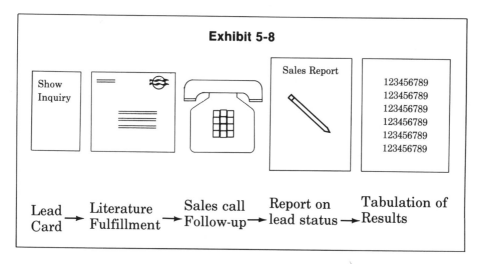

Exhibit 5-8

tracking system. The variations on this theme are only limited by the exhibit manager's needs and imagination. In Exhibit 5-9 you'll see some variations to this flow of information.

The Inquiry Form. This is often called the lead card and is a critical component of the lead tracking system because it is the tool that staffers use to gather information and record follow-up requests at the show. Chapter 6 covers the "how tos" of creating good inquiry forms in detail.

Literature Fulfillment. Decide now what literature will be offered to show visitors and how it will be distributed. It is not recommended that literature be handed out at the show, since most of it ends up in the trash can before it ever leaves the show hall anyway. (4) You have two options for fulfilling literature requests. One is to do it internally, and a second is to hire a fulfillment house to handle it for you. Time is of the essence here, and literature requests must be fulfilled within two weeks of the show.

Sales Call Follow-Up. Decide who will be following up on the leads generated at the show. Typically they are distributed to field sales offices and salespeople handle that step or an internal group or external service uses telemarketing to pre-qualify them before they go to the field. If you are sending them to the field without telemarketing, it is a good idea to show the salespeople that you respect their time by sending only qualified leads for follow-up.

Reports on Lead Status. If you have tried this, you know that it is the potential weak link in the process, what with salespeople loving paperwork and all. But this information allows you to create actual return on investment figures as a measure of your program's success. When justifying show participation is important, this is the information that will make your case. Think now about how you will facilitate gathering this information. Some exhibitors create multiple copy lead forms, using the copies for distribution and include an area for follow-up information that is completed by the salesperson. Others call salespeople regularly for status reports on their leads. The more sophisticated managers have created computer programs, and request updates on disk.

123456789
123456789
123456789
123456789
123456789
123456789

Tabulation of Results. Think about how you will want to tabulate the results of the show. Will you want reports on the number of leads generated by geographic region, job function, product interest, exhibit staffer? If you use a computer to tabulate leads, you can sort them on any function that you include on the lead card and in the computer system.

If you are not using a computer, keep the sorts to a minimum. Two essential reports will probably be as much as you can produce, depending on your support staff. These types of tabulations can provide quality control measures for your program (by identifying top performing staffers), product interest (by identifying those products generating the most inquiries), or any measure you find appropriate to your program.

Now consider a few variations on these basic components. The chart in Exhibit 5-9 illustrates where some of these variations fall into the standard flow of information.

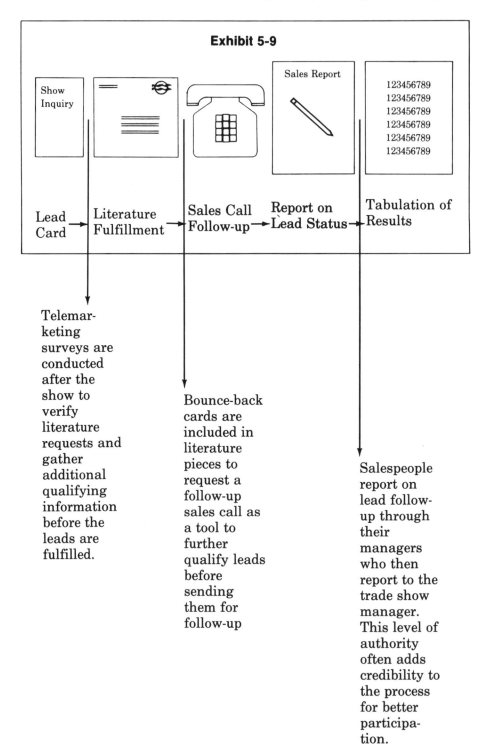

Exhibit 5-9

Show Inquiry

Sales Report

123456789
123456789
123456789
123456789
123456789
123456789

Lead Card → Literature Fulfillment → Sales Call Follow-up → Report on Lead Status → Tabulation of Results

Telemarketing surveys are conducted after the show to verify literature requests and gather additional qualifying information before the leads are fulfilled.

Bounce-back cards are included in literature pieces to request a follow-up sales call as a tool to further qualify leads before sending them for follow-up

Salespeople report on lead follow-up through their managers who then report to the trade show manager. This level of authority often adds credibility to the process for better participation.

Key to Success: Input from Participating Departments

It is obvious that the inquiry processing function doesn't operate in a vacuum. In most cases at least two and maybe four departments will need to contribute to its success: the exhibits department, the sales department, the marketing department, and maybe the MIS or information processing department. So include the key people from those departments in the planning process.

The Sales Department. Talk to a few sales managers about what type of information their people will need on the lead card to facilitate efficient follow-up. Discuss how you might motivate them to report back on the status of leads.

The Marketing Department. The information you gather through a computerized lead processing program can be useful to marketing managers. Discuss your plans with them to see if any special report formats would be useful for their programs.

The MIS Department. Although it may be very difficult to get five minutes with these people, unless you know the software program you will be using, they can provide valuable guidance on setting up your program. If it will be implemented by the MIS department, be sure to get their input before making any plans.

Pros and Cons of Computerizing Lead Tracking

If you process just a few hundred leads at one or two shows each year, it probably isn't necessary to computerize your lead tracking system. Most of the information you need can be easily tabulated from hard copies of the lead. And while computerizing leads does speed up the fulfillment process, it can also complicate your program a bit. Here are a few factors to watch for.

PROS: Availability of information is the primary advantage here. Speed in fulfilling leads is not necessarily a benefit since, unless you input lead data in real time at the show, you need to enter the information afterward for literature fulfillment anyway. Computerizing the process simply allows you to manipulate the information gathered at shows more quickly and efficiently. You can set up the program to sort and print reports on any function you need.

CONS: The down side of having all of this information at your fingertips is the upfront investment to get the system functioning and then the investment in personnel required to keep the system going. You will need someone to be responsible to:

  □ Input the leads after the show
  □ Generate and distribute reports on demand

☐ Update the file as status reports are submitted

☐ Troubleshoot problems with the system

Depending on the scope of your show program, this can be a sizeable job.

Six Steps to Computerizing Lead Tracking

If you do decide to computerize your inquiry tracking function, the procedures for most systems follow these six steps.

Step #1 Input leads.

Step #2 Generate labels for literature fulfillment.

Step #3 Generate and distribute reports.

Step #4 Solicit status reports from salespeople.

Step #5 Update files based on status reports.

Step #6 Generate report updates on a pre-determined schedule (e.g., each quarter).

If you don't get the lead processing system in place right away, don't give up. The trade show world is full of unanticipated problems that can throw the best laid plans into chaos. One exhibitor spent a good deal of time perfecting the first phase of their inquiry processing system which was based on using the inquiry forms and imprinting machines provided by show management. However, once they got to the show they discovered that show management had changed systems and neither the forms nor the imprinters were available. They found themselves taking notes on 3×5 cards and business cards until they could get the right inquiry forms to use.

Congratulations! You have now made some of the critical decisions that will move your trade show program forward on schedule. In Chapter 6 you will see how to keep juggling all of the apples that you have set in motion.

Chapter 6: You are here:

↓

	5 Mo.	4 Mo.	3 Mo.
Planning			
Goal-Setting			
Budgeting			
Promotions	Create promotion strategy	Create pre-show direct mail package	Implement promotions strategy
Product Demos			Plan formal live presentation
Exhibits	Begin design process for new structure	Final decisions on new exhibit design	Manage new construction Find portable supplier
Installation	Plan transportation Select contractor	Plan installation	
Staffing	Create sales action plan for staffers	Select staffers	Prepare pre-show memos
Inquiry Processing	Plan inquiry processing procedures	Set up inquiry processing system	
Measuring Results			

6

Keeping the Wheels Turning
(4 Months in Advance)

At this point if you look at the tasks that need to be completed before the show, you might feel a bit panicky. That's okay. If you are keeping up with the schedule, you will have plenty of time. If not, begin prioritizing the remaining tasks in order of importance. You may or may not find time to accomplish them all, but if you need to leave some out, at least you will know which have the greatest priority for a specific program.

In this chapter you will finalize some decisions, and begin digging deeper in other areas. You will cover:

1. EXHIBIT DESIGN: Making the final decision
2. PRE-SHOW DIRECT MAIL: Steps toward creating the package
3. LEAD PROCESSING: Getting a system in place
4. EXHIBIT INSTALLATION: Getting the information you need
5. STAFFING: Selecting exhibit staffers

EXHIBIT DESIGN APPROVAL: THREE FINAL POINTS TO CONSIDER

If you are having a new custom exhibit built, at this point in the process there have probably been a host of changes made from your original design objectives. Before signing off on the design and going into construction, get the project back under control by reviewing goals and objectives, changes to the original plan, and related costs.

The three factors here are primarily cost-related. *First, were there any deviations from the original goals you had requested?* In most cases, once the dialogue between the exhibit designer and the client gets going, new ideas are brought to the table which hadn't been considered previously. These often change the direction of goals that had been established (or, in the excitement of the moment, they can ignore goals completely.)

Go to your Plan Notebook and pull out the original goals. Note any deviations in the final design and reasons for those.

Second, what changes are required to accomplish your goals? Designs are rarely approved in the first draft. There are typically a series of changes made as the design evolves. Review the changes that have been made from the original concept to assure that everyone understands the requirements for the structure.

Third, are there any additional costs because of those deviations? Good designers don't build additional costs into a project randomly, but changes and improvements can require an additional investment. If they do, your designer or account executive should discuss them with you and get your approval, by signature, before building them into the budget. Be sure you are aware of those additional costs before agreeing on the design concept.

Sometimes at this stage it can be difficult to remember exactly what has been decided on and the project feels a bit out of control. Taking time to review these factors will contribute a great deal to keeping your costs in line.

The worksheet in Exhibit 6-1 is designed to help you review the goals for the new exhibit and consider any changes and related costs. The first one is listed as an example. This completed sheet can be filed in your Operational Plan under Exhibit Design.

Exhibit 6-1

New Exhibit Goal	Goal Met? Yes	No	Description of deviations	Related costs
Storage space		√	*Need three additional cabinets*	*$1,500*

CREATING THE PRE-SHOW DIRECT MAIL PACKAGE

The pre-show direct mail campaign can be the workhorse of any show program. It provides one of the very first exposures show attendees have to your company, and show plans. It creates an image, sets a theme, and motivates attendees to put your exhibit on their "must see" list. It requires targeting your show audience, creates a message closely linked to their interests, and provides a measure of response.

Unfortunately, it will be impossible to begin to cover the subtle complexities of using direct mail efficiently. Volumes have been written on the subject. Here, instead, you will see some of the critical components of creating a direct mail promotion specifically for a trade show. Because your audience is more targeted, and your results easily measured, creating direct mail for a show is slightly easier.

Three Critical Steps

Begin by going to your Show Plan Notebook and reviewing the theme you have selected for show promotions. The impact of your mailer will increase significantly when you use a theme, and a creative incentive. So review that theme and decide how you want it incorporated into the mailer and the incentive.

Step #1: Defining Your Target Audience

You might think that you have already done this step when you calculated the show's potential audience. Actually you have completed an important part of the process, but that is just the beginning. If you need to, refer back to your Strategic Plan to review the potential audience for this show. Any audience research statistics available are also helpful in identifying the target audience. A few key breakdowns that will help you here include:

- Job functions
- Job titles
- Industry representation (medical, accounting, etc.)
- Geographic distribution
- Product interest

This research has a twofold purpose. First, the past research you have gathered will help you to define your target audience at the show a bit more clearly. For example, our glassware manufacturer from Chapter 1 might see that they are targeting primarily retailers whose job titles will typically be "buyer" or "assistant buyer", at a store in the Midwest. This will help you create copy for the mailer that will stimulate a higher level of interest and motivation for people to visit your exhibit. It will also help you select an incentive that will have a high perceived value among your target audience. Third, it becomes the criteria by which you judge potential mailing lists.

Step #2: Finding and Evaluating Direct Mail Lists

The following five sources for direct mail lists are prioritized by those that will probably be closest to representing your show audience. Obviously, the objective is finding the list that provides the greatest number of people in your target audience. It may seem apparent that you would want to purchase the show pre-registration list, or last year's show list, but these can have their drawbacks.

Show Pre-Registration List. Registration companies often provide the registration list to exhibitors for a fee. This list will, in most cases, provide you the best profile of your show audience. The only problem is that often the highest percentage of registrations comes in the last two to three weeks prior to the show. And many of those are exhibitors and their personnel. You will need the list at least three weeks prior to the show to allow time to review it and send out your mailers. Thus you could miss a high percentage of the show audience.

Timing is critical here, and the registration company's projections of what your list will look like don't necessarily match what you end up getting. Be sure to inquire about what percentage of that list is exhibitors and personnel, and what percentage of the total attendees pre-register. If they don't know, ask about previous years.

The Show's Previous Year Registration List. If an annual show has a fairly steady attendance from year to year, consider using the previous year's registration list. Be aware of whether the show is considered a National show (over 60% of the show audience from outside a 200-mile radius of the show city) or a Regional show (over 40% of the show audience from within a 200-mile radius of the show city) and whether it travels from city to city.

This will affect your registration list. If the show is very regional and travels from city to city each year, the attendance list will change quite a bit from year to year and the previous year's list will not be very useful.

Association Membership List. Many shows are sponsored by associations rather than by a show management company. For example the American College of Physicians holds an annual convention for their membership, of which exhibits are a part. In these cases the association membership list will provide an excellent source of names for mailing. You might find that the membership list is greater than the show registration list and you will see a bit of overkill, but it will assure that you reach a high number of your target audience.

Trade Magazine Subscriber Lists. If a trade magazine in your industry sponsors a trade show, chances are good that you will find a high number of your targeted attendees on their subscriber list. Many publications rent their list for a one-time use. If the publication is not a show sponsor, it is important to cross-check the percentage of show attendees that reads their publication (typically available through show management), or the percentage of their readers that attend the show (typically available through the publication.) This information is usually only available at larger shows where money is spent to do the necessary audience research.

Corporate Sales Network. This is a bit more time consuming, but you can create your own pre-show mailing list by asking representatives in your sales network to submit lists of key customers and prospects that they know will be attending the show. Your list will probably be smaller but will be much more targeted to your key prospects at the show than any other list available.

List Brokers. Finding a list to meet your needs is like looking for that special sauce at the grocery store. There is a host of lists available through brokers (companies that rent and sell mailing lists). But finding the one that matches your target audience for a specific show is extremely difficult. Here, more than with any other list, you are taking a shotgun approach: mailing to a large list that fits your audience profile and hoping that a good percentage of them hit those folks who attend the show.

One company used a broker's list and then asked their salespeople to review it, highlighting those companies with which they were familiar in the industry. This helped to refine the list a bit, but is extremely time consuming for the sales staff.

Step #3: Evaluating Lists

If you have a variety of lists from which to choose, it is definitely worth your time to evaluate them carefully. Just for review, in the chart below, on the left you see the variety of sources, and on the right you see the variety of evaluators you can use as criteria for judging the list.

List Sources	**List Evaluators**
1. Show registration list	1. Are exhibitors included?
2. Previous year pre-registration list	2. Geography/show location
3. Association membership list	3. Job function
4. Trade magazine subscriber list	4. Publication readership
5. Corporate sales network	5. Industry representation
6. List brokers	6. Product interest
	7. Buying plans

In evaluating show lists, look for three criteria: the show attendance representation, the product interest representation, and psychographics of the audience. For example, for show attendance representation, you want to know how many people on the list attend the show. For product interest representation, you want to know what percentage of that list is interested in the products or services you will be exhibiting at the show. And finally, psychographics tells you information about the people on the list such as their industry representations or job titles/functions, that you can match with your pre-defined target audience.

The chart in Exhibit 6-2 provides a worksheet for compiling that information if you must research available lists for your direct mail campaign. Simply write yes or no in each box to indicate whether that information is available from the list supplier. By comparing the chart with the guidelines you used for your attendee profile, you can see which list will provide the most information needed to get closest to your target market. The first entry in italics is an example.

NOTE: The chances of finding a list that meets all of the above criteria is rare. Prioritize by importance and look for lists that provide the most high priority information.

Three Essential Components of the Pre-Show Mailer

Once you have set your target audience and selected a list, you need to create the mailer. Successful direct mail campaigns all include three essential components: the invitation, the incentive, and the response mechanism. We have discussed the response mechanism quite a bit in previous chapters so we will focus here on the other two components.

The invitation is the copy on the mailer that invites attendees to your exhibit, and most importantly, lets them know why they should bother. If

Exhibit 6-2 Direct Mail List Evaluation Chart

List Source	Attendee Representation			Interest Level		Psycho-graphics	
	Exhibitor Included?	*Geogr. Breaks?*	*Readership?*	*Product Interest?*	*Buying Plans?*	*Industry?*	*Job Title?*
1. Show Pre-registration	Yes	Yes	No	No	No	Yes	Yes

you have a new product they should see, let them know. If you will have a special demonstration or presentation, let them know. Your objective is to get on their list of "must see" exhibits. Let them know how it will benefit them to visit you. And make the booth number prominent so they can easily find you.

The incentive takes the invitation a step further and offers them a potential reward for visiting the exhibit. Incentives can take a variety of forms, from inexpensive premiums offered to anyone who responds, up to sophisticated contests and drawings. Keep in mind that the more sophisticated your incentive, the higher your audience interest level will have to be to assure attendance. One company sent out a pre-show mailer as an invitation to a pre-show scavenger hunt, with clues stationed around the show city. Their response was low as a percentage of the total show audience, but represented a high percentage of their target audience.

> WARNING: If you are using a contest or drawing as an incentive, be sure that it is within not only show regulations but also local gaming regulations for the show city. They are quite strict in Las Vegas (as you might imagine). One company had to adjust their promotion the day before the show opened to comply with local guidelines. The city's chamber of commerce should be able to direct you to the local gaming commission for guidance.

The chart in Exhibit 6-3 offers a checklist of reminders to consider as you plan for each of these essential components in your program.

THE PRE-SHOW PRESS RELEASE

How to Write It, Who Should Receive It

If yours is a relatively large company, you probably have PR people on staff, or a PR agency who handles the releases for your shows. If so, you can disregard this section. This information is designed to be a basic primer for those of you who find yourself wearing many hats and writing your own releases. Press releases for a trade show follow the same basic format as those for any publications event. There are just a few additional details that will be important because of the nature of shows.

When creating the press release, be sure to distinguish it from the press advisory. The release is information about your company or products that you want to see in print. The advisory is like an invitation to editors, making them aware of opportunities to gather more information about your company and products while they are at the show. Both are essential at shows where you expect press coverage.

For the advisory, be sure to let editors know all of the opportunities

Exhibit 6-3

The Invitation	The Incentive	The Response Mechanism
☐ Does it tell the reader what they can expect to see in your exhibit? ☐ Have you included the booth number (and a map if necessary)? ☐ Do you tell them what's in it for them? ☐ If you are using a contest or drawing, have you explained how it works? ☐ Are there special timeframes to consider such as when a drawing will be held? ☐ Does it have energy and excitement?	☐ Does your incentive have high perceived value among your target audience? ☐ Is it within your budget? ☐ Does it relate to the theme you have selected for the promotions and the show? ☐ Does it echo a message about your company or products? ☐ How will the incentive be distributed at the show? (Visitors shouldn't have to wait long.) ☐ Is it within show regulations? ☐ Is it within the city's gaming regulations?	☐ Have you designed in a perforated tear-off if the response card will be returned at the exhibit? ☐ Does the response card ask visitors to fill in the vital statistics? (Name, company, title, address, phone, etc.) ☐ Does the response card include qualifying information you would like to gather on participants? ☐ Have you determined how the response cards will be collected and verified? ☐ Have you considered using the response mechanism to connect the visitors with the exhibit sales staff?

available. Timing is especially important at shows, because it is limited. If you are hosting a special presentation, let the editors know all of the available times to see it. If you have executives available for interviews, encourage editors to set an appointment for that interview prior to the show. Specify any photo opportunities available and best times to shoot.

Location is important here too. Especially at larger shows, finding some of the press rooms and conference rooms is difficult. Busy editors might not take the time if they don't know exactly where to find you. A map might be helpful.

For the press release, follow the basic journalistic 5 W's: Who, What, Where, When, and Why. The closer your release conforms to journalism industry standards the better chance you have of getting it published as written. (Associated Press and United Press International have created detailed guidelines (1).)

Put the most important information in the first paragraph, with additional information in descending order of importance. This is the old "inverted pyramid" style still used by most journalists, since editors tend to cut stories from the bottom up.

MOST IMPORTANT: Identify the News Angle. Just as your show program targets a specific audience, so too should your news releases. If, for example, our glassware company was writing a press release about a new line of unbreakable plastic glassware available, we would feature its unbreakable durability to a pool and spa audience, and perhaps its new fashion color and style to a kitchen boutique retailer. Always ask the question: Is it newsworthy? To be newsworthy, the information must be new, or have a new angle which will have an effect on the publications' readership. A more direct question to your idea may be, "So What?"

There are three places your press releases and press kits should go when you plan for a show.

- Mail kits and releases to all editors on your promotions target list early enough for show issue publication when that is appropriate, or so they will receive them before leaving for the show.
- Distribute kits in the show press room prior to the show and check periodically to assure the supply is replenished.
- Keep extra kits in your exhibit. Editors often like the convenience.

Depending on the size of the show, press rooms and press kit distribution can run from extremely informal (a few press kits on a table) to very complex (categorized alphabetically by company name and organized in slotted shelves). Some shows do not have facilities for press kits at all. Check with show management when planning press kit distribution.

IMPLEMENTING THE LEAD PROCESSING FUNCTION

You spent some time in Chapter 5 thinking about lead processing and how it should function for your program. Now is the time to make decisions and get the system in place because lead processing takes a bit of planning up front to run smoothly.

Five Vital Components of the Lead Card

The first point for the lead card is a warning: don't fall into the trap of taking the easy way out. It will only dilute the effectiveness of your program. By the "easy way" I mean using the generic lead forms provided by show management or the registration company.

Many larger shows use badge imprinter systems to make lead gathering more efficient for the exhibitor. In this system, each attendee is given a show badge that resembles a credit card with their company, name, and address, printed in raised letters. Exhibitors can then rent imprinters and carbon forms to make imprints of the badges.

The forms used in these imprinters are usually called "lead forms" and they are very generic. It's tempting to use them because you don't have to go to the effort of producing your own lead cards and bringing them to the show. However, these generic forms do nothing to encourage exhibit staffers to gather key qualifying information about the people who visit your exhibit. Thus with the imprinter forms you rarely get more information than you would if you simply collected business cards.

Whether you use the imprinter system or a manual system for gathering leads, you can create your own custom lead card to gather just the information you need. Keep the lead card small and concise, about the size of a vest pocket brochure is recommended so that staffers can carry them in coat pockets and have them readily accessible. Visitors only spend on the average three to five minutes in an interaction, and won't take a lot of time completing a lengthy questionnaire. Choose those qualifying questions carefully. The sample lead card in Exhibit 6-4 illustrates seven vital components to include on the custom lead card. You can further customize it to your needs.

Three Options for Lead Distribution

Once you have created the lead card, the next step is to determine *exactly* what is going to happen to the leads after they are collected at the show. A favorite legend amongst veteran exhibitors is about the company who was taking their exhibit out of storage to prepare it for the show, and opened a drawer to find all of the lead cards from the previous year's show still inside! To avoid that, or a lesser evil, plan how leads will be handled. There are three basic options.

Hand-Carry the leads back to the office after the show is over. Then generate the mailing labels and follow-up literature and distribute literature. This requires the longest follow-up time, and, depending on the efficiency of your literature distribution, you can expect show participants to receive literature 2 weeks to 30 days after the show is over.

Exhibit 6-4

Inquiry Card	→ Show Name and Date
Show name: _____ Date: _____	
	→ Vital Statistics
Name: _____	Be sure phone number is
Company: _____	included here. You can
Title: _____	gather this information
Address: _____	by stapling a business
City: ____ State: __ Zip: __	card to the form, if you
Phone: ( ) _____	are using just single copy forms.
**************	
Visitor profile ———————	→ Visitor Profile
☐ Retail	
☐ Distributor	This reflects what you
☐ Wholesaler	want to know about your visitors. May include job function, applications for
Visitor need/interest	products, titles, business
☐ Custom glassware	or industry, etc.
☐ Luxury line glassware	
☐ Nonbreakable outdoor glassware	
	→ Visitor Interest
Call to action:	
☐ Have salesperson contact	What products or services
☐ Send literature _____	are they interested in? Check-off boxes make
Comments: _____	completing the form
_____	much easier for exhibit
_____	staff.
_____	
Staffer: _____	

Action ◄
What type of follow-up action should be taken on this lead? This may vary according to your follow-up procedures.

Comments This is the most frequently neglected, yet the most important section of the lead card. This is where staffers note important details of the conversation that will help the person following up on the lead.

Signature

A place where the staffer who took the lead can sign his or her name for checking on missing details.

Overnight-Mail the leads back to the office at the end of each day. This speeds up the response time a bit by allowing you to get them processed sooner. In a very efficient system (where leads are input to a data base and mailing labels generated quickly), the leads from the first day of the show can often go out before the show is over and recipients see the response literature the week they return from the show.

On-site-input leads to your computerized data base. This requires having your data base established in advance and either bringing a portable computer to the show or renting a compatible system in the show city. Then you can either overnight-mail disks back to your office and avoid the input time, or send them via modem right onto your office computer. Keep in mind that this system requires having someone at the exhibit dedicated to inputting the leads as they come in and sending them back to headquarters at the end of the day.

Depending on the complexity of the lead and the data base, an experienced person can input one lead in about 20 seconds. That should give you a rough idea of the personnel required to assure leads are input regularly. Be careful not to ask a booth receptionist to input leads at the same rate that a full-time person would do the job. Interruptions will greatly reduce the speed with which he or she will be able to accomplish the task.

The Essential Link: Assigning Responsibility

Reviewing the steps in lead processing that were outlined in Chapter 4, we will be focusing now on the fourth step: reporting back on lead status. The chart in Exhibit 6-5 will refresh your memory.

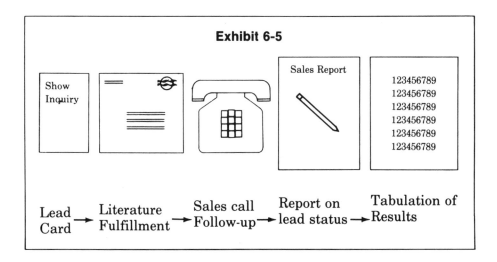

Exhibit 6-5

Lead Card → Literature Fulfillment → Sales call Follow-up → Report on lead status → Tabulation of Results

If you remember, this is frequently the weakest link in the chain. Therefore success of lead tracking will depend on having one person dedicated to that tracking function. The question is: Who should be responsible? There are a variety of considerations, but no single solution. Each has its built-in pros and cons, and you will find additional pros and cons to each, based on how your company operates. Take a few minutes to review the options outlined below and decide on the person who will work best for your program.

Secretary or Administrative Person

Pros: If this is written in as one of this person's job responsibilities they will best be in the position to be sure the job gets accomplished. They will have the time, and they rarely travel for business so they are able to focus on making the necessary contacts with the salespeople.

Cons: It is rare for a person at this level in the company to have the authority to demand performance from salespeople. Short of continual nagging, they will have little control over whether or not salespeople actually report back on leads.

Exhibits Manager

Pros: This gives exhibits managers one additional level of control over the trade show function. It allows them to see results from shows on a regular basis and use them in show evaluations.

Cons: It is difficult for exhibits managers to find time to execute this function efficiently. Due to their travel schedules, connecting with salespeople becomes a nearly impossible task.

Sales Manager

Pros: A sales manager has the authority to ask salespeople for reports and be assured that they will be returned. This also provides the sales manager with a system for monitoring the action on at least one type of lead that salespeople receive. The sales manager also often has regular reporting contact with salespeople which would better facilitate the process.

Cons: The sales manager must provide an additional link between those salespeople working on the leads, and the exhibits manager, to report on results of show leads. This sets up an additional chain of communication which can in fact further weaken that link in the chain.

Keep in mind that *who* is responsible for this function is not nearly as important as the fact that *someone* is responsible. It typically works best to set up a reporting schedule so that the responsible person knows that each 30, 60, or 90 days, a report on lead status will be expected. Don't expect this function to fall into place immediately. Companies spend years perfecting the system. One company with a very efficient system has been constantly improving and upgrading the system for nearly ten years.

Two Options for Follow-Up Literature

Select the literature well before the show to assure that you have the right quantity and they can be processed immediately following the show. There are two choices to consider here.

The first choice is to use existing literature that you have on file. This is typically done when you only want to be able to supply visitors with samples of product literature after the show is over.

The second option is to have literature specially created for the show. This is important if you are working to build a special image message at the show. Keeping the theme consistent from the point of the pre-show mailer, to the message in the exhibit, and all the way through to the follow-up literature after the show, is going to strengthen the message that you are communicating in the show effort. If you are considering having a piece of follow-up literature created, now is the time to get that process started.

A few pointers on creating special follow-up literature for the show:

- Be sure it echoes the theme established for the show.
- Keep the message simple; include just one or two key points in the follow-up literature.
- Leave a door open. As a result of sending the follow-up literature we want to motivate people to request a sales call. Remember to facilitate that in the follow-up literature. Some companies include bounce-back cards that highly interested prospects can return to request more detailed information, or a sales call.

THE SITE VISIT: PREREQUISITE FOR A SMOOTH INSTALLATION

The information in this section focuses on making a site visit to the show hall prior to your participation in the show. This will give you details that will guide not only your set-up, but many details of your show plan.

The site visit is considered by some to be a bit of a luxury. Some exhibit managers consider that this is not worth the time and expense. Admittedly, if you are very familiar with the show hall and city, then the site visit is not as important. However, if you are not familiar with it (and a vacation trip to the show city five years ago doesn't qualify), it will be worth your time to go out and check the site. Especially if you are planning hospitality events and a variety of ancillary promotions (billboards, hotel door fliers), the site visit will provide you an opportunity to work out some of those details.

If you are planning a site visit, be sure to find out in advance what type of event is going on at the time you plan to be there. If there is a show in progress, you might need special permission from that show's manager, or from the convention hall to get into the hall and check on your space location.

Checking out that booth space location is a priority. Unfortunately, although many of the floorplan drawings for shows are very good, you could run into a situation where posts, outlets, or fire alarms are not indicated on the show floorplan. You may show up at the hall with one exhibit plan to discover that you have to rebuild parts of it on the spot to accommodate unexpected "details" in your booth space.

> TRUE STORY: One exhibitor, fully aware of a large column in his exhibit space, had very carefully planned the exhibit structure to fit within the space and around the column. What he didn't know was that built into that column was a fire alarm box that had to be accessible throughout the show. Unfortunately he had planned an exhibit that was going to be built right up next to that column making the fire alarm inaccessible. He had to do a bit of redesigning on-site to be in compliance with the show regulations.

The checklist in Exhibit 6-6 will guide you in establishing the details you want to focus on during your site visit. If some of the items seem obvious, be forewarned. Making assumptions is the first step toward getting into trouble. Take checking the loading dock freight doors and elevators, for instance. It would stand to reason that they would be created to accommodate display shipments. However, especially if the show is in a hotel, this is not always the case. One exhibitor ended up unpacking crates and hand-carrying components into a show hall, because their crates would not fit the hotel's limited freight elevators!

Exhibit 6-6   Site Visit Checklist

☐   Booth Space
  ✔ Poles
  ✔ Columns
  ✔ Plumbing access
  ✔ Electrical junction box location
  ✔ Lighting (can it be changed?)
  ✔ Loading docks and freight elevators

☐ Service Locations
  ✔ Where are service desks typically located?
  ✔ Where will phone service be?
  ✔ Electrical contractor's office
  ✔ Union contact and offices
☐ Hotel Contact
  ✔ Double-check reservations
  ✔ Check meeting rooms for appropriate size and lighting
  ✔ Locate catering offices
  ✔ Confirm A-V equipment
  ✔ Confirm catering orders
☐ Coordinate Local Promotions
  ✔ Billboards
  ✔ Taxi cab placards
  ✔ Hotel room door fliers
  ✔ Airport advertising
  ✔ Local spot TV ads

As you can see, especially if you are planning a fairly complex show strategy, much can be accomplished during the pre-show site visit.

Pointers for Product Delivery

In planning for shows, a great deal of thought is often given to *which* products will be displayed. But as to where they will come from, how they will get there, and how they will be maintained...this is often a last-minute detail. Here, Lize Culbertson, CES, offers some advice from her own experience coordinating product deliveries and installations at hundreds of shows.

ADVICE FROM THE EXPERTS

Tips on Product Shipping

Lize Culbertson spent ten years as the trade show manager at computer company Triad Systems, Inc. where she coordinated over 200 shows each year. The sheer volume of products required for these functions forced her to create systematic procedures for coordinating transportation and maintenance.

Depending on your products and the number of shows you do a year, financial resources dedicated to trade show product inventories are lost revenue on the books. It rarely appears in your show budget, but you may need to consider it in your quarterly or annual department budgets.

Especially if you are taking the financial responsibility, the responsibility for all products *must be a one-person job.* While a committee might decide on show participation and what to display at a show, the rest of the product-related decisions must be made by the person in charge of the show. You will need to determine:

- How much should be shipped?
- Whether or not to display a prototype product or just what we are selling now.
- How to get it to the show and back again (in one piece).

How Much Should Be Shipped? The overall average size of your booth is the factor that guides the number of products to display. If you have a demo product about the size of a vacuum cleaner in a 10-foot in-line exhibit, bring two for show and one for product failure. Just multiply this by each 10-foot booth size.

For larger and smaller products your decisions will require a bit more thought. If you can get statistical breakouts on the product interest of the show audience, you can allocate products and product space in the exhibit according to the level of interest attendees have in them. (2) Or you can go back to your potential audience figures (see Chapter 1) and determine how many prospects you might see per hour in your exhibit. Then allocate product space, assuring that you will have 25 sq. ft. of *open space* per visitor (and for each staffer) in your exhibit at any given time.

Should We Send Prototypes? The best advice here is show what you can sell today and use photos and graphics to show what is coming. Prototypes *never* perform like they are supposed to, especially under show conditions (Murphy's law).

Getting It to the Show and Back in One Piece. HANDLE WITH CARE, THIS SIDE UP, FRONT, BACK ... recognize any of these phrases? Whatever the instructions on the carton, crate, or case, package it as if they WILL NOT be adhered to (Murphy's law).

Identify each product container clearly with your company name, show name and booth number. Remove all labels each time it comes in from a show, before it leaves for the next show. Keep the information simple to read, since your goal is to instruct with a minimum of errors. Have outbound labels available for tear-down to eliminate confusion.

Color-code each container by products to identify easily what is inside. You may also want to number them according to show and coordinate the numbers with booth properties.

Pack each crate, carton, or case as if it will be the only one that might show up. (Whenever possible, do not ship in cardboard cartons; containers cannot be stored at your booth and must be taken off the floor to drayage. Chances of seeing cardboard cartons in usable condition again are zero to minus one zillion.)

Keep a complete inventory and repacking information sheet inside each container. This helps to identify missing items before products are sent out, along with a security check upon their return. This also helps during tear-down, in case the person who sets up is not the same one who packs up. Leave a complete inventory at your office with someone you can reach in an emergency to help you fix problems. Carry three copies with you: one for set-up, one for tear-down, and one for salespeople who want to know what's there.

Systematize the entire procedure so that you handle it the same way for every show, whether your schedule is three shows a year or thirty. Loss, theft, damage, and upkeep are product-shipping nightmares that can be offset by doing the same thing the same way for the booth every time you do a show. Ultimately that means less planning, less hassles, and fewer communications problems. It also gives you more confidence that things are where they are supposed to be. It may not be easy to capture dedicated product for shows, but it is worth the effort.

HOW TO SELECT A WINNING TEAM OF EXHIBIT STAFFERS

Six Qualities of a Top-Performing Staffer

Many companies like to send their crack salespeople to the show hoping for the type of performance they provide in the field. Unfortunately, the traits and skills required to succeed in trade show interactions aren't always the same ones that those experts use out in the field. Exhibit selling requires teamwork, and thus a variety of factors to consider when you select your staff.(3)

Personality

The best candidates are extroverts who enjoy people. A sense of humor is essential. Here you are looking for someone who is outgoing, highly energized, easy to meet and talk with. Avoid the "lone rangers" since they are not typically team players.

Attitude Toward Shows

Every staffer should have a positive attitude about shows. A negative attitude about shows will greatly affect their performance in the exhibit. Admittedly, they may not all be pleased about leaving the field to attend a show, but they should generally see shows as worthwhile events.

Previous Performance

If you know that in the past people have spent most of their booth duty shift chatting with other staffers, taking breaks, talking on the phone, or, worse yet, being rude to customers, they should not be considered for future booth duty regardless of their product knowledge or expertise.

Product/Industry Knowledge

If you *had* to choose, it would be preferable to bring people that are a little less knowledgeable about the products but have great communications skills, than those product experts who have trouble relating to people. A blend of both skills is the best option.

Territory: National vs. Regional

If your company has a national sales force, deciding whether to have just regional, or full national representation among your staffers can be tough. Unfortunately, local reps selected for booth duty often have agendas separate from the show activities and are trying to manage their day-to-day responsibilities as well as booth duty. If you are worried that national representatives will only talk to visitors from their regions, don't. This is a myth about trade show staffers that rarely rings true.

Previous Experience

There is an obvious advantage to using people with previous trade show experience, because they understand what to expect and how the medium works. Always include at least a few staffers with previous trade show experience on your booth duty roster.

Getting Cooperation from Sales Managers

All too often those responsible for trade shows are put in the position of having to "beg, borrow, and steal" people to staff their exhibits. Unfortunately, begging sales managers for people to staff the exhibit puts you in the position of requesting "favors" from that person . . . not a very strong position.

Exhibit managers who succeed at this suggest that being more *proactive* rather than *reactive* puts them in the best position to manage the staffing function. Even if you have ready and willing sales managers and sales personnel, using the open lines of communication effectively is an important first step toward building the best team to staff your exhibit. The following process will help.

Step 1: Determine Your Needs

I. Numbers

Go back to your show-by-show Operational Plan and review the calculations you made about how many people you will need in the exhibit.

Keep in mind that you will want to adjust this to accommodate staffing shifts. If, for example, you know you will need five staffers to handle traffic, you probably will need at least ten people assigned to work the show (five staffers for each of two four-hour shifts or rotating two-hour shifts).

II. *Types of Staffers*

Technical experts
Experts at interpersonal communications skills (extroverts)

Step 2: Communicate Your Needs

Communicate your needs as early as possible to avoid schedule conflicts. Identify exactly how many people you will need, what types of people would work best, how long they will be at the show. Ask the person assigning booth duty to generate a memo informing staffers of their assignments. Request a roster of candidates by a specified date.

Step 3: Create the Booth Duty Schedule

Once you have received a roster, create the booth duty schedule as early as possible. Once again, ask the person making assignments to distribute the roster, but specify that changes to the roster must be made through you. Remember, if once the booth duty roster is created, you ask people to find their own replacements should they not be able to fulfill their obligation, you lose control over the quality of staffers you get.

Get Optimal Performance with Staffing Shifts

One critical error that even the most experienced exhibitors make in planning for the exhibit staff, is not establishing staffing shifts. Typically companies ask salespeople to work full eight-, nine-, even ten-hour days in the exhibit with just a break for lunch. Based on their observations of literally thousands of staffers in trade show exhibits, the staff at Communique Exhibitor Education determined that after about four hours on a shift, the staffer becomes a negative factor in the exhibit. The chart in Exhibit 6-7 is an illustration of how staffers perform over time.

Staffers, especially those who have been trained for show participation, get off to a good start and performance accelerates rapidly. They hit their peak performance after about two hours, and then performance begins to decline. After four hours performance has declined to a point where it begins to be more negative than positive. Therefore, you will see optimum performance among staffers if they work two hours at a time with a two-hour break between shifts.

The key to being effective in an exhibit is the ability to tune in to the

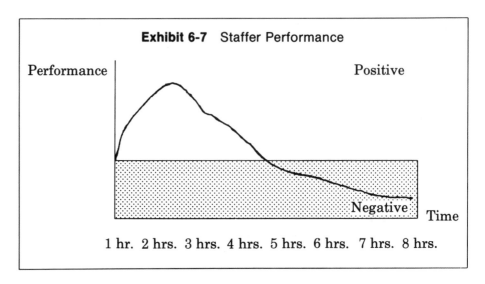

Exhibit 6-7 Staffer Performance

visitors' needs during the conversation. Fatigue tends to distract staffers from their ability to do so, therefore reducing their effectiveness in each individual interaction.

NOTE TO MANAGERS: Impact of Management on Staffer Attitudes. If you are a management person who is going to be assigning staffers, this information is for you. Your attitude about the show will significantly affect their performance. The following true life examples illustrate the point. One company had a sales manager who didn't believe in shows. He sent people because someone higher up said he had to. He showed up at the show for about two hours and joked around with the staffers. He made no contact with visitors. Staffers tended to follow that manager's unfortunate style. In contrast, at a smaller company the company *president* participated from the pre-show meeting through full staffing shifts in the exhibit every day of the show. The staffers followed suit being assertive out on the show floor in a positive way.

A few techniques for creating a positive attitude:

- An enthusiastic pre-show memo
- Attendance at the pre-show meeting
- Work staffing shifts
- Meet with show visitors during your time in the exhibit

The exhibit staffers are the only part of your exhibit that are going to make those person-to-person contacts that visitors will remember. It's worthwhile to take the time and care to select the very best people to staff exhibits and represent your company at every show.

You have made some critical progress in this chapter. Most of your plans are in place and Chapter 7 takes you to just three months prior to show participation. As deadlines approach, details have a greater tendency to slip through the cracks—and in the next chapter you will receive some guidelines for keeping up with the details of each component of the show program.

Chapter 7: You are here:

↓

	4 Mo.	3 Mo.	2 Mo.
Planning			
Goal-Setting			
Budgeting			
Promotions	Create pre-show direct mail package	Implement promotions strategy	Check direct mail costs
Product Demos		Plan formal live presentation	
Exhibits	Final decisions on new exhibit design	Manage new construction Find portable supplier	Exhibit preview Select portable structure
Installation	Plan installation		Prepare site book
Staffing	Select staffers	Prepare pre-show memos	
Inquiry Processing	Set up inquiry processing system		
Measuring Results			

7

Managing the Details
(3 Months in Advance)

As a wise prophet once said, "It's not the mountain you have to climb, it's the grain of sand in your shoe." At this point you probably feel as if you are well on your way up the mountain. But it's easy to get bogged down in details. In this chapter you consider and manage the details with timeframes, checks, and balances.

Also, if you intend to use a portable exhibit for the show rather than a custom exhibit, now is the time to begin planning for this new structure. Here you will consider the pros and cons of purchasing a portable exhibit, and how to find and work with a supplier for your portable exhibit.

In Chapter 7 you will be working on:

1. EXHIBIT CONSTRUCTION: Working with your supplier to manage the project construction.
2. PROMOTIONS: A Ten-Point Plan for organizing and implementing your promotions strategy.
3. STAFFING: How to prepare pre-show memos.
4. PORTABLE EXHIBITS: Selecting and working with a portable exhibit supplier.
5. PRODUCT PRESENTATIONS: Planning for the formal presentation.

MANAGING THE NEW EXHIBIT PROJECT

If the relationship between an exhibit supplier and the client can be compared to a marriage, the construction process is, in many cases, "post-honeymoon." The glow of the selection process has worn off a bit. By now a few stumbling blocks have already been worked through. You are beginning to get a good feel for how the other person operates, and a trust level is beginning to build.

Typically clients operate one of two ways during the construction

193

process. Very busy managers count on the trust level they've built with the account executive and completely leave the project in his or her hands. Others prefer to stay on top of the project and check its progress regularly. Striking a happy medium here is important.

Leaving the project totally in the hands of your account executive could bring surprises when the exhibit is completed. Decisions need to be made along the way, and if you are not available to make those decisions, you will either slow the construction or open yourself to unexpected results. The question, of course, is what is the right balance?

Identifying Key Responsibilities

There are two "projects" that will need to be completed before your new exhibit leaves for the show. The first is construction. The second is packaging and preparing the exhibit for shipment. Many of the details of packing and shipping cannot be left until after the exhibit preview (which is discussed in Chapter 8). It must be clarified at this point in the planning process. The chart in Exhibit 7-1 outlines for you a series of considerations to make, and who, generally, is responsible for each one.

Five Questions to Ask Before Making Expensive Changes

During the construction process it seems that changes to the exhibit are inevitable. In most cases, changes you initiate after signing off on the design, will incur additional costs. Therefore, it's important to consider each change carefully, but particularly those expensive ones. The following five questions will guide you in making the decision about whether the change warrants the additional investment.

1. *How will it affect the timetable?* Exhibits are typically produced under fairly stringent timeframes. When the producers are working against a deadline, changes to the plan could significantly affect their ability to meet that date. If the production will need to go into overtime hours or be rushed, you may pay for not only the changes, but also the additional production costs to get the job done on time. Review this possibility before deciding on the change.

2. *What are the long-term effects?* When you are producing an exhibit that will premier at a selected show, it is easy to become myopic about it and think of the structure only in terms of that show. But when you decide on changes, be sure that they won't negatively affect your long-term plans for using the structure. If, for example, you decide to build in a spotlighted pedestal to showcase a product that is being introduced, consider the long-term value of that investment and how that showcase will be used at future shows when there isn't a new product to introduce.

3. *Can it be justified in light of budgetary constraints?* Take time to review your goal evaluation worksheet from Chapter 6 to know *exactly* how far

Exhibit 7-1 Responsibilities Chart

Exhibit Production

Your Responsibility

√ Establish your expectations for communication throughout the process

√ Be available to approve each phase and any changes

√ Provide camera ready art for graphics

√ Double-check for compliance with show rules and regulations

√ Notify ASAP of changes to equipment or products displayed

√ Be prepared to pay for changes initiated after you've given approval

√ Be prepared to pay for services performed in the event of cancellation

√ Submit and agree to changes in writing

The A/E's Responsibility

√ Inform you of potential cost overruns

√ Inform you of any changes in materials used

√ Monitor the quality of the construction

√ Update you periodically on the construction progress

√ Inform you immediately of difficult time constraints

√ Discuss any problems that arise with solution suggestions

√ Trouble-shoot

√ Oversee graphics production

Transportation*

Your Responsibilities

√ Supply addresses for all pick-up and delivery points

√ Provide a list of materials in addition to exhibit structure that will be shipped. (e.g., products, literature, press kits, etc.)

√ Review and approve estimate of shipping rates

√ Inform A/E of any schedule changes for product or literature delivery

Your A/E's responsibilities

√ Oversee preparation of exhibit for shipping

√ Secure a weight certificate & bill of lading for shipment

√ Oversee completion of paperwork for shipping

√ Tracking shipments

√ Communicate schedule changes to transportation provider

*Your Account Executive can be expected to handle these responsibilities ONLY if you have requested that they handle shipping arrangements as part of your contract. If not, those additional responsibilities fall to you.

you have deviated from your original budget for the exhibit. This will shed that cold, hard light on the necessity of an expensive change.

4. *What are the alternatives?* Since the cat can be skinned several ways, it will be worth your time, on any change, to sit down with your account executive and brainstorm *all* alternatives. Just as an example, if you decided that you wanted a granite look for your pedestals rather than an adobe finish, you could use real granite (yes, some exhibitors really do) or a granite-look laminate, or a variety of paint finishes that have a similar effect.

5. *Is it functional or cosmetic?* In many cases the functional changes are more critical. If you're talking about improving lighting, increasing storage space, providing for an extra demonstration area, these types of changes can greatly affect the exhibit performance. Cosmetic changes, such as colors or surface materials, are less critical to performance.

ADVICE FROM THE EXPERTS: What Every Exhibit Manager Should Know About Graphics Production

Charlie McMillan is president of the McMillan Group, an exhibit design and marketing firm. During his experience as an exhibit designer, and now as principal of his own firm, Charlie has become an expert on graphics production options. Here he shares two fundamental facts about graphics production that he wishes every exhibitor knew (and followed).

Fundamental #1: The quality of your reproduction hinges on the quality of your original. It is too common to see exhibitors in a rush show up with a business card as their only source of original art, and want an exhibit graphic produced from it. To produce the *best* quality graphics the artwork must be original. That means original typeset copy. Original photographs that have not been screened. Original drawings that have not been photographed. A small spot on that 35 mm transparency becomes a gaping, black hole in an enlarged photomural.

Also, it is much more expensive to reproduce good results from bad artwork. For example, if you submit a 35mm slide with copy stripped in, you will pay extra for the retouching required to clean up that artwork. It, in fact, might be cheaper to reshoot the art in a different format.

Fundamental #2: There are three elements in any graphics project that must be considered: time, cost, and quality.

Quality	Cost	Time

All elements of the project have to be in balance and then a predictable result will occur; that is, good quality at a reasonable cost in a normal time of production and delivery.

When one of the elements is squeezed, as in this example of the time frame being too short, the result is that the cost goes up to allow for rush and overtime charges to keep the quality the same, or . . .

. . . the quality will be reduced if time is cut without added funds for rush and overtime. In many cases it won't even be possible to do the work without the right balance of these three items.

Thus, when one item is off, compromises must be made in the other two categories to produce the graphic. For example, the least flexible item to manage is cost. If the cost is reduced, it doesn't mean time can be extended to accommodate less money.

In contrast, the level of quality provides the most flexibility. When cost is reduced, there are options that can be used which will affect the quality of the finished piece, but not necessarily render it unacceptable. Alternate materials can be used, or less color or simpler construction methods to make up for lesser cost or time. These compromises don't always mean poor quality. They may only require a simpler or less involved solution to a given problem.

Time is the element most commonly out of proportion here. Exhibitors frequently spend much more money than they need to on graphics, or sacrifice quality, simply by not planning far enough in advance. Avoid this by planning graphics early and getting artwork produced early enough to control the quality of the original art.

When you do face a time crunch, explore solutions with your designer to provide the best quality graphic that you can within your budget constraints. Your designer should be able to help you there. That's what design is about: solving problems.

TEN-POINT PLAN FOR IMPLEMENTING THE PROMOTIONS STRATEGY

You have invested quite a bit of time in *planning* your promotions strategy and have probably begun working on several of the components. And you've probably begun to see the magnitude of the details required to accomplish it. The chart in Exhibit 7-2 is designed to help organize those

Exhibit 7-2

	Trade Ads	Direct Mail	Give-Aways	Press Kits	Bill-Board	Other:
1. Interface with agencies or other departments.	Name: Date:	Name: Date:	Name: Date:	Name: Date:	Name: Date:	Name: Date:
2. Select suppliers.	Name: Date:	Name: Date:	Name: Date:	Name: Date:	Name: Date:	Name: Date:
3. Scheduling.	Name: Date:	Name: Date:	Name: Date:	Name: Date:	Name: Date:	Name: Date:
4. Creative and copy.	Name: Date:	Name: Date:	Name: Date:	Name: Date:	Name: Date:	Name: Date:
5. Production.	Name: Date:	Name: Date:	Name: Date:	Name: Date:	Name: Date:	Name: Date:
6. Purchasing and ordering.	Name: Date:	Name: Date:	Name: Date:	Name: Date:	Name: Date:	Name: Date:
7. Approvals.	Name: Date:	Name: Date:	Name: Date:	Name: Date:	Name: Date:	Name: Date:

	Trade Ads	Direct Mail	Give-Aways	Press Kits	Bill-Board	Other:
8. Distribution.	Name: Date:	Name: Date:	Name: Date:	Name: Date:	Name: Date:	Name: Date:
9. Follow-up.	Name: Date:	Name: Date:	Name: Date:	Name: Date:	Name: Date:	Name: Date:
10. Cost tracking.	Name: Date:	Name: Date:	Name: Date:	Name: Date:	Name: Date:	Name: Date:

details. Vertically, down the left side of the chart are ten points that generally outline the remaining tasks (your Ten-Point Plan). Across the top you will list the promotion media you are using. (In the example, these media have already been listed.) When using this chart, select only those media you are using.

To use the chart, identify for each medium the tasks that have to be accomplished. In the square where the task and the medium intersect, write down your deadline, and the initials of the person responsible to complete that task. As tasks are completed you can draw an X through each box. If one of the ten tasks is not required for a certain medium, simply draw an X through the box where that task and medium choice intersect. Following the chart is an explanation of each task that identifies what typically needs to be accomplished. Be sure to adjust these as you read them to fit within your own needs and situation.

Whether or not you need this chart, and the extent to which you use it, will depend on the complexity of your program. If you only use trade publication advertising before the show and add a tag line to an existing ad, much of this planning won't be necessary. However, as more promotional tools are used, the number of details seems to increase exponentially. The chart will help you keep them organized.

1. *Interface with agencies or other departments.* Almost any promotional media used may require that you interface with another company department or with an agency to produce the media. For example, your company may work with a public relations agency who could produce press kits and press releases. You might find it useful to get your advertising manager or agency involved in producing show-related ads. Discuss your plans with these contacts and define responsibilities for task accomplishment.

2. *Select suppliers.* Depending on your existing working relationship with ad agencies, premiums suppliers, and direct mail list suppliers, this could be very simple or a bit time-consuming. Take time to identify all of the new suppliers you will need. For example, direct mail requires someone to write the copy, produce the artwork, produce the mailer, supply a mailing list, and package and send mailers. If you are using giveaways such as coffee mugs or frisbees, you will have to locate a source for those. Suppliers will help you further define production deadlines.

3. *Scheduling.* Whether you are placing an ad, writing press releases, or just handing out pens, you will have deadlines to meet in using the promotions effectively. Take time up front to identify the deadlines for each promotion and assure that everyone involved knows their role in meeting those deadlines. For help with scheduling, you can refer back to the chart in Chapter 5 on building your promotions strategy.

4. *Creative ad copy.* Those special ads and direct mail promotions will need copy and artwork. Identify who will be responsible to produce those and when they will be completed.

5. *Production.* Nearly any promotional media requires some sort of production. Ads, direct mail, billboards, press kits all require special production. Here again, identify who will be responsible for the production of each medium, and when it will need to be completed. Keep in mind that production of media that will be shipped to the show such as press kits or giveaways must be completed a week in advance of the ship date to allow time to double-check the quality and make any required changes.

6. *Purchasing and ordering.* This relates primarily to giveaways and/or contest prizes. These items must also be ordered well in advance of the ship date if you are planning to send them to the show with the exhibit.

7. *Approvals.* At times approval must be sought for new advertising campaigns, press events, or direct mail projects. If copy or artwork needs to be approved by upper management, schedule an additional week for the approval process and changes that need to be made.

8. *Distribution.* Target the dates that your direct mail must be sent, or that your final artwork needs to be at the publisher's, or that the billboard art

needs to be to the supplier. Identify how the premiums and press kits will get to the show and when they need to leave your facility.

9. *Follow-Up.* If each detail isn't double-checked and followed-up, one or two are sure to slip through the cracks. Plan to assign one person to follow up on the details and assure all promotions are in place a week prior to leaving for the show.

10. *Cost tracking.* Double-check all costs as you implement components of the promotions plan. When you are managing several promotions a few cost overruns are easily overlooked, but they can add up to a surprising shock when the bills come in.

Use a separate worksheet for each show, and once completed, file it in your Show Plan behind the promotions plan.

PREPARING PRE-SHOW MEMOS THAT STAFFERS READ AND USE

If you participate in one or two shows a year with a 10′ linear exhibit, staffed by one or two salespeople, you'll probably be tempted to skip the pre-show memo altogether. Don't. This memo provides the first opportunity for you to communicate the show plan (modest though it may be) to *everyone* who will be involved in working at the show. For smaller shows you will just have shorter, simpler memos. But this is a critical tool for informing participants about your expectations and their job at the show.

A well prepared pre-show memo saves time by accomplishing the following:

- *Establishes guidelines* for behavior and expectations for all staffers.
- *Informs staffers* of the housekeeping details they need. This should cut down on phone call inquiries you receive about show procedures. At the very least it will help you keep those conversations short by simply referring inquiries to the appropriate page of the pre-show memo.
- *Raises issues* for which there may be conflict or concern well in advance. For example, if there is a staffing conflict, this allows plenty of time to handle it.
- *Raises confidence* level of the staffers, especially for those who don't travel a great deal. An exhibits manager recently shared the story about a rather frantic staffer from a small town who called to express several fears and concerns about going to New York for the first time. (How would she get to the hotel, where was the convention hall, how much do you tip the cab driver? . . .) Well-traveled exhibits managers tend to take these details for granted.

Six Improvements for the Pre-Show Memo

A few considerations to make in preparing the pre-show memo. The greatest challenge, of course, is getting busy salespeople and staffers to read them. A few tips that exhibit managers have used effectively:

- *Packaging,* as they say in the world of consumer goods, is *everything.* Try putting the memos in brightly colored folders so they look interesting and stand out from the typical clutter on a desk or in a briefcase.

- *Personalize* them with name tags on the cover. People tend to give more attention to items addressed to them personally.

- *Use an "Urgent" stamp* or sticker on the cover or a label that says "Dated Material: Vital XYZ Show Information."

- *Specifically request* that they read the memo prior to leaving for the show. Salespeople tend to stick those files in their briefcases to read on the airplane on their way to the show. For some types of information (shift scheduling, hotel assignments) that may be too late.

- *Include a cover letter* over the signature of an upper level management person. It's best to put the cover letter over the signature of the person to whom most of the staffers report. This adds a significant level of endorsement to the information.

- *Organize the information* in categories and use tabbed dividers for quick reference. Especially if you have quite a bit of information to communicate, make it easy for staffers to find the details they need most. The balance between complete and brief is tough to maintain but important.

The checklist in Exhibit 7-3 outlines a variety of items to include in the pre-show memo, organized for you by category. Use it to check off those items appropriate to your show, and add anything pertinent to your program that's not included here.

Selecting the Pre-Show Meeting Location

A brief review of the types of pre-show meetings will refresh your memory as you consider scheduling:

The Orientation Meeting is conducted by the exhibits manager and covers the basic details of the show.

The Training Meeting is conducted by an exhibit selling specialist and covers selling skills for trade shows.

The Rally Meeting is conducted each day prior to the show to motivate staffers.

The very best time to conduct an orientation or training pre-show meeting is shortly before the show opens at the show site. Not in the

Exhibit 7-3   Pre-Show Memo Checklist

Section I—Site Information

☐ Show name, dates, location

☐ Map of the show city

☐ Hotel address, phone number

☐ Ground transportation information

☐ Restaurant list

☐ Other _____

Section II—Staffing Logistics

☐ Booth duty schedule

☐ Hotel rooming assignments

☐ Demonstration assignments

☐ Booth duty captains (names and roles)

☐ Pre-show meeting (date, time, location)

☐ Rally meetings (date, time, location)

☐ Dress standards

☐ Registration and badge pick-up procedures

☐ Other _____

Section III—Show Strategy

☐ Show goals

☐ Exhibit Selling Action Plan

☐ Show promotions and advertising

☐ Literature for at-show and post-show distribution

☐ Sample lead card

☐ Samples or premiums that will be handed out in the exhibit

☐ Hospitality functions planned

☐ Other _____

Section IV—Exhibit and Hall

☐ Hall floorplan indicating your booth location and those of competitors

☐ Exhibit floorplan

☐ Exhibit photos

☐ Other _____

exhibit, but in the show city. If you are including exhibit staff training in your pre-show meeting, the staffers will remember and assimilate the material they learn more efficiently if training is conducted just prior to the show.

Also, as a matter of convenience and economy, especially for larger shows, this is perhaps the only time when you will get all of your salespeople together in one place at one time. Plan to take an entire morning or afternoon the day before the show opens to conduct your pre-show meeting. If you have considered holding the meeting the evening before the show, keep in mind the time zone changes for people who are traveling and how that can affect participation and attention span.

Rally meetings are best conducted in the morning before the show opens, on the second and/or third days of the show. This is when enthusiasm, energy, and focus tends to dissipate and the symbolic shot of pep in a rally meeting can boost performance.

Where Should the Meeting Be Held?

It's easiest to begin with places where the meeting shouldn't be held:

Don't hold the pre-show meeting in your exhibit. In most cases the pre-show meeting needs to take place during exhibit installation hours. That means you will be vying for attention with forklift trucks and union laborers. You will also have a difficult time controlling staffers who become bored and begin exploring different parts of the exhibit while you are trying to review the staffing schedule. And, it's risky to share information of a confidential nature when your discussions are so easily "overheard" as they can be in the exhibit. Your best bet is a meeting room in the show hall or at a nearby hotel.

Don't hold your meeting in a restaurant. Restaurants don't work well for larger groups. Restaurants are set up for a relaxed environment and rarely can accommodate your audio-visual requirements well.

The best place to conduct the meeting is at a meeting room in the hotel where a majority of your staffers are staying. It's easy for staffers to find and easy to facilitate set-up arrangements. Most of the major show halls around the U.S. have meeting rooms as well. Unfortunately, the quality of these rooms varies dramatically from hall to hall and can be pretty gloomy. Services in the hall can fluctuate as well when the same A-V people set up your room as those setting up the show hall. Show demands can take priority leaving your meeting needs wanting.

As budgets for trade shows increase, so too is pressure for perfor-mance and results. In the period from 1978 to 1987 the average show budget went from $73,000 to $212,600. In this same time period, the percentage of exhibitors who felt that booth staffing and training techniques would be helpful in improving show participation jumped from 21% to 33%.(1) To stay competitive, exhibitors are increasingly investing time to prepare their personnel for show participation. Pre-show orientation meetings, training meetings, and rally meetings can contribute significantly to those efforts.

CONSIDERATIONS FOR SELECTING A PORTABLE EXHIBITS SUPPLIER

"Fifteen years ago . . . it was nearly impossible to find a low cost, lightweight, portable display that you could check as airline luggage, carry into a convention hall, set up yourself, and be ready to go to work in less than an hour." That quote from the *Exhibitor Magazine* best illustrates how far the portable side of exhibits has come. In fact less than ten years ago, in 1981, only $2 million worth of 10' portable exhibits were sold in the U.S.(2)

In 1986, according to an *Exhibitor Magazine* survey, sales of 10' portable exhibits climbed to $48,327,000. Just three years later the magazine reported over 80 different portable display companies in the U.S. and Canada. That's quite a bit of choice. In some ways, finding a good portable display is easier than ever. In other ways, though, it's tougher. More choices mean more complexity.

As one person has said, the portable did for exhibiting what the Apple did for computing: made the tool accessible to a group who could never before afford the investment in time and resources previously required to use it. But be careful about automatically assuming it will be the best, most economical exhibit source. The list of pros and cons in Exhibit 7-4 outlines some common benefits of portable displays as well as their limitations.

Services Portable Exhibit Suppliers Can Provide

If you used the analogy of restaurants, custom exhibit suppliers range from all-American to five-star gourmet in terms of the products and services they supply. Portable exhibit suppliers fall more into the fast food category, in that the solutions are pretty much the same and the services are limited.

But services do vary among suppliers, and knowing what you can expect up front helps to find the best ones. Recently, at least one portable exhibit company has begun offering a variety of show services; among them are inventory control, shipping, and on-site installation. For exhibits managers who use portables at a host of regional and vertical market shows, and simply don't have the staff to support the shipping, inventory,

Exhibit 7-4   Pros and Cons of Using Portable Displays

Pros	Cons
+ Transportability	— Limited space sizes
+ Variety of uses	— Not a custom solution
+ Graphics flexibility	— Limited dimensions
+ Lightweight	— Less support (storage
+ Ease of installation	inventory, etc.)
+ No drayage required	— Product weight limits
+ No union labor required	— Potential for "me too" look
(for most installations)	— Limited graphics options
+ Minimal transport costs	
+ Interchangeable parts	

and installations involved, tapping into the service offerings of the portable suppliers is an efficient way to expand resources.

Therefore, the list of what you can expect from a portable exhibit supplier has been divided into two parts. The first five are the basics, which you should expect when you purchase a display. The second lists extra services that a few suppliers are offering for additional fees.

The Basics

- Graphics Design. The supplier should be able and willing to help you design graphics for your display. Depending on their expertise, this type of help can include tips on the use of color, copy size and location, content of copy, guidelines for using photographs and drawings, and even help in clarifying your exhibit message.

- Graphics Production. Some suppliers produce graphics in-house, others job them out to local photo labs. Keep in mind when purchasing a display that the price you are quoted in most cases includes just the structure itself, and graphics design and production is an additional cost. The graphics can actually represent an investment equal to or greater than that of the structure.

- Service. The supplier should be available for repairs. Look for those that have a network of resources around the country so that you can get spare parts easily in any show city. Some portable exhibit suppliers have an 800 number for customer service. Also, check on the written directions they provide for setting up the display. If you will be sending the display out to the field and asking sales representatives to set it up, the clarity of those instructions can make all the difference in their attitudes about using it.

- Exhibit Preview. When the exhibit is delivered, does the rep simply ship it to your office or does he hand-deliver it and demonstrate the set-up? Does he allow you time to preview the exhibit once it is set up to assure that everything is in place?

- Follow-Up. Once the sale is made, do they follow up to assure that the exhibit met expectations? Does the sales rep follow up periodically to see whether graphics needs have changed or expanded? Check with references on this one to evaluate it accurately.

The Extras

- Warehousing. For companies who attend hundreds of shows each year in which portable exhibits are used, simply warehousing the structures can be a pretty big job. At least one portable supplier offers that service to their clients.

- Inventory Control. With any significant number of shows, routing both the structure and the graphics is sure to present logistical headaches. If your department is a bit short-staffed to handle these logistics you might look for a portable supplier that offers these services.

- Shipping. If your supplier is handling warehousing and inventory, the next logical step is to have them coordinate shipping as well. Most portable displays can be shipped UPS or through an overnight service. Turning this over to the supplier, however, requires a bit more pre-planning, organization, and communication.

- Display Scheduling and Reservations. Along with inventory control, the supplier can also schedule and coordinate which structures are where, to assure the correct structure and graphics are available for any given show.

The Federal Express company has a two-person exhibit department responsible for 300 trade shows and events where portable exhibits are used. They are able to meet this demanding schedule primarily because they utilize these services through their portable exhibit supplier. In Chapter 8 you will see how they organize the company side of the information flow to make the working relationship most efficient.

Sources for Portable Exhibit Suppliers

With the growth of demand for portable exhibits has come the growth of suppliers. A few of the types of suppliers you will find include:

- Exclusive distributors (companies dedicated to a single manufacturer).
- Custom exhibit houses who provide their own models of portable exhibits.
- Custom exhibit houses that rep a variety of lines of portable exhibits.

- Portable companies that carry only portable exhibits but represent a variety of lines, often in a showroom where you can see several options in a single location.

The ways of finding these suppliers is almost as varied as the types. A few suggestions are listed here, in order of their comprehensive coverage of the offerings.

1. The Illustrated Buyer's Guide to Exhibits. The third edition of this catalog, published by Exhibitor Publications, Inc. in 1986, lists over 100 systems.(3) Along with the source it lists specifications such as the frame construction, panel options, panel coverings and colors, setup time, price, strength, weight, lights, accessories, and others. It is the most comprehensive one-stop shopping guide.

2. Trade Shows. There are two major trade show industry trade shows, one sponsored by the International Exhibitors Association called TS2 (The Trade Show About Trade Shows) and another called The Exhibitor Show sponsored by Exhibitor Publications, Inc. There are also a variety of smaller vertical market shows such as the Health Care Exhibitors Association annual meeting. Portable exhibit suppliers are often in abundance at these shows and there you can meet with a variety of manufacturers.

3. Publications. Portable companies advertise in small business magazines, marketing publications, card decks, trade show industry trade publications, and even in-flight magazines. These are good first-step resources.

4. Local Phone Directories. Check the yellow pages under exhibits or displays for local listings.

PLANNING THE FORMAL PRODUCT PRESENTATION

If you are planning on using a formal presentation at the show, now is the time to begin planning. Because of the dynamics of trade shows using formal presentations successfully is a bit tricky. The presentation area has to be open enough to draw traffic, yet the open environment means a less-controlled audience. People can come and go as they please. Lighting, staging, sound, even the scripts have special considerations at a trade show. While much of the planning for any live presentation will have to be done by the exhibits manager, your best bet is to hire a professional for scripting and production.

ADVICE FROM THE EXPERTS: Successful Live Presentations

Elaine Cohen, president of Live Marketing, Inc., has contributed significantly to the professionalism of producing live presentations for trade shows in her 15 years in the business. Her company now averages 350 shows a year in virtually every industry from caskets to computers, for companies ranging in size from Fortune 100 to small start-ups.

Elaine coined the phrase Live Marketing and pioneered the concept of marketing-based live presentations for trade shows as opposed to entertainment only. She is a recognized expert in the trade show industry on conducting live presentations at show. Here she guides you, step by step, through the considerations to make when planning for a live formal product or corporate presentation in your exhibit.

It is essential to create the live presentation based on objectives set for show participation. Those objectives will have to be interpreted into goals for the presentation. This requires thinking about what you want the audience to hear, and, equally important, what you want them to *do* after viewing the presentation. When planning for the presentation, consider the following five factors:

1. What *tone* and *style* do you want the presentation to have?
2. How will you *motivate* the audience to *view* the presentation?
3. What do you want the audience to *do* after viewing the presentation?
4. What *presentation techniques* will best help you accomplish your goals?
5. How will you *set the stage* for the presentation?

#1: Establishing Presentation Tone and Style

With presentation goals established, you can begin to decide on the tone and style of the presentation. This requires that you understand the personality of your audience, the level of sophistication of the industry, and the image that your company wants to project. This information then becomes the basis for the presentation and must be accurate. For instance, you don't sing a song at an American College of Surgeons Show (a very serious group) and you don't do scientific demonstrations at the National Restaurant Show.

There are three commonly used presentation styles. The first is the "corporate spokesperson" presentation where the information is delivered in a straightforward, professional, conservative style. Here the presenter is perceived as a salesperson who works for the company.

The second is the theatrical presentation where there is usually a story with character and a lot of humor.

The third style is a combination of spokesperson and theatrical. All three styles work. The key is to understand when and where to use which style, and for whom.

Regardless of the style you choose, always keep the *product message* as your main focus. People have to go away understanding and remembering your product message, not a presentation gimmick.

#2: Motivating the Audience

You can't just rely on traffic at the show being self-motivated to view your presentation. And, especially if you want to reach a certain market segment, you have to invest time and resources in motivating visitors to participate. You can maximize the response to your presentation by promoting it prior to, and during, the show. A few suggestions:

1. Send out pre-show mailers which include a lead card to bring to the booth and exchange for a giveaway after they have viewed the presentation.

2. Advertise the presentation and any incentives given on-site in trade journals.

3. Provide an immediate incentive during the presentation. For example, if they complete a lead card and view the presentation, they will be eligible for a prize drawing at the close of the presentation.

4. Hire professional crowd gatherers or use your own staffers to tell people about the presentation, escort them to chairs, get them to complete the lead cards, and collect the cards and assist in the drawing.

5. Provide comfortable chairs, music, and promotional graphics to draw aisle traffic into the presentation.

#3: Directing the Audience

As a result of the presentation, you may want visitors to talk to sales reps, see a product demonstration, place an order, or set up an appointment for future meetings. Define the action you want them to take clearly. There are two techniques that will facilitate their taking the identified action.

One technique is to use your incentive to motivate them after the show. Instead of having a drawing after the presentation, make them eligible for a gift after having viewed a presentation or talked with a sales representative.

A second technique is to train your booth staff to take an assertive approach and initiate a dialogue with key visitors immediately following the presentation. Professionals who specialize in exhibit staff training know how to train exhibit staffers to take advantage of audiences drawn by live presentations.

#4: Selecting Appropriate Presentation Techniques

In reviewing techniques to use in your presentation, always be sure they don't overshadow the message, and use them only when their cost is justifiable. Perhaps instead of using a $25,000 video wall, you could accomplish the same goal with a 40' television monitor for $1,500.

To select the proper presentation technique, first ask yourself these questions:

1. What type of product do I have and how is it best displayed?
2. What is the best way to understand my product . . . through a demonstration, hands-on interaction, or some other technique?
3. What are the standard ways the salespeople are currently using to sell the product?
4. Can these techniques be incorporated into a presentation?

The following gives a quick overview of the types of techniques available.

- Live trained professional presenters. Live is important because unless people are related to in a live, personal, direct way they will walk on by. It's easy to be rude to a video or A/V screen, but it's hard to be rude to someone speaking directly to you, calling you by name. Be sure your presenter is skilled at working with trade show audiences. A lecture (especially read from notes) is certain death.

- Music. Music can be used as song to get people to remember information (like a commercial jingle) and is a great attention-getter. It can also be used as a background to the dialogue to help create the atmosphere you want instantly. Imagine what a slide show would be like without music. That's what a presentation at a trade show is like . . . empty and sterile. Music also makes a presentation seem shorter and can work to pull concepts together.

- Audio/visual. As a rule, A/V by itself will not sustain audience interest for more than two to three minutes. It is not immediate or personal enough. But when A/V is combined with a live professional presenter it becomes a powerful marketing tool. Now the audience is brought in and made to feel a part of the presentation by the presenter.

Note: When using A/V be aware of the physical requirements which include:

*Adequate projection throw from behind the screen. This can vary from 3 to 15 feet based on the screen size. It is different for each set-up so talk to A/V specialists to make the right determination.

*Provide a way to eliminate ambient light.

*Use a method to light presenters that won't wash the screen.

- Video wall. A video wall needs to be combined with a live presenter to be totally effective. The more interaction between the presenter and the video wall the better. For example, you could use testimonials with questions asked by the presenter and customer responses on the video wall. Video walls are extremely expensive. There are at least nine types on the market in a variety of price ranges. Take time to find the best system for your needs.

- Lasers. Lasers are also expensive and require extra safety precautions. Unless you can provide the proper environment (preferably an enclosed theater), you run the risk of not getting a maximum return on your investment because ambient lighting and environment greatly impact their effect.

- Puppets. Puppets must be treated as human beings with sophisticated stage movement and sophisticated dialogue. They need to be in the caliber of Jim Henson's Muppets or they can't be expected to come off as anything but corny. Puppets work best when the company already has a spokesperson in its ads such as Ernie Keebler®, Snap Crackle and Pop®, or a celebrity imitator.

- Magic and illusions. Be careful here that the tricks don't detract from the message. Use the tricks as part of the message so that the audience remembers the pay-off as part of the product story. An example would be to name several parts of a featured product and put those parts into a container. After the magician shakes the container, the product appears whole.

- Product demonstrations. Product demonstrations are one of the best ways to get audience attention and keep it. People love to see how things work, and, if you conduct the demonstration quickly and professionally, you will get a great deal of response immediately because a demonstration, like a picture, is worth a thousand words.

- Video. Video, like A/V, needs to be combined with a live presenter to make the audience stop, listen, and react. Having interaction with the video on the monitor is a great way to involve the audience. If you use one large Mitsubishi tube monitor whenever possible as opposed to a video projector, you will not have to worry about ambient light washing the screen or the 10′ throw distance necessary behind the screen for video projectors. The cost is considerably less and you get a crystal clear picture with a tube monitor.

#5: Setting the Stage

The proper booth logistics are essential to a successful live presentation. Most any exhibit, even as small as 10 linear feet, can be adapted to accommodate a live presentation. Consider the following points:

Placement of the stage

1. Don't obstruct the stage or view of it with any other exhibit properties or products.

2. Never put the stage on the aisles. Leave plenty of room for the visitors inside the booth.

3. Make sure there is easy access to the rest of the booth.

4. Make sure there is a backwall to the stage to control sound, lighting, and viewing.

Lighting

1. Use a general stage wash.
2. Use separate lighting from the general wash to emphasize specified areas.

Sound

1. Use a professional company to set up the sound.
2. Avoid feedback *at all costs.*
3. Use directional speakers.
4. Use separate sound controls for music and each of the presenters' microphones so that sound levels can be adjusted individually to maintain the best balance and not disturb neighbors.
5. Be aware of any sound restrictions set by show management.

Others

1. Use a show clock to indicate when the next presentation will begin.
2. Have enough comfortable chairs available to accommodate a reasonable-sized audience.
3. Provide pencils or pens for them to complete lead cards if you are asking them to do so.

Open vs. Closed Environments

There is quite a bit of debate as to whether you should use an open or closed environment for your presentation. Both methods work, but you have to understand the conditions required to make them work and how the advantages of each differ.

Advantages of using an open environment

1. The presentation is instantly visible from the aisles.
2. More people can view the presentation.
3. It is easy for staffers to spot good prospects during the presentation.
4. It creates excitement in the exhibit.

Advantages of using a closed environment

1. You can control the total environment including sound, lighting, and A/V.
2. You can do more sophisticated presentations, especially video and A/V.
3. You have a captured (but not captive) audience.

4. It is easier for the audience to concentrate on the message as there are no outside distractions.

However, a closed environment will require more booth space dedicated only to that purpose. You will also need to hire several trained crowd gatherers to build an audience and plan pre-show promotion to let people know about why it will benefit them to visit the presentation. Consider using exhibit graphics to draw traffic off of the aisle too.

This is only a brief overview of considerations to be made in planning for the live formal presentation. The most important ingredient is a professional producer *who knows trade shows*. There is much more to a live presentation than the five or ten minutes you see performed. It is not just the script, just the presenter, or just the techniques used, but it is a combination of these and a variety of details along with experience with the quirky trade show crowds that come together to create a successful presentation.

Conclusion

From this point on, your planning becomes less and less sophisticated, and more a matter of assuring that the plans are carried out. You've organized many of the details in this chapter, and in Chapter 8 you will see how to finalize direct mail promotions, exhibit set-up plans, and how to conduct the exhibit preview. You're counting down to the show date, and every detail counts.

Chapter 8: You are here:

	3 Mo.	2 Mo.	1 Mo.
Planning			
Goal-Setting			
Budgeting			
Promotions	Implement promotions strategy	Check direct mail costs	Cross-check all promotion needs
Product Demos	Plan formal live presentation		
Exhibits	Manage new construction Find portable supplier	Exhibit preview Select portable structure	Portable exhibit preview
Installation		Prepare site book	Double-check installation plans
Staffing	Prepare pre-show memos		Prepare orientation meeting contents
Inquiry Processing			
Measuring Results			

8
Finalizing the Details
(2 Months in Advance)

When your program is operating on schedule, two months prior to the show most of the components will be in place. Use this remaining time to fine-tune. Tasks such as previewing the exhibit, and preparing the site book need to be planned into your schedule, and this bit of breathing room between accomplishing the planned tasks and handling the last-minute details is the best time to finish those items.

In this chapter you will review four optional tasks. Depending on your plans, you will most likely not need to accomplish all of the four tasks. For example, if you had a new custom exhibit built you would want to conduct the exhibit preview, but probably won't be looking for a portable display.

1. EXHIBIT DESIGN: How the Exhibit Preview Can Save You Money
2. PROMOTIONS: Keeping Direct Mail Costs in Line
3. EXHIBIT SET-UP: Preparing the Site Book
4. PORTABLE EXHIBITS: Selecting the Best Structure

HOW THE EXHIBIT PREVIEW CAN SAVE YOU MONEY

If you are having a new exhibit built, previewing it prior to the first show will help to avoid as many hassles as possible come set-up time. It will also, eventually, save you money. Consider for a moment just a few of the hassles that an exhibit preview will help to avoid:

- *Expensive Airfreight.* If missing components are not discovered until set-up day, they will have to be air-freighted to the show.
- *Graphics Changes.* If graphics are dirty, fuzzy, misspelled, or just wrong, they'll have to be replaced. It's an expensive mistake to discover on-site. Lighting in the booth can affect readability of graphics and those changes are most economically made prior to the show.

- *Set-Up Overruns.* If you set up the exhibit prior to the show, you can see the best *order* for the process and time your labor and electrical services accordingly. If electricians are waiting for work to be completed, you are being charged for that waiting time. A preview will help you to schedule more accurately.
- *High Repair Bills.* It can cost twice as much (and more) to have components of an exhibit fixed or altered at a show site as it might at your supplier's facility. Save the additional expense (not to mention potential headaches) by taking care of it during the exhibit preview.

You may have to pay for an exhibit preview, so discuss this with your A/E. The exhibit firm can incur a great deal of expense to get the exhibit completely set up in their facility prior to the show. This could be a point of negotiation in your contract.

Goals of the Exhibit Preview

The following are ten goals that you can expect to accomplish during the exhibit preview. You may have some additional goals of your own.

1. *Quality Check.* Check the quality and workmanship of the structure. Be sure everything that was promised is there and that all components *work.* The Exhibit Preview Checklist on page 219 offers guidelines for this.

2. *Graphics Check.* Be sure that all of those graphics promised are complete, and to your expectations.

3. *Estimate Set-Up Time.* Ask the exhibit house to track the number of workers and time it took to set up the exhibit for your preview. This will provide guidelines for planning on-site labor requirements. Keep in mind, though, that at the exhibit house experienced people familiar with the structure set it up. At the hall this will not be the case—adjust the requirements slightly to accommodate.

4. *Review Set-Up Drawings.* Ask your A/E to provide a complete set of drawings at the exhibit preview. Use them to identify each component in the exhibit and get an overview of the set-up process. You will gain more respect from on-site workers if *you know your exhibit.* Keep copies of the set-up drawings for the site book. (See sample in Figure 8-1.)

5. *Obtain Crate List Inventories.* If your structure is shipped in crates, request a list of the components *in each crate.* They should be packed and repacked in the same crate each time. This will help you organize crates as they are delivered to the exhibit during set-up. It will also help identify where missing pieces are.

6. *Review Goals for Compliance.* Prior to the preview pull out the list of goals you had created for the new exhibit. As you preview the exhibit, review them point by point to assure they have all been met. Double-

check compliance with show regulations. It is frustrating to get to the show site and discover your exhibit is 2′ too tall for the ceiling height.

7. *Test Demos and Live Components.* Assure that they work. Consider back-up plans should one of them fail at the show.

8. *Organize Set-Up Procedures.* As you are reviewing the set-up drawings be thinking about how you would like to organize the set-up yourself. You can orchestrate the exhibit set-up from the start (by identifying where the crates should be located when they are delivered) to the finish (by outlining when each component is installed). Create your plan, then be flexible.(1)

9. *Prepare Your Utilities Kit List.* Always ship a utilities or hardware kit with your exhibit. For complex exhibits you can even purchase these kits already filled with goodies such as extension cords, tools, tapes, touch-up paint, cleaning supplies, and more. The preview is the perfect time to determine any special tools, paints, or cleaners needed for the kit.

10. *Provide a Management Preview.* This is also a good time to make a "formal" unveiling of the exhibit for management. Some exhibitors turn it into a regular "event" complete with cocktails and hors d'oeuvres.

    Warning: Be sure to make it very clear to all participants that this unveiling is not the time to make changes. Provide opportunities earlier in the process for those reviews.

If you are purchasing a fairly large structure you and your A/E will probably be tempted to set up and preview only part of it. (For example, some smaller firms may not have the facilities to put up your entire 20′ tower.) Don't succumb to that temptation. You can be sure that the problems will only be found in those sections you had chosen not to set up in advance—hence aggravating your first on-site set-up.

Exhibit Preview Checklist

Now that you have identified exactly what you want to accomplish in the exhibit preview, the following checklist will serve as an on-site guide to accomplishing these tasks.

☐ Goals. First, go back to your show plan book and pull out the goals you have set (both logistical and image goals). Check to assure that all goals were accomplished to your satisfaction.

☐ Graphics. Are all of the graphics clean and clear? Are they readable from the appropriate distances? (Occasionally, dimensional graphics are not readable from a distance when their color is too close to the background color of the structure.)

Figure 8-1

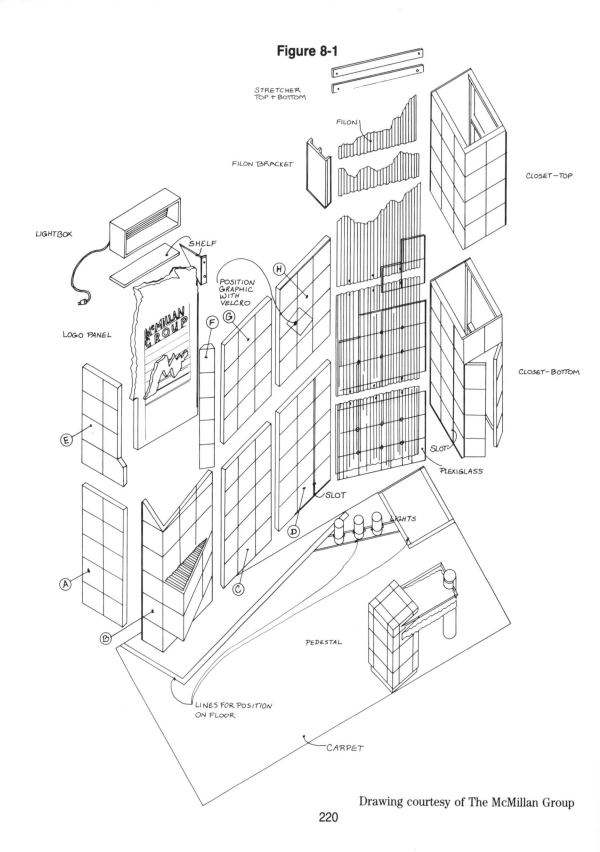

STRETCHER
TOP + BOTTOM

FILON

FILON BRACKET

CLOSET—TOP

LIGHTBOX

SHELF

POSITION
GRAPHIC
WITH
VELCRO

Ⓗ

LOGO PANEL

McMILLAN
GROUP

Ⓕ Ⓖ

CLOSET—BOTTOM

Ⓔ

SLOT

PLEXIGLASS

SLOT

Ⓐ

Ⓑ

Ⓒ

Ⓓ

LIGHTS

PEDESTAL

LINES FOR POSITION
ON FLOOR

CARPET

Drawing courtesy of The McMillan Group

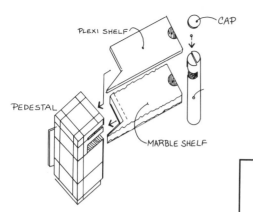

PLEXI SHELF

CAP

PEDESTAL

MARBLE SHELF

PEDESTAL ASSEMBLY

1. Position pedestal unit.
2. Remove cap from column (friction fit).
3. Slide marble shelf into pedestal.
4. Slide plexiglas shelf into pedestal.
5. Fit round column slots over shelf ends.
6. Bolt in place in both pedestal and column.
7. Refit column cap.

SET UP INSTRUCTIONS

1. Lay carpet in position.
2. Position panels A and B at left side of exhibit, bolt together.
3. Bolt panels C & D. Rear edge of A and D should be 1″ in from back edge of carpet.
4. Bolt panel E to panel A.
5. Panel F and G to panel C. Panel H to panels G and D.
6. Using tabs, bolt logo panel in place behind panels E and F.
7. Position closet bottom. Bolt closet top to closet bottom.
8. Bolt stretchers to back of panels H and D to closet unit.
9. Pivot closet unit to outside of space (see floor plan).
10. Slide bottom two plexi panels into slot on panel D.
11. Using chromed acorn nuts, bolt three filon panels together. (the center panel is the longest panel) Slide filon into panels D and H slots.
12. Position three white cam lights on floor between plexiglas and filon.
13. Pivot closet unit in to mate plexiglas with slot in closets (don't worry about filon position at this point).
14. Bending filon, snap into position in slots of closet unit.
15. Fit wedge clips behind filon.
16. Bolt filon bracket to panel H and fit top two pieces of filon.
17. Bolt light track vertically to closet unit.
18. Remove shelf support from inside light box bolt to panel G. Position shelf and light box behind McMillan Group logo.
19. Position graphics.

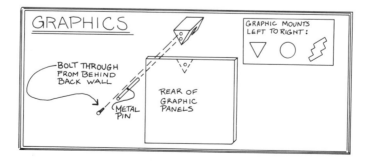

GRAPHICS

GRAPHIC MOUNTS LEFT TO RIGHT:

BOLT THROUGH FROM BEHIND BACK WALL

METAL PIN

REAR OF GRAPHIC PANELS

☐ Color. Are the colors true in the fluorescent light of the shop? Lighting definitely changes colors and since lighting varies among halls it is impossible to guarantee a color's accuracy even in the exhibit preview. But this will give you a very different read than any color samples provided.

☐ Finishes. Are the finishes all as you had agreed upon in the proposal and contract?

☐ Electrical. Does it work? Is any requested pre-wiring complete and to code?

☐ Lighting. Is it too brassy? Too dark? It is typically difficult to identify the effects of lighting from a rendering or model. Here you will be able to judge the full effect. Check backlit graphics to assure that they are not too bright or too dark.

☐ Display Stands. Do display stands have requested features such as slots for lead cards, locked storage, mouse holes for wires and cables?

☐ Carpet. Is it the right size and color? (One exhibitor got to the exhibit preview and was fortunate to have measured the carpet. She discovered it to be 12″ too small for their space—on all four sides!)

☐ Workmanship. Does everything work? Preview the A-V program and be sure that the exhibit truly accommodates all required equipment as planned. (One exhibitor got to the show and set up his A-V monitor in a tower designed to house it and the entire structure collapsed.) Check that doors and drawers close flush as they should.

☐ Accessibility. Is everything accessible? (This may sound ludicrous, but remember the exhibitor who discovered that a graphic panel blocked the opening to their central storage area.)

☐ Controls. Where are the electrical boxes and any other controls (lights, A-V, sound) that you will be using? Will it be easy to use during the show?

☐ Set-Up Drawings. Review your set-up instructions and assure that you can identify each part inventoried on them. Try to get at least a working knowledge of how the structure goes together. The better you know your exhibit, the more confident you will be during set-up.

☐ Photos. Take photos of the structure completely set up to use for the workers who will install the exhibit on-site. A picture can be worth more than a thousand words. It can save thousands in time.

☐ Inventory. Request that an itemized list of contents be included in each crate, and an additional copy provided for you to include in your site book.

NOTE: Plan several hours for the exhibit preview. Since some changes may be required, be sure to schedule it early enough so that the changes can be made without incurring rush charges. Two months prior to the show should be adequate for any minor changes.

KEEPING DIRECT MAIL COSTS IN LINE

Because of the sheer number of components you must manage in any direct mail campaign (copy writing, mailing list, artwork, production, mailing costs), it is an area where overruns easily creep in. Since nearly all costs are related to the *number* of pieces you mail, let's look at how to analyze the mailing list to assure that as many superfluous names as possible are eliminated from the list.

Four Questions to Answer When Selecting a List

1. *How current is the List?* By way of example, in the trade show industry, exhibit managers tend to stay in their jobs less than three years. If you were mailing to a list of names (not job titles) for exhibits manager, chances are you would be mailing to people who have already moved on if the list is more than a year old.

2. *How narrowly* can the list be segmented? If you need to reach only two of ten job titles among the show attendees, can the list be segmented so that you mail to just *those* job titles? You may still end up paying for the entire list, but the money saved on production, mailing, and incentives will make it worth the effort.

3. *What is the geographic distribution* of the list as compared to what's anticipated for *this year's* show audience? For example, if last year's show was held in Chicago and this year's show is in Los Angeles, chances are good that many of the people on last year's list will not be attending this year's show. (Studies show that only 48% of the attendees at an average show travel over 400 miles to attend a show, and 20% travel less than 50 miles.(2)

4. *How was the list compiled?* Show lists are typically compiled from pre-registration or registration lists. If you are purchasing a show attendance list from the previous year, the best option is the on-site registration list, since many people pre-register and never make it to the show.

Tips for Producing the "Budget Conscious" Direct Mailer

The range of quality of trade show direct mail promotions runs from the bland, nearly pointless, printed invitation to kits and boxes filled with tantalizing treasures such as magic kits, building blocks, and boxing gloves. Price ranges fall along the same lines . . . inexpensive to exorbitant.

Unfortunately, as pre-show direct mail promotions are used more widely, it becomes more of a challenge to stand out among the crowd of mail, while reigning in the budget. The following is far from an exhaustive list, but it represents a few techniques exhibitors have used to create direct mail promotions with impact on a limited budget. They are organized by the major cost-intensive components of your direct mail program: Producing the Mailer, The Incentive, The List, and Mailing Costs.

ADVICE FROM THE EXPERTS

The following collection of tips are offered by David Taylor, senior manager of marketing services and information at BF Goodrich, where he has implemented a host of pre-show promotion activities.

Producing the Mailer

$ Check with your internal printing department, if you have one, to see what their costs would be. (This can require advance planning to get on their schedule.)

$ Consider producing a creative black-and-white piece or use one color with screens as opposed to using the more expensive four-color printing process.

$ Don't underestimate the role of your envelope in the overall impact of your mailer. Include copy on the envelope to motivate recipients to open it.

$ Avoid sinking a lot of money in original artwork. Consider using stock photographs or artwork from computer clip art files. One company built an extremely successful direct mail promotion from an old *Life Magazine* photograph.

$ Use simple stock type that is common to most typesetting equipment and avoid additional charges for special fonts. (Most computerized typesetters offer a wide range of type from which to choose.)

WARNING: The area you won't want to scrimp on is copywriting. In the professional world of direct mail, it is commonly accepted that copywriting will make or break the success of your mailer. The copy must have a strong appeal to your audience and define quickly and clearly what's in it for them. Good copywriting is an art and it is worthwhile to get the input of a professional here.

Selecting the Incentive

$ Consider what type of item will provide the most bang for your buck: one flashy incentive (awarded through a grand prize drawing), a few well-chosen prizes (awarded daily or hourly), or an inexpensive incentive awarded to each respondent (a t-shirt, ball cap, etc.)

$ Get more motivational mileage out of your incentive by showing a photograph of it on the mailer.

$ Be directed by your theme in the selection of an incentive. Themed incentives often open the door to fun, inexpensive giveaways. The company who used a "mystery theater" theme in their exhibit, for example, gave away magnifying glasses and Sherlock Holmes hats.

$ Don't limit your hunt for a premium to standard premiums/ incentives catalogs. Instead, select your premium to match the theme and then go out and find it. You might, in fact, get a very good deal at your local discount stores.

$ Unless you sell Lear Jets, the obvious incentive to use at a reasonable cost is your own product. If you do give away your own products as an incentive, create some excitement around the prize (a "hunt", a live presentation, a contest, etc., will raise the interest level).

$ Or you could exchange products with a related vendor. If your products are designed to be used with those manufactured by another company (hardware and software for example) consider exchanges. One company exchanged their software packages for the portable computers on which they are run. Rather than giving away just software, they also held a drawing for the portable computer.

Mailing Costs

$ Be careful about the design of your direct mail package. Just the shape and size of a dimensional mailer can significantly affect mailing costs.

$ Pre-sort the mail by zip codes (this can be done easily with computer-generated labels) and consider applying for a bulk mail permit. Pre-sorted bulk mail can be sent for a fraction of the cost of first class mail. Keep in mind, though, that mail dates will have to be scheduled earlier, since bulk mail can take up to three weeks (and more) for delivery.

CREATING THE INSTALLATION PLAN

This information on exhibit set-up is directed toward a custom set-up. (Setting up a custom display of any size.) If you only use portable displays and set them up yourself, this section will not pertain to your program.

The Site Book: An Organizational Tool

The site book is a binder that contains all of the information that relates to set-up. Include in the site book copies of every order you placed—from the space contract to the shipping bill of lading.

Why a Site Book?

A site book may seem like a lot of work for an eight- (or 16- or 24-) hour installation. But the aggravation it saves is worth every minute invested. This site book simply provides you with easy access to information. And information can be your strongest tool toward getting things unstuck, unstopped, or accomplished.

For example, say you show up at your booth space, ready for installation, and discover the power has not been hooked up. You have to run the power lines to different display areas before you can put down the padding and carpet. You go over to the service desk, locate a representative from the contractor, and they claim they have no order from you for electrical service. You *know* you placed the order early to get an advance discount. But, rats, you didn't bring a copy to prove it. Now you have to reorder, pay the full rates, and be last in line for electrical service which could sure make a difference in whether the exhibit gets installed in time.

Now, consider all of the orders you have placed and how they could be misplaced and you will appreciate the value of the site book. Some exhibitors even send their orders "return receipt requested" and keep the receipt in the site book as proof that the order was received.

The following outline will help you determine what to put into the site book and how to organize it for easy access during the show.

SITE BOOK CONTENTS

PART I: THE STRUCTURE

- ☐ Photos of the exhibit
- ☐ Set-up drawings
- ☐ Crate inventories
- ☐ Set-up plan
- ☐ Names and contact numbers of technicians involved in product installation

PART II: THE SERVICES
(Include copies of all order forms)

☐ Labor order form
☐ Electrical services
☐ Cleaning services
☐ Drayage price sheet and service order
☐ Orders for floral, furniture, photography, etc.
☐ Names of contacts who promised any variances or special accommodations
☐ Copy of your badge registration list

PART III: ESSENTIAL CONTACTS
(Name, address, and phone number)

☐ The show general contractor
☐ Show manager
☐ Exhibits representative if different than show manager
☐ A/E from your display house
☐ Representative from independent service contractor if using one
☐ Contact at company for technical product information
☐ Contact for persons who furnished payments if other than yourself

TIP: Put your essential contacts' numbers on a 5×7 card and tape it to the inside cover of your site book. That will make it easier to access the frequently used information.

PART IV: TRANSPORTATION INFORMATION

☐ Weight certificate(s)
☐ Copy of bill of lading
☐ Name and contact number for representative at the transportation company (home phone number)
☐ Airbill number for all airfreight shipments
☐ Crate inventories

The Step-by-Step Installation Plan

If you will be supervising the exhibit installation yourself, prior to leaving for the show, take some time to think through your exhibit installation step-by-step and write out a set-up plan. The set-up plan is important for each show, because the exhibit configurations and product displays typically change from show to show. Here again, this will prepare you for the basics so that you can best deal with the unexpected. The following step-by-step photos will give you a good idea of the steps involved in a custom set-up.

1. Set your crates on the edge of the exhibit (Photo 8-1).

Photo 8-1

Photo by Robyn Gillespie, courtesy of I&D, Inc.

2. Run electrical cords out to product display areas (Photo 8-2).

Photo 8-2

Photo by Robyn Gillespie, courtesy of I&D, Inc.

3. Lay carpet pad, carpet, and protective plastic (Photos 8-3A and B).

Photo 8-3A

Photo by Robyn Gillespie, courtesy of I&D, Inc.

Photo 8-3B

Photo by Robyn Gillespie, courtesy of I&D, Inc.

4. Begin construction (Photo 8-4). For an in-line backwall, begin at one end and work across to the other end. For an island display, work from the center out to the aisles.

Photo 8-4

Photo by Robyn Gillespie, courtesy of I&D, Inc.

5. Begin wiring for any necessary electrical installations as product display areas are set (Photo 8-5).

Photo 8-5

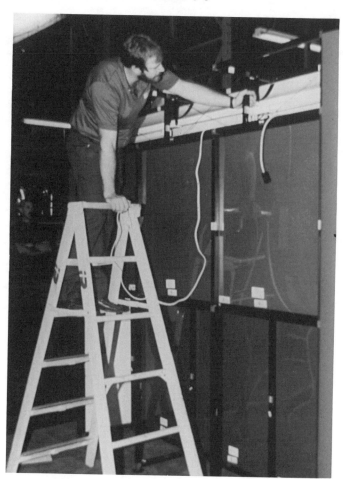

Photo by Robyn Gillespie, courtesy of I&D, Inc.

6. Install products on display pedestals and shelves (Photo 8-6).

Photo 8-6

Photo by Robyn Gillespie, courtesy of I&D, Inc.

7. Hang graphics and set finishing details such as plants, wastebaskets, furniture, literature, lead imprinters, etc. (Photo 8-7).

Photo 8-7

Photo by Robyn Gillespie, courtesy of I&D, Inc.

8. Clean structure and displays (Photo 8-8). Touch up any knocks or scratches caused during set-up.

Photo 8-8

Photo by Robyn Gillespie, courtesy of I&D, Inc.

This plan, thought out in advance will give you a head start on:

- Knowing where you want crates set when the drayage team arrives to deliver them.
- Knowing when to order different labor services. (For example, in Chicago, you will need carpenters to set up the exhibit, decorators to hang graphics, and electricians for wiring.)
- Estimating how long each stage should take.
- Scheduling product installation technicians.

Options for Coordinating Product Installations

Depending on your products, installation can be as simple as shelving books, or as complex as installing and networking a series of computers or a mine excavating system complete with diggers, haulers, and conveyors. If you lean toward the "book" variety, then you needn't take a great deal of time with this section. But if you require any more complex activity than taking items from a box and placing them on a shelf, spend some time here.

Your first tasks involve recruiting—both products and people. For products, you have at least three ways to handle the task.

- *Out and Back.* If your product displays differ at each show, you'll probably need to get inventory from your factory or warehouse and ship it out and back for each show.
- *Local Sources.* To save on shipping costs you can use inventory from local offices, facilities, or showrooms in the show city. This requires a bit more advance planning to locate sources, secure their cooperation, and facilitate product transport to the show hall.
- *Dedicated Inventory.* If you participate in many shows with the same products, it will be most efficient to secure a dedicated inventory of products that travels with the exhibit. If you do, plan for the following:
    *Packaging—Use crates *not* cardboard boxes. Consider having special crates made with jigs to hold the products securely, increase safety during shipping, and reduce the amount of packaging required.
    *Spare Parts—These must be shipped with the equipment in case of the inevitable.
    *Spare Extension Cords—Also include these with the products and ship them from show to show since electrical service and installations vary.
    *Rotating Inventory—The products will have to be "taken off the road" periodically for upgrade and repair. Be sure to accommodate those down times in your schedule.
    *Keep Equipment Clean and Presentable—Schedule regular equipment checks to assure it is in top presentation condition.

*Inventory and Equipment Tracking—You will need to create an inventory system to track equipment as it travels from show to show.
*Scheduling Equipment—Create a schedule to assure that equipment needs don't overlap and leave you short at the last minute.

WARNING: INSURANCE COVERAGE. Be sure to check and assure that your corporate insurance covers products that are taken *off the corporate premises.* You may need to secure additional insurance or a rider to your policy to cover products when they are in transit or at a show.

When it comes to recruiting *people* you have the same three options, but a different group of considerations.

- *Out and Back.* Here again if you participate in a limited number of shows you can recruit one or two technicians from your facility to travel to each show and install the products. Their expense will be an additional budget item to cover.
- *Local Source.* If you have technicians in the city where the show is held, you can save on that expense money by recruiting these local people to help with installation. You will need to schedule further in advance here since it will require the cooperation of management at that local facility. It will also require that you double-check to assure that they have adequate knowledge of all of the products you are asking them to install.
- *A Dedicated Team.* If you participate in more than two shows a month you might want to consider a dedicated team of technicians for show installations. This will require salaries for the team (and consideration about what department will supply the budget for these salaries), travel expenses for the team, someone to coordinate scheduling and support communication for the team . . . and burnout. When people travel under the time-related stresses of trade shows for an extended period of time (over six months in a row), they tend to get burned out. You might want to consider rotating these technicians on a regular basis to avoid losing your technical team altogether.

The chart in Exhibit 8-1 summarizes your options for both people and products and the key points to consider for each.

USING PORTABLE DISPLAYS EFFECTIVELY

As the popularity of portable displays increases, so too does their misuse. The common shortfall of companies using portable displays is to underestimate the planning required to use the display successfully at a show. Because the structure itself is so simple, it is easy to overlook the necessity of a strategy for its use. But quite to the contrary, these smaller, simpler exhibits take thoughtful planning.

Exhibit 8-1   Options for Coordinating Product Installations

	Products	People
Option #1 Out & Back	Products are shipped to and returned from each show individually. • Provide backup parts • Assure in working order • Plan well in advance to coordinate product availability	People travel to and return from each show. • Best for a limited number of shows • Consider travel expenses and housing arrangements • Schedule well in advance • Plan for backups in the event of illness or emergency
Option #2 Local Source	Products from local offices or warehouses are used for display. • Arrange for special transport and delivery to show • Plan to double-check working order well in advance • Plan for backup products	People from a facility in the show city handle product installation. • Schedule well in advance • Secure cooperation of their managers • Assure knowledge of all products
Option #3 Dedicated Team and Inventory	An inventory of products is set aside just for show displays. • Special packaging • Inventory • Rotate and upgrade for repair • Scheduling and shipping	A dedicated team of technicians travels to shows and handles all installations. • Salaries • Expenses • Scheduling • Burnout

How to Make the Small Space Work

A small space is a bit like a small closet, in that you can get a decent functional use out of it by simply filling it with things, but you can make it much more functional by organizing the space according to your needs and strategy.

Thus the first question to ask in using your space most efficiently is, "What is our strategy?" for the exhibit and the show.

For example, if your strategy is simply exposure—to get as many of the show attendees to see your product or discuss your services as possible—you will want most of the displays and activity to be located near the aisle for maximum visibility and attraction.

However, if you want to reach just one segment of the show audience and conduct fewer but more in-depth interactions about your products, plan to use the aisle area as a prequalifying area. Then move the products toward the backwall of the display and invite those qualified prospects in for a closer look.

The second question to ask is "How will we use our 'front porch'?" in the booth. The front porch is the area where your exhibit carpet meets the aisle carpet, and about a 2-foot depth into your exhibit. Do you want to conduct product demonstrations right out there on the front porch, or would you rather use it to prequalify attendees? Would that be a good area to initiate conversations with your giveaways, or to locate products to attract attention?

The third question to ask is "How will we display our products?" In a small booth space you might even want to consider whether it is essential to have your products in the exhibit. Will large photo-graphics do the same (or an even better) job? This can be true if you manufacture any type of large equipment. It can also be true for equipment or instruments that are extremely small and difficult to identify at a glance (computer chips, for example.) If you can display your products on backwall shelves, this increases floor space in the exhibit since you won't need display stands.

Finally, ask yourself "What is the primary message of our exhibit?" Two factors are at work with the small space that force you to use a clear and focused message. First, you are competing for attention with a host of larger displays and other distractions. Your message *must* be discerned in less than seven seconds. Second, in such a small space you are forced to be selective about what can be communicated.

The list of "Don'ts" in Exhibit 8-2 provides more tips for using the small space efficiently.

Exhibit 8-2

TEN "DON'TS" FOR USING A SMALL SPACE EFFICIENTLY

DON'T block the entry to your space with a table. That puts a barrier between you and the visitor, and between the visitor and your communications message.

DON'T put graphics and copy below the sightline. The lower 36″ of your backwall will not be seen when people or products are standing in front of it. Don't count on that space for communications.

DON'T overcrowd and over-display. It is better to use one or two products chosen to support your communications focus rather than to splatter the backwall with a confusing array of the entire product line.

DON'T create a self-service exhibit by spreading literature, giveaways, and product samples on a table, or using a fish bowl for collecting business cards. The purpose of your presence at a trade show is *to talk to visitors* and the self-service display sabotages those efforts.

DON'T overstaff the exhibit. Especially in a small space, the presence of too many company representatives will keep visitors out instead of making them feel welcome. According to Exhibit Surveys, Inc., the optimum traffic density in a booth is one company representative per 50 sq. ft. of open space. That assumes that each rep will be working with a visitor and allows 25 sq. ft. of open space for each person. That means in a 10′ × 10′ exhibit you should have just two company representatives.

DON'T clutter the space with literature, and especially personal effects. Keep the coats and briefcases to a minimum, and if there is no storage in your space, try to check them.

DON'T neglect the lighting of your exhibit and booth space. Even the smallest displays in the most remote areas can stand out if the lighting is sufficient.

DON'T waste precious space on inefficient communication tools. Graphics with copy that is too dense or too small will not be read.

DON'T try to tell the whole story. Select key benefits designed for your audience and focus on those. Use words sparingly in your graphics.

DON'T over-attract. Work to draw your audience selectively. Each component of your plan—especially promotions—should be designed to attract only your target audience, not the entire group of show attendees. That way you can avoid crowding your space with nonqualified visitors.

The Role of Graphics: Attract, Inform, and Direct

A classic mistake made by new exhibitors using portable displays is to try to economize by blowing up existing advertising artwork to use as backwall graphics for the display. Unfortunately, the principles for advertising layout, and those for strong, effective exhibit graphics differ so much that trying to economize that way can be counter productive.

When planning graphics for the portable display there are three basic components of the graphics to consider: the images, the colors, and the words. The choices you make for each will affect the most important element of your graphics: their stopping power. The chart in Exhibit 8-3 outlines the three components and what they can accomplish for you. The accompanying illustration in Exhibit 8-4 diagrams how and where each component can be used most effectively.

Whether you are building a large custom exhibit, or simply creating graphics for a 10′ in-line portable display, the *quality of the original artwork* will determine the quality of the graphics. Especially for large-scale photomurals, clean, crisp original art is essential for a quality reproduction.

Exhibit 8-3 Graphics Elements

Use Color To:	Use Words To:	Use Images To:
• *Attract attention* Since bright colors attract attention, use them as accents, where they will be visible from the greatest distance.	• *Identify* The header, or upper-most area of your backwall should use your company logo as a sign to identify your company.	• *Attract* Single, large, bold images are most effective for attracting the kind of attention that will stop the passerby.
• *Create a mood* Do you want your space to be warm and inviting? Use colors on the warm end of the color scales such as peaches and mauves.	• *Differentiate* Just below the header, use a tag line to describe what your company does and to set you apart.	• *Support a message* The image you use should work, not only to attract but to begin communicating your key message for the show.
• *Reinforce a product or company message* A company used an acid green color to promote a new bile medication.	• *Inform/Instruct* Additional copy in the small exhibit should be sparse, but can be used to point out key benefits about the product or service.	• *Explain key benefits* of your product or service that can be communicated quickly through the right visual image.

Exhibit 8-4 Elements of Effective Backwall Graphics

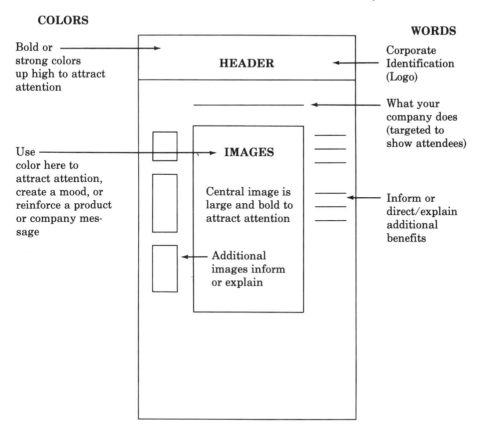

CASE STUDY: HOW FEDERAL EXPRESS PRODUCES 300 ANNUAL EVENTS WITH 38 PORTABLE DISPLAYS

To appreciate the complexity of this task, consider tracking 38 portable displays and five different categories of graphics used at 300 events. Then consider coordinating the premiums and literature to be used at over 100 of these. And finally, consider the task of communicating with and supplying these support items to field marketing representatives who initiate the request to participate in these events. That's the task that Mary Padron, senior marketing specialist, and Doug Williams, administrator at Federal Express, have pared down to a science.

There is no magic here. The pointers they offer are simple organization techniques. And if you find yourself in a similar situation (or one of slightly less magnitude but equal complexity) this information will simply keep you from reinventing the wheel.

COMPANY:	Federal Express
STRUCTURES:	38 truss frame portable exhibits, a modular structure, a custom exhibit.
EVENTS:	Trade Shows Open Houses Receptions Forums
GRAPHICS:	Designed to target markets served: 1. International Services 2. Airfreight/Heavyweight[sm] 3. POWERSHIP 2® 4. Corporate Marketing Campaigns to introduce new services 5. Generic Show audience and target market guides the decision on graphics used.
SERVICES:	Provided by their portable display supplier: 1. Warehousing the structure and graphics 2. Structure inventory 3. Exhibit installation and dismantling at local shows 4. Graphics design 5. Graphics inventory 6. Repairs and parts replacement 7. Ordering related show services (i.e., electrical, plants, etc.)
SCHEDULING:	Padron keeps her own schedule of shows and the displays and graphics used at each show. She uses these tools to organize scheduling logistics: 1. Display Legend 2. Calendar 3. Display Request Log

Under the "DISPLAY TYPE," she indicates vendor and the display types (e.g., Portable, Modular, or Custom). Under each vendor she writes the name of the graphics packages available. She then assigns the graphics package a color-coded line under the "Code" column and indicates the quantities available in her inventory under "Quantity." She leaves room under each vendor to add new graphics packages as they become available.

The Display Legend is a chart that has three columns:

DISPLAY TYPE	CODE	QUANTITY
Vendor A (Portables)		
International Earth Photomural	Red	12
POWERSHIP 2®	Green	4
Generic Full Service	Blue	6
Vendor B (Modular)		
International Flag Pkg.	Orange	6
Vendor C (Custom)		
Heavyweight[sm]	Yellow	2

The Calendar works hand in hand with The Display Legend. The following example illustrates how it is organized.

SEPTEMBER

1 2 3 4 5 6 7 8 9 10 11 12 13 14 15 16 17 18 19 . . .

0901-91 (red)   0910-91 (green)

0905-91 (orange)   0930-91 (red)

0911-91 (blue)

0907-91 (red)   0902-91 (blue)

For each show/event, an appropriate color-coded line from the Display Legend is graphed on the calendar. Each line indicates one exhibit structure and one set of graphics for the dates it covers. (This line also has the show Control Number which can be referenced in the Display Log for complete information.) This way, by taking a quick glance at the calendar she can count the number of graphics from any single category, and the number of display structures used for each day of the month. Since Padron has a total of 38 structures, she knows she can't do more than 38 shows in any given time period. In addition, she also knows the amount of graphics packages she can schedule at any given time via the quantity indicated on the Display Legend.

Scheduling Steps: Here are the steps used to schedule trade shows.

1. Once a request is received it is immediately recorded in the Display Request Log and is assigned a six-digit Control Number.

    The Control Number is significant because it helps the communication process between Federal Express and the display company. The first two numbers represent the month, the third and fourth indicate the scheduling number and the last two represent the year. For example, the first show scheduled in September would have a Control Number of 0901-91; the second show scheduled for September would be 0902-91; and so on. Since many shows often take place simultaneously, Padron does not include the dates in the Control Number. And, the scheduling number (this is the third and fourth number) *is not dependent on the chronological dates of the shows.* It merely indicates the order in which the request was received by Marketing.

2. By color, the display type is graphed on the calendar. The line begins at the ship date and ends when the unit should be back in the warehouse.

3. The Display Order Form is submitted to the appropriate display house when all necessary information is available via receipt of the exhibitor kit. (See Communicating with the Display and Services Supplier on page 254 for more information.)

4. Once the display house receives an order and confirms that unit will ship on the requested date, a Display Confirmation Form is returned to Padron.

COMMUNICATE: To facilitate the flow of information and record-keeping Padron communicates regularly with:
Field marketing representatives
Exhibit display and services suppliers
Internal resources

The following forms keep the maze of shows, services, and requests organized:

Communicating with Field Representatives

Form #1 (see page 248)	The "Tradeshow Request Form" gets the process started. Field representatives use it to request participation in a show. It also asks the requestor to provide preliminary information about the show, along with the exhibitor manual if available.

| Form #2
(see page 249) | The "Notification of Action" Form is sent to the person requesting participation to let them know that marketing will provide trade show support. It also outlines guidelines for the participating representative on literature, giveaways, A-V and staffing. |

| Form #3
(see page 250) | The "Tradeshow Job Aid Memo" is sent to the field two weeks prior to the show to inform them about the supplies they will receive, the exhibit they will use (along with a photocopy illustration), details about the exhibit, and tips on how to use giveaways supplied. This ensures that the participants are familiar and comfortable with expectations for the show. Padron calls the requestor a week before the show to discuss the Job Aid and any last-minute details. |

| Form #4
(see page 252) | The "Tradeshow Evaluation Form" is used to evaluate the show. All field representatives who participated are asked to complete the form. It requests information about the quality of the audience, competitors at the show, and its overall value in terms of leads generated and business booked. |

| Form #5
(see page 253) | The "Account Tracking Request Form" asks field representatives to identify new business from existing customers, as well as new accounts opened as a result of participation in the show. It aids in evaluating sales results from shows and to determine the value of future participation at that event. |

Form #1

TRADESHOW REQUEST FORM

INSTRUCTIONS

1. Complete the information below.
2. Attach show information or exhibitor manual if available.
3. Submit to Convention Services Dept. *six weeks* prior to event if possible.

♦ SHOW INFORMATION

Show Name _____
Show Dates _____
Show Site: Building _____
　　　　Street Address _____
　　　　City _____ ST _____ Zip _____
Show Audience _____
Estimated Number of Attendees _____ No. of Exhibitors _____

♦ FIELD REQUESTER INFORMATION

Field Contact _____ Phone (___) _____
COMAT _____ EMAIL _____
Street Address _____
City _____ ST _____ Zip _____

♦ LOCAL MARKETING APPROVAL

The above-mentioned tradeshow will not interfere with any other Local Marketing OR Convenience Network event.

Sr. Local Marketing Specialist Signature _____

|||||||||||||||||||||||||||||||||||||||||||||||||||||||||||||||||||||||||||||||||||||||||||

FOR CONVENTION SERVICE USE ONLY

Show Manager _____ Phone (___) _____
Company Name _____
Street Address _____
City _____ ST _____ Zip _____
Booth Number _____ Booth Size _____ Booth Badges _____
Booth Cost Includes: __ Draped Table __ Two Chairs __ Carpet
Electricity _____ Other _____
Union Restrictions _____ ___ Certificate of Insurance

|||||||||||||||||||||||||||||||||||||||||||||||||||||||||||||||||||||||||||||||||||||||||||

Form #2

INTER-OFFICE MEMORANDUM

DATE: TO:

FROM: Mary E. Padron   cc:

SUBJECT: TRADESHOW NOTIFICATION OF ACTION

Your request to participate in:

Show Name: _____
Date: _____
Location: _____
Booth Number: _____

has been approved by your Sr. Local Marketing Specialist.

CONVENTION SERVICES RESPONSIBILITIES

The Convention Services Department pays for and
coordinates the logistics listed below provided we are given at
least 4 to 6 weeks prior notice of the event:

- Handling of contract and payment of exhibit space
- Reserving a FEDEX display for the event
- Ordering and payment of these show services:
  - —Electricity
  - —Booth clearing/vacuuming
  - —Drayage
  - —Furniture and carpet rentals as required
  - —Labor for booth installation & dismantling
  - —Show directory listing
- Shipping of tradeshow bags, drawing prize, and other
  handout items as required

FIELD RESPONSIBILITIES

BOOTH MANNING

*The local sales and operations personnel are responsible for
manning the booth at the trade show.* We recommend
scheduling personnel in three- to four-hour shifts if possible.
(When people have to work over four hours, they are often too
tired to practice effective selling techniques.)

Form #3

INTER-OFFICE MEMORANDUM

DATE: TO:

FROM: Mary E. Padron   cc:

SUBJECT: TRADESHOW JOB AID

Attached are copies of the forms which I have completed for
your involvement in:

Please review these so you will be familiar with what has
been ordered/handled for you. Also, please read the enclosed
Trade Show Job Aid. It should answer the majority of your
questions.

I will be calling you soon to discuss any last-minute concerns
or questions.

Form #3 (Cont'd.)

FEDERAL EXPRESS
TRADE SHOW JOB AID

INTERNAL PRE-SHOW MEETING

You will find it advantageous to schedule a pre-show meeting with the personnel whom you have scheduled to man our booth. At your pre-show meeting, you may want to:

♦ Review the "Federal Express Boothmanship Skills" communique attached, especially the section about Closed- and Open-ended questions.

♦ Go over the manning schedule so everyone is reminded of the hours which they are required to work.

♦ Establish the procedures on how sales leads are to be handled.

WHAT YOU NEED TO BRING TO THE SHOW

We recommend that you bring the following items to the show:

♦ Tape Gun
♦ Scissors
♦ Stapler
♦ Markers & Pens
♦ Note Pads
♦ Box Cutter (very important)
♦ Extension Cord
♦ Powerstrip
♦ First Aid Kit
♦ Breath Mints

In addition, we encourage you to bring some FEDEX packaging and airbills, especially if your show is regional or national in scope. You will usually get attendees and exhibitors who want to use our services right there at the trade show.*

*NOTE: Sometimes convention centers are ruled by the union. If you plan on taking packages at the exhibit booth, you will need to get prior approval from show management.

YOUR DISPLAY

Attached is a photocopy of the display reserved for your event. For more specific information about where and when the display is being sent, please refer to the attached Display Order Form.

If your display is being sent to a Federal Express facility, don't forget to make arrangements with a courier to deliver it and the sales support materials on set-up day.

Set-Up and Take-Down

Whenever feasible and geographically possible, we try to arrange for the set-up and take-down of the display. If we are able to secure installation and dismantling of the booth, I will call you later with the specifics.

Form #4

FEDERAL EXPRESS
TRADESHOW EVALUATION FORM

Instructions: Please complete the information below and
submit within a month from the date which the
show took place.

◆◆◆

Submitted By _____ Title _____

Show Name _____ Dates _____

Location _____

■ To fulfill Legal requirements for drawings, please provide
us with the name and phone number of the person who won
the drawing.

Winner's Name _____ Phone (___) _____

Company Name & FEC Acct. # (if any) _____

■ VERY IMPORTANT

To help us determine our return-on-investment, please list
below the account numbers from which you gained or
strongly expect package/volume commitments: (Attach
additional sheets if necessary.)

ACCOUNT NUMBER	COMPANY NAME	VOLUME COMMITTED

■ Which of our competitors were at the show? Check all that
apply.

☐ Emery ☐ Airborne ☐ UPS ☐ Post Office ☐ DHL

■ Please list any NEW account numbers opened on the show
floor.

NEW ACCOUNTS OPENED	COMPANY NAME

■ How many POWERSHIPs did you place? _____

■ Which of our services were the attendees most interested in?

☐ Domestic   ☐ International   ☐ Heavyweight

☐ Air Cargo   ☐ POWERSHIP   ☐ Other _____

252

TRADESHOW ACCOUNT TRACKING REQUEST

REQUESTOR
NAME: MARY E. PADRON   PHONE:

TRADESHOW NAME _____

TRADESHOW DATE _____ LOCATION: _____

HOW LONG TO TRACK _____

INDICATE TYPE(S) OF REPORT WANTED:
        _____ SUMMARY REPORT
        _____ INDIVIDUAL REPORT FOR SELECT
        ACCOUNTS WITH AN "X"

INSTRUCTIONS TO FIELD:
In the "Existing Accounts" category, write the account numbers of already established customers from which we may see increased activity as a result of tradeshow selling. Or, if you are made aware of any accounts who may be switching to one of our competitors, please list that also. Under "New Accounts Opened . . ." write the account number of each new customer who applied for an account at the trade show. *If there are any accounts expected to have substantial volume jumps, either high or low, please put an "X" by them.*

NOTE: Trade shows allow us to come in contact with many accounts. This Tradeshow Account Tracking Form is not intended to track every customer who comes to our booth. Therefore, please do not write the account numbers of everyone who registered for the drawing prize. This would be non-productive for our Business Analysis group who is responsible for tracking.

ACCOUNT NUMBER	ACCOUNT NUMBER	ACCOUNT NUMBER

Existing Accounts:

_____	_____	_____
_____	_____	_____
_____	_____	_____
_____	_____	_____

New Accounts:

_____	_____	_____
_____	_____	_____
_____	_____	_____

USE ADDITIONAL SHEETS IF NECESSARY

Communicating with the Display and Services Supplier

| Form #6 (see page 255) | The "Display Order Form" is sent to the display supplier to reserve a structure. One is sent for each show or event. It indicates the number of structures needed, a request for graphics and an option for installation/dismantle services. |

| Form #7 (see page 257) | The "Display Confirmation Form" is returned to Federal Express to confirm that a structure has been reserved for the show. It indicates whether the system is confirmed as ordered, or if units requested are not available. It also indicates the person who will assist in installation/dismantle if it is requested. |

Form #6

LOCAL MARKETING & CONVENTION SERVICES DISPLAY ORDER FORM

Instructions: This form is to be submitted when a portable display is needed for a Local Marketing event other than trade shows. Please give two weeks notice if possible.

☞ NAME OF EVENT _____ EVENT DATES _____

☞ SHIPPING INFORMATION

ATTN: _____ PHONE ( )_____
COMPANY _____ DEPT. _____
STREET _____
CITY _____ STATE _____ ZIP _____

☞ DISPLAY INFORMATION

How many displays are needed for your event? (The Skyline Mirage display is 8′ tall by 10′ wide and about 1′ in depth.)
    ONE _____   TWO _____   THREE _____
Indicate below your 1st, 2nd, and 3rd choice for the message you would like promoted on your display.
    GENERAL FEDEX _____   INT'L _____
    AIR FREIGHT _____   POWERSHIP _____

☞ BOOTH SET-UP AND TAKE-DOWN (INSTALLATION & DISMANTLING)
Skyline representatives are available in most major metropolitan areas to set up and take down your display. Would you like *installation and dismantling* service if it's available?

YES _____ NO _____

IF YES:

SET-UP DATE _____ Start Time _____ End Time _____
TAKE-DOWN DATE _____ Start Time _____ End Time _____
    Location for Meeting Display Representative

FEDEX CONTACT _____ PHONE ( )_____
BUILDING _____ ROOM _____
ADDRESS _____ CITY _____ STATE ____

☞ REQUISITIONER INFORMATION

YOUR NAME _____ DATE _____
MANAGER: RIDINGS __ GOLIGHTLY __ OTHER _____

Form #6 (Cont'd.)

★★

FOR CONVENTION SERVICES USE ONLY

PROPERTIES TO RESERVE   ____ SKYLINE MIRAGE
                           EARTH PHOTOMURAL
          ____ RADIUS TABLES   ____ FEDEX CHAIRS
          ____ BAG STAND

OTHER _____

SHIP DATE	RETURN DATE	CONTROL NUMBER

Form #7

DISPLAY CONFIRMATION

NAME OF EVENT: _____

CONTROL NUMBER: _____

REQUISITIONER: _____

CONFIRMED AS ORDERED _____ *

PARTIAL CONFIRMATION _____

THE FOLLOWING UNITS ARE NOT AVAILABLE: _____

_____

*Because the field sometimes does not return displays as scheduled, there are occasions when we have to send a display with a different message than what was originally confirmed.

BOOTH SET-UP AND TAKE-DOWN

ASSISTANCE IN SETTING UP AND TAKING DOWN YOUR DISPLAY IS AVAILABLE.

               YES _____ NO _____

NAME OF REPRESENTATIVE: _____

PHONE: (   )_____

LOCATION: _____

CONFIRMED BY: _____ DATE: _____

NOTE TO FEDEX PERSONNEL: IF YOU ENCOUNTER PROBLEMS WITH YOUR BOOTH OR EXPERIENCE DIFFICULTIES AT THE BOOTH SET-UP OR TAKE-DOWN, PLEASE NOTIFY LEX HORTON OR DENNIS DOWN, PLEASE NOTIFY OUR DISPLAY REPRESENTATIVE

110888

Communication for Internal Supplies and Record-Keeping

Form #8 (see page 259)

The "Trade Show Supply Order Form" is used to request supplies internally, such as literature, premiums, registration cards, special banners, etc. This initiates the process of getting those supplies shipped to the show.

Form #9 (see page 260)

The "Trade Show Checklist" is stapled to the inside of the file created for each show. Padron uses it as a prompt to record the process as all tasks are accomplished for that show. It includes administrative details, display information, show services, premiums orders, field communications, and special requests and comments.

Form #10 (see page 262)

The "Display Request Log" is used to list each show or event for which a display is needed. It is a prompt for such information as the control number, event name, location, properties reserved, and the reserve dates.

Form #8

TRADESHOW SUPPLY ORDER FORM

SHIPPING INFORMATION
Show Name _____ FedEx Booth # _____
Contact Name _____
Company _____
Address _____
City _____ ST _____ Zip _____
SHIP DATE _____   ___ P-1   ___ Economy   ___ COMAT

Quantity	Description	Part Number	Pack
Literature			
_____	8 Impt. Reasons Acct.	CSLD000001	1
_____	POWERSHIP 2	CSLD107005	1
_____	Service Guide	CSLD204173	1
_____	Int'l Quick Guide	CSLI102961	25
_____	Heavyweight Brochure	CSLH102000	25
_____	Heavyweight Guide	CSLH119546	50
_____	SOS Brochure	CSLD204174	100
Giveaways			
_____	Plastic Bags	CSP1001150	200
_____	Jelly Bellies	CSP1000012	150
_____	Highlighter Pens	CSP1107002	250
_____	Magnetic Clip	CSP1107004	250
_____	Disposable Stapler	CSP1107005	250
_____	WW Memo Writer	CSP1107007	100
_____	Globe Key Chain	CSP1000008	120
_____	Acrylic Key Chains	CSP1107011	100
_____	Golf Tees	CSP1107012	100
Drawing Prizes and Support Tools			
_____	5" Magnavox TV	CSPP000131	1
_____	Seiko Clock	CSPP000132	1
_____	Registration Cards	CSS0107000	100
_____	Trade Show Organizer	CSS0107773	1
_____	FEDEX Banner	CSS0107004	1
Other			
_____	_____	_____	____
_____	_____	_____	____
_____	_____	_____	____

REQUESTED BY ____ Mary Padron ____ Doug Williams
Date _____

Form #9

TRADESHOW CHECKLIST

ADMINISTRATIVE

_____ Log show and
assign control number ☐ ☐ ☐ ☐ ☐ ☐ ☐ ☐
_____ Create manila and pendaflex folder
_____ Complete Contract _____ Complete Check Request
_____ Submit Invoice
Contract sent via _____
Date Submitted _____
_____ Send Notification of Action Memo to field requestor and a
copy to Sr. Specialist
_____ Call Primary Field Contact and review objectives for show
_____ Send field Manning/Registration Form
Due Date _____

LOGISTICS

DISPLAY INFORMATION
_____ Submit Display Order to Appropriate Display Co.
_____ Graph Display Order on Booth Reserve Chart
_____ Display Confirmation Received

SHOW SERVICES   Exhibit Orders Due by _____
_____ Submit Payment Policy Form if required
_____ Complete Electrical   _____ C/R   Date Submitted _____
Form
_____ Complete Rentals   _____ C/R   Date Submitted _____
Form
_____ Complete Drayage   _____ C/R   Date Submitted _____
Form
_____ Complete Labor Form if unable to use Skyline
Representatives

PREMIUM/SUPPLY ORDER
_____ Complete Delta Request for Shipment Form
_____ Submit to Delta on _____ D/T
Ship Date _____ Airbills Rcvd. _____

COMMUNICATIONS

INTERNAL

_____ Send Tradeshow Job Aid to field/copy to Sr. Specialist
by _____ D/T
    copies of all forms ☐
    booth plan ☐   show info. ☐
_____ Send Commercial Video Yes ☐   No ☐
_____ Send Skyline Video Tape for Set-Up and Take-Down
    Yes ☐   No ☐
_____ Call field to discuss show and verify supplies/booth received

PROMOTION AND PUBLICITY

_____ Submit Directory Listing
_____ Submit Directory Advertising (if appropriate)
_____ Special Requests (Explain in Comment Section)

COMMENTS:

FEDERAL EXPRESS
Convention Services
DISPLAY REQUEST LOG

CONTROL NUMBER	EVENT NAME	LOCATION	PROPERTIES RESERVED	RESERVE DATES

Conclusion

If you are still following the schedule outlined here, you have left yourself one month prior to the show to recheck all of the details you have already set into place. In Chapter 9 you'll get a very specific list of details to check, along with guidelines for conducting a pre-show meeting.

Chapter 9: You are here:

↓

	2 Mo.	1 Mo.	On-Site
Planning			
Goal-Setting			
Budgeting			
Promotions	Check direct mail costs	Cross-check all promotions needs	
Product Demos			
Exhibits	Exhibit preview Select portable structure	Portable exhibit preview	
Installation	Prepare site book	Double-check installation plans	Managing on-site installation
Staffing		Prepare orientation meeting contents	
Inquiry Processing			
Measuring Results			

9

Checking and Cross-Checking (1 Month in Advance)

The person responsible for the show had recently joined the company. Since it was her first show, she was especially careful to assure that all details were covered. Unfortunately on Thursday she received the call that exhibitors lose sleep over. Due to an oversight the exhibit had not been shipped. The show opened on Monday. All of the plans had been made, she just *forgot to double-check*.

By this time in the planning process most of the strategy for the show has been set into place and with the exception of a few extra details, all of the planning and execution of the plan has been carried out. So it would seem the natural time to breathe easy, assured that all components are in place. Unfortunately, since the logistics of show planning involve so many different vendors there are a host of tiny cracks that are difficult to see, through which things tend to slip. Hence the need to check and recheck.

BEFORE YOU LEAVE THE OFFICE: 13 CONFIRMATION CHECKPOINTS

- **Assure that the exhibit has been shipped.** Get a scheduled date of departure from your transportation company (or exhibit house if they are handling transportation) and check with them on that date to assure that the exhibit and products have gone out as scheduled.

- **Confirm all service orders.** Call the official contractor and other vendors involved to assure that all service orders have been received.

- **Assure notification of intent to use independent contractor.** If you are planning to use an independent contractor for the exhibit installation rather than the one appointed by show management, some shows require notification of that fact 30 days prior to show set-up.

265

- **Assure that your products and literature have been shipped.** If they are shipping with the exhibit, check to confirm that they were received by the shipper and included on the truck. If literature is shipped from anywhere other than your office (divisional offices, agencies, etc.), call to check on the progress toward its production and shipping. Try to get a firm shipping date and check again to confirm it has been shipped. Missing literature is one of the most common nagging problems.

- **Assure premiums and giveaways have been shipped.** Did you order special premiums or incentives for the show? Have you checked to make sure they have been produced and delivered as requested? Are they being shipped with the exhibit or under separate cover? If not with the exhibit, try to get a ship date for those and double-check to be sure they went out. Nothing will sabotage a direct mail campaign more quickly than not having the promised premiums on-site when show visitors arrive.

- **Confirm air/hotel reservations.** Rumor has it that exhibitors have lost entire blocks of rooms to computer errors. If you are responsible for flight and hotel arrangements, double-check reservations, and get confirmation numbers. This is also the time to double-check hospitality arrangements.

- **Assure press kits have been shipped (and have arrived).** If press kits are being shipped directly to the show press room, about a week in advance of the show it is a good idea to call and confirm that they have arrived.

- **Confirm arrival of the exhibit.** If you shipped the exhibit in advance to be stored at the show warehouse, call one to two weeks prior to the show (depending on when you expected it to arrive) to confirm that it has been received at the warehouse.

- **Complete your site book.** What are those things that you had planned to get together for your site book, but hadn't had the chance to slip in there yet: set-up drawings, key contacts, phone numbers, crate inventories?

- **Double-check all documents.** Do you have copies of:
  - ☐ Service order forms (with copies of checks for proof of payment)
  - ☐ Weight certificates
  - ☐ Shipment bill of lading
  - ☐ Set-up drawings (and photos of the exhibit when available)
  - ☐ Crate inventory list
  - ☐ Product inventory list (if shipped separate from the exhibit)
  - ☐ Airbill numbers for airfreight shipments
  - ☐ Copies of letters from management indicating any variances granted.
  - ☐ Phone numbers (home and office) for
    Exhibit firm A/E
    Show management contact
    Transportation company contact
    Set-up contractor contact
    Product technician (for technical products)

- **Confirm Your Set-Up Team.** If you are using an independent service contractor, call to confirm that you are on their schedule and get the name and contact number of your supervisor there. If you are using the show contractor, call to confirm that you are on their schedule.
- **Check billing arrangements.** Some contractors are now requesting payment in full for services (such as drayage) before they will move your exhibit out of the hall. You can occasionally make arrangements prior to the show to be billed, but it is much more difficult to do so on site.

Exhibit 9-1   Checklist for Exhibit Installation

☐ Sent form to show management notifying of intent to use independent service contractor

☐ Exhibit shipped

☐ Exhibit arrival at warehouse confirmed

☐ Service orders confirmed

☐ Literature shipped

☐ Products shipped

☐ Premiums and incentives shipped

☐ Press kit arrival confirmed

☐ Hospitality arrangements confirmed

☐ Hotel bookings confirmed

☐ Move-in and installation times confirmed

☐ Checked billing arrangements for services

☐ Set-up supervisor and phone number confirmed

☐ Telephone included

☐ Site book complete with copies of:
　____Service order forms
　____Weight certificates
　____Shipment bill of lading
　____Set-up drawings
　____Crate inventory
　____Product inventory
　____Phone numbers for key contacts

NOTES: _____

_____

_____

_____

_____

_____

Double-check their payment policies and be sure you will be able to meet the requirements.

- **Consider taking your own phone.** At most shows, if you have telephone service, you rent the phone separately. Bring a small telephone and you can plug it into your service right away which is handy if you have to trace missing shipments or truly last-minute details.

ASSURING SUCCESS OF THE IN-BOOTH PROMOTION

While 89% of all exhibitors use some form of pre-show promotion in their exhibit efforts, it is interesting that only 10% include with them the promise of a gift to selected booth visitors. And about 37% use direct mail in quantity to motivate visitors to stop by their exhibits.(1) Any attempt to identify reasons for this are pure speculation, but it would be fairly safe to say that time and money are two primary factors.

The pre-show direct mail campaign takes a significant investment of resources. Unfortunately, much of the investment concerns the production of the mailer and not enough concerns the logistics of how the program will function *in the exhibit.* For example, how will those visitors who show up at the exhibit to receive their promised gift be connected with staffers? The exhibitor who is merely handing out giveaways to a line of waiting participants is missing the opportunity their direct mail promotion has been designed to create: not just to draw a crowd, but to facilitate the connection between visitor and company repesentative.

This, too, requires planning. But this type of planning involves the more mundane task of simply defining how it is all going to work. If your incentive is a simple giveaway, you have one set of considerations. Where will giveaways be distributed? If your incentive is a contest or drawing, it requires a different set of considerations. Who will handle the drawings? How frequently will they be held?

The checklist in Exhibit 9-2 walks you through some of those considerations. If you are conducting a drawing or contest in the exhibit look over the considerations under that category. If each person who responds to the mailer will receive a giveaway, review the considerations under "Giveaways."

HOW TO LEAD THE ORIENTATION MEETING

Whether it is a group of two or three people over cocktails the evening before the show, or 40-50 people in a formal setting, the pre-show orientation meeting is a necessary component of a successful show. It's the last opportunity for all of the players to be briefed on their role in the exhibit. Even if it requires budgeting for participants to get to the show

---

Exhibit 9-2   Checklist for a Smooth Promotion

If You Are Using . . .

A Contest or Drawing:	A Giveaway:

1. **The Booth Number.** Before the piece goes out the door, be sure to check that the booth number is accurate.

2. **Drawing Details.** Consider exactly how the details of the drawing will be handled. When will it (or they) be held? Who will do the drawing? How will the winners be notified? Will the drawing be public in the exhibit, or private?

3. **Word of Mouth** When word gets out about a contest or drawing, it inevitably draws crowds of people. Do you want to have additional entry forms in the exhibit for those people, or limit entry to the people on your mailing list?

4. **Entries vs. Leads** Will the entry forms also be considered leads? It is rare for any contest entry (especially those filled out by the contestants) to be complete enough to double as lead cards. If not, consider follow-up for these.

1. **The Booth Number.** Before the piece goes out the door, be sure to check that the booth number is accurate.

2. **Giveaway Distribution** How will the giveaway be distributed? Is there one station that will keep confusion to a minimum? Or will they be handed out by staff at the end of an interaction? Will visitors be required to provide any qualifying information before receiving the gift?

3. **Staffers' Roles** What is the staffer's role in making this promotion a success? How will they connect with visitors requesting gifts? Have they been apprised of their role?

4. **Crowd Control** Where will the giveaways be distributed? Do you anticipate that it might interrupt the flow of traffic into other areas of the exhibit? Into your neighbor's exhibit? How will you handle potential crowds?

If You Are Using . . .

A Contest or Drawing:	A Giveaway:
5. Press Opportunities. Depending on the size of the show and the type of drawing you are holding, the awarding of prizes might be an event covered in the show daily. News of the contest might be covered as well. Do you want to take advantage of this by inviting editors or making them aware of the contest?	5. Two techniques. Giveaways can be used most effectively when they help the staffer either break the ice with visitors, or thank them for stopping by the exhibit. If no other conditions are put on receiving the giveaway, let staffers know how your giveaways can help them break the ice and open the conversation or serve as a token of thanks.

city a day early, the investment will pay off significantly in performance and productivity in the booth. This time also saves you, the exhibit manager, from a stream of questions about expectations and details.

The orientation meeting should be kept as brief as possible. For a small group and simple show strategy it can be accomplished in about 30 minutes. For a larger group it may typically go to an hour or 90 minutes. If you are conducting just an orientation meeting with no exhibit staff training, it's not wise to go longer than 90 minutes. Use the following considerations to organize your thinking about the pre-show meeting. Then use the outline in Exhibit 9-3 and the checklist in Exhibit 9-4 to prepare the meeting. With these tools, preparation should take just a few hours from start to finish.

Who Should Be on the Agenda?

There are two people who must be on your pre-show meeting agenda: a key management person (typically from either sales or marketing) to whom a majority of the staff reports, and the exhibits manager or person responsible for putting the show program together. After that, contributors will vary based on your program, but avoid boring participants with lengthy discourse from, say, product managers or technical experts. A few people you might also include:

- *Third-Party Vendors.* If your distribution network involves Value Added Resellers (VARs) who will display their services in the exhibit, consider giving them each five minutes on the agenda to *briefly* explain their participation.

- *Divisional Marketing Managers.* If several divisions of your company are participating in a show together, and staffers are not familiar with products from each other's division, have a marketing manager from each division provide a *brief* layman's explanation of the product. Marketing people tend to work better here than product experts or technical experts because they are good at translating product features into a few key benefits that those unfamiliar with the products can quickly grasp and use.
- *Coop Vendors.* Occasionally exhibiting companies coop their space with other vendors. For example, a major dealer/distributor rents an exhibit space and coops with two or three manufacturers whose lines they carry. Give representatives from those coop companies a few minutes to explain their product displays.
- *PR Representatives.* It is usually beneficial to at least introduce the primary press contact within your company so that staffers know where to direct inquiring editors.

One primary purpose of the pre-show meeting is to build your exhibit staffing team. The more staffers who are acquainted with one another and know who to ask for information, the more efficiently the exhibit will function.

Those who you select to participate on the agenda need to be briefed about what is expected of them. By memo (so they have something to refer to when they are planning their input on the airplane) outline:

- The time and location for the meeting
- An agenda for the meeting
- What you would like them to talk about
- How much time they will have
- A note about how strictly you will adhere to timeframes
- A-V equipment available for their use (or lack thereof)

Options for a Meeting Place

Small groups, of course, can meet almost anywhere. The pre-show meeting can be discussed over pizza at a local restaurant or a hotel suite reserved for the show. Larger groups require a bit more planning, and when you considered a pre-show meeting in Chapters 4 or 7, you might have scheduled a meeting room at that time.

Five Useful Support Materials

While preparing, consider the support materials you will need at the orientation meeting. Staffers should all receive:

- copies of literature used in the exhibit
- samples of literature that will be sent after the show (when appropriate)

- a copy of the lead card
- a sample of any premiums that will be used
- registration badges (when they can be secured in advance)

Eight Components of the Orientation Meeting

To make the meeting as efficient and thorough as possible, plan to include these eight topics.

1. **Introduction.** Introduce yourself and your role in putting the show together, and the content and timeframe for this meeting. And most importantly, if the staffers do not know one another, take time to have them introduce themselves. Provide name tags for the staffers if they don't already have them.

2. **Review of the Exhibit.** Make an overhead transparency of the exhibit floorplan and review how you anticipate traffic will flow into and through the space. You can also review here station staffing assignments, storage areas, reception areas, and lead collection points.

   If you have a slide of the exhibit from a preview or a previous show, use it to point out these areas since most people relate better to an actual photograph than they do to a floorplan drawing. To provide a context for your own exhibit, create an overhead transparency of the show hall floorplan and indicate your location, that of competitors, and details such as snack bars and restrooms.

3. **Review the Booth Duty Schedule.** An overhead transparency of the booth duty schedule is also helpful here. Present it to the group and see if there are any conflicts. Review guidelines for booth duty responsibility, reminding them that if they are not available they *must* find a replacement. This is also a good time to remind them to arrive at the exhibit about 15 minutes before their assigned shift and familiarize themselves with all of the selling tools in the exhibit (lead cards, literature, premiums, graphics, product displays, etc.)

4. **History.** Provide a quick snapshot of your performance in this same show during previous years. A few areas you could discuss include:
   - Lead count from previous year
   - Any formal surveys or analysis conducted on your show participation
   - Why and how you would like to see performance improve this year
   - Differences about previous year that will affect this year's show (a change in location, for example)
   - Success stories from last year. If you know of any major sales associated with the show from last year this offers a great motivational boost.

5. **Show Goals.** Make goals as quantifiable as possible. In most cases this will be a specific number of leads or orders written at the show. You can take this a step further, and personalize it a bit for your staffers by calculating how many leads or orders each person has to write in order to achieve your goals. This is also a good time to review any key prospects that salespeople anticipate seeing in the exhibit.

The less tangible goals are more difficult to personalize, but be sure to review them as well. For example if you have a special theme or product emphasis for the show, or image goals, discuss that with the group. If you are planning on evaluating competitors at the show or gathering any additional industry information, discuss how that will be accomplished.

6. **Review the Contact/Lead Form.** Be prepared with an overhead transparency of a blank lead card, and a sample for each participant to follow along. Explain each category on the lead card and not only what type of information you want them to gather there, but why that information is important. Emphasize the importance of filling out the leads neatly and completely, getting the phone number, and including detailed remarks or comments.

Review logistics of gathering leads. If you are using an imprinter, be sure that everyone knows how they work. Let the staff know where blank lead cards are stored and where the completed lead cards will be collected.

Finally, review the follow-up process for the leads. Let staffers know the timing in which you expect requests for literature and sales calls to be fulfilled, and encourage them to let the visitors know in turn. (For example, staffers should close the interaction by assuring visitors that the literature they requested will be out to them within the next couple of weeks, or that a salesperson will be contacting them within ten days). Take a minute to explain why the lead card and follow-up system works to emphasize the importance of their participation in making it work.

7. **Review Standards and Do's and Don'ts.** Most people know that they probably shouldn't smoke in the exhibit, or eat hot dogs and let mustard drip on their suits. They know it, but if they are not reminded, they tend to fall into bad habits. Remind them of the standards that are expected of them when they are in the exhibit. This is your show and you have a right to have high expectations. If it means outlining for them exactly what "appropriate business attire" means for your company, then do so. First impressions are made repeatedly at trade shows and making a good one counts. Also plan to review your policies for handling competitors who come fact-finding in your exhibit, complainers, and press representatives.

8. **Close.** Save any housekeeping details such as rooming assignments, shuttle buses, and hospitality functions for the close of the meeting. Even

at the end you will be sure to have the attention of the group for details that are important to them. Finally, inspirational anecdotes or success stories from previous shows put a nice motivational finishing touch on the meeting.

Exhibit 9-3 Orientation Meeting Outline

*NOTE: This outline does not include any additional participants whom you might have on the agenda. Be sure to slot those people in at the appropriate points in the outline.

I.   Introductions
    A. The meeting leader
    B. Meeting content
    C. Meeting timeframe
    D. Meeting participants

II. Exhibit Review
    A. Booth floorplan
       i. Product stations
       ii. Staffing assignments
       iii. Traffic flow
       iv. Storage areas
       v. Reception area
       vi. Lead collection points
    B. Hall floorplan
       i. Booth number and location
       ii. Competitor's locations
       iii. Traffic flow
       iv. Snack bars, etc.

III. The Booth Duty Schedule
    A. Problems and conflicts
    B. Arrive early
    C. Familiarize with exhibit and selling tools

IV. History
    A. Results from previous year
    B. Formal survey or observation reports from previous year
    C. Changes that affect this year's strategy

V.   Show Goals
    A. Sales goals
       i. No. leads/sales expected
       ii. No. leads per person
       iii. Key prospects expected

B. Image Goals
   i. Market theme or product emphasis
   ii. Image goals (change/establish/maintain)
   iii. Evaluating competition
   iv. Gathering industry information

VI. Review the Contact/Lead Form
  A. Completing the lead card
    i. Explain each category
    ii. Emphasize phone number and critical data
    iii. Encourage use of comments area
  B. Review lead card logistics
    i. Using the imprinter (when appropriate)
    ii. Where lead cards are stored
    iii. Where completed lead cards are collected
  C. Lead follow-up
    i. The process
    ii. The timing
    iii. Why it works

VII. Review Standards and Do's and Don'ts
  A. Standards
    i. Dress
    ii. Proprietary information
    iii. Handling competitors
    iv. Talking to the press
    v. Handling complainers
  B. Do's and don'ts

DO'S	DON'TS
[ ] Know the products	[ ] Chat in small groups
[ ] Practice your presentation	[ ] Leave station empty
[ ] Arrive early	[ ] Ignore visitors
[ ] Bring a positive attitude	[ ] Ask "Can I Help You?"
[ ] Dress in business attire	[ ] Smoke
[ ] Approach visitors courteously	[ ] Drink
[ ] Ask open-ended questions	[ ] Eat
[ ] Qualify quickly	[ ] Chew gum
[ ] Make presentation benefits-oriented	[ ] Sit down
[ ] Get commitment for follow-up	[ ] Look like you'd rather be somewhere else
[ ] Thank the visitor	

VIII. Close
  A. Extra housekeeping details
  B. Motivational anecdote or success story

Exhibit 9-4 Pre-Show Meeting Checklist	
To Plan for the Meeting:	**To Bring to the Meeting:**
☐ Time and date confirmed	☐ Lead cards
☐ Meeting agenda complete	☐ Literature samples
☐ Participants confirmed	☐ Premiums samples
☐ Meeting room reserved	☐ Badges
☐ A-V ordered	☐ Booth duty schedule
☐ Memo to participants	☐ Exhibit floorplan
☐ Memo to staffers	☐ Hall floorplan
☐ Overhead transparencies complete	☐ Visuals
☐ Other _____	☐ Other _____

Tips for Encouraging Participation

Particularly if you are working with a large group of independent salespeople, getting them together for an orientation can be a task in itself. Excuses run from "my time would be better spent in the field or contacting my customers," to "I can't come to the show a day early because it's my son's birthday." A bit of extra effort can go a long way toward getting maximum participation.

Tip: Make the meeting mandatory. Some exhibits managers go so far as to allow only those people who participate in the meeting to work in the exhibit. Depending on the commitment level of your staff, complexity of the show plan, and timeframe for the meeting, this could be an important factor. For a fairly complex show program, those staffers who do not participate in the orientation meeting may never fully participate in the exhibit as they should.

Tip: Get upper management to mandate participation. Ask them to send a letter to the staffers involved indicating that the meeting is mandatory. If the budget for the meeting or an additional night's lodging has to come from the sales or marketing manager, be sure you have their cooperation on this in advance.

Tip: Schedule the meeting to be as convenient for the staffers as possible. When the show doesn't open until 10:00 or 11:00 a.m., you can schedule a breakfast orientation meeting. Or you might plan a late afternoon meeting followed by cocktails or dinner the evening before the show opens.

Tip: To keep up the enthusiasm level from show to show (if you have the same group working) let them know you appreciate the extra effort they put into the show with a token gift. One company president handed out gold pens to each person who participated in the meeting as a thank you for their commitment.

Tip: Highlight some of the benefits to them of attending the meeting. For example, if the group is rather small indicate that you'll be looking for their input on key accounts they are planning to see at the show. If it is large, let them know that the meeting will outline how they can get the most out of the show.

PREVIEWING THE PORTABLE EXHIBIT: SIX REASONS NOT TO SKIP THIS STEP

Previewing the portable exhibit is such a simple task that many exhibitors overlook it completely. Those sales reps who demonstrate how quickly the portable display can be set up make it look so easy that most people never consider they need to *practice* such a thing. And the fact of the matter is that *not* practicing before the show would not lead to any dramatic catastrophes. But it could provide a few unnecessary hassles.

And if field sales representatives set it up, you'll need to make a few additional considerations. These people need good installation instructions, and guidelines for packing it up and returning it (or sending it on to the next show).

If the person who sold you the exhibit calls to let you know it will be shipped soon, ask them if they would mind coming in to drop it off and guide you through a set-up. And then double-check some of the following points.

1. **Set it up yourself while they are there.** Make note of any quirks in the set-up that people would need to know about. Time yourself and see how long it takes. In most show cities the union rules state that you don't have

to hire union labor to install the exhibit if one person can set it up in under 30 minutes.

2. **Ask for copies of set-up instructions.** Try to follow them yourself as you are settng up the exhibit and be sure they are very self-explanatory. Remember, if the supplier doesn't have written set-up instructions, then you will have to write them up before sending the display out to the field; a mundane task that could be avoided.

3. **Hang your graphics.** Don't just set up the frame. Hang the graphics and check them for alignment, clarity, durability (any tears or ripples?), and accuracy.

4. **Practice repacking the display.** If you have ever taken a shirt out of its package and then tried to put it back in, you know what a challenge repacking can be. For most portable displays repacking follows a step-by-step procedure in order for all components to fit neatly into the compact cases. Check the instructions for repacking guidelines.

5. **Check on backup parts.** If the exhibit includes snaps or fasteners, check to be sure there are backup parts included with the display. If not, order some.

6. **Confirm an emergency contact.** Double-check who your contact will be if replacement parts are needed quickly. (Inevitably, someone will be setting up the exhibit a few hours prior to the show opening and be missing essential components of the display.) If they have offices in a variety of show cities, ask for a list of contacts and phone numbers.

By now you have planned, implemented, checked, and cross-checked every detail of your show participation. You are ready to head out to the hall for your exhibit installation. And the best way to succeed in that environment is to be armed with knowledge. Knowledge about how the set-up environment works (do we need to use union labor? and which unions?), who the important players and contacts are, how to solve on-site problems, how to work successfully with union laborers, and problems and pitfalls to avoid. Chapter 10 includes a primer on succeeding in the set-up environment.

Chapter 10: You are here:

	1 Mo.	On-Site	Post-Show
Planning			
Goal-Setting			
Budgeting			Audit invoices and prepare final budget
Promotions	Cross-check all promotions needs		
Product Demos			
Exhibits	Portable exhibit preview		
Installation	Double-check installation plans	Managing on-site installation	
Staffing	Prepare orientation meeting contents		
Inquiry Processing			
Measuring Results			Report on show results

10

On-Site Set-Up

Okay. You've planned. You've implemented. You've checked and cross-checked. You've created and used more checklists than you thought could ever exist. You have prepared for the inevitable. But at on-site set-up it's not the inevitable that happens. Only the one thing for which you did not prepare will actually happen. Regardless of the efficiencies with which you planned and prepared for the show, unexpected details always seem to pop up during an exhibit installation. This chapter is designed to help you deal successfully with these eventualities. You'll learn about:

1. THE PLAYERS: The key people involved in on-site show installations, and how they can help you.
2. THE RULES: Both written and unwritten rules of set-up.
3. HELPFUL HINTS: A selection of tips you won't find in the exhibitor's manual.
4. TROUBLE-SHOOTING: A guide to solving on-site problems with an appendix "What to do if. . ."

HOW TO SUCCEED IN THE SET-UP ENVIRONMENT

"Imagine 2,000 trucks delivering 3 million pounds of freight, the equivalent of about 8,570 [NFL football players] or eight Boeing 747s in thousands of crates. Then imagine you were ultimately responsible for making sure the crates got unpacked and their contents arranged over an area the size of about 40 football fields, all in 48 hours. In the hours before a big convention that's what faces the guy managing it if it's at McCormick Place, the nation's largest temple devoted to that sacred American institution: the trade show."(1)

That description from a *Chicago Tribune* writer aptly describes the heart of the set-up environment. True, the scenario he described was for one of the largest trade shows in the United States. But to varying degrees those are the logistics that have to be contended with in any set-up.

Hundreds of trucks need to be unloaded at the docks, thousands of pounds of freight have to be delivered throughout a show hall, and then hundreds of work hours will be put into setting up the exhibit structures within the allotted time frame (usually two to four days).

For the person who has never installed an exhibit at a trade show before, the organizational machine that accomplishes this task can be overwhelming, confusing, and downright frustrating. But there is definitely a machine in place, and the trick to succeeding here is to understand how the machine functions and how to use it to get your tasks accomplished.

The Players

There is a definite cast of players at all on-site installations that remains fairly constant among shows. Knowing who those players are and their responsibilities will take you a long way toward calmly and expediently solving any problems that come up during the installation or dismantle process. The diagram in Exhibit 10-1 illustrates the players and, generally, their relationships to one another.

- **Show Management and Exhibitors.** The relationship between show management and exhibitors is unique. In one sense, show management works for the exhibitors since technically the exhibitor is a client of theirs (having purchased their exhibit space from them). However, show management typically sets all of the rules about how the show will run, by which exhibitors must abide. Therefore they are illustrated here in a give-and-take relationship, on an equal level.

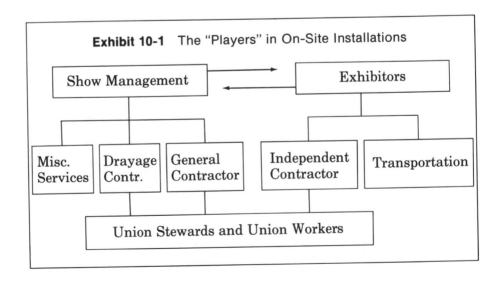

Exhibit 10-1   The "Players" in On-Site Installations

- **Show Management and the Contractors.** To accomplish all of the tasks in setting up a show, most management companies bring in contractors, typically referred to as general contractors or official contractors. Official contractors prepare the exhibit hall for set-up (set pipe and drape, divide booth spaces, lay aisle carpet) and provide the union workers who do set up work for exhibitors (carpenters, riggers, etc.) Sometimes a separate contractor is hired to handle drayage (getting crates from the hall docks to the booth spaces) and sometimes that is handled by the official contractor. Show management also typically contracts out most miscellaneous show services from furniture and carpet rental to plant rental and photography.

- **Exhibitors and the Contractors.** For exhibit installation and dismantle, labor exhibitors have the choice of using the official contractor (provided through show management) or hiring their own contractor. Contractors hired by exhibitors are typically called independent contractors, exhibitor-appointed contractors, or non-official contractors.

- **Contractors and Union Workers.** Contractors, in turn (whether official or independent), hire the union workers who actually show up to install and dismantle your property. Whether you use the official contractor, or an independent contractor, the union workers all come from the same source: the local union labor pool.

Don't confuse this chart with a chain of command chart or a hierarchical chart. All of these organizations are independent entities, but they are motivated (or should be) to please their customers. Thus, the most direct customer of the unions are the contractors, and the most direct customer of the contractors is show management, and their most direct customer is you, the exhibitor. As you can see then, to solve a problem, it makes sense for you to go to the person for whom you are the most direct customer (for exhibitors who have not hired an independent contractor, it is typically the show manager).

Supervising an exhibit installation is essentially a management job and like any management job requires good communication skills. Get the names of all of these people as they are involved in your installation as a first step to opening the channels of communication. The second, is knowing the rules.

Understanding the Written Rules

Exhibitors who have years of experience supervising elaborate exhibit set-ups can quickly get to the heart of why inexperienced people tend to have problems. As one exhibitor said in an *Exhibitor Magazine* article about working with unions at trade shows, "Too many [exhibit] coordinators don't make it their business to know what unions are out there and what the rules are. . ."(2) On the trade show floor more than anywhere else that knowledge can ensure your success. We'll begin here with the written rules, and then discuss some of the unwritten rules and nuances of which you will want to be aware.

1. **Using Union Labor.** Unless you are exhibiting in a right-to-work state, you will be required to use union workers to set up the exhibit. Many shows have a rule that if one person can set up an exhibit in less than 30 minutes by themselves they don't need to hire union workers for the installation. For anything else, plan on it.

   Without spending too much time on the repercussions of trying to do work on your own, suffice it to say they can range from having to take parts of the exhibit down and install them again, to having to do so on overtime, and incur exorbitant costs. It is typical for unions to protect the work they feel is theirs by having union stewards walk the show floor during set-up to identify people taking work away from them (whether it be other unions usurping their jurisdictional rights, or exhibitors trying to do the work themselves).

   If you are questioned by a union steward, don't argue with them. If you know you are doing work they have a right to, let them know that you will hire union workers to complete the job. If you think it is something you have a right to do, take it up with the official contractor or show management.

2. **Union Jurisdictions.** In union terms a jurisdiction is the category of work they feel is rightly theirs. For example, in Chicago carpenters have jurisdiction over all exhibit construction, but teamsters have jurisdiction over freight delivery.

   The number of different unions that have jurisdiction over different functions in the exhibit set-up range among cities from eight in New York City to just one in Baltimore. If you are involved in a fairly complex set-up in a major show city like New York or Chicago, you might find that representatives from two different unions are claiming jurisdiction to a job in your exhibit. If that is the case, locate the show manager or general contractor to get to the bottom of who really should be doing the work for you.

   How can you learn about the jurisdictions in a particular show city? In most cases the exhibitors manual for the show provides this information. If you are interested in a ready reference, the National Association of Exposition Managers publishes a guide to show labor in major convention cities around the U.S.(3) Knowing in advance which unions have jurisdiction over which jobs will help to clarify appropriate vs. inappropriate challenges.

3. **Union Straight Time and Overtime.** Union wages are based on very rigid scales which define their straight time hours, overtime hours, and even meal and coffee break times. In most cases 8:00 a.m. to 4:00 p.m. from Monday through Friday are considered straight time hours. That

means they are paid a standard wage rate for those hours. Keep in mind the fact that union workers are not paid the full hourly rate that you are charged because contractors typically mark up the rate.

Any hours after 4:00 p.m., weekends, and holidays are considered overtime hours and billed at a different rate. Some overtime hours are time and a half, while others are double time. It varies among show cities, so check with your contractor or show manager on questions regarding overtime rates. As you can see, it's more economical to try to schedule installation on straight time hours. (Although for some shows, Saturday, Sunday, and/or holiday set-ups are unavoidable.)

4. **Drayage Procedures and Fees.** Drayage is one of those givens in trade show life, like space rental and show rules. If you need to get anything into the hall that you can't carry in your own hands, you will be relying on drayage to do the job. Drayage is the process of moving freight from the dock of the show hall where it is delivered by trucks, to your booth space. Typically show management contracts for this service with either the general show contractor, or a different drayage contractor.

Drayage services are charged by weight. The rate is usually quoted "CWT" which translates "per hundred pounds." So, for example, if the show manual indicates that drayage rates are $50 CWT, that means you will pay $50 for every hundred pounds of materials. If your shipment weighs 1,000 pounds, the drayage bill will be $500 (1,000 ÷ 100 = 10. 10 × $50 = $500).

Unfortunately, however, drayage rates are rarely that simple. Drayage contractors often charge additional fees for materials that are not in crates, or a different fee for shipments that are half-crated and half-blanket-wrapped.

There is typically a minimum weight on any incoming shipments, as well. And you will be charged this minimum for each separate shipment that comes into the hall. If, for example, your literature was shipped separately from the exhibit, you will pay the minimum drayage weight fee for this shipment separate from your exhibit shipment. If the minimum weight is 200 lbs. (and they vary from show to show), even if you have only two boxes of literature that weigh 20 lbs. you will be charged the 250 lb. minimum. Obviously, it is more economical to have everything included in a single shipment to the show hall.

Since the drayage contractor also uses union labor, their fees are subject to overtime rates. Thus, if your truck does not check in at the drayage desk until after the designated time, you will be charged overtime rates for drayage services. In most situations, if your driver checks in on straight time, you will be charged straight time rates even if the truck is not unloaded until overtime hours.

5. **Fire Codes.** Most shows now have very stringent flammability regulations for all exhibit materials and products. A typical statement about fire regulations is "all objects or materials used for decorations must be

non-flammable. If requested, a certificate of non-flammability must be made available by any exhibitor for inspection." Check your Exhibitor's Manual for more specific guidelines. In many cities, fire marshals have been known to test flammability on-site with their own lighters, so don't try to skirt around this regulation.

Special Note: If you are bringing any motorized vehicle or gasoline-powered equipment or tools onto the show floor, fire regulations often state that the batteries must be disconnected, gas caps sealed, and fuel tanks empty or less than one-quarter full.

6. **Electrical Codes.** Faulty electrical wiring is a major fire hazard and shows halls are strict about electrical installations and equipment wiring being up to code. Chicago's McCormick Place has some of the strictest codes in the U.S., and if you are doing any pre-wiring, check in advance to assure that your exhibit and equipment are up to code. Electricians are able to cut off power to your exhibit if it is determined that it constitutes an electrical or fire hazard. (Be especially careful here with transformers with neon lighting in the exhibit. Sometimes transformers must be enclosed in special fireproof housings.)

7. **Ordering Services.** Service contractors plan for the amount of people and equipment they will have at a show based on advance orders. Therefore, it may be difficult for them to accommodate last-minute on-site orders expediently. Being put "at the end of the line" for services you order on-site may feel like a type of punishment, but it is done so to accommodate first those exhibitors who placed advanced orders. That's why copies of service orders and canceled checks will prove priceless, should any of your paperwork be lost by the suppliers.

8. **Show Management Regulations.** The show regulations published in the Exhibitors Manual range from restrictions on heights and depths of exhibits, to promotional techniques, to hanging signs, to noise levels in exhibits. If you try to usurp these regulations, consequences can be as simple as having to turn down loudspeakers, or as difficult as having to take down and reconstruct your exhibit.

It is common for show managers to demand that an exhibitor take down an exhibit that exceeds height restrictions and blocks another exhibitor's visibility. It's also been seen that exhibitors leave the hall in the evening with their overhead signs neatly hung (an expensive task considering the rigging labor and equipment required) only to find it resting in their booth the next morning because show management had it removed. If you have a reasonable exception to a show rule, you can request a variance from show management, but the best time to get agreement on that is long before the show (in writing) and not on-site during set-up. (4)

Understanding the Unwritten Rules

1. **The Power of Knowledge.** Surprises catch us off guard and make us feel out of control. If, for example, the labor team on your exhibit starts to pack up at 3:30 and you didn't know for sure what time they were supposed to quit, you'd be less reluctant to call them on it than if you knew the work hours. If a union representative challenges you on installing your own light bulbs, you might embarrass yourself trying to argue with them about it because you didn't know that was part of the union jurisdiction.

   Aside from avoiding surprises, your knowledge about your exhibit and its installation goes a long way toward gaining the respect of the workers you may be supervising during an installation. Learn how to read blueprints and set up drawings for the structure. (5) Have a set-up plan laid out in advance and review it with the workers. The more you know in advance about how things operate, the more you will remain in control.

2. **Supervision.** The importance of supervising your exhibit set-up, or hiring an independent contractor to supervise the installation and dismantle can't be overemphasized. No matter how small the exhibit or how simple the installation, not being there is giving responsibility carte blanche to whomever happens to be assigned to your exhibit.

3. **Attitude.** If you are new to trade shows, it won't take long at all before you begin hearing the horror stories about working with unions during an installation. In a study conducted by *Exhibitor Magazine,* when readers were asked whether their attitude toward union workers at shows was positive, negative, or neutral, only 11.6% said positive. Neutral was next with 48.5% and then 39.9% said their attitude was negative. (6) Going into a set-up with a negative attitude about the people you will be working with can be a self-fulfilling prophecy. In the frenzy of show set-ups it's easy for tempers to flare and patience to run thin. The more positive your attitude about being successful in the experience, the better chance of reaching your goals with less hassle.

4. **Communication.** Opening and maintaining the channels of communication among all of the players at your show will also go a long way toward an efficient installation. Communicate your needs and expectations to workers, your concerns and grievances to show management, your specific problems and complications to the service suppliers involved.

5. **Tipping.** In the trade show industry exhibitors are quick to differentiate a "tip" from a "bribe." A tip is a reward given to a worker for superior performance. A bribe is money given to a worker to get the job done more quickly (or at all). Experienced exhibitors adamantly oppose bribing workers to get work accomplished and unions are coming down with strict regulations for their workers about accepting bribes. In short, don't get caught in that trap. If you are having trouble getting something

accomplished, go through the proper channels. Most workers don't have the authority to speed your job along anyway.

6. **Incentives for Workers.** Some exhibitors find that incentives such as baseball caps, coffee and doughnuts in the morning, crew t-shirts, all help to motivate workers and facilitate teamwork during a lengthy set-up, and don't consider these bribes. In the *Exhibitor Magazine* study, 81.5% of the respondents said they have used incentives to encourage team spirit and cooperation among union set-up crews and other workers, and 86.5% of those respondents said they found them effective. (7)

7. **Camaraderie Amongst Exhibitors.** During set-up, exhibit managers in even the most competitive of companies pull together to get the job done. Tap into the resources around you of other experienced exhibit managers. If you run into a problem, ask someone nearby if they've run into the same problem and how they've handled it.

Finally, the list on page 290 and 291 is a summary of tips on the installation/dismantle process that will save you time, money, and exasperation in the process.

What to Do If: A Special Problem-Solving Section

Some people say that Murphy wrote his law after trying to supervise an exhibit installation. The nature of the environment just presents so many opportunities for the unexpected. The following list identifies a variety of typical problems that exhibitors face during an exhibit installation or dismantle, and suggestions for solving the problem on-site. You might want to photocopy these pages and include them in your site book as a ready reference.

What to Do If . . . You Show Up at the Booth but Your Crates Don't

A few things could have happened here: Your shipper has for some reason not delivered the shipment yet, the truck is still in line to be unloaded, the exhibit has been delivered but drayage has not delivered it to your booth space yet, or it was delivered to the wrong booth space.

Begin at the drayage desk. Check to see if your driver has checked in. If he or she has, then find out where they are on the drayage schedule. You probably don't have to worry if they are on the drayage schedule, it will only require patience.

If drayage has recorded that your crates have been delivered to your booth, find out the booth number they were delivered to (there might have been a mixup in the delivery). If you can't find it you will have to begin searching the halls.

If your truck driver has not checked in yet, you must begin tracing the shipment from the shipper's end. Call your transportation agent and let them know the shipment has not arrived. They will track down your driver.

Keep in touch with them regularly about the status of your shipment. In the meantime begin preparing for the possibility that the shipment may not arrive in time. Find out if the show contractor has rental structures that you could use in place of your own exhibit structure. Consider calling a local office or your exhibit supplier for backup graphics (but don't actually have anything shipped until you are confident that the exhibit is not going to arrive).

Some desperate exhibitors have located art stores to purchase adhesive letters, mounting board, and supplies to create their own handmade backups for missing displays. Other have resorted to tearing ads out of industry publications and show issue magazines to mount as graphics in their rental exhibit. The point is, alert everyone involved of the situation and begin planning for a backup. Better to have one and not have to use it than to need one that you don't have.

What to Do If . . . Your Exhibit Structure and Equipment Arrived but Your Literature Boxes Are Nowhere to Be Found

Begin at the drayage desk to see if there are any loose boxes around the receiving docks that were missed. Then, call the person who was responsible for shipping them to assure they are not sitting in an office or warehouse somewhere. Double-check the shipping address, to assure they were sent to the hall and not to your hotel or to a local office.

Then begin having them traced. Depending on the timeframe and necessity of the materials, begin to consider a backup plan. You may want to alert your office that the information is missing and that an airfreight shipment might be required. Keep in mind the expense of a last-minute shipment and weigh the pros and cons of going without vs. spending the money for a rush shipment.

What to Do If . . . One Crate from Your Inventory Is Missing

Again, return to the drayage desk and cross-check with their delivery list to see if they have a record of delivering that item. If they have no record of it, chances are it was either not on the truck or for some reason not unloaded. Then you will have to begin tracing the crate through your shipper. Call the warehouse where the delivery was picked up to assure that the crate was included. If the shipper off-loaded at consolidation

Exhibit 10-2 On-Site Installation/Dismantle Tips

Labor Tips	Time-Saving Tips	Cost-Saving Tips
• Introduce yourself to your labor crew first thing, and get to know names. People respond much better to their own name than to "hey you."	• Arrive at the hall early to assure your freight has arrived.	• Report any damage incurred during the drayage process immediately. If you can, document the damage with photographs.
• Know your installation process backward and forward (literally.)	• Double-check your service orders and start times as soon as you can.	• Cross-check your drayage charges with your weight certificate while you are at the show to clarify any discrepancies while you are still on-site.
• Organize your set-up in advance of the show.	• If you are required to pick up your workers, arrive just before start time (typically 8:00 a.m.), if you are ready for them, to assure you get a good, fresh crew.	
• Take time to think through each step of the process while reviewing blueprints.	• Be on-site to supervise crate delivery to your exhibit, and try to get them to arrange the crates in order, around the periphery of your space (facing in toward the space).	• Schedule as much of your installation and dismantle as possible during straight time hours. It may be worth putting dismantle off until the day after the show closes.
• Know the union jurisdictions in the show city.		
• Have photos of your completed exhibit to review with the labor team.	• Use your inventory checklist (in Exhibit 10–3) to check inventory as it arrives at your space.	• If you can see that your installation is running behind schedule, adjust your labor start times so that you won't be paying workers to stand around and wait.
• Review blueprints with the labor team.		
• Address slow workers and bad performance individually, out of range of the other workers.	• Use pre-printed labels or a stamp for crates to address them for outbound shipping.	• If you are installing heavy equipment, be sure that your padding and carpet are in place before the equipment is delivered to avoid additional charges for re-setting the equipment to lay carpet.
• Take problems to show management rather than getting into arguments yourself.	• Don't put empty labels on your crates until they are, because that's a sign for drayage to remove them from your exhibit.	
• Consider using incentives to build team spirit and motivate workers.	• Use unique markings or colors for your crates to make them easy to locate.	• Measure your space before beginning installation to assure it is as expected.

Personal Safety	Exhibit Maintenance	Dismantle
• Be aware that the set-up environment is full of dangers similar to those on any construction site. • Things to watch for: —Overhead signs —Overhead structure —Work being done overhead that could fall —Loose headers —Workers in cherry pickers —Forklift trucks —Leaning crates and panels —Loose electrical wiring —Paints and chemicals —Wood, wires, carpet packing papers, and plastic on which you could slip and fall. • Don't strain your back by trying to lift items yourself that are too heavy. • Don't try to stop falling items, they may be heavier than they appear (crates and many exhibit panels are very heavy).	• Checklist for On-Site Exhibit Maintenance. ☐ Replenish literature ☐ Replenish lead cards ☐ Check working order of imprinters ☐ Replenish giveaways ☐ Keep supply of pens and/or pencils for staffers and visitors. ☐ Spot-clean carpet (May want to take along or pack a hand-held vacuum for this purpose.) ☐ Store and replace items needing special security. ☐ Touch up and polish any chrome, plexiglas, or laminates that show fingerprints. ☐ Police the exhibit regularly for stray cups, cans, papers, etc. ☐ Assure ashtrays are clean. ☐ Assure personal effects are properly stored.	• Once the exhibit is all set up begin planning to dismantle it. • Confirm your plans for shipping products and equipment. • Make arrangements for any split shipments required. Think about how they can be organized for drayage pick-up so they are not confused. • Complete your outbound bills of lading. • Inform the drayage contractor of any special timing requirements. • Place or check on your dismantle service orders. • Prepare labels for outbound crates. • Check with drayage on crate return schedule to get an idea of when your crates will be delivered to the exhibit. This will affect your start time for dismantle labor. • When crates are returned, assure that all empty labels and old shipping labels are removed. • Supervise outbound shipment pick-up.

Exhibit 10-3

D—Delivered to exhibit
P—Picked up at exhibit
L—Loaded onto outbound truck

INVENTORY CHECKLIST

ITEM	D	P	L	NOTES
(Include crate #s, loose items, carpets, pads, equipment, etc.)				
1.				
2.				
3.				
4.				
5.				
6.				
7.				
8.				
9.				
10.				
Shipping Contact:				
Exhibit Firm Contact:				

terminals, have them check those terminals to see if it might have been left behind.

If they do have a record of delivering it, then it's time to start looking around. The first possibility is that it is in a neighboring exhibit. It could also have been delivered to an exhibit with a similar booth number. Or it could have been inadvertently left behind at the receiving docks. Before taking any desperate measures, take a walk through the show hall to see if it was delivered to the wrong exhibit by mistake.

What to Do If . . . A Worker on Your Labor Crew Is not Performing to Acceptable Standards

The following guidelines from the *Exhibitor Magazine* are a composite of suggestions from seasoned exhibits managers.(8)

- **Step One:** First give the worker in question a chance. Pull him or her aside and discuss your concerns and the consequences if you don't see improvements.

- **Step Two:** If the problems persist and you want the worker taken off your job, go to the service desk and ask to speak with the official contractor representative on-site. Describe your problem as calmly and objectively as possible. Identify the problem worker by name or badge number. Avoid an emotionally charged blanket statement like "he's driving me crazy." It probably won't get you what you want.

- **Step Three:** Usually the official contractor will then contact the union steward on-site to have that problem worker taken off your crew. If you get no action, you can contact the steward yourself (don't let the fact that this step is sometimes frowned upon by contractors deter you). After you have determined that you are talking to the right person, once again explain your grievance calmly and objectively.

- **Step Four:** If you still get no cooperation, go to the show manager. You are his customer and he is the contractor's customer. Ask that he contact the show contractor again to have the person taken off your crew. By that time, if the worker hasn't been removed, your set-up will probably be completed anyway. But contractors tend to be responsive and chances are good that Step Two will be as far as you'll have to go.

If you are concerned about repercussions from taking this type of action, you can arrange to have the worker removed after a lunch or coffee break. Those are natural breaks in the work flow when the contractor can simply request that the worker move to another site.

What to Do If . . . Someone Damages Your Exhibit Structure During Set-Up

First, of course, is identify who that person represents: the drayage contractor, the general contractor, the transportation company? It is the company which they represent that you will contact for adjustments or compensations.

Second, record the damage as best you can. Identify when it occurred, how it occurred, and take photos when possible. If you can get an estimate of the cost to have it repaired, do so. Next contact a person in authority at the representative company (your account representative at the transportation company, the key contact at the general contractor company) and let them know of the damage.

Don't wait until you return to the office or even after the show to seek compensation for damages. Report the incident as soon as it happens and get as much resolved on-site as you can.

What to Do If . . . Services You Ordered Have not Been Supplied

Go to the service desk and check again to confirm that they have your order. If they do not have a record of your order, show them your proof of ordering the service (copy of the order and canceled check which you have in your site book) and find out when your order will be filled.

If they do not have a record of your order and you cannot find a record of having ordered the service, you will need to place another and will be put at the end of the list for having it filled. You may be asked to pay for the service up front, but not in every case.

If they do have a record of your order and have simply not gotten to your exhibit yet, ask them where you stand in the process and how long they think it might be. Then check again if the services have not been delivered close to the allotted time.

What to Do If . . . You Discover You Are a Few Bolts Short, Need an Extension Cord, or Miscellaneous Hardware Supplies

For any hardware supplies, time vs. cost is the issue. In many cases the general contractor will be able to supply you with what you need on-site, but it will cost more than double what you might pay for it at a local hardware store. If you are working with an independent contractor, they can be counted on to come up with almost anything you need, but again you will pay for it. If you must take the time to scout local hardware stores for difficult-to-replace items, start in the phone directory, and call to find the closest store and assure that they have the item you need in stock.

What to Do If . . . Your Graphics Didn't Arrive

The solutions to this problem are as varied and creative as the exhibit managers who have had to come up with them. The standard options are to trace the shipment at the drayage desk, through the transportation company, and then at the exhibit firm.

In the meantime, backup plans can range from having graphics reproduced locally on a rush basis, reproduced at the exhibit firm and shipped via overnight carrier to the show hall, or finding clever ways to cover the gap created by the missing graphic (large, leafy plants have saved many an exhibitor an exorbitant airfreight bill). Large, vinyl press-on letters substitute for missing logos or explantory copy.

Take another look at your structure to see if it can be rearranged to close up the gap created by the missing graphics. If you have a local office or factory, consider bringing in a few additional products to take up the slack created by the missing graphics.

What to Do If . . . Display Equipment Is Missing from Your Crates

First, check *every* crate to assure that it wasn't simply packed in a different crate than indicated on the inventory. Then check at the warehouse where the shipment was loaded to assure that it wasn't inadvertently left behind. If you still can't locate it or won't be able to get it to the show on time, consider a few backup options:

- call nearby offices to see if they have one you can borrow.
- check to see if any of the salespeople coming to the show have access to demo models they could bring along with them.
- for prototype or difficult-to-get equipment, consider having a graphic made to illustrate components of the equipment in lieu of having it on-site.
- for very large equipment, see if there is an on-site installation nearby that might cooperate in a site visit for key customers and prospects at the show.

What to Do If . . . You Have Products or Structures That Must Be Shipped Out Immediately After the Show to Accommodate Tight Time Frames?

After the dust has cleared and most of the freight is delivered, talk to a representative at the drayage desk and explain your situation. See if you can arrange to have your crates delivered to the exhibit early (this often requires having them stored last or in a separate spot), and picked up for delivery to the docks early.

Be sure to coordinate this schedule with your truck driver so that person will be available to load as soon as the shipment is delivered to the docks. Get the name of the person you talked with, and toward the closing hours of the show go over and meet him or her again as a reminder. Just ask if there is anything you need to do to help expedite the procedure.

What to Do If . . . You Have Ordered Labor to Install Your Exhibit, but Workers Don't Show Up at the Designated Time

At most shows you are required to go to the service desk and pick up your workers, so don't panic if they don't show up on time. Just walk over to the labor desk and find out what the situation is. If there are no workers available (which occasionally happens at very busy shows), find out how long they expect it will be before you can get your crew. Then be sure to adjust the other components of your installation strategy accordingly.

What to Do If . . . Your Crates Don't Seem to Be Returned Expediently?

Crate return can be one of the exhibit manager's great frustrations. It simply takes time for the drayage crew to get all of the crates out of storage and return them to the correct exhibits. The frustration is often compounded when exhibitors schedule flights to get out of the city, expecting that they will be able to begin dismantling their exhibit the moment the show closes.

If you are wondering about your crates, go to the drayage desk and see if they have a schedule for returning crates. Find out where your exhibit is on the schedule and how far they've gotten. A calm demeanor works best here, since ranting and raving will only alienate you from the people who you rely on to get the job done. But don't be afraid to check periodically because crates have been known to get lost or left out in the post-show hustle.

What to Do If . . . You Realize at the Last Minute That You Need Special Security for Products or Components in the Exhibit

There are typically two options for security at the show halls: most offer security guards that you can hire on an hourly basis, and some offer security cages. Cages are large, lockable metal cages that you can store in a designated security area during off hours. Both of these services are offered in the Exhibitor's Manual, but can be ordered on-site as well.

What to Do If . . . A Service You Desperately Need Demands On-Site Payment in Cash or Company Check

You have just a few options here:

- call your office and see if you can get cash wired
- tap a credit card account for a cash advance (and don't forget to get a copy of the receipt before you leave)
- talk with a manager at the general contractor to see if you can arrange to be billed for the service (you might try a 50% cash deposit and 50% billing depending on how much cash you can afford to put down)

What to Do If . . . You Have Split Shipments Going to Various Locations After the Show

During dismantle, pack the shipments and physically separate them in the exhibit according to destination. Complete a separate bill of lading for each shipment. Color coding the shipment with markers, ribbons, paper, or tape will help to further differentiate them. Supervise drayage as they pick up the crates and boxes in the exhibit to take them out in their respective groupings. And supervise their loading onto the truck (checking off your inventory sheet) to assure that they all go in the right places.

What to Do If . . . You Discover That No Arrangements Have Been Made for Outbound Shipping

Contact the transportation company that delivered your exhibit and see if you can make arrangements with them for the return shipment. Many shows appoint official show carriers and claim the right to ship any freight left over at the end of the show with the official carrier. Check with show management to see if there is an official carrier and make arrangements with them for the outbound shipment.

What to Do If . . . Two Unions Claim Jurisdiction over the Same Job in Your Exhibit

Avoid a confrontation by putting a stop to any work that is currently taking place. Let the workers know that you will be going to get someone who can solve the dispute. Go to the general contractor's service desk (where you picked up your workers) and let them know what is going on. Ask them for a representative who can come to your exhibit to solve the dispute. You may find by the time you return that the conflict has been solved. But don't try to solve it yourself. Get the backup of an objective and authoritative party.

What to Do If . . . A Union Representative Claims You Are Doing Work over Which They Have Jurisdiction

Here's where it helps to know up front about union jurisdictions. If you know you are wrong, apologize and ask them how to go about getting a union worker to take care of the job. If you are not sure, but suspect it is something you can do yourself, *don't* argue with the union representative. Tell them you want to check it out, and return to the labor desk and ask a representative of the general contractor about the situation. Once again, if you do have the right to do the work yourself, ask that person to come and talk to the union representative and back you up.

What to Do If . . . You've Ordered Electrical Services, but No One Shows Up to Do the Work

Check at the service desk. Because of the technical nature of some exhibit installations (especially when there is a great deal of equipment), it is difficult to anticipate how long the electrical service will take. As a result the electricians get backed up and exhibitors are left waiting. The only recourse is to check periodically on their progress. If electricians are forced to work overtime because of their delays (not yours), you shouldn't have to pay the overtime rates.

The End?

Well, now it's over. You've successfully planned for the show, shipped and installed the exhibit, experienced a rewarding show, and packed it up for the trip home. You probably want to put this effort behind you and move on to the next job. Unfortunately, to manage the most profitable trade show, the task isn't over. Two jobs that still need to be done will be covered in the next chapter. Upon returning from the show it will be important to complete your show budget (including actual cost figures to compare with your estimates), audit invoices, and to gather post-show evaluations and write up a post-show report.

Chapter 11: You are here:

	1 Mo.	On-Site	Post-Show
Planning			
Goal-Setting			
Budgeting			Audit invoices and prepare final budget
Promotions	Cross-check all promotions needs		
Product Demos			
Exhibits	Portable exhibit preview		
Installation	Double-check installation plans	Managing on-site installation	
Staffing	Prepare orientation meeting contents		
Inquiry Processing			
Measuring Results			Report on show results

11
After the Show

A 1986 Trade Show Bureau Study indicates no less than 22 different performance measures that exhibitors use to evaluate their success at trade shows. They range from the number of qualified leads to something as nebulous as "Evaluation of Exhibit Attributes."(1) This comprehensive listing however is not a testimony to the efficiency and expertise with which trade show performance is being evaluated. It instead points to the frustration on the part of exhibitors in doing so. No established system of measurement exists, and among those that do, exhibitors continually struggle with refining the measure to find a standard.

Yet post-show performance measures are increasingly important. "What are we getting for the money we're spending on this show" seems to echo down the halls of large and small companies alike as profit margins decrease, competition heats up, and allocation of resources is carefully scrutinized.

While post-trade-show evaluation has not been perfected to a science, several useful and valuable measures are available to shed an objective light on the value of the show. Here you'll see how to finalize your show budget as a foundation for making return-on-investment calculations. And then review a variety of typical performance reports used by exhibitors to stay on top of show participation results.

In this chapter you'll see how to:

1. AUDIT INVOICES: A checklist of items to review for miscalculations and overcharges.

2. FINALIZE THE SHOW BUDGET: Nine checkpoints for finalizing the post-show budget.

3. REPORT ON SHOW RESULTS: Sample evaluation tools, preparing the summary report, and who should receive the summary report.

HOW TO AUDIT SHOW INVOICES

A story was reported in *Exhibitor Magazine* years ago about an exhibitor with a large installation who noticed he had been billed on his drayage invoice for one additional *entire van load* of materials more than he had actually had delivered at the show. Catching this error on the invoice saved him 15% of his total freight bill.(2)

Auditing invoices is a straightforward, no-nonsense money saver that many exhibitors simply overlook. Unfortunately, invoices come in at their own pace. Some must be handled right at the show sight. Others dribble in after the show. So there is never a time when you can sit down for a morning and audit all of the invoices and tie up the exhibit budget in a tidy package. But taking a few moments to review them and check for errors *as they come in* can realize a return on that time investment by finding just one or two overcharges. Use the checklist in Exhibit 11-1 as a reminder of items to review for each invoice.

As you are auditing invoices, begin to complete the show budget by filling in the actual figures.

FINALIZING THE SHOW BUDGET

The Value of a Complete Final Budget

It is the rare manager who demands justifications of budgets immediately following the show. It's not until resources are allocated for the next show that budgets come under painful scrutiny. But remember, if you are planning for shows on an efficient timeframe, it is almost time to prepare a working budget estimate for participating in this show next year. Therefore, taking the time to finalize the show budget and record all of the actual expenditures has a few advantages.

- The final show budget drives Return-On-Investment Calculations. Any return-on-investment calculation you want to make in evaluating this show relies on an accurate record of the investment made. Cost per lead, cost per sale, cost per contact . . . all measures rely on the final budget.
- The final show budget helps to justify show costs. A $100,000 lump sum show budget can appear astronomical to skeptics questioning the costs. But itemized breakdowns of where the money was spent paint a very realistic picture when doing battle for allocations.
- The final show budget helps to plan for next year. This is the time to establish a preliminary budget for next year, and realistic budgets from this year's show will simplify that process exponentially. Adjust for changes in strategies, changes in location (for example union wages differ in different cities and may affect your installation costs), and for inflation, and you have a good working idea for next year's budget requirements.

Use the final budget worksheet in Exhibit 11-2 (which you should have in your Operational Plan for this show from Chapter 4), and the following nine steps, to complete the show budget.

Exhibit 11-1 Invoice Audit Checklist

Exhibit/ Handling	Transpor- tation	Drayage	Show Labor	Misc. Services
√ On a new exhibit cross-check your itemized bid with your invoice. At some firms they are the same format. √ Account for any additions or deletions from the original bid (cross-check with worksheet in your show plan). √ Double-check handling charges (warehous-ing and outbound/ inbound prep). √ Cross-check any additional services such as installation supervision, rush charges, etc. with pre-established estimates.	√ Review list on bill of lading for accuracy. √ Check to assure that weight and load/ unload points are accurate. √ Cross-check charges for additional pick-ups or deliveries with estimates. √ Check on any additional fees for insurance coverage to assure you had agreed on them previously.	√ Check that the shipment weight charges are accurate. √ Review the itemized bill of lading to assure it matches your itemized inventory. √ Double-check any extra deliveries you are being billed for to assure they were made. √ Compare inbound and outbound rates, checking for any dis-crepancies. (If you are charged more for outbound than inbound without any additions to your ship-ment, check into it.)	√ Are the hours accurate to your record of the set-up? √ Is the no. of workers you are being charged for the same no. you used? √ Are you only being charged for the union services you used? (This is especially important in those cities where several unions have jurisdiction over set-up.) √ Are all overtime charges legitimate? √ Are you paying a supervision fee, and is it accurate?	√ Double-check quantities for which you are being charged. For example: * Size and type of carpet if you rented carpet. * No. of security guards and their hourly rates if you used security. * Number of days and types of service for booth cleaning. √ Were there any services that were not delivered or were cancelled for which you are being charged?

Exhibit 11-2 Budget Worksheet

	Budget Item	Cost/per	Needed	Estimate	Actual

Charge-Back

Exhibit Structure

☐ _____ _____ _____ _____ _____
☐ _____ _____ _____ _____ _____
☐ _____ _____ _____ _____ _____
☐ _____ _____ _____ _____ _____
☐ _____ _____ _____ _____ _____
☐ _____ _____ _____ _____ _____

Set-Up Services

☐ _____ _____ _____ _____ _____
☐ _____ _____ _____ _____ _____
☐ _____ _____ _____ _____ _____
☐ _____ _____ _____ _____ _____
☐ _____ _____ _____ _____ _____
☐ _____ _____ _____ _____ _____
☐ _____ _____ _____ _____ _____
☐ _____ _____ _____ _____ _____
☐ _____ _____ _____ _____ _____
☐ _____ _____ _____ _____ _____

Promotions

☐ _____ _____ _____ _____ _____
☐ _____ _____ _____ _____ _____
☐ _____ _____ _____ _____ _____
☐ _____ _____ _____ _____ _____
☐ _____ _____ _____ _____ _____
☐ _____ _____ _____ _____ _____

Staff

☐ _____ _____ _____ _____ _____
☐ _____ _____ _____ _____ _____
☐ _____ _____ _____ _____ _____
☐ _____ _____ _____ _____ _____
☐ _____ _____ _____ _____ _____
☐ _____ _____ _____ _____ _____
☐ _____ _____ _____ _____ _____
☐ _____ _____ _____ _____ _____
☐ _____ _____ _____ _____ _____

Charge-Back	Budget Item	Cost/per	Needed	Estimate	Actual
	Hospitality				
☐	_____	_____	_____	_____	_____
☐	_____	_____	_____	_____	_____
☐	_____	_____	_____	_____	_____
☐	_____	_____	_____	_____	_____
☐	_____	_____	_____	_____	_____
☐	_____	_____	_____	_____	_____
☐	_____	_____	_____	_____	_____

Miscellaneous (Use for post-show final budget)

_____	_____	_____	_____	_____
_____	_____	_____	_____	_____
_____	_____	_____	_____	_____
_____	_____	_____	_____	_____
_____	_____	_____	_____	_____
_____	_____	_____	_____	_____
_____	_____	_____	_____	_____

TOTALS   _____ _____

Percent
change (+/−) _____

Notes on special circumstances (Use for post-show final budget)

_____
_____
_____
_____
_____

Budget Summary (Use for post-show final budget)

_____
_____
_____
_____
_____
_____
_____
_____
_____

Nine Steps to Completing the Final Budget

- Step #1. Complete the actual costs under the "actual" column as the invoices come in.
- Step #2. Flag major differences between estimates and actual costs (either higher or lower) by highlighting them with a marker or circling them with a red pen. It will be important for future planning to note whether those differences were a fluke that didn't represent a typical situation (for example high labor costs because set-up problems forced a great deal of overtime) or whether this difference should be anticipated for future show planning.
- Step #3. Itemize unaccounted-for miscellaneous expenses in the designated columns. This will help to identify items that might be necessary to include when planning for the following year.
- Step #4. Add major expenditures that were last-minute additions under the miscellaneous column. (For example, last-minute air freight, extra drayage shipments because of late literature, on-site problem solving.)
- Step #5. Use the "special circumstances" area on your budget worksheet to note extenuating circumstances that might have caused significant increases in the budget. (This explanation can be especially important if the budget is challenged. You will want to be able to outline in detail the unforeseeable problem that forced this increase.)
- Step #6. Flag any budgetary items that were charged back to another group. Use the boxes in the left column to check off those items that will be charged back. For example you might charge back expenses to sales, product groups, or marketing groups within company divisions. You can write in the group on the left side of the box. This is also a good time to route the invoices for those charges.
- Step #7. Calculate the actual total and compare with the estimate total (if you hadn't already done so). Calculate the percent increase or decrease of the actual total as it compares to the estimate.
- Step #8. Calculate "lost opportunity costs." This is optional, but if you anticipate being challenged by sales managers who don't want to take their people out of the field to work at shows, you can calculate in opportunity costs to see if they justify doing so. For example, once you have your total budget figure, calculate the daily cost of a sales representative (salary, bonuses, and benefits). Multiply it by the number of days they worked at the show and add that into your total before calculating ROI measures. If they still show a reasonable return on investment you have further information to justify ongoing support. Even if the figures aren't spectacular, you still have a realistic picture of the total cost to the company.
- Step #9. Write a budget summary. In the space provided on your worksheet summarize the key points. A sample budget summary might read as follows:

"The total budget estimate for this show was $59,600, and actuals came in at $65,769.24. The final budget was about 10% over estimates. The bulk of that 10% was incurred because of late shipments due to problems in getting the product and literature on time. (See notes on special circumstances.) There was also a slight overage in the labor area, which does not appear to be an exception and should be adjusted for the next show where this exhibit structure will be used."

File the budget summary in your Show Plan notebook under the Operational Plan for this show.

HOW TO MEASURE AND MANAGE SHOW RESULTS

An Introduction to Evaluation Methods

In Chapter 2 you did some work on establishing realistic, measurable show goals. You saw a general review of categories of measures you could use to evaluate your performance at a show. A more detailed list of methods that exhibit managers use to measure their performance follows. It may appear obvious, but the important factor in selecting the evaluation tools is using only those that help to identify how well you've reached established goals.

The lion's share of performance measures can be facilitated one of three ways:

- **Lead tracking** will help you to identify the number of qualified leads, the number of visitors to your exhibit who requested follow-up, the number of inquiries for information, the number of booth visitors who requested follow-up, evaluation of booth personnel, profile of booth visitors, cost per qualified lead, and the remaining "cost per" measures.

  Note: Lead tracking systems only provide information on those visitors who stopped in your exhibit and requested follow-up. This may not be reflective of the total show audience. For information and statistics on the entire show audience you need to go to a survey of the attendees.

- **Formal surveys** customized to your needs will help evaluate total traffic to your exhibit (as opposed to just those who requested follow-up), exhibit attributes, show attendance, audience demographics and quality, attitudes of visitors, reaction of attendees, awareness, memorability, and comparisons with your competitors at the show.

- **Internal feedback** from company representatives in attendance at the show can provide an evaluation of exhibit attributes, attitudes of booth visitors, activity at competitors' exhibits, reactions of attendees, along with their own reactions to the show.

In reporting on show results, cull the key points from each evaluation tool used that summarize and illustrate the performance. What follows is a review of detailed information that can be gathered from the most commonly used evaluating methods, and guidelines on preparing and distributing the post-show summary.

Six Types of Computerized Lead Tracking Reports

To generate these types of composite reports, you must have set up a lead tracking system in advance. For more information on creating a lead tracking system see Chapter 5, Section IV, "How to Plan for Inquiry Processing," and Chapter 13, "Managing Lead Processing and Tracking." For each of the six following types of reports, you will see an example of that report with ideas on how it can be used to evaluate the show.

1. Report on Geographic Distribution of Leads

Example: Each lead card will include the complete address and phone number of the attendee. Therefore geographic sorts can be done based on any of that information: by zip code, by state, by city, by area code. The following example shows a format for a report on geographic distribution by state.

Glassware Expo   Geographic
June 29–July 1
Long Beach Convention Center

Arizona (10)

John Doe	Sam Smith	Mary Jones
Owner	Buyer	Owner
Pool City	Glasses Unlimited	Jones Rest. Supply
100 Water Way	58 S. Flower	6634 First St.
Scottsdale, AZ 00000	Phoenix, AZ 00000	Phoenix, AZ 00000
123/456-7890	123/098-7654	123/890-1234

Use this report to:

- Distribute leads to the field if sales regions are divided geographically.
- Track results on leads after they are distributed.
- Evaluate the geographic distribution of interest.
- Check the "regional" nature of the show audience.

2. Report on Product Interest Categories

Example: As with most of these reports, you can typically generate a synopsis of totals for each category or actual listings for each category.

The report can list product categories across the top with name and address listings beneath each (illustrated here), or for several products, a separate listing for each product (as with the states in a geographic sort).

Glassware Expo June 29–July 1 Long Beach Convention Center	Product Interest	
Unbreakables (125)	Luxury Line (55)	Custom (150)
John Doe Owner Pool City	Sam Smith Buyer Glassware Unlimited	Mary Jones Owner Jones Rest. Supply

Use this report to:

- Distribute leads if your sales force is organized by product line.
- Inform marketing management of product interest trends.
- Plan for product displays for future attendance at this show.

3. Report on Staffer Performance

Example: When staffers initial or sign the leads they generate, you can include a category for their names on the computer data base. Then you can sort by staffer for sheer numbers, or use multiple sorts to evaluate by lead quality. The examples here show both a summary by staffer and a complete listing with totals by staffer.

Glassware Expo June 29–July 1 Long Beach Convention Center	Staffer Summary		
	Monday	Tuesday	Wednesday
Eric Martin	65	32	48
Sharon Bold	33	105	52
John Samson	42	65	36

```
Glassware Expo                    Staffer
June 29–July 1                    Listing
Long Beach Convention Center

Eric Martin
Total (145)

John Doe          Don Stanford        Sara Styles
Owner             Buyer               Buyer
Pool City         Glass Boutique      Fellows Department
100 Water Way     425 5th Ave.        245 Main Street
Scottsdale, AZ    New York, NY        Peoria, IL 00000
  00000             00000             345/678-9012
123/456-7890      234/567-8901
```

Use the reports to:

- Apprise sales management of staffer performance.
- Select top staffers for future shows.
- Keep records for incentives or reward programs.
- Distribute leads when each staffer follows up on leads they generate.

4. Reports on Exhibit Visitor Profiles

Example: The information gathered on the lead card will generate this report. In Chapter 6 you saw a sample lead card for our glassware company. On that card, staffers collected information on whether the visitors were retailers, distributors, or wholesalers (which pertained to the glassware manufacturer). Therefore, our visitor profile will be broken out by those categories. You might choose to make your information gathering a bit more specific, looking for such information as product application, job title, or function depending on your needs. The more specific your lead card is, the more specific your reports can be. The example here shows a listing sorted by profile category.

```
Glassware Expo                    Visitor Profile
June 29–July 1
Long Beach Convention Center

Retail            Distributor         Wholesale
(230)             (465)               (78)

Sam Smith         Mary Jones          Bob French
Buyer             Owner               Owner
Glasses Unlimited Jones Rest. Supply  Glass Imports
```

Use this report to:

- Evaluate the quality of your show leads.
- Evaluate your success at reaching your target audience.

5. Report on Lead Quality Profiles

Many exhibitors like to rate the quality of their leads in terms of timing or purchase potential. The "A,B,C" lead rating is commonly used on lead cards to separate hot leads (A's) from leads with a high level of interest but longer term buying plans (B's) from people just requesting information or literature with no follow-up sales call required (C's). You, of course, can define the letters in whatever way is most appropriate to your sales cycle. The following example shows a listing by quality rating.

Glassware Expo   Quality Rating
June 29–July 1
Long Beach Convention Center

"A" Leads
(198)

Mary Jones	Bob French	Sara Styles
Owner	Owner	Buyer
Jones Rest. Supply	Glass Imports	Fellows Department
6634 First St.	56 Figueroa	6634 First St.
Phoenix, AZ 00000	Compton, CA	Peoria, IL 00000
123/890-1234	00000	345/678-9012
	234/567-8901	

Use this report to:

- Identify the quality of leads generated at the show.
- Prioritize leads for follow-up.

6. Reports Using Combined Sorts

Example: You can make reports much more sophisticated once you begin combining sorts. For example, you might sort by lead rating and geographic territory to provide the sales reps a list of their leads already sorted by follow-up priority. The combinations are only limited by the input and sort capacity of the computer software used. Most of these sorts can be done on off-the-shelf software for personal computers (given that the lead numbers are not too large).

```
┌──────────────────────────────────────────────────────────────┐
│                                                                │
│   Glassware Expo              Geogr. Distribution              │
│   June 29–July 1              and Quality                      │
│   Long Beach Convention Center                                 │
│                                                                │
│   Arizona (10)                                                 │
│                                                                │
│   A(2)                B(6)                  C(2)               │
│                                                                │
│   Sam Smith           John Doe              Mary Jones         │
│   Buyer               Owner                 Owner              │
│   Glasses Unlimited   Pool City             Jones Rest. Supply │
│   58 S. Flower        100 Water Way         6634 First St.     │
│   Phoenix, AZ 00000   Scottsdale, AZ        Phoenix, AZ        │
│                       00000                 00000              │
```

Use these reports to:

- Distribute leads by priority.
- Identify quality of leads by staffer.
- Identify product interest by geographic category.
- Further refine your information gathering.

In summary, you can generate nearly any type of report that you will find useful, just by setting up your inquiry processing system, and creating the lead card accordingly. But don't go overboard with statistics. Select the types of reports that will be most useful in evaluating and justifying show participation.

Two Types of External Performance Reports

The Post-Show Survey. This can be conducted by your own staff or telemarketing department if you have the expertise and resources to create and facilitate the surveys. Or you can use an outside research firm to conduct and evaluate the surveys for you.

Any survey, whether conducted internally or by an outside firm, should be customized to gather the specific information you need. A typical post-show report conducted by Exhibit Surveys, Inc., a firm that specializes in trade show research, can provide the following types of information on show performance.

- **Potential Audience.** The percentage of the total show audience who have an interest in your products and a good chance of visiting your exhibit.
- **Product Interest.** The percentage of show attendees that had an interest in the products or services you displayed.

- **Purchase Plans.** The percentage of attendees planning to purchase your products.
- **Buying Influence.** The percentage of attendees who have a role in purchasing your products.
- **Memorability.** The percentage of attendees who remembered visiting your exhibit.
- **Exhibit Attraction.** How well your exhibit drew your potential audience at the show.
- **Exhibit Efficiency.** How many of the visitors that your exhibit drew actually talked to a staffer in your exhibit.
- **Staff Performance.** How visitors rate the helpfulness of your exhibit staffers.
- **Sales Call Percentages.** The percentage of your visitors called on by a salesperson from your company within the past year. This can be evaluated to determine the percentage of new personal contacts being made.
- **Post-Show Calling.** The percentage of your visitors called on by a salesperson from your company within a given time after the show.
- **Image Perceptions.** How the attendees perceive your company or specific products.
- **Comparisons with Competitors.** Comparing booth traffic, memorability, and perceptions with those for your competition provides a point of reference for your performance scores.

These types of statistics are useful not only for justifying, but also for refining show participation. For example, a report on the percentage of visitors interested in specific products could guide you in selecting products to display at the next show, and in allocating booth space to different product categories. A reading on potential audience will be a helpful tool in setting goals for show participation.

The second type of post-show evaluation is the *staffer evaluation*. These are really at-show evaluations because they must be conducted on-site. Like the post-show surveys, the staffer evaluation can also be conducted by a company representative or by an outside firm. Where post-show surveys identify the symptoms (for example, not reaching your potential audience), staffer evaluations get closer to the disease (identifying where staffers lack skills in engaging exhibit visitors in conversation, or qualifying them to uncover needs).

To conduct the staffer evaluation, a fairly objective observer will need to spend about four hours watching the exhibit personnel and noting their skills at welcoming visitors, qualifying them to uncover needs, their use of basic booth etiquette and nonverbal communication, and their presentation skills.

Professionals who do this can identify a host of subtleties that are at the heart of poor performance in the exhibit. At Communique Exhibitor Education, where performance reports are part of their show training packages, trainers observe behaviors and document them with photographs in a post-show evaluation report. Key points can be culled from this report to include in the post-show summary.

Another valuable type of evaluation is often overlooked: *internal evaluations* or feedback evaluations from company representatives who worked in the exhibit. This type of evaluation is easily facilitated by sending out short evaluation forms to exhibit staffers to get their reactions to the show. This adds another dimension to understanding why facets of the program might not be working as intended. For example, a post-show survey might identify that staffers are only considered fairly helpful by show visitors. The staffer evaluation report might indicate that they are not doing a very good job at product presentations. But the staffers might tell you that the products kept breaking down, and they finally just gave up trying to present them.

Exhibit 11-4 is a sample Post-Show Survey that you can send to staffers to solicit their feedback. (See page 317.)

Because the human element is such a strong factor at a trade show, all three levels of evaluation—statistical evaluations, judgment observations, and feedback—are important contributions to an overall view of the show's success.

How to Select and Interpret Data for the Post-Show Report

Preparing the post-show report requires *interpreting* and consolidating all of the results and feedback on the show. These need to be presented in a format that will provide a quick overview for both management, and for yourself, as you use the summary to prepare the show for the following year. Avoid just lumping all of your reports together and calling it the post-show report. Here's some guidelines for synthesizing the information and creating a standard post-show report.

To put the post-show report together, review each evaluation you have on the show, and draw out only the most relevant performance information. The following lists identify key pieces of data to gather from each type of report, with periodic notes on how that data can be synthesized.

- From the show plan:
  * Review show goals
- From the post-show budget:
  * total show costs
  * percentage over or under budget estimate and allocation
  * budget summary

Exhibit 11-3   Internal Show Evaluation Survey

Post-Show Evaluation Survey

Show: _____   Dates: _____

Thank you for your participation in making this trade show a success. We are now evaluating the value of this show and would appreciate your input in the following areas.

1. How would you rate the quality of the visitors to our exhibit?
   - ☐ Excellent   Please explain: _____
   - ☐ Good   _____
   - ☐ Fair   _____
   - ☐ Poor   _____

2. How would you rate the exhibit as a selling environment?
   - ☐ Excellent   Please explain: _____
   - ☐ Good   _____
   - ☐ Fair   _____
   - ☐ Poor   _____

3. In which products did you find the visitors most interested?

   _____
   _____
   _____
   _____

4. Please give us your suggestings for improving corporate participation in this show? _____

   _____
   _____
   _____

5. Would you recommend participating again? ☐ Yes   ☐ No

- From the lead tracking reports:
  * total number of leads generated
  * geographic area from which the most/least leads were generated
  * products with most/least interest among visitors to your booth

- Synthesis:
  * From the budget totals and lead totals, calculate the cost per lead
  * Compare the cost per lead for this show with that of previous years
  * Determine whether your visitors represented one region of the country more than others and how that relates to previous years and show location

  Note: When you are evaluating leads, consider some variables that may affect fluctuations in lead counts. For example, show variables such as attendance, location, or industry strength in specific regions can all affect leads generated in your exhibit. Variables in your exhibit can affect lead counts as well. For example the number of staffers on duty, attention-getting techniques you are using, the location of the booth in the exhibit hall (if you get stuck in a poor location, lead counts could drop significantly). When you see dramatic changes in leads, evaluate these variables to consider how they might have impacted lead counts.

- From the External Evaluations
  * Exhibit performance (how well your exhibit drew your target audience)
  * Personnel performance
  * Potential audience for the show
  * Product interest statistics
  * Statistics on image or perception changes
  * Key recommendations from staffer evaluations
  * Comparisons with your competitors

  Synthesis: Compare the product interests from the post-show surveys with those in your lead tracking reports for similarities and differences. Compare your potential audience as identified by the surveys, with the actual number of leads you generated from the show. If there are major discrepancies, consider additional factors that might have affected the number of leads generated, such as staffer performance.

These are just samples, and the more you work with your own shows, the more you will know the pertinent data to collect and areas of observation to synthesize for the report. With that done, the following outline will help to organize the information.

Exhibit 11-4

POST-SHOW REPORT

Show Name:_____ Show Dates:_____

Show Location:_____

I. Goals/Results Synopsis

In chart format, review and list show goals and related results

SHOW GOALS   SHOW RESULTS
_____

II. Return on Investment
  A. Report on the budget
  B. "Cost per" analysis
     (Cost per lead, per contact, etc.)
  C. Comparison to previous shows

III. Strengths and Weaknesses

Again, in chart format, summarize the remaining performance evaluations under strengths and weaknesses. (For example, staffers, exhibit structure, promotion, presentation, etc.) It is not necessary to review each component of your show program, only those which require special mention because they were extremely strong, or in need of improvement.

STRENGTHS   WEAKNESSES
_____

IV. Recommendations
  A. Recommendations on whether to attend in the future
  B. Budget allocation changes recommended
  C. Strategy changes recommended
     (Goals, target audience, products displayed)
  D. Program changes recommended
     (Exhibit, staffers, promotions, presentations, etc.)

Conclusion to Section I

Planning strategy and tactics, implementing the program, and evaluating results—this section of the book walked you through the three basic components of using trade shows successfully as a sales and marketing tool. Learning to use this system is like learning any system for the first time; it appears complex and feels unmanageable. But just like learning a new software program, or taking a course in auto mechanics, after using the system a few times it begins to make sense. After using it five or six times, it almost becomes second nature. And after you've successfully managed the logistics of a year's worth of your company's trade shows you'll have a fairly predictable system down. Instead of saying, "How am I ever going to get all of this done?" you will find yourself saying "How can we do this better?"

Improving on the existing program, managing the function to make it more efficient, successful, and, yes, even profitable, is what the next section of this book is about. You will learn how to manage components of your program, from creating and structuring a trade show department within your company to gaining ongoing management support for the program. It requires a shift in your mindset as well. You will move from "coordinator," keeping the wheels turning and putting out fires, to "manager," planning, evaluating, and managing the program.

Frankly, the managing side is tougher, because it often requires implementing change. You see something that could be improved, and you have to *justify* the change that improvement will take to people who *like* the status quo. It also requires vision. You have to get outside of the day-to-day workings periodically to reflect on the tasks, then the function, as they relate to corporate goals and direction. And, of course, you have to be willing to risk being wrong. The following section is designed to provide some direction on how to make calculated improvements that will reduce the risk, improve performance, and hopefully, make your work more fulfilling, and your job a bit easier.

II

MANAGING THE
EXHIBITS DEPARTMENT

12

Building the Exhibits Department

Section I of this book was about coordinating. It guided you through the steps of a trade show strategy. And that is as far as many companies go with their trade show programs today. As each show arises, management finds someone who can handle the logistics of making the event happen. However, if your company is going to use trade shows successfully as a marketing medium, it will be essential to have someone in place who does more than coordinate show details. The company needs a designated person to *manage* the company's trade show efforts.

It is the responsibility of the trade show manager to look for ways to make the show program more efficient, and useful. That person deals with departmental budgets instead of just show budgets; multi-show lead tracking systems instead of just show-by-show inquiry processing; managing an exhibit staff and a league of vendors. This chapter will guide you through some of the preliminary decisions required to create and manage such a department. Here you will see:

1. MANAGEMENT: An introduction to management.
2. DEPARTMENTAL STAFFING: Setting task goals and finding the right people to staff the department.
3. ACCOUNTABILITY ISSUES: Solutions to the sales vs. marketing tug of war.
4. STRUCTURE: How to position the department within the organization with typical lines of reporting.
5. BUDGETING: Guidelines for determining the department's budget requirements.

INTRODUCTION TO MANAGEMENT

Whether your trade show program includes just two or three shows a year or hundreds, the entire program must be managed to be effective. If you have little knowledge of the basic theories of management, this section will introduce you to common sense management concepts as they relate to the trade show function. If you are versed in management theory and experience, this section will help you see how to interpret those skills for the trade show or exhibits department.

Functions of the Trade Show Manager

It is typically agreed that a manager's functions fall into four categories: planning, organizing, directing, and controlling.(1) The chart in Exhibit 12-1 categorizes specific areas of exhibits management as they fit within the functions.

Create your own chart to get a quick snapshot of your management functions. Begin by taking a few minutes to brainstorm all of the responsibilities in your job. Your list might include items such as: set budgets, select shows, process leads, order show literature, or oversee new exhibit design/construction. List not just the things you do directly, but everything for which you are responsible whether you actually carry out the task or not. Then begin to categorize them into each column. The completed list will identify and organize your function requirements.

Use this as a tool to evaluate where you are at vs. where you would like to be. If you are weighted heavily in organizing and only slightly in planning, consider whether planning is an area where you would like to gain more responsibility. What would it take to do so? Will you have to reduce your involvement in one of the other functions to allow you the proper balance to incorporate more planning?

STAFFING THE EXHIBITS DEPARTMENT

How to Define Essential Task Responsibilities

Along with your functions as a manager (planning, organizing, directing, and controlling), it will be important to also review the areas that need to be managed. Management areas also typically fall into four categories. The chart in Exhibit 12-2 outlines where trade show tasks fall within those four areas.

In areas of management, as well, not all managers have an equal balance of functions under their jurisdiction. For example, if you have a large show program with a small staff (unfortunately, typically the case) you probably spend the bulk of your time managing materials and finances (represented by quadrant #1 in Exhibit 12-3). The dominant areas are usually a function of the size of your program (the number of shows in which you participate) and the size of your department (the number of staff available to you). The grid in Exhibit 12-3 provides a framework to plot your current situation, and where you would like the program to be as you plan for the future.

Exhibit 12-1 Functions of the Trade Show Manager

Plan	Organize	Direct	Control
• *Strategic Planning.* The trade show manager is responsible for creating a strategic plan that outlines the general objectives of trade show participation as they relate to long- and short-term corporate objectives	• *Shows.* The exhibits manager organizes participation details on a show-by-show basis.	• *Staff.* The exhibits manager delegates tasks to staff and assures they are being accomplished.	• *Budgets.* The exhibits manager is responsible for keeping show and departmental programs within budget.
• *Operational Planning.* The trade show manager must create a plan for each show setting goals and tactics for participation in that particular show.	• *Staff.* The exhibits manager organizes the staff to most efficiently accomplish all tasks.	• *Vendors.* The exhibits manager constantly communicates expectations and needs with vendors.	• *Resources.* The exhibits manager also controls exhibit properties, graphics, support materials such as giveaways, display products, literature, and other resources required for shows.
• *Departmental Planning.* The trade show manager must plan for the growth of his or her department and its contribution to corporate objectives.	• *Vendors.* The exhibits manager organizes a team of vendors supplying a variety of services.	• *Company Participants.* The exhibits manager communicates needs and expectations to other departments within the company (R&D, for example when a new product will be introduced, or advertising for input on a show promotion campaign or sales management to assign staffers.)	• *Exhibit Staff.* Although staffers are often from other divisions, at shows they are under the control of the exhibits manager.
• *Personal Planning.* The trade show manager must also plan for individual career growth.	• *Administration.* The exhibits manager organizes administrative details such as order processing, budgeting, etc.		• *Evaluations.* The exhibits manager justifies his or her programs through regular show evaluations.
	• *Departmental Organization.* The exhibits manager organizes the functions and day-to-day operations of the trade show department.		

Exhibit 12-2

Management Area	Related trade show functions
Information	Selecting shows, ordering services, communicating goals, lead tracking, educating/training exhibit staff, briefing management.
People	Delegating responsibilities, working with vendors, working with show management, motivating departmental and show staff.
Finances	Establishing budgets, obtaining resources, allocating resources, paying/processing invoices, justifying budgets, controlling costs.
Materials	Producing exhibits, graphics, live presentations, managing structure and product inventories, warehousing, and shipping.

Exhibit 12-3

Program Size (# shows)

#1 Materials and finances	#2 People and Information
#4 Materials	#3 People

Department size (# staff)

As you can see, if you manage a large program with multiple staff your primary areas of management are people and information (quadrant #2). In the rare case that you should have a small program (just a few shows) and a large staff, you probably spend the majority of your time managing people (quadrant #3). With a smaller program and small staff, you probably spend the majority of your time managing materials (the exhibit properties and product displays) (quadrant #4). Obviously, if you have the disadvantage of a small staff, you will need to be more creative to work in the important function of information management.

If you are fortunate enough to hire staff for your department, this tool can be helpful in identifying tasks that you can delegate. For example you might discover that you are heavily weighted in the area of materials management, and you would like to hire someone to take on a group of those tasks. To find the best person, consider what skills are used most in managing this function: organization of properties and schedules, communication with vendors, and delegation of tasks to vendors. Look for someone with strengths in these skill areas.

Skills to Look for in the Exhibits Department Staff

The skills set for various tasks within exhibits management varies a bit. Review your own skills as they relate to various areas of the function and consider how you might build on your strengths and improve on weak areas. Hiring staff people provides an opportunity to balance your strengths and weaknesses with those of your support staff so it will be useful to evaluate their strengths and weaknesses in each of these areas.

To manage people, a successful manager must be skilled in:

- Written communications
- Interpersonal communications
- Delegating

To manage information, a successful manager must be skilled in:

- Data processing
- Data interpretation

To manage finances, a successful manager must be skilled in:

- Organization
- Goal-setting
- Decision-making

To manage materials, a successful manager must be skilled in:

- Organization
- Goal-setting
- Delegating
- Communicating

When selecting a manager for the position, or starting out on the management of a new department, be careful not to rely too heavily on a limited skills set. For example, people frequently view exhibits management as managing materials and put heavy weight on those skills. But with this aspect of management as well, a balance among all of the management skills is essential for the exhibits department to be more than just a "show mill" pumping out one show after another with little direction or results.

POSITIONING THE DEPARTMENT WITHIN THE ORGANIZATION

The Sales vs. Marketing "Tug of War"

In the question of where the responsibilities for trade shows should fall within an organization, the choices typically boil down to sales or marketing. Some companies consider it a sales function since its primary purpose is to generate sales leads. Others see it as a marketing function, since many of the functions involved in trade show planning are marketing- or marketing-communications-oriented (selecting shows, creating promotions, creating the exhibit, etc.).

Over the past five years there has been a dramatic shift in emphasis from sales to marketing as the place where trade shows are managed. In a 1982 study conducted by the Trade Show Bureau, 36% of the companies surveyed reported that the sales department is responsible for the trade show function within the organization. Only 8% of the companies reported the trade show function to be the responsibility of the marketing department. Yet in the same survey, conducted in 1987, only 20% said it was the responsibility of sales while 41% said responsibility for the exhibits function fell under marketing.(2)

Regardless of where the bulk of responsibility falls, there is a gap in the lines of communication between the two groups common to most companies that significantly affects trade show performance. Exhibit 12-4 illustrates the gap.

Generally, a lack of communication between these two groups sabotages the efforts of either group if they are responsible for the show. For example, if marketing has primary responsibility, but does not communicate the show strategy to the sales staff effectively, the staff (the key to making the strategy work) is not participating fully in making the show

Exhibit 12–4

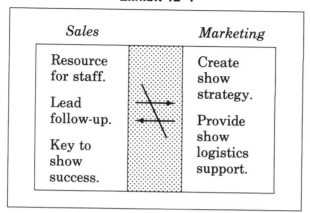

successful. By contrast, when the primary responsibility lies in the sales department and they go to the marketing group only for logistical support, it results in a strategy that lacks cohesion with other marketing communications efforts (at best . . . at worst it results in no strategy at all).

To further exacerbate the problem, the exhibits manager who is often held accountable for return to the trade show investment has no authority over the sales department to hold them accountable for converting leads generated at shows into sales. Nor does the exhibits manager have authority to motivate sales representatives assigned to exhibit duty to go out of their way to generate a good number of quality leads.

Therefore, it is essential to have a representative from each group (sales and marketing) responsible for their group's contribution to show participation. As a result, the goal in placing the department within the organization is to place accountability for the success of *all components of the program . . . both sales and marketing efforts . . .* and authority to get the job done under the same management, to the greatest degree possible.

The following three charts illustrate how the trade show function is positioned in a variety of different corporate structures. After each chart there is a description of where responsibility for certain show-related jobs fall, along with comments about their strengths and weaknesses. These illustrations do not represent any specific company, but serve as representative samples.

Chart #1: Company Organized by Function

- **Strategic Planning** is done by the trade show manager, with support and sign-off by both the marketing communications manager and the sales manager.

- **Operational Planning** is done by the trade show manager with input and sign-off from the marketing communications manager.

- **Logistics** of show participation are managed by the trade show manager, with cooperation and support from sales, advertising, and public relations.
- **Staffing** is supplied by the sales manager. On-site meetings and accountability are managed by the trade show manager with visible support from the sales manager.
- **Lead Fulfillment/Tracking** is managed by the trade show manager
- **Lead Follow-Up and Results Reporting** is managed by the sales manager who supplies status reports to the trade show manager. This must be supported by the vice president of sales and marketing.
- **Accountability.** The trade show manager is accountable for budgets and logistics management. The marketing communications and sales managers are accountable for return on investment.

Advantages: The advantages to this structure are that all support and direction for the trade show program comes ultimately under the same person, the vice president of sales and marketing. Support from this person will drive the rest of the program. The sales department is held accountable for the results from the show, and also participates up front in setting sales objectives in the strategic plan and incorporating their goals into the planning process. The trade show manager works within his or her division (marketing communications) to coordinate support functions such as advertising and public relations.

Disadvantages: This structure relies on a great deal of communication and cooperation between sales and marketing communications. Budgets come from the marketing communications department, but sales is held accountable for sales results. When the vice president of sales and marketing is a strong and visible supporter of trade show participation, this structure incorporates both the responsibility and accountability at both the sales and marketing levels. But if that person is not a strong supporter of trade shows and accountability of sales, the sales department can be a weak link in the shows' cumulative success.

Chart 2: Company Organized by Product Divisions with Autonomous Trade Show Departments

- **Strategic planning** is done by the divisional marketing manager with input from the trade show manager and support from the corporate sales and marketing manager. This structure, by its nature, makes the process more complex, because rarely does a division operate in a vacuum. You might find overlaps of divisions at shows, so the big picture must come from a manager who oversees all divisions.
- **Operational planning** is done by the trade show manager with support from and sign-off by the divisional marketing manager. Here, too, the trade show manager will rely on support from the advertising and public relations managers within the divisions.

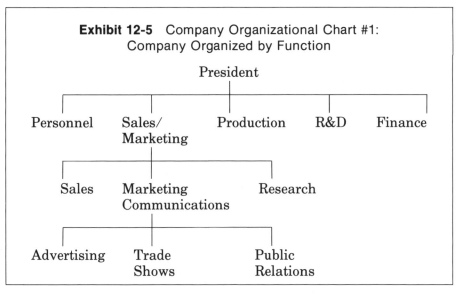

Exhibit 12-5 Company Organizational Chart #1:
Company Organized by Function

President

Personnel Sales/ Production R&D Finance
Marketing

Sales Marketing Research
Communications

Advertising Trade Public
Shows Relations

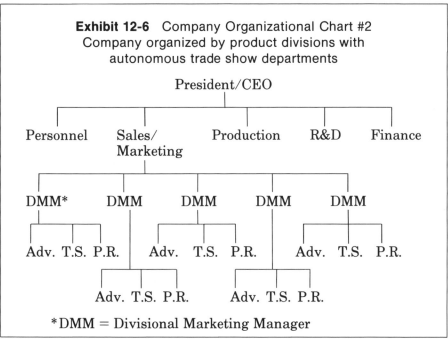

Exhibit 12-6 Company Organizational Chart #2
Company organized by product divisions with
autonomous trade show departments

President/CEO

Personnel Sales/ Production R&D Finance
Marketing

DMM* DMM DMM DMM DMM

Adv. T.S. P.R. Adv. T.S. P.R. Adv. T.S. P.R.

Adv. T.S. P.R. Adv. T.S. P.R.

*DMM = Divisional Marketing Manager

- **Logistics** are all managed by the trade show manager. Several trade show managers might be involved here, and in the case of several divisions participating in a show together, one division must be named as the lead division. (Typically it is the division with the most dominant product offerings among the show audience.) The lead division's trade show manager then manages the participation of all other divisions.

- **Staffing** is typically supplied from a balance of sales, R&D, and marketing people. This requires an interface with the divisional sales department and the divisional R&D (or corporate, if there isn't a department within the division).
- **Lead fulfillment and tracking** is managed by the division trade show manager, and each division is accountable for their own performance.
- **Lead follow-up** is managed by the divisional sales manager.

Advantages. For a multi-product company there are several advantages to this structure. Each division can select shows and create strategies for the shows they feel will be of value to them. They are not forced to participate in shows, but each division is also accountable for their performance at each show. This is especially advantageous when divisions maintain their own identity separate from the company. (When brand or product identity is stronger than corporate identity in the marketplace.)

Disadvantages. As you might imagine, there is a phenomenal duplicity of efforts in this structure. Each division has their own exhibit, graphics, lead processing function, and each handles shows in their own way. There is little to no corporate unity amongst show structures, promotional messages, or show performance. Each division also works with their own vendors. Several divisions could be participating separately in the same show. Companies who have tried to shift from autonomous structures to centralized structures find it difficult to get the buy-in of divisional trade show managers who have found a system that works for their division.

Chart #3: Company Organized by Divisions with Centralized Trade Show Department

- **Strategic planning** is done on two levels here. Overall strategic planning on the role of trade shows and the contribution they make to the organization is done by the corporate trade show manager. Here policies are set on considerations such as unified corporate image, graphics guidelines for exhibits, creating one unified exhibit structure for use by all divisions, procedures for show participation and ordering services, guidelines for setting show goals and measuring results, and support for all divisional show activities. On the second level, strategic planning is also conducted within the divisions by the divisional trade show or marketing manager. This person creates a strategic plan for their division's specific show participation. They may do this in conjunction with the divisional sales manager depending on their role in shows.
- **Operational planning** is all done at the divisional level. With the aid of guidelines set in place through corporate input, the divisional trade show or marketing manager makes all decisions about individual show strategies, from products displayed to budget allocations.

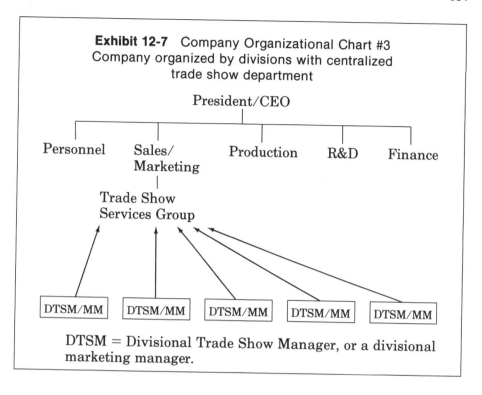

Exhibit 12-7 Company Organizational Chart #3
Company organized by divisions with centralized
trade show department

President/CEO

Personnel   Sales/   Production   R&D   Finance
            Marketing

Trade Show
Services Group

DTSM/MM   DTSM/MM   DTSM/MM   DTSM/MM   DTSM/MM

DTSM = Divisional Trade Show Manager, or a divisional
marketing manager.

- **Logistics** are all handled by the corporate trade show services department. Typically the divisional trade show or marketing manager orders the exhibit components, graphics, and services required from the corporate services department, which acts almost as an outside agency, billing out their services back to the divisions. The corporate trade show services group then manages all of the details from transportation to exhibit installation, to ordering premiums and lead cards.

- **Staffing** is managed by the divisional trade show or marketing manager in cooperation with the divisional sales manager. The trade show manager sends out pre-show memos and conducts the pre-show meeting, with input and support from the sales manager.

- **Lead fulfillment and tracking** can be handled in the divisional trade show or marketing department or at the corporate level. If a system is put into place at the corporate level to process all inquiries, it relieves the divisional trade show or marketing manager of this responsibility and provides continuity for how leads are handled throughout the company. When the responsibility is left to the divisional trade show managers, it also gives them more control over lead fulfillment and tracking.

- **Lead follow-up** is handled by the divisional sales manager. That person is responsible for distributing leads for follow-up, managing the tracking of leads, and reporting back to either the divisional or corporate trade show manager depending on where the lead processing function is handled. The divisional or corporate manager is responsible, in turn, for providing the sales manager with ongoing updates (quarterly, semi-annual, or annual) on sales generated from trade show leads.

Advantages. The primary advantages to this structure are unity and control. Guidelines for image, procedure, and participation are all provided by the corporate department, offering a consistent corporate image message in all trade show efforts. Much of the hassle of show participation on the logistics side is taken off the shoulders of the divisional managers, providing them more time to spend on strategic and operational planning, and managing their program.

This structure also provides economies of scale as all services and materials are purchased in one place. All services and materials are ordered and invoiced through the corporate department. Therefore they can take advantage of quantity orders and find multiple uses for tools and materials.

For example, a corporate trade show department could purchase a customized pre-show meeting leader's guide which could be used by all divisions, or purchase a quantity of portable exhibits at a discounted rate to be used by all divisions rather than have each division purchase these tools and materials independently.

Disadvantages. It is easy for divisions to feel their identity is lost to the corporate cause. Especially if a division has strong product or brand awareness with a particular show audience, it is important that enough flexibility is incorporated into exhibits and graphics guidelines to allow them to emphasize that recognized brand name.

A great deal of communication and people management is required on the part of the corporate trade show manager to keep all of the divisional managers informed. Some corporate managers hold regular quarterly or semi-annual meetings to discuss new procedures and guidelines, get feedback from the divisional managers, and even provide educational seminars on trade show management topics. And, most important, it requires cooperation and buy-in from divisional managers. They must believe that guidelines and policies will benefit, not detract, from their program. "Selling the program" becomes a primary job of the corporate trade show manager.

Also, depending on the size of the exhibits program, a separate set of procedures will need to be implemented for accounting and billing back services to divisions. This could require an additional full-time person.

If you have tried to evaluate your own corporate structure in light of these three examples, you have probably found that yours is a variation on these themes with components of several or all of them defining your structure. Weigh the disadvantages and advantages of each as they relate to your program to determine the best solution.

COMPONENTS OF THE DEPARTMENT BUDGET

In Chapter 2 you learned how to prepare working show budgets. Here you will see how to consider budgetary requirements beyond show-by-show budgets, for the company's total trade show participation. When it comes to establishing departmental budgets, there are very few guidelines in the trade show industry to follow. The Trade Show Bureau published a report in 1988 on corporate expenditures on trade shows. The report indicated that the average annual budget for trade shows was $212,600 in 1987. It also indicated that trade shows were allocated about 27% of the advertising and sales promotion budget.(3)

Smaller companies tended to allocate a greater portion of the sales and promotion budget to trade shows. Those companies with annual sales of up to $25 million allocate 21% of their sales and promotions budget to trade shows while those with revenues of over $100 million spend 13% of the sales and promotions budget on shows.(4)

While there is that slight bit of information on budget sizes and allocations, there is little to illustrate how that budget is spent. We know about the separate categories as they relate to specific shows (which was covered in Chapter 2), but not much more about other expenses incurred in the trade show department (such as staffing expense, education, exhibit properties management, and others). But if you are managing the department, chances are you must divide that pie into more slices than just individual show participation budgets. The following categories represent a composite of typical departmental expenditures for the exhibits or trade show department.

Departmental Staff. Does your departmental budget need to accommodate administrative personnel? Even at large corporations, division trade show departments typically have just two people, an exhibits manager and a coordinator or administrative support person. In many cases these people have additional responsibilities beyond just shows.

Those corporations with centralized trade show services departments often have larger support staffs, with clear divisions of responsibilities. One person, for example, handles ordering all show services; another manages invoices and payments, and yet another manages lead processing. Or each person is responsible for a specified group of shows. This, however, is the exception rather than the general rule.

Another consideration for departmental staff is continued education. Have you budgeted for seminars, books, publications, and courses for yourself and your staff?

Properties. In many cases new exhibit construction, warehousing, and handling can be budgeted on a show-by-show basis. But if components of the exhibit are used for corporate events, how is the handling and transportation budgeted? Where does the budget for warehousing between shows come from? What about insurance? Your exhibit property (and any product inventories you use) may be covered by your company insurance policy, but you might have to pay for a rider when those items travel. Does that come out of your budget? Do you have to pay for product inventories for display purposes? Also, budgeting for new exhibit properties can be considered a one-time capital investment and come out of the departmental budget rather than a show budget.

Program Development. Managing your program efficiently can raise expenses as well. An investment in a computer and software for a lead processing function or program management can represent a significant investment. Also consider any manuals you might like to have produced for show management, such as a guidelines manual.

If you manage a centralized trade show services department, consider strategic planning meetings, educational opportunities, and consulting services. Consider the investment for a resource library for those divisional people including published show schedule books, study courses, and periodicals. Finally, when you are evaluating shows for future participation, it often makes sense to visit the show and evaluate it as an attendee. How are expenses for those visits accommodated in the budget?

The following two checklists will help you to itemize and evaluate your own departmental budgetary considerations. The worksheet in Exhibit 12-8 is a cost evaluation worksheet to itemize those functions outside of typical show budgets that you must currently include, and those for which you would like to budget in the future. The worksheet in Exhibit 12-9 is a departmental budgeting tool to trace all departmental costs, including show-by-show expenses.

Creative Financing

If you are a visionary manager with future plans and goals for the company's exhibits department, you could easily become frustrated by limited resources. When planning for programs, take some time to consider creative ways to get resources to turn goals and objectives into actions.

If you are a trade show services department, divisions might participate in some continuing education or program management expenses. Before investing in a computer system, see what already exists within the company and if there are computer resources available that you could use. See if you can share administrative personnel with another department to

Exhibit 12-8 Departmental Cost Evaluation Worksheet

Budget Item	Current	Future
Staff Expenses		
Salaries	☐	☐
Books/publications	☐	☐
Continued education	☐	☐
Properties Expenses		
Warehousing	☐	☐
Handling	☐	☐
Product inventories	☐	☐
Insurance	☐	☐
New properties	☐	☐
Program Development		
Lead processing program	☐	☐
Computer hardware	☐	☐
Computer software	☐	☐
Show guidelines manual	☐	☐
Pre-show meeting guides	☐	☐
Consulting	☐	☐
Inter-departmental meetings	☐	☐
Strategic planning meetings	☐	☐
Show visits	☐	☐
Other		
_____	☐	☐
_____	☐	☐
_____	☐	☐
_____	☐	☐

defray salaries or additional overhead costs. See how the advertising or public relations department can share in show-related promotion costs.

In summary, whether or not your company *needs* an exhibits department depends on the volume of trade show activity. If you are participating in more than five major shows each year, you probably need one person devoted exclusively to trade shows to assure that the function is *managed* for success. Even if you don't have an official exhibits department, consider where you as the manager are placed within the corporation and how it affects your job. In the following chapters you will consider management strategies and techniques that will be influenced by where the exhibit function is located within the company.

Exhibit 12-9   Departmental Budget Worksheet

FY _____

Budget Item	Estimate	Actual	Totals
Show-by-Show Budgets			
Show #1 _____	_____	_____	
Show #2 _____	_____	_____	
Show #3 _____	_____	_____	
Show Budget Totals			_____
Staff Expenses			
Salaries/benefits	_____	_____	
Books/publications	_____	_____	
Continued education	_____	_____	
Staff Expense Totals			_____
Properties Expenses			
Warehousing	_____	_____	
Handling	_____	_____	
Product inventories	_____	_____	
Insurance	_____	_____	
New properties	_____	_____	
Properties Totals			_____
Program Development			
Lead processing program	_____	_____	
Computer hardware	_____	_____	
Computer software	_____	_____	
Show guidelines manual	_____	_____	
Pre-show meeting guides	_____	_____	
Consulting services	_____	_____	
Inter-departmental meetings	_____	_____	
Strategic planning meetings	_____	_____	
Program Development Totals			_____
Fiscal Year Departmental Budget Total			=========

If you don't have an exhibits or trade show department, managing instead of just coordinating is not necessarily something that will be assigned in your job responsibilities. But it is something you must decide to do.

13

Managing Lead Tracking

The roadblock to managing an efficient lead tracking system for most exhibitors is not how to process the leads, or how to tabulate results, or even how to distribute leads for follow-up. The roadblock is the actual *tracking* of leads . . . getting salespeople to report back on the action taken and sales that result. And as you saw in previous chapters, this is the key to lead tracking. Therefore, in this chapter you will take a look at how to set up a lead tracking program for the trade show department, with special emphasis placed on strategies for facilitating the *tracking* function. Here you will see how to:

1. DETERMINE REQUIREMENTS. How to determine your lead processing needs based on your sales and distribution structure, and information requirements.

2. SELECT THE BEST TECHNIQUES. How to select the best techniques for tracking leads.

3. COMPUTERIZE YOUR SYSTEM. Nine questions to ask before computerizing the lead processing and tracking functions.

HOW TO DETERMINE LEAD TRACKING REQUIREMENTS

Two terms are commonly used interchangeably when people discuss trade show leads, and they actually mean two different things. The terms are *lead processing* and *lead tracking*. It is important to define them as they will be used here to assure that we are speaking a common language.

- **Lead processing** is simply fulfilling whatever requests have been made by show visitors. Typically that involves either mailing requested literature, or making follow-up sales calls. But depending on your distribution network and selling cycle, it can involve sending out price quotes, mailing or delivering samples for evaluation, telemarketing follow-up, or any combination of post-show sales efforts.

- **Lead Tracking** is following the distribution of leads to the field, the action taken, and sales that result. It is an essential component to calculating return on investment from a show.

Lead processing systems can be relatively simple and straightforward. Lead tracking, in contrast, is more complex and difficult to implement, since it involves the cooperation of people outside of the trade show department. The chart in Exhibit 13-1 outlines the basic requirements for both lead processing and lead tracking, to help you evaluate your ability to implement one or both of these functions, based on your resources.

Exhibit 13-1   Lead Processing and Tracking Requirements

Lead Processing Requirements	**Lead Tracking Requirements***
√ A lead card for compiling inquiries.	√ A copy of each lead for tracking records.
√ A person responsible for collecting leads at the show and returning them to the office for processing.	√ A procedure for prioritizing leads by urgency.
√ A system for generating mailing labels	√ A format for salespeople to report on action they have taken on leads and resulting sales.
√ A person to oversee collection or production of follow-up literature.	√ A person to monitor communication from the field and update files.
√ A person to prepare and mail literature.	√ A person to compile and calculate figures on a pre-set schedule (monthly, quarterly, etc.) and generate reports on results.
√ Procedures for distributing leads to the field for follow-up.	
	*These are in addition to the lead processing requirements which are also needed here.

NOTE: Do You Need Help with Lead Processing?

You might find that you are still at the point of just getting the processing function in place before you can concentrate on lead tracking. If you don't have the staff to operate an efficient lead processing program, you might want to consider having leads fulfilled through an outside fulfillment agency. The following few quick questions will help you determine if it's time to seek help:

- Are you finding leads from old shows stuck in files, under piles of work or on a secretary's desk, or worse yet left in the cabinets of the exhibit?
- How long is it taking for inquiries to be processed? More than one week is too long.
- Are leads getting fulfilled without any records being compiled on lead numbers and breakdowns?
- Are salespeople complaining that they are not getting leads on a timely basis for follow-up?

Yes answers to most of these questions are sure signs that either you do not have the resources to handle lead fulfillment yourself, or there is no efficient system in place. Consider the potential revenues lost in sales from those leads, and an outside lead fulfillment service might look like a viable solution. If you are considering it, these questions can help in evaluating firms.

12 Questions to Ask a Lead Fulfillment Service

1. Have they handled trade show leads for any other companies?
2. What is the average turnaround time on those leads?
3. What turnaround time will they guarantee for your leads?
4. Will they store your filfillment literature at their site?
5. How will they organize fulfillment to assure the correct literature is sent to each respondent from each show?
6. How will they collect leads from you? (Will they pick them up at your facility, will you overnight mail them to their facility from the show, or will you have to deliver them?)
7. How will they record your leads and generate mailing labels?
8. If they use a computerized system, can you get sorted reports on the leads?

9. How will their system accommodate a variety of product choices and literature fulfillment from show to show?

10. Will they distribute leads to your sales offices?

11. How will you be updated on the status of leads from each show?

12. How do they charge for their services?

Now that the distinction between these two terms has been made, the remaining content of this chapter will address the entire process of *lead tracking* inclusive of *lead processing*. So as you are reading about how to determine your requirements, and potential uses for a program, keep in mind that these guidelines pertain to the complete lead tracking program. There are four points to consider when planning for lead tracking. The first two offer some background on your company and procedures that will affect the lead tracking function, and the second two consider your own goals and expectations for lead tracking.

VARIABLES THAT INFLUENCE LEAD TRACKING

#1 Define Your Distribution Channels

The way your products are sold becomes a guiding influence on the lead tracking system. If your products are sold through distributors, you will have to make different considerations for lead tracking than if they are sold through your own internal sales force. If the selling cycle is a long one (a year or more), this brings different considerations to lead tracking than if the selling cycle is short (60–90 days).

Let's first look at channels of distribution and how they influence the lead tracking system. For our purposes, we will divide distribution channels into three general categories: 1. direct sales, 2. distributors, dealers, and wholesalers, and 3. OEMs, VARs, and retailers.

Direct Sales. If your company has its own direct sales force, the lead tracking system may be challenging, but it is infinitely simpler than if you are dealing with a third-party sales network. It is simpler because you need to get cooperation and support from only one or two central management people to facilitate the feedback process. It is also simpler because the sales department should report regularly on sales made, and it is only a matter of connecting sales to leads from shows.

Wholesalers, Distributors, and Dealers. If you are dealing with this type of network, be ready to face a few of the following hurdles in your lead tracking program. First, you have to get a group of otherwise independent entrepreneurs to take time to report back to you on action taken from show leads. Depending on your corporate culture and the company's relationship with these people, it can be tough to "demand" that they do anything.

You do have a couple to options to consider here: you can use a program to motivate these resellers to report on sales, or you can go around them and do your own telemarketing follow-up on show leads that were passed on to these folks. At least one company gives their third-party resellers a time limit to follow up on leads after which it is understood that the manufacturer will follow up on them and make the sales directly.

OEMs, VARs, and Retailers. This, too, is an altogether unique situation, and will depend on how you choose to measure your results from the show. They are in a separate category, because this structure can include three steps to the end user. The manufacturer could sell to a wholesaler who then sells to a retailer who sells to the end user. Or the manufacturer could sell components to another manufacturer (say truck axles) who then builds the product into equipment that is sold through a dealer or retailer.

The goals of lead tracking are to determine the influence of your efforts on the show attendees wherever they are in the distribution chain. The difficulty is that the further they are from you in the chain, the more difficult it is to get information by which to measure show efforts.

If you are attending a show for the express purpose of recruiting or selling to dealers, distributors, or OEMs, for example, then results will be measured simply by how many new resellers you sign, and how much they buy. But if you are marketing at shows to end users, you will need a bit more sophisticated lead tracking system to see how the inquiries generated are being followed up, and the business that results.

#2: Define Types of Markets Show Audiences Represent

These factors lead to the next consideration. If you work with third-party vendors, are most of your show efforts directed to your primary or secondary market?

The primary market is the group to which you sell directly. In other words, the glassware company we've been using as an example may sell a line of products to restaurants. But they sell to restaurateurs through restaurant supply companies (wholesalers). Therefore the wholesaler represents their primary market.

The secondary market is the end user of the product in this reselling chain. So in our example above, the restaurateurs, even though they are the ones using the product, become a secondary market for the glassware manufacturer.

"Primary and secondary" are not used to reflect the relative importance of this group to the manufacturer. They simply indicate the distance from the manufacturer in the sales chain. This is illustrated in Exhibit 13-2.

If the audience at most shows represents a primary market for you, lead tracking is easier, because you see the direct sales that result internally. If the audience at most shows represents a secondary market, lead tracking is more difficult, because you either have to get the reseller's cooperation to report on sales generated from show leads, or go directly to the end users who inquired at the show to see if they purchased any products as a result.

Lead tracking is a rather new concept in trade show marketing, and it is the rare company that has found a system that works well. What the industry has collectively discovered to date, are a variety of tracking techniques that are adapted to individual situations, and tweaked to do the best job. Therefore, a large part of the process of finding a lead tracking program that works successfully for you is working with different tracking techniques to find the best solution for your situation.

The chart in Exhibit 13-3 puts the two variables (type of distribution and primary or secondary markets) on a grid with tracking techniques that companies have used with success under the appropriate categories.

#3: Determine the Optimum Tracking Techniques

The tracking technique (the function of reporting back sales resulting from trade show leads) is the key to making a lead tracking program work. Therefore, your relationship, or rather your collective company's relationship, with the key participants in the distribution channels will also affect the type of tracking technique you can use. For example, do you or does someone within your company have the authority with internal sales representatives or third-party vendors to demand that they report back on the status of show leads, or even on sales generated from show leads?

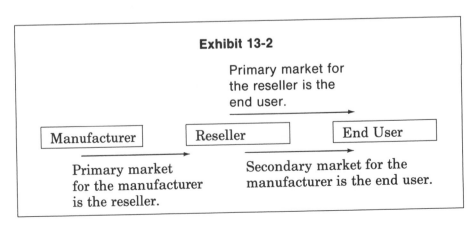

Exhibit 13-2

Primary market for
the reseller is the
end user.

| Manufacturer | Reseller | End User |

Primary market
for the manufacturer
is the reseller.

Secondary market for the
manufacturer is the end user.

Exhibit 13-3

	Direct Sales	Wholesalers, Distributors, Dealers	OEMS, VARs, Retailers
Primary Market	• Measure show based on sales made from leads generated. • Must have cooperation of sales management. • Must have a system for reporting on follow-up results. • Could use telemarketing to track.	• Can measure show based on vendors signed, or business signed by vendors as a result of show. • Can use show specials to encourage sales at or as a result of show. • Need internal person to track these results.	• Measure show based on new vendors or orders signed at show. • Use show specials to encourage sales at or as a result of show. • Need cooperation from management responsible for third-party vendors.
Secondary Market	Not applicable.	• Measure show based on leads generated and resulting sales through third-party vendors. • Use telemarketing or direct surveys to track results through to end users. • Use incentives to get vendors to report back action taken on leads and resulting sales.	• Measure show based on leads generated and resulting orders from vendors. • Package bounce-back card with products for user to return to you and compare with show leads. • Involve vendor in show to make on-site connection with prospects.

Do you have a communications system in place to facilitate that reporting? (One manufacturer has an on-line computer system with all of their dealers which allows the manufacturer to input leads on a data base, send them via modem to the dealers, and call up the dealer files to check their status regularly.)

Have you been providing the sales teams or resellers with quality leads so that they take them seriously and see the value of responding to them?

If you have the authority to put a reporting system in place and are assured that the sales team or resellers will participate, then the lead tracking system can be based on their reports on lead status. You will simply need to facilitate the tracking and reporting function from your department. We will call this technique "tracking through the sales channel."

If you cannot anticipate cooperation from your sales department or resellers, then you probably need to incorporate some type of post-show survey or telemarketing into your program to track the results of show inquiries yourself. We will call this technique "tracking through the source."

Each tracking technique has its own specific needs:

Tracking through the sales channel requires:

- A system for distributing leads for sales follow-up.
- A record of leads generated for the trade show department.
- A record of lead distribution for the trade show department.
- A system for reporting back the status of leads.
- A person in the trade show department to gather information and update lead records.
- Cooperation of salespeople, whether internal or third party.

Tracking through the source requires:

- A system for distributing leads for sales follow-up.
- A record of leads generated for the trade show department.
- A person to create a telemarketing script or post-show survey.
- Staff or a vendor to distribute surveys or conduct telemarketing.
- A system for tabulating results from surveys of telemarketing efforts.
- A person to compile results and reports from telemarketing efforts or returned surveys.

These requirements assume that a system is in place for processing leads and distributing requested literature immediately following the show.

#4: Determine Your Goals for the Lead Tracking Program

Your primary goal for the lead tracking program is to determine revenues generated from show leads. A secondary goal is to calculate the return on that trade show investment. But are there additional ways that you could use the lead tracking system to manage your program? In Chapter 11, for example, a series of reports that a computerized lead system could generate were illustrated. Generating lead summary reports might be one additional function of the lead tracking program.

A second function might be to compare leads or inquiries generated from shows, with those generated from other marketing media such as ads or direct mail campaigns. This requires processing of all your inquiries on the same data base and providing a source code to identify whether the inquiry came from a trade show, a trade ad, etc.

Companies that track multiple media can then make dollar comparisons on the cost to generate inquiries among media. They can see, for example, their cost per lead at a trade show vs. the cost per inquiry from a trade ad. This becomes a valuable tool in deciding how to allocate those promotion dollars (or how to justify getting the dollars you need for your program).

Another requirement of your system may be that you can merge and purge files from multiple shows to search out duplicate leads. This will be important to establish up front because if you are using a computerized system for lead tracking, it will be an important function to establish at the beginning.

You might also want to be able to sort active leads from inactive leads. Show leads have a definite life, and when you get leads back from the field that are clearly "dead," you might want to have a separate file to record inactive leads. This too will need to be established up front if you are planning to put your lead tracking program on a computer system.

Other requirements you choose to add will be dependent on your program. Before establishing the system, discuss it with the salespeople who will be following up on the leads to see what kind of information they would find most useful. Talk to marketing management and product managers to see if they have any input. But most importantly, establish the system based on the needs of your own department.

An efficient lead tracking system will be one of your most valuable tools in "exhibiting smart" (choosing the most profitable shows in which to participate) and in justifying show expenditures as you begin to demonstrate return-on-investment measures from your shows. The worksheet in Exhibit 13-4 walks you through the steps we just discussed on determining lead tracking requirements.

Exhibit 13-4 Determining Lead Tracking Requirements

Step #1: Define Distribution Channels

☐ Internal Sales   ☐ Distributors   ☐ OEMs
                    ☐ Dealers   ☐ VARs
                    ☐ Wholesalers   ☐ Retailers

Step #2: Define Markets Represented at Shows

☐ Primary market only
☐ Secondary market only
☐ Primary and secondary markets combined

Step #3: Determine the tracking technique to use

☐ Tracking through the sales channel
    ____ Salespeople respond on report forms
    ____ Salespeople respond by telephone
    ____ Other _____

☐ Tracking through the source
    ____ Post-show mail surveys
    ____ Post-show telemarketing
    ____ Other _____

Step #4: Consider additional requirements

☐ Generate lead status reports
☐ Compare leads from all media sources
☐ Merge/purge files between shows
☐ Sort active and inactive leads
☐ Other _____
☐ Other _____
☐ Other _____

After you've thought through the basic requirements for the system, you are ready to begin the process of putting the system into place. The following 12 steps follow a basic formula for establishing the system, but you will no doubt use a variation of these steps and this order to get your own system up and running.

Be forewarned that this is not a project that can typically be established in a few months and run smoothly for the rest of your shows. It takes the first year just to get the system in place, and running efficiently, and perhaps longer to get all of the participants cooperating. Be patient. Know that after each show you will see new ways to improve on the system and increase the percentage of salespeople who report back as the procedures become more accepted.

Exhibit 13-8 (page 353) is a worksheet that includes each of these 12 steps. You might want to make a copy of it to use while you read this material to jot down notes and ideas you consider for each step.

NOTE FOR MANAGERS: As with any new program, lead tracking will become more successful over time *if you don't give up.* It will be up to you to be consistent in expecting post-show tracking reports from salespeople and following up on their input.

12 STEPS TO PUTTING THE LEAD TRACKING SYSTEM IN PLACE

Step #1: Establish the Types of Leads that will be tracked through this system. Do you want to include leads from a variety of media (advertising, direct mail, PR, etc.) or only from trade shows?

Step #2: Determine How the Leads Will Be Generated. You will most likely use a lead card to generate leads at the show. Decide whether you will use an imprint system, or collect business cards to staple to the lead form, or hand-write vital statistics onto the card.

Some shows use magnetic card readers for lead gathering. The visitor's registration information is encoded on a magnetic strip on their name badge. Exhibitors can rent the computer systems that read these cards and store information, along with additional data the exhibitor collects. Consider *all* systems you might use because they will vary from show to show and you want the lead tracking system to be compatible with any of them.

Step #3: Determine Information Required. What will you need to know about this inquiry to facilitate lead tracking? The minimum information required is name, company name, address, phone number, product interest, and follow-up action requested. After that a variety of information from budget allocations to competing products used may be necessary. The checklist in Exhibit 13-5 will help you uncover your information needs for the lead tracking system.

Exhibit 13-5   Checkpoint: Is Your Lead Card Doing
the Job?

✔ **Can your lead card be used as a "report back" form?** Many companies use multi-copy forms and include sections for indicating the status of the lead right on the form. The salesperson then gets two copies of each lead, one which they keep for their records and one they send back to the trade show department to report on action taken and resulting sales.

✔ **Does your lead card have a sense of urgency?** Consider not just how it will be used at the show, but how it will be used after the show for follow-up. To give it that sense of urgency consider printing **Sales Lead** in large bold type along with **Please process immediately.** You might even include a date by which the lead must be returned to your department if you are using it as a reporting form.

✔ **Have you listed questions on the card in order of priority,** or indicated priority in some other way to separate "must get" answers from optional ones?

✔ **Is there anything you would like to know about your prospects** that could be included on the lead card? Be careful that the lead card doesn't turn into a marketing survey. Three or four key questions is about all you will have space and time for. But don't overlook this opportunity to learn information such as applications for your products, competing products they are using, or annual volume used of your product or a competitor's.

✔ **Have you considered inquiring about budgets and purchasing timeframes?** For most large purchases, budget dollars are allocated before serious shopping begins. Those budget questions can tell a salesperson volumes about where that prospect is in the decision-making process. Inquiring about purchasing timeframe can uncover similar information.

✔ **Does the lead card include a question about the decision-making authority of the prospect?** Whether the person is an influencer, a sole decision-maker, or part of a decision making team can also be valuable information for the person assigned to follow up the inquiry.

✔ **Does the lead card help you monitor results from your promotion?** You might consider including an area to indicate whether the visitor participated in a contest or promotion you conducted in the exhibit, and how they learned about it. This provides feedback on the effect of your promotional dollars.

✔ **Have you included a generous area for comments?** Much of the information gathered by exhibit staffers defies the standard format of a lead card. Yet it is the most valuable information a salesperson could receive on the lead. These are the free-form comments that come up in the conversation about experience with competing products, problems, and concerns of the prospect. Does your lead card include a generous amount of space for staffers to record this type of information?

✔ **Will the lead card work with a variety of imprinting systems?** Some imprinters supplied by show management will take a variety of forms, others will only take the small credit card type forms. Be sure your lead card will work with the imprinters you will be using, and that the area for imprinting is large enough. One smart exhibitor purchased his own imprinters to ship with the exhibit. He went to a local bank and asked if they had used imprinters they would like to get rid of. They were more than happy to "dispose" of them at a fraction of the cost of new ones.

✔ **Are you using multiple carbonless forms** for easy distribution? If you distribute actual lead forms to any departments or divisions other than your own, you will want to use multiple part carbonless forms.

✔ **Is it small enough to fit in a coat pocket?** The best size for a lead card is one that makes it easy for salespeople to carry them and use them anywhere at the show (not just in the booth). Making them small enough to fit in a jacket pocket increases the chances of salespeople having them when they need them.

✔ **Is it sturdy enough to write on?** Consider printing the lead cards on a sturdy stock, or ordering them on pads so that staffers can write on them without having to walk over to a counter.

Step #4: Establish How Leads Will Be Processed. There are a few considerations to make here. Will you process the leads in the trade show department, will each division process their own leads, will you use another group within your organization to process the leads, or will you hire an outside agency to handle this task?

If you will be managing the function within the trade show department, determine who will be responsible for that job.

Will you use a computer system for processing leads, or a manual system? If you are using a computer system, do you have the hardware and software resources you need or will you have to get the system set up? Most computerized lead tracking systems use either the trade show department's personal computer(s) with off-the-shelf data base software packages, or, in a few cases, the corporate MIS department's computers with customized software.

Step #5: Determine Task Responsibilities. Take time now to assign responsibility for each of these tasks:

- Returning leads from the show
- Fulfilling literature requests
- Inputting lead information on a data base (if you are using a computerized system)
- Distributing leads for follow-up

Step #6: Determine Your Departmental Record Needs. How will you retain and store lead information? Will you need to? If you are going to track leads, you will need a record of all of the leads generated in order to follow up on the action taken. Do you want to keep a set of hard copies of each lead? Do you want to input the leads onto your data base and then send off the hard copies to their respective salespeople or sales offices? If you are not using a computerized system, do you need a master list of leads for tracking follow-up, or will you use hard copies of the lead cards for that record-keeping?

Step #7: Decide on Reporting Procedures. How do you want salespeople to report on lead status? Will you create a section on the lead card where they complete this information to mail back? Will you have a person in your department responsible to call each salesperson for status reports? Will salespeople receive computer-generated lists of leads on which they can list action taken? Can salespeople update lead status on a computer file and return it to your department?

Step #8: Decide on Reporting Timing. How often do you want salespeople to report on lead status? Should they report each sale made as it is closed? Or would intervals of 30, 60, and 90 days after the show be a good follow-up report time span. Keep in mind that if salespeople follow up leads from a variety of shows keeping track of these timeframes can be confusing. You may want to go with monthly or quarterly reports on the status of all trade show leads.

Step #9: Determine Recording and Tabulating Methods. If you are setting up a computerized system you will need to decide what types of reports you want to use, how you want them formatted, and who will be responsible for generating these reports and updating the files. If you are using a manual system, it will be worthwhile to create some summary sheets for gathering and tabulating lead tracking status information. The worksheets in Exhibits 13-6 and 13-7 are simple examples of tracking record forms. The form in Exhibit 13-6 would be used to track leads on a 30-, 60-, 90-day timeframe for a single show. The form in Exhibit 13-7 would be used to track monthly show results for several shows.

To use the form in Exhibit 13-6 get reports on lead status in 30-day increments after the show is over. Plan to record after each contact the status of the lead, and the amount of any sales that resulted. You might want to use a code for lead status such as: NC = no follow up call has been made yet; IP = a call has been made and the sales cycle is still in process; NS = a call has been made and it is determined that no sale will result, but continued follow-up will be made; and DEAD = a lead that requires no further follow-up.

To use the form in Exhibit 13-7 for multiple show tracking, plan to list the leads chronologically by show, and then alphabetically by company name. You can then just continue adding leads to the list as you complete shows. Depending on the number of shows in which you participate, you

Exhibit 13-6 Lead Tracking Record Form (Single Show)

Show name: _____   Show date: _____

	30 days	60 days	90 days	+ 90 days	Totals
Companies and contact name listed alphabetically by company name.					
TOTALS					

Exhibit 13-7 Lead Tracking Report Form
(Multiple Shows)

Form start date: _____   For quarters: _____
Shows included: _____

	January	February	March	April	May	June
Leads listed chronologically by show and then alphabetically by company name.						
TOTALS Tabulate totals for each show monthly.	═══	═══	═══	═══	═══	═══

might want to create a separate form for each show, or start over after a specified time period. This form is set up on a quarterly system, with two quarters (six months) on each form. As lead status is reported, simply indicate in the appropriate time block after each contact whether a sale was made and the amount of the sale.

Step #10: Plan to Calculate Return on Investment. One of the first questions to ask when calculating return on investment from a show is how long should you wait? That will depend on your selling cycles. If a typical sales cycle is 90 days, then calculate return on investment 90–120 days after the show. If it is up to a year, you might want to make periodic calculations until you are satisfied that you know the status on a significant number of leads that were generated at the show.

The return-on-investment calculation is a simple one:

$$\text{Total sales generated} \div \text{Total show costs} = \text{ROI}$$

Typically ROI is reported on a sales-to-investment ratio: sales/investment. For each dollar spent, how much was returned? While there are no hard-and-fast rules about acceptable return on investment for trade shows, 10:1 is a generally accepted minimum standard. What will your minimum acceptable ROI ratio be?

Step #11: Decide Who Will Receive Reports. Your post-show reports can provide visibility and program justification to a number of people: sales management, product management, marketing communications management. Much of the decision about who should receive reports will depend on the structure of your company and who participates in decision-making about shows. It is useful to decide on this up front, so that it is not a consideration that needs to be made after each show.

Step #12: Communicate. Determine how you will communicate the policies and procedures on lead tracking to everyone involved. A guideline sheet for all participating parties (salespeople, trade show department staff, sales management) will be useful, particularly as new salespeople join the ranks. One exhibitor made personal visits to each field sales office to explain the new lead tracking system just prior to launching the operation.

Exhibit 13-8   Lead Tracking System Planning Worksheet

Step #1: What types of leads will be tracked:

- ☐ Trade show leads
- ☐ Advertising leads
- ☐ Direct mail leads
- ☐ Other_____

Exhibit 13-8 Lead Tracking System Planning Worksheet
(Cont.)

Step #2: How will leads be generated?

☐ Show supplied lead cards and imprint system
☐ Our own custom lead cards and imprinters
☐ Our own custom lead cards and business cards
☐ Our own custom lead cards and hand-written information

Step #3: What information is required?

_____

_____

_____

_____

Step #4: Where will leads be processed?

☐ Trade show department
☐ Other divisions
☐ Outside agency
☐ Other_____

Step #5: Who will be responsible to:

Return leads from the show:_____
Fulfill literature requests:_____
Input data:_____
Distribute leads:_____
Monitor reporting:_____
Update files:_____

Step #6: How will you retain records?

☐ Hard copies of leads
☐ Computer data base of leads
☐ Computer-generated reports
☐ Other_____

Step #7: How will salespeople report back on leads?

☐ Return copy of lead form
☐ Written lead status reports
☐ Update computer files of leads
☐ Telephone
☐ Other_____

Step #8: How often will salespeople report?

☐ 30-60-90 days
☐ Monthly
☐ Quarterly
☐ Other_____

Step #9: How will results be recorded and tabulated?

- ☐ Manual forms
- ☐ Update computer files
- ☐ Other_____

Step #10: How often will ROI be calculated?

- ☐ Monthly   ☐ Semi-annually
- ☐ Quarterly   ☐ Annually
- ☐ Other_____

Step #11: Who will receive reports?

- ☐ Trade show manager   ☐ President
- ☐ Marcom manager   ☐ Other
- ☐ Sales managers
- ☐ Product managers
- ☐ Vice Presidents

Step #12: Communications plan

- ☐ Guidelines sheets
- ☐ Field sales office visits
- ☐ Guidelines announced at pre-show meetings
- ☐ Other_____

_____

_____

_____

_____

_____

_____

_____

_____

_____

_____

NINE QUESTIONS TO ASK BEFORE GOING ON-LINE

If you are considering putting the entire lead tracking function on a computer system, your primary consideration will be resources. Do you have the financial resources and personnel to plan, install, operate, and maintain a computerized lead tracking system? If you can answer "yes" to the following nine questions, you are probably ready and able to create a computer-based lead tracking system.

1. Do you have the hardware? Do you currently have computer hardware either in your department or through your company's MIS department on which to set up this system?

Don't just assume that because your company has an MIS department that you will be able to get computer time and space for your function. Go through the necessary channels to be sure. If you do not have the hardware, do you have the financial allocations to purchase the necessary hardware?

2. Do you have the software? Do you have a good data base program and enough working knowledge of it to produce an efficient lead tracking system?

3. Has this already been done? Is there anyone else in the company who is using a similar system (maybe sales or advertising) that you might be able to simply adapt to your needs, rather than investing time and resources to reinvent the wheel?

4. Do you have a communication link? Is it possible for you to link your hardware and software with that of other divisions within the company with which you will need to communicate for the lead processing function? If you can communicate via modem, or even by exchanging disks on a compatible system, you will be able to take more advantage of the time savings offered by a computerized system. If not you will still find yourself generating and distributing a host of reports which can be time consuming.

5. Do you have staff to operate the system? Will you be able to have one person in your department dedicated to operating and maintaining the computer files? Giving the job to an already overworked secretary will only sabotage the system by pushing the tasks to the bottom of an already very deep stack of work.

6. Will you use the computer on-site? The *most* efficient way to input leads is to do so right on-site as they are generated in the exhibit. This requires taking a computer to the show or renting a similar system on-site, both of which require additional financing, and a person to input the leads.

7. Are all participants computer literate? If you are counting on salespeople to update their files on a computer data base, check to see what percentage of these people use computers on a day-to-day basis. It will be frustrating to get an efficient system set up that relies on computer input from a group of people who have a very low comfort level with using the computers and are reluctant to do so.

8. Do you have a backup plan? Plan for the unexpected. What will your backup plan be should the system fail you?

9. Is it more efficient to handle it in-house than through an outside supplier? If you find that you don't have the staff or financial resources to computerize the function, you might consider going with an outside firm which offers the services. There are companies devoted exclusively to lead processing and tracking that will handle the entire function for you, from creating a lead card, through to tracking the leads to final sale. They typically charge an initial set-up fee and an additional "per lead" price.

Aside from the exhibit property itself, lead tracking can be one of the most time-consuming components of a show program. But managed well, the statistics and reports pay big dividends. With this function in place the success of shows, and justification for participation in them, becomes a clear reality. It provides the only way to get a true measure of the return on your trade show investment.

14

Managing
Exhibit Staffing

Quite simply, the exhibit staff will make or break your show. As an exhibit manager you can invest countless hours preparing the optimum selling environment for your marketing-based show strategy, only to find the entire effort submarined by a team of staffers who have more important things on their mind than breathing life into the show strategy. Common complaints voiced by exhibit managers include:

"They just stand around in the booth and talk to each other."

"They just come and go as they please. . ."

"They don't fill out the lead cards correctly. . ."

"They think trade show assignments are just a few fun days away from the office."

"They don't take booth duty seriously."

By contrast you might find that nothing else seemed to come together at a particular show, but you were fortunate to get a staff with a great attitude who made the effort a huge success.

The issue here is: Can you have any influence on the quality of your staffing team or is it just left to luck?

It is common to see two extreme reactions to staffing problems. The first is an opinion on the part of the exhibit manager that "nothing can be done about these people" and a resignation to muddling along with what exists. The polar extreme is to incorporate a host of strategies for improving the staffing function and then throwing in the towel when all of the staffers don't come along 100% of the time.

Instead, consider improving the staffing situation gradually. Implement a few techniques and don't throw them out the window when two people complain. Continue to review and revise based on input and your own observation about the effectiveness of the program. For example, you might decide to implement pre-show meetings as a standard procedure for all shows. Yet at your first two shows, only a handful of staffers show up. The knee-jerk response is to say, "Well, this certainly isn't working." But when you are dealing with people, changes must be gradual. Find out *why* the staffers didn't show up and work to increase attendance for the next show. As procedures become more routine, more and more people will buy-in to the program.

This chapter covers a variety of techniques for improving staff performance. In previous chapters you saw how to implement basic staff management strategies such as preparing pre-show memos and staffing schedules and conducting pre-show meetings. Here you will take a more analytical look at how to evaluate the source of staffing problems, and a broad range of solutions, from reconsidering your staffing team to educating staffers and soliciting management support. Here you will see how to:

1. EVALUATE PERFORMANCE PROBLEMS: Identify sources of staffing problems as a foundation for making improvements.
2. BUILD A STAFFING TEAM: Alternate sources within your company for exhibit staffers.
3. EDUCATE THE STAFF: Equip your chosen staffers with the knowledge and skills to be top performers in the exhibit.
4. GAIN CONTROL: Identify your own weak links in management and strengthen them to better control the function.

Note: This is not a chapter on how to sell in an exhibit. There are a variety of resources available on that subject. For more information check the resource list in the Appendix.

ADVICE FROM THE EXPERTS: Taking Control of Staffing

Diane K. Weintraub, president of Communique Exhibitor Education, Inc., has specialized in exhibit staffing education for the past eight years, consulting with exhibit managers in a variety of different-sized companies from the IBM Corporation to small start-ups. Here she highlights a few primary considerations for the exhibit staffing function.

"If you want to make a big change, an immediate change, in your show results, look in the direction of your staffing team. I have seen many companies double, even triple or quadruple, the number of leads they wrote at a show by fine-tuning the structure of what staffers did.

"But, on the opposite side, I have also seen a host of excuses and traps exhibitors fall into that actually diminish the quality of the staffing team and reinforce unproductive behavior. Exhibit and sales managers too often look the other way when staffers don't show up . . . ignore visitors . . . sit around eating or reading the newspaper . . . talk mostly to each other . . . and on and on. When I see an exhibit like this I see money thrown away. I see someone who doesn't care. I see someone too lazy, behind the times, or ill-informed to do anything about it. But mostly I see a wasted opportunity.

"Exhibitors sometimes fool themselves. They think that just because salespeople are first class in the field, they will be first rate in the exhibit. But why should it be so? Consider the environment alone. The exhibit sales environment is completely different than the field sales environment. Then consider the pace of an interaction. The average interaction in the exhibit lasts from three to five minutes. While sales calls vary in length, they are usually much longer than five minutes. Can we not conclude from these two facts alone that both the place and time differences would indicate a degree of adjustment is needed if we are to expect staffers to succeed?

"Still other exhibitors fool themselves when they assume that everyone assigned to work a show will be self-directed and know where they should be and when they should be there for maximum utilization of their time. Unfortunately, the unstructured nature of shows means exhibitors must work extra-hard to stem the tide and thereby make the best use of staffer time. People don't need less direction at shows—they need more direction.

"Some exhibitors miss going the full distance when they don't face issues of staffer management and motivation. Working shows is challenging, difficult, exhausting work. Staffers need to feel that they are giving their all because their leader asked them to and their company needs them to. Then they will go the extra mile. And when they do, you need to reward them so they feel good and are likely to do it again and again.

"If I could give you just one piece of advice about how to be *very* successful at exhibiting, it would be about *taking control of your staffers.*

"Here are a few ways this works out practically. Be responsible for staffer selection; pick and choose carefully. Structure the booth duty schedule and fine-tune it. Get a team leader others would want to follow and brief him or her on what needs to be done. You must have a pre-show meeting both to make certain the staffers know what is expected of them and to give them a time and place to shift gears and skills from whatever they do day-to-day in the exhibit. And by all means, evaluate their performance.

"Your staffers are your single most important resource. They can be a wild card that ruins your exhibit, or your ace in the hole. In order to play that card just right, you must be ready to take full responsibility. That means seizing every opportunity to calculate, manipulate, poke, and prod your recruits into the crack team that you need."

EVALUATING PERFORMANCE PROBLEMS

If you want to improve the exhibit staffing function, your primary job will be motivating. The first step to motivating is understanding the source of the problem.

When entire groups of people are involved, this process can be complex. Issues won't be the same for any two people involved. So when you are evaluating the staff, think in general terms about what exists with the highest percentage of people.

Staffing problems tend to fall within one of three categories: attitude, knowledge, or skills. For example, if you are working with a sales manager who believes that trade shows are a waste of time, then that *attitude* will probably be communicated through the ranks. The staffers will probably feel unspoken expectations that they need to work in booth duty around their daily account management responsibilities. Of course they won't be at all focused on *your* expectations for their performance in the exhibit. And who could blame them? You have here an attitude problem, and the source of the problem is the staffers' manager. This is a common problem when experienced salespeople are selected for booth duty.

Or, you may find that staffers love to work shows. They volunteer for booth duty with great enthusiasm. They dress for success and generally adhere to the hours that you've asked them to be in the exhibit. They stay fairly busy with booth visitors, yet when you evaluate the lead cards, they are only filled in with cursory information. You know that you are not even getting close to maximizing show results. This is most likely a skills problem. Staffers have a positive attitude about working shows, but they don't have an understanding and grasp of the *skills* required to do the job. This is a common problem when inexperienced marketing or technical staff are assigned booth duty.

Or, the problem may be simple knowledge and communications. The staff has simply *never been told* what is expected of them. This accounts for much of the restless chatting in small groups and lack of adherence to schedules seen in exhibits. Staffers are only asked to "be there," have received few guidelines for their participation, and no person has been appointed to whom they will be accountable for their participation in the show. This is most common when groups from outside the corporate ranks (such as third-party vendors) are requested to staff an exhibit.

Lack of knowledge raises an additional problem. Perhaps the staffers from within the company have been given a set of guidelines in a pre-show meeting, but the vendors were not required to attend. Then a vendor violates one of the guidelines (smoking or drinking sodas in the exhibit for example) and is scorned for doing so (even though they had no knowledge of the guidelines).

Lack of knowledge is the easiest problem to remedy. Lack of skills can be remedied, but takes a bit more time and energy. A bad attitude is the toughest illness to cure and may even require *replacing* staffers whose attitudes continue to drag down show efforts.

The chart in Exhibit 14-1 is designed to help you evaluate some of your own staffing concerns, and consider whether they are primarily attitude, knowledge, or skills issues. There is also a completed chart to illustrate how you might consider some of these problems. The following section provides strategies for approaching each of these types of concerns.

Dealing with Attitude Problems

If you have determined that your staffing issues are primarily attitude-related you can take your choice of steps toward improving the situation.

- *Change the team.* The most drastic approach is to change the group of staffers selected to participate. If salespeople have trouble devoting their energies to show participation, consider using people from the marketing, product, or technical departments. One exhibit manager switched from purely sales staffers to using marketing technicians (people who troubleshoot equipment problems for customers) with great success. These people knew the products, had day-to-day dealings with customers, and found show duty to be a welcome break in their regular routine.

  Keep in mind, though, that replacing a sales-oriented staffing team with people from other areas within the company can raise its own set of problems. The exhibit manager who used technical people found a gap in their skills base that had to be closed with exhibit staff training. You will need to thoroughly prepare the new team with training and education.

- *Demonstrate value.* Much less drastic is working to change attitudes by demonstrating the value of the show to staffers individually, and to the company as a whole. Use success stories generously in pre-show memos, pre-show meetings, and even in post-show newsletters or follow-up reports. Communicate the financial investment that the company makes in the show and the staffers' roles in realizing a return on the investment.

  Give staffers opportunities to see how they could benefit from their participation at the show by attending conference sessions, arranging appointments with key clients, learning more about the industry and their competition, and even enjoying the show city. Then be sure to create a realistic booth duty schedule that allows them time to do so.

	Exhibit 14-1A Evaluating Staffing Concerns		
Concern Defined	**If it's attitude . . .**	**If it's knowledge . . .**	**If it's skills . . .**

Concern Defined	If it's attitude . . .	If it's knowledge . . .	If it's skills . . .
Exhibit 14-1B Evaluating Staffing Concerns			
1. Don't adhere to schedules.	1. They might be getting negative input about shows from their managers. They might have additional expectations for their time from their direct bosses.	1. If you don't have a booth duty schedule and staffers are not told what's expected, it might be a simple knowledge issue.	1. This is not a skills-related problem.
2. Lead cards are missing vital info.	2. Staffers might not appreciate the value of the contacts made at the show.	2. Staffers don't know how this information affects the follow-up process and why it is important.	2. Staffers don't have the skills or experience to ask what they might consider sensitive qualifying questions.
3. Staffers chat among themselves and ignore visitors.	3. Staffers don't have a sense of personal goals or ownership in show participation.	3. Staffers haven't been told that it is expected that they be proactive instead of reactive in the exhibit.	3. Staffers are not skilled or experienced in opening techniques that will give them the confidence to approach visitors.
4. Over-present. Spend too much time in product presentation.	4. Technical staffers often have a disdain for "sales and selling" that keeps them from any communications techniques they consider sales-oriented, such as qualifying.	4. Staffers who come from areas other than sales often don't know the value and importance of qualifying, listening, and eliciting feedback from visitors.	4. Staffers may need work on basic listening skills and non-verbal communications techniques.

- *Create ownership.* When planning shows get input from sales management about their expectations for the show and for their people. Ask the staffers to set specific individual achievement goals for the show. Getting sales management involved at this level will set the stage for getting staffer involvement and cooperation.

- *Use incentives.* Incentives are tricky and have to be carefully crafted, but can work to motivate a dragging team of staffers. This can be a significant psychological boost if salespeople are asked to spend three to five days out of their territories and maintain monthly quotas. Rewarding them for top-notch performance can motivate them on a short-term, personal level, which is exactly what you need at the show. For more information on using incentive programs, see the "Advice from the Experts" section on incentive programs.

- *Get support.* It is no surprise that staffer attitudes are significantly influenced by management support and participation in the show effort. Go as high as you can to get a cooperative ear and supportive voice for the expectations of exhibit staffers.

    When dealing with attitude problems it is essential to keep a good attitude yourself. Too frequently exhibit managers begin to focus on the poor performers and complain about them as much as those folks complain about the show. Focusing on the poor performers will only drag down your own attitude. Instead, focus on the top performers, work to replace the poor performers, and try to bring that large group in the middle up to speed as much as you can.

ADVICE FROM THE EXPERTS: Using Incentive Programs

Phyllis Fox is a faculty member with Communique Exhibitor Education, Inc. and works with a variety of clients to implement effective incentive programs for their exhibit staffers. Prior to joining Communique, Phyllis worked as exhibit manager at Texas Instruments where exhibit staffers were known to comment on how much they enjoyed working at trade shows where she had instituted incentive programs.

"If your trade show program suffers with a staff performance problem or if you are serious about meeting a show goal, then an incentive program could help assure your success. Incentive programs are powerful tools for motivating staff and improving show performance. Although the booth must be conducive to sales activity, exhibits don't sell, people do. Show staffers much be enthusiastic, knowledgeable, productive, confident, and professional to be successful. If your trade show program suffers from a staff performance problem or if you are serious about meeting a show goal, then an incentive program could help assure your success. Here are a few guidelines for creating an incentive program that counts.

Set Goals and Measure Performance:

Clearly defined quantitative show goals such as lead count or sales volume will boost morale and motivate exhibit staffers to exceed your expectations. Many companies resist accountability and do not establish show goals. But the best example a trade show program can set, is one that isn't afraid of performance measures.

Whatever your reason for considering an incentive program, all contests have three basic components: teams, program administration, and awards.

Teams:

Divide your staff into two teams. Balance each team with an equal number of sales, marketing, and technical personnel to provide a blend of personalities and expertise. Since leadership is vital to a successful incentive program, select team captains who can be the role models of superior booth behavior. They are typically selected from the ranks of sales management and are respected for their selling and negotiating skills. When traffic gets heavy and staffers get weary, Team Leaders provide support and enthusiasm. They handle all problems from customer complaints to schedule changes. And, equally important, they assist with the incentive program administration.

Program Administration:

Incentive programs are contests and should include:

A Coordinator: A non-biased, neutral party to develop and oversee the program.

Guidelines: A written copy of the program's rules to be given to participants that should contain show dates, eligibility requirements, show goals, award criteria, and bonus opportunities.

Documentation: The paperwork for the contest—show lead or inquiry form, sales or purchase orders, applications, sales agreement, etc. Whatever the document, it should have space for: Name/address, telephone number, qualifying questions, comments, and staffer's signature.

Awards:

It's no contest unless something is given to the winners. Consider these elements when selecting the awards and prizes.

There are two types of awards: monetary/merchandise and ego boosters. With a physical award, it is essential to remember that what counts is not actual dollar worth but the perceived value of the prize. Some staffers will be delighted with a desk set or company calendar, while others require cold, hard cash or an exotic vacation to get them motivated. Ego boosters motivate staffers through peer and management recognition. One Fortune 100 company allows each staff member the opportunity to nominate an 'outstanding show staffer.' The nominees are awarded a beautiful plaque with their name and show date engraved upon it.

Successful contests allow for multiple winners throughout the show period. Limiting the contest to one prize for the entire show is demoralizing, actually encouraging staffers to give up before they try. Programs can be based on daily, hourly, or shift periods. Staffers should receive their prizes as soon and as often as possible. The timing of award distribution can be as motivational as the actual prize. Programs that require staffers to wait for a show lead to result in a sale are losers.

Incentives entice action and provide encouragement. They are inspiring and stimulating. Chances are that your staffers will *enjoy* working shows with incentive programs. And your greatest reward, as trade show manager, will be increased productivity and improved results from trade shows."

Dealing with Knowledge Problems

There is an old saying about working with people that you can't change other people, you can only change the way you deal with them. This is especially true if you are facing primarily knowledge-related problems. A few communications strategies and a little extra effort on your part can quickly alleviate these problems.

The Pre-Show Memo. In Chapter 7 there are specific guidelines for the pre-show memo. Plan to make the pre-show memo standard operating procedure for every show. Simplify the process by using boiler-plate forms as much as possible. Create stationery with a trade show or exhibits department logo that identifies all of your correspondence as show-related and separates it from the other piles of paper staffers receive. *Most important,* don't give up if it seems no one reads them. Refer questions back to the memo.

Pre-Show Meeting. If most of your problems are knowledge-related, you must also make the pre-show meeting standard operating procedure. In Chapter 4 you can find guidelines for planning the pre-show meeting. If you don't attend all of the shows, it will be necessary to find someone who has the authority to run the pre-show meeting and equip them with the tools to do so.

Many companies now use off-the-shelf resources such as exhibit selling courses and tapes for pre-show meeting content. Others have produced their own pre-show meeting leaders guide to assist field sales or marketing managers in leading those meetings. For more detailed information on those, see Section III of this chapter on training and organizing staffers.

Define Your Expectations. If the problems are knowledge related and you take time to reflect on the situation, you may discover that you haven't clearly defined your own expectations for booth staffers, not to mention communicating them. Take time to quickly review the checklist in Exhibit 14-2 and clarify your expectations. Then check those which you think have not been clearly communicated in the past, and must be considered in the future.

Follow-Through. A quick way to sabotage performance expectations is to communicate them and then not follow through when staffers don't adhere. For example, if you are asking staffers to show up 10-15 minutes early and a handful don't, let them know they were missed. If you are asking that lead cards be neat and complete, check them periodically and go back to staffers to get more information if necessary. It does not require a critical or nagging approach—just consistency and follow-through.

Dealing with Skills Problems

It is common (and understandable) to assume that salespeople have the skills required to work trade shows effectively and don't need any further training. Yet it is also common to find that field salespeople have the toughest time successfully adapting to the trade show environment. When you take some time to realize how dramatically the trade show environment differs from the typical field selling situation, the reasons for this are easier to understand. The chart in Exhibit 14-3 outlines some of these differences.

Because the trade show provides such a unique selling environment, the skills required to succeed will be different than those skills that staffers use on a day-to-day basis—regardless of their jobs. For that reason it is common to see skills problems among staffers.

If the problems you face are primarily skills related, then training and education are the best solutions. For more detailed information on trade-show selling skills, training content, and meeting leaders' resources, see Section III of this chapter on Educating Exhibit Staffers on page 377.

As you take time to evaluate your group, you will probably find that the issues and concerns don't fall neatly into one of the three categories: attitude, knowledge, and skill. You will most likely find it is a combination

	Exhibit 14-2 Staffer Expectations Chart		
	Expectations	**Is it currently being communicated?**	
	(Check those that apply)	Yes	No
☐	Attend pre-show meeting	☐	☐
☐	Arrive for booth duty shift 10–15 minutes early	☐	☐
☐	Adhere to a booth duty schedule	☐	☐
☐	Greet all visitors to the exhibit	☐	☐
☐	Gather specific qualifying information	☐	☐
☐	Fill out lead cards neatly and completely	☐	☐
☐	Turn in completed leads at a specific location	☐	☐
☐	Staff a hospitality function	☐	☐
☐	Use giveaways or premiums	☐	☐
☐	Help to draw an audience for live presentations		
☐	Report when leaving and returning to exhibit	☐	☐
☐	Demonstrate specific products	☐	☐
☐	Cover specific stations or areas of the exhibit	☐	☐
☐	Hand out literature or not use literature	☐	☐
☐	Not spend time with competitors	☐	☐
☐	Follow-basic etiquette guidelines (no eating, etc.)	☐	☐
☐	Adhere to a dress code	☐	☐
☐	Not chat amongst themselves	☐	☐
☐	Not use the conference area for staffer meetings	☐	☐
☐	Install equipment	☐	☐
☐	Install the exhibit structure	☐	☐
☐	Secure the booth and products in the evening	☐	☐
☐	Open the exhibit and set out displays in the morning	☐	☐
☐	Pack up and return the exhibit after the show	☐	☐
☐	Other _____	☐	☐
☐	Other _____	☐	☐
☐	Other _____	☐	☐
☐	Other _____	☐	☐
☐	Other _____	☐	☐

Exhibit 14-3

Field Interactions	Trade Show Interactions
Time	
Interactions in the field often allow a great deal of time to develop a rapport with and learn about the customer.	The average trade show interaction lasts just 3–5 minutes. Trust level must be built quickly and the staffer must work harder at learning about the visitor.
Place	
In field interactions the environment is fairly controlled. There are few distractions and interruptions to deal with.	Trade shows present a host of distractions to dilute the quality of the presentation effort. The best staffers work to control even this environment.
Quality	
The field interaction is typically prepared in advance and planned for. The salesperson has a good idea who they are talking with and what their needs are.	Interactions at trade shows are random and "pot luck." The staffer must work to discover the prospect's level of interest and specific need.
Depth	
Field interactions can go into a great deal of depth. Salespeople learn quite a bit about customers and also have the opportunity to present detailed solutions.	Interactions at trade shows tend to be shallow. In the short timeframe of most discussions, at best just a few key points can be addressed.

---

of these. If that is the case, take time to evaluate your resources and begin implementing changes gradually, starting with those you can use without too much resistance (for example it takes no financial resources or approval to begin sending pre-show memos) and then build toward the more demanding techniques.

BUILDING THE STAFFING TEAM

How do you approach the staffing needs for a show program? Do you simply say, "We'll need about ten people to work the exhibit for this show?" If so, you are missing the opportunity to build a team that will perform exactly as you need them to.

Trade show selling by its very nature is a *team selling* function. You as the exhibits or sales manager are responsible for pulling together an otherwise totally independent group of people and building the team that's going to bring your show strategy to life.

Instead of approaching staffing from a numbers point of view, consider approaching it from a project management point of view. Look at the show as a project. Define the tasks that will need to be accomplished in this project, and then the types and numbers of people you will need to accomplish those tasks. In other words, stop soliciting warm bodies, and start building a team for show participation.

Options for Structuring the Team

Basically, three options for exhibit staff team building have been bandied about among exhibitors, but they tend to settle on just one. Let's review the three options and some of the problems they could raise.

A Dedicated Group. Many exhibitors who take time to think through their staffing needs consider what on the surface seems to be a viable solution to the ongoing problem of staffer resources. Their idea is to create a team of people whose sole job is trade show selling. They would travel from show to show to demonstrate products and represent the company. It appears to make sense because then you can train the team, you have a pool of resources at the ready, they use the same skills over and over, and they become experts in the medium of trade show selling.

Companies have used this with mixed success.(1) The inherent problem with this approach is burnout. Trade show selling is extremely demanding. Asking a team of people to do it regularly means asking that they do essentially the same tasks repeatedly, on an ongoing basis, in an atmosphere that by its nature causes high stress and fatigue.

A second problem to consider is the seasonal nature of trade shows. It is rare for a company to have a regular schedule for trade show participation that would keep the same number of people busy over any given period of time. Therefore you would have to deal with shortages of staffers in the peak months, and finding something else for them to do during the slow months.

The "Certification" Approach. Other companies have tried training their people once on exhibit staffing skills and then considering them "certified" exhibit staffers. This means when planning for a show the exhibits manager would go to the sales manager and request a team of certified staffers. Only those who had been through trade show training qualified for booth duty. This approach has its pitfalls as well. Trade show selling skills are used intermittently, and need to be refreshed just prior to participation in a show for optimum assimilation. Therefore, training a group once and then expecting them to draw on those skills, when they are not using them every day, is unrealistic.

When the strategy for participation changes from show to show, staffers need to be reminded of how to adapt skills to function efficiently within that particular show strategy.

Show-by-Show Selection. The solution that most exhibitors use is to select and prepare a team for each show in which they participate. Here the staffing team can be selected based on the needs of the project, and they can be prepared for their assignments with training that is specific to the tasks they are asked to perform.

Team Selling and Staffer Selection

One of the best ways to satisfy visitors is through team selling. The concept has a variety of interpretations based on product demonstration and selling strategies for an exhibit. The following description outlines a basic team selling format. You will be able to create variations of the team selling concept that meet your needs.

In team selling each staffer is either a *presenter* or a *floater*. Prior to the show, each staffer needs to know what role they are assigned so they can adequately prepare.

A *presenter* is assigned to a particular product or service area and is responsible for presenting the capabilities of that product or service.

A *floater's* job is to work in the open areas and the exhibit perimeter, engaging and qualifying visitors. After qualifying to find the product need, the floater will match up the visitor with the correct presenter. Typically a team selling interaction involves three steps.

- **Step 1: Opening and Qualifying.** A visitor strolls casually into the exhibit and is engaged by the floater. After a quick qualification, the floater identifies the visitor's area of interest.

- **Step 2: The Cross-Referral.** The floater then walks the visitor over to the appropriate presenter, or gathers the appropriate presentation team. This action is called cross-referral and prevents the visitor from wandering aimlessly about or leaving without being contacted. If the presenter is tied up, the floater will catch the presenter's eye and tell him that he has someone the presenter should meet. The floater will then keep the visitor interested with warm-up conversation.

- **Step 3: The Pass-Off.** The floater then introduces the visitor to the presenter, restating a summary of the information gathered in the qualifying process. At that time the floater might also give the presenter the partially completed lead card the floater has started.

  This introduction, or *pass-off*, avoids asking the visitor to repeat all of the information again. The floater is then free to disengage and return to his or her post. If the qualifying process uncovered more than one area of interest, it is important that the floater let the presenter know this so the visitor can be passed off again when his or her presentation is complete.

If you were using a live presentation in your exhibit, team selling would take on another variation. The staffing team might consist of floaters, live presenters, and product demonstrators. The floater's job is to draw visitors in to view the live presentation, and perhaps qualify them in the process. They would then also be required to greet visitors after the presentation, to see if they wanted a more in-depth product presentation. At that point they might cross-refer them to a demonstrator and conduct a hand-off.

Your staffing team might also include PR representatives, receptionists, hostesses, guides, or management representatives, all of whom would need to be considered in the selling strategy.

Therefore the first step in creating the team is to identify the tasks to be accomplished in the exhibit and the types of people who can best fill those tasks. In any group you will find some extroverts and some introverts. The extroverts excel at certain tasks and the introverts at others. Of course it makes sense to use people's strengths.

If you most often work with 10′ in-line exhibits and two staffers this will be fairly simple. The following diagram in Exhibit 14-4 identifies

---

Exhibit 14-4   Team Selling Tasks and Personality Types

Floater ───────────────────────▶ Extrovert
   Welcomes the visitor   Enjoys people
   Learns visitor's interest   Good communication
   Uncovers needs   skills required
                                     Only cursory product
                                     knowledge

Presenter ─────────────────────▶ Introvert
   Demonstrates the product   Fewer communications
   Closes the interaction   skills required
                                     In-depth product
                                     knowledge is essential

personality types that work best with the two basic team selling functions. You won't find too many surprises here, it is simply something that exhibitors don't take time to consider.

However, if you are working with large exhibits and a complex plan, your job in identifying tasks will be a bit more complex. The chart in Exhibit 14-5 will aid you in identifying typical roles to fill that are often required in the size exhibits indicated. These divisions are general and should be adapted to your situation.

Exhibit 14-5 Exhibit Staffing Roles		
100-200 sq. ft.	**200-600 sq. ft.**	**600+ sq. ft.**
☐ Balance of product knowledge and communications skills essential in staffers selected. ☐ Staffers will most likely fill both roles, greeting and qualifying visitors and presenting products. ☐ Plan for one staffer for each 50 square feet of open space in the exhibit.	☐ Sales staff with good communications skills. ☐ Product experts to conduct demos. ☐ One support staff person to serve as a receptionist at the information counter. ☐ Management personnel. Define their role on the team. ☐ Third-party vendors. How will they contribute to the team? ☐ Do you need to consider geographic representation among staffers?	☐ Sales staff. ☐ Product experts. ☐ Technical experts to keep demo equipment trouble-free. ☐ PR representative to handle press inquiries. ☐ Third-party vendors. ☐ Models, hostesses, receptionists, guides. ☐ Presenters for formal presentations. ☐ Management and executives. ☐ Others _____ _____ _____ _____

Using the Staff Team Planning Worksheet

When the number and variety of people working in the exhibit increases, so does the difficulty of organizing those needs. Use the Staff Team Planning Worksheet in Exhibit 14-6 to keep track of the types and numbers of staffers required for each show. Complete this as early as possible (note that you will be determining staffing requirements early in the planning process as you create the operational plan for the show) and file it in your Show Plan notebook.

Word of Warning: A common danger that companies fall into is using new hires to staff the exhibit. Their reasoning is that it will

Exhibit 14-6   Staff Team Planning Worksheet

SHOWS

Team Members	#1	#2	#3	#4	#5	#6	#7	#8	#9	#10	#11	#12
Sales personnel												
Product experts (Total) (By product)												
Third-party reps												
Receptionists												
PR staff												
Technical spprt.												
Management												
Executives												
Others: _____												
_____												

give the new hire quick exposure to the industry and "trial by fire" experience presenting and demonstrating products with a support staff right there to help them. Do you want to position someone who knows the least about your company and products as the person who will make a first impression on show visitors? Would you send that person out on a string of sales calls to important prospects?

Studies indicate that lack of product knowledge is one of the primary complaints show visitors make about exhibit staffers when they are not satisfied with their experience in an exhibit.(2) Putting new recruits on booth duty usually only results in a staffer with a low level of confidence and resulting lesser quality performance in the exhibit. Avoid it.

When You Have to Limit Participation

It is one of life's ironies that some exhibit managers find themselves begging, borrowing, and stealing to get enough staffers to create a sufficient team, while others find themselves having to say no to hosts of people who can't wait for show opportunities. Keep in mind, however, that the staffing function is your responsibility and it is okay to say no. If you are fortunate and have to deal with large numbers who want to participate, begin to be selective and make trade show work a bonus by:

- Establishing the number of staffers you will need early.
- Selecting only top performers for participation.
- Giving participants specific assignments for booth duty.
- Establishing a booth duty schedule, and not allowing off-duty personnel to hang around the exhibit.
- Evaluating performance and replacing staffers who are not meeting expectations.

The threads of continuity that you have begun to see repeated over and over in this chapter are *responsibility and control.* The next area we are going to cover, which will allow you another level of control over staffer performance is their education and training.

EDUCATING EXHIBIT STAFFERS

As companies are expecting more from the trade show function, the level of sophistication with which exhibitors are approaching shows and their staff is also on the rise. Booth staff training techniques are becoming more accepted among exhibits and sales management as a prerequisite to successful show participation. In 1982 23% of exhibits managers surveyed said they needed more information on booth staffing and training techniques to improve their show participation. Within five years that percentage had risen to 33%.(3)

What Type of Training Is Required?

To get a good picture of the type of training to look for, consider first the basic selling strategy common to most exhibits. It follows these four steps.

- **Engaging the visitor.** The first step is for the staffer to open the interaction with visitors. This appears simple but is actually very difficult to do on a continued, repetitive basis. In fact, most salespeople in their day-to-day jobs do nothing like that at all. Even the most extroverted people benefit from strategies that help them open interactions successfully without threatening or intimidating visitors, and in a way that opens the door to further conversation.
- **Qualifying the visitor.** The next step after the visitor has been welcomed is to qualify them. Doing an adequate job of qualifying requires learning basic information about the visitors such as company affiliation, and job responsibilities, but most important it requires the staffer to learn about visitor needs. Many crack salespeople fall down here because they are used to having plenty of time with customers to learn this information, and at trade shows it must be gathered within the first 90 seconds of the interaction. Staffers need techniques for uncovering this information in a short timeframe, while continuing to keep the visitor's comfort level high and build a trust level.
- **Presenting/Demonstrating Products and Services.** A group of staffers is usually selected for booth duty based on their product expertise, so most staffers excel at product presentations. But the weak link here is knowing how to streamline those longer presentations used in the field to accommodate the typical trade show visitor's short attention span. The average exhibit interaction lasts just three to five minutes. Staffers also need techniques for breaking through the visitor's fatigue, and getting them involved in the presentation to increase their recall of your company's products vs. all of the other products they have seen that day.
- **Closing the interaction.** The skill level here can vary dramatically from the experienced sales staffer who closes on a dime to the technical representative who is uncomfortable asking visitors to commit to any type of follow-up. But all staffers need to be reminded about how to use the lead card in the close, how to gather the information requested for the lead card, and the types of follow-up options that can be offered. Salespeople, generally being the broad brush types of people that they are, often think that getting the name and address is sufficient, and gloss over other vital information that needs to be collected on the lead card.

Nonverbal Communications and Basic Booth Etiquette. Staffers also need to be reminded of any etiquette standards you have set for the exhibit such as no eating, drinking, or smoking. And, illustrating for them how nonverbal gestures can influence the communication content of the interaction can make a significant contribution toward their efforts to successfully communicate nonverbally.

In fact, 93% of what is communicated in an interaction is done so nonverbally, either through gestures, tone of voice, or facial expression. Even more than many field selling interactions, the trade show interaction involves full-body, nonverbal communications. A sophisticated group of staffers must understand how to use this powerful communications tool.

That description covers the most basic exhibit selling skills that staffers should be equipped to use. Depending on the strategy for your show the skills level required could be more sophisticated, including team selling skills, relational selling skills, formal presentation, or demonstration skills.

Training and Education: Options

The training solutions you select will most likely be influenced by your time, level of expertise, and financial resources. If, for example, you are a one-person department, and don't have the time or the resources to conduct training sessions yourself, you might prefer to hire an outside firm to handle the training. If you are fairly experienced at shows and familiar with the concepts of show selling, you might prefer to use off-the-shelf courses to conduct your own pre-show meetings. If you manage a large program and will be relying on someone else (divisional exhibit managers, sales managers, etc.) to conduct pre-show meetings, you might prefer to have a custom pre-show meeting leader's guide produced that can be used show after show.

Self-Study Options. A variety of resources exist from pamphlets to audio and video tapes to full courses for self-study skills-building in exhibit selling. These are the most economical solutions and can be implemented in a variety of ways.

- Tapes or self-study courses purchased for all staffers.
- Tapes or self-study courses purchased for building a "library" of resources that can be used on a loan basis.
- Educational brochures on exhibit selling included in pre-show memos or handed out at pre-show meetings.
- Training meetings where self-study materials are studied in small groups facilitated by group leaders.

Pre-Show Meeting Support Materials. The following are a variety of materials that you can purchase to include skills training in your meetings. They are listed from the most general to the most custom solutions.

1. *Video tapes.* Several trade show organizations produce video tapes on exhibit selling. (See Appendix for a list of training resources.) These are usually designed to be presented at pre-show meetings. Be sure to view the tapes yourself and plan your introduction prior to using them.

2. *Subject brochures.* Literature on subjects related to exhibit selling briefly covering topics such as "Nonverbal Communications," "Qualifying Probes for Trade Show Selling," and others is also available. You can pass these out at the pre-show meetings.

3. *Meeting Leader's Guides.* The Meeting Leader's Guide is a custom-produced document that you, or other managers, use as a resource for preparing pre-show meetings. It can include guidelines on everything from room planning to speaker participation to exhibit selling skills. The guides are formatted in such a way that a person with little experience leading pre-show meetings could open the guide and step through the process of preparing for a pre-show meeting.

   Some of the more in-depth guides also include detailed content on skills training with guidelines and samples for interactive workshops and skill drills. Consider a custom Meeting Leader's Guide if you need help preparing pre-show meetings, or want to equip other people within your organization to lead these meetings.

Pre-Show Training. There are also a variety of sources for formal exhibit staff training, ranging from independent consultants to firms exclusively committed to these services. "Training" as a term is used loosely to describe these services as they do vary in content and structure from motivational lectures to purely content lectures to interactive-skills-based workshops. If you are talking with exhibit staff trainers, clarify their approach to assure that it meets your requirements.

SUMMARY

If there is a single theme for this chapter it would be to encourage you to take responsibility for and control over the staffing function in your exhibit. You can do this by: identifying the problem areas, incorporating techniques to overcome the problem areas, improving communications with sales management, and motivating staffers to become top performers in your exhibits. The resources for accomplishing these tasks continue to improve in depth, breadth, and sophistication. A bit of research will provide you with the tools. For more help on implementing the changes required, see Chapter 17 on managing growth in the exhibits department.

15

Managing
Exhibit Properties

If you own a single exhibit structure, store it at your exhibit house, have them control inventory, and ship it to shows for you, most likely you needn't spend a lot of time on this chapter. But, if you are beginning to wonder whether you have sufficient properties, or whether your properties are being managed as efficiently as they could, this chapter will be useful to you.

These days corporate exhibit programs and options for exhibit structures are growing simultaneously. As many corporate exhibit managers are finding their needs for display structures changing, they are also discovering the options for filling those needs are expanding.

And as properties inventories grow, the complexities of managing them increase as well. Preparing for shows is no longer as simple as saying, "Let's get the exhibit ready to ship." You often have to ask: which exhibit, how much of that exhibit, in what configuration? Managing exhibit properties can be a full-time job. In fact at some large companies it is a full-time job for several people. In this chapter, you will find guidelines to help you discover the best solution to meet some of these growth needs . . . for today. Keeping up with properties management requires ongoing review and adjustment. Here you will see.

1. HOW TO DETERMINE YOUR NEEDS: Guidelines for determining if, and by how much, you need to expand your properties inventory.

2. OPTIONS FOR FILLING THE NEEDS: Structural options and a cost evaluation worksheet.

3. OPTIONS FOR MANAGING EXHIBIT PROPERTIES: Three choices for properties management and factors to consider for each.

HOW TO DETERMINE WHEN IT'S TIME TO EXPAND
EXHIBIT PROPERTIES

Not long ago I talked with an exhibit manager who saved his company tens of thousands of dollars by scrapping a new custom exhibit after its first year of use and converting his entire show program to rental structures. Shortly after that I read about an exhibit manager who saved her company tens of thousands of dollars by giving up her practice of renting most of her exhibit properties and purchasing an exhibit system. Confused?

Lately, making the best decision about exhibit properties has been a bit confusing. Up until the early 80s there weren't a great deal of choices. There were custom exhibits, and pipe and drape, with a few portable and systems options tossed in. Now, selecting an exhibits structure is like walking up to the salad bar and trying to make the most nutritious choices.

And the choices are phenomenal. Now you can select from custom structures, custom-built system structures, off-the shelf system structures, rented custom structures, rented system structures, portable exhibits, used exhibits, and redesigns or refurbs of your existing structure.

To complicate matters still more, as your program expands in size you will probably find a need for more than one type of structure. Many large programs (more than ten shows each year) use a combination of custom-built structures, modular system structures, and portable exhibits.

Three Common Reasons for Expanding Properties

But first things first. Before deciding on a type of structure, first invest the time in determining exactly what you need. If you find yourself putting off facing the trade show schedule because there is going to be a lot of juggling and negotiating to distribute properties fairly, there's a good chance you may need to expand inventory. But there's a much more practical, even systematic, way to approach the need for more exhibit properties. Here are a few reasons exhibitors typically expand their inventory. See if any of these fit your situation.

Volume. It may be impossible to meet the sheer number of shows and requests for exhibits properties that are anticipated for the coming year. That problem isn't too difficult to identify. But what is difficult to identify is exactly how much more inventory and what types of exhibits will most effectively meet those needs. It might be worthwhile to project out to the following year as well. Is this spurt in growth temporary or stable enough to warrant an investment in new property?

Economics. As you saw in the introduction, pure economies might warrant an investment in more exhibit properties. It has been common recently to hear exhibitors laud the value of modular system exhibits in helping them to supplement and stretch custom displays to accommodate more needs in the department. Cost comparisons may reveal for you significant savings of one type of exhibit property over another, to warrant expanding your inventory in that type of property. For example, you may have purchased some system structure and found that the savings in set-up and services warrants an investment in more of that property so that it can be used more frequently. (For help in making some of those comparisons, see Exhibit 15-5 on page 391 in this chapter.)

Efficiencies. Perhaps your earliest exhibiting efforts were at major national shows in your industry and now you are moving into regional or vertical markets with your trade show efforts. It might then be impractical to send a custom exhibit out to be set up for these smaller shows. This can be true even if you own a 10' custom display.

At the smaller shows, if you use portable exhibits, local salespeople can set them up and save you the time and effort of ordering labor or hiring a set-up firm, or traveling to the show yourself to supervise set-up. The efficiencies realized by shipping portable exhibits to the smaller shows can justify the investment in these properties.

The list in Exhibit 15-1 offers a series of "signposts" that point to a need for expanding exhibit inventories. If these apply to your program it will be worth the time invested to identify the needs more clearly.

Exhibit 15-1   Signposts That Point to a Need

- Do you see shows on your schedule for which no structure is available?
- Are overlapping shows common in your schedule?
- Is your show schedule shifting from primarily national major shows to more smaller vertical market or regional shows? (Or vice-versa?)
- Are you finding requests for a wide range of exhibit sizes?
- Are show demands making it impossible for you to supervise all installations?
- Are budget constraints restricting participation in important shows?
- Do you plan to begin attending international shows?
- Is your structure no longer accommodating necessary product displays?
- Do you want salespeople to begin setting up displays themselves?
- Are service costs on your structure too high?
- Are expanded needs long-term or temporary?
- Are you using exhibit properties in areas other than shows (board meetings, corporate events, etc.)?

The obvious question here is, "Do you have enough properties?" If the signposts are all pointing to the fact that inventories need to be expanded, spend some time on the worksheet in Exhibit 15-2. It is a schedule that allows you to view, at a glance, properties required to meet the demands, and identifies whether you currently have as much as you need.

One worksheet covers one month. To view the entire year, complete a worksheet for each month. It lists three different types of structures that you could have in your inventory: custom structure (which is usually configured in fairly limited space sizes), modular system structure (which is usually configured in linear feet), and portable exhibits (which are usually configured in 10′ linear segments).

On each worksheet the days of the month are listed in the left column. Under each title on the worksheet, one box represents one component. For example, there is only one box that represents the custom exhibit with a space to write in the size required. Under the modular system exhibit each box represents 10 linear feet of structure. So, in our example, we would have 60 linear feet of that property in our inventory. Under the portable exhibit, each box represents one 10′ structure. In our example, we would have five portable exhibits in our inventory. You will have to make up your own sheet to represent the actual amount of property in your inventory.

To use the chart you need to have a completed show schedule for each month, and identify the type of exhibit structure preferred for each show. A sample show schedule for the completed chart in Exhibit 15-3 is listed here.

SHOW SCHEDULE: January

Date	Show	Exhibit
Jan. 3–5	Midwest Restr. Supply	Portable
Jan. 3–8	California Outdoor Retailers	System/10 × 20
Jan. 4–6	Glass Expo	Portable/10 × 10
Jan. 2–7	Int'l Glassware Show	Custom
Jan. 6–11	Pool & Spa Retailers	Portable/10 × 20
Jan. 7–12	National Home Show	System/10 × 30
Jan. 7–15	Gourmet International	Portable/10 × 10

Working off of the completed schedule, shows can be plotted on this chart to see very quickly where property needs overlap. You can also see, by looking across the chart, what quantities of properties are in use at any given date. In our example in Exhibit 15-3, we are able to accommodate all shows, but January 7 and 8 we will only have two 10′ portables left to fill any additional requests for properties.

Exhibit 15-2 Properties Scheduling Model Worksheet

January	Custom	Modular System:						Portable Exhibits				
	Size:	10′	10′	10′	10′	10′	10′	#1	#2	#3	#4	#5
1												
2												
3												
4												
5												
6												
7												
8												
9												
10												
11												
12												
13												
14												
15												
16												
17												
18												
19												
20												
21												
22												
23												
24												
25												
26												
27												
28												
29												
30												
31												

Exhibit 15-3 Properties Scheduling Worksheet

January	Custom		Modular System								Portable Exhibits					
		Size:		10′	10′	10′	10′	10′	10′			#1	#2	#3	#4	#5
1			1								1					
2		20′×30′	2								2					
3			3								3					
4			4								4					
5			5								5					
6			6								6					
7			7								7					
8			8								8					
9			9								9					
10			10								10					
11			11								11					
12			12								12					
13			13								13					
14			14								14					
15			15								15					
16			16								16					
17			17								17					
18			18								18					
19			19								19					
20			20								20					
21			21								21					
22			22								22					
23			23								23					
24			24								24					
25			25								25					
26			26								26					
27			27								27					
28			28								28					
29			29								29					
30			30								30					
31			31								31					

When plotting the use of properties, don't just plot the date of the show, plot the dates from when the structure leaves the warehouse to when it returns.

Plot out usage for each month for the next year to provide a realistic picture of short-term needs. To adequately address the need, however, review your show schedule over at least the following two years. This will also help you to identify whether increased requirements are just temporary, or sufficient to justify an investment in additional properties.

SEVEN OPTIONS FOR MEETING STRUCTURAL NEEDS

Up to this point you might be using just one type of structure, a modular exhibit, or strictly portable exhibits. Don't limit the possibilities for expanding properties to just buying more of what you already have. There are options for expanding your inventory, and as was referenced earlier, exhibitors with large programs often have a mixture of structure types in their inventories. The following list of options includes the needs that they *typically* solve in an expanded exhibits program. These are not restrictive however, just explanations to give you an idea of where they can help in your program.

Custom Structure. A custom-built structure is typically used by companies when they participate in larger shows, frankly to present a strong, solid image for the company. Exhibitors often choose custom structures when, as the name implies, they need a unique custom solution for their exhibits marketing strategy.

General opinion is that custom structures are more expensive than modular systems or portable exhibits. But this isn't necessarily true. When you are considering a 10' linear structure, custom exhibitry will typically cost more than portable displays, but as you move into larger exhibits, custom structures can be in line with the cost of other solutions.

Custom structures are built for a limited number of configurations and tend to be less flexible than other options. There is a hybrid solution called the custom system. It's becoming increasingly popular for exhibit houses to propose custom-designed system structures for companies who need a great deal of flexibility yet don't want an off-the-shelf system.

Modular Systems. System exhibits usually consist of some combination of poles, connectors, and panels. They are becoming an increasingly popular solution for companies that exhibit in many shows and need a system that can meet a variety of structural needs, without being limited to pre-designed configurations. Companies that have exhibit departments to service the trade show needs of their divisions often find systems a good solution because they can use the components in a different configuration for each show.

Exhibitors are also using systems to extend the use of their custom exhibitry among more shows. As show schedules increase, rather than buying a large custom structure, or just purchasing a new system exhibit, exhibitors supplement the custom structure with system components.

And some exhibitors have experimented and realized such a cost savings by using system exhibits over a custom structure, that they have changed inventory completely.(1)

> **NOTE:** Exhibit systems are not necessarily portable. People often confuse these terms. If you purchase an exhibit system you will most likely still need to use scheduled transportation, and drayage and installation/dismantle services.

Portable Exhibits. Portable exhibits are designed to pack in a carrying case and ship as baggage on airlines. Many cost savings can be realized with portable exhibits because they can often be carried right onto the show floor and set up by one person without the help of show labor. For companies with relatively small exhibit programs, the portable exhibit might be the only structure they own. Increasingly, companies with large exhibit programs are using portable displays at regional and vertical market shows.

If you participate in several shows where one or two field salespeople staff the booth, a portable exhibit would allow them to handle installation and dismantle, as well as the selling in between. The exhibit manager would not have to attend the show at all. The only key factor here, if you are considering investing in portable structures, is implementing a system for shipping the exhibit, ensuring that salespeople know how to set it up, and ensuring that it is returned to you or sent on for the next show in tip-top condition. (For more information on that, see Chapter 8 on getting the most from your portable exhibits.)

Rental Structures. Rental structures can be lifesavers. If you find that you just have one time slot on your schedule where you won't have enough exhibit properties, rather than making the investment in another property that won't be used for the rest of the year, consider renting a structure to fill that slot. If most of your shows are scheduled nearby, but you have one overseas, you might rent a structure from a supplier there to avoid shipping and customs hassles. This is especially useful if you don't have to ship products.

Keep in mind with rental structures, however, that you will either have to find a structure that will accommodate your existing graphics, or invest in new graphics for the exhibit. But when your inventory is stretched to capacity, investing in graphics would most likely be more economical than investing in an entirely new structure.

Refurbish an Existing Structure. You might have an old work-horse exhibit that has just seen one too many shows, but could really be useful to beef up your inventory a bit. Would it be more economical to refurbish the existing structure or build an entirely new structure? That depends on the type of refurbishing the exhibit needs. Where does it fall in these three categories?

Touch-Ups of course are fairly economical. If you only need new laminate in a specific area, or new carpet, or a new light box, it will probably make sense to do a minor refurbish and put the structure back into circulation.

Re-Skin. This is a term used in the exhibit industry to describe the process of removing the covering (or skin) on the structure, such as a laminate or paint, and putting a new covering on. This can be considerably more expensive, but as compared to the cost of building a new structure might make sense. While it will depend on your structure and require-ments, re-skinning an exhibit can be done for one-third to one-half of the cost of building a new structure.

Rebuild. If the exhibit needs major structural repairs or quite a bit of rebuilding to get it up to usable standards again, this is the time to seriously consider investing in a new property. The cost to rebuild could easily be comparable to the cost of a new modular system or a group of portable displays.

The worksheet in Exhibit 15-4 is designed to help you consider some of the costs involved in bringing an old exhibit up to usable standards again. Use the check-boxes on the left to indicate the types of changes you would have to make to the structure. Then indicate in the spaces cost estimates from your exhibit supplier for making those changes. You can use this to compare the cost of an entirely new structure to make some calculated decisions.

How to Anticipate Structural Operating Expenses

While volume and efficiencies influence the decisions about the amount and types of structures to have, costs are usually the most influential factor. But the cost savings to be realized with different types of structures are found more frequently in costs that are incurred *after* the exhibit is purchased. It is the ongoing cost of the structure such as warehousing, transportation, drayage, installation, and dismantle that can make an exhibit structure expensive.

While it is difficult to anticipate those costs, estimates can be made based on information you gather from your transportation and exhibit

Exhibit 15-4   Exhibit Refurbish Cost Evaluation
Worksheet

Item	Estimated Cost
☐ Pieces rebuilt	$ _____
_____	
_____	
_____	
_____	
☐ Graphics removed from panels	$ _____
☐ New graphics on panels	$ _____
☐ New flooring or carpeting	$ _____
☐ New laminants	$ _____
☐ New paint	$ _____
☐ New lighting	$ _____
☐ Electrical rewired	$ _____
☐ New component construction	$ _____
☐ New set-up drawings	$ _____
☐ New crates	$ _____
TOTAL	$ _____

suppliers. The worksheet in Exhibit 15-5 can help you make some comparisons between exhibit structures to see where cost savings can be realized. If you already own several structures, this worksheet can provide some management guidelines on which are most economical to use. You might find some surprises.

To complete the worksheet you will need to record costs for the specified categories for each show in which you participate. Use the "structure" column to indicate what type and size of structure was used. You can use a shorthand here. For example S = the system structure,

Show Name	Structure	Storage	Trans.	Dray-age	I&D	Svs.

Exhibit 15-5   Structure Expense Comparisons

P = the portable structure, and C = the custom structure. So a 10′ linear portable display would be coded P/10×10. Scanning the list, you will be able to quickly spot highs and lows and begin to see some expense patterns.

When the Structure Is Too Expensive

Determining whether transportation and service costs are in line can be based on what your budget can tolerate, and measured against past history benchmarks.

For some independent guidelines, you can refer to the Trade Show Bureau study on how the show budget is distributed. These 1987 figures show that for an average of companies surveyed (typically those with larger programs), 14% of their show budget is spent on transportation, 21% on show services such as installation/dismantle, drayage, electrical, etc., and 8% on refurbishing. (For a more detailed breakout see Chapter 2 on preparing budget estimates.)

THREE OPTIONS FOR MANAGING EXHIBIT PROPERTIES

There are three choices here: external, internal, or a combination. External management means turning over all of those logistics to your exhibit supplier. This is often the best solution for the one-person exhibits department. Internal properties management, at the opposite extreme, means that everything from the decision and construction of the exhibit, to warehousing, inventory, transportation, show set-ups, and return, are handled by a company employee. This is not the most common way to manage properties, but extremely efficient for some larger programs. Most exhibits programs fall somewhere in between, with a combination of internal and external management. For example the exhibit is built by an outside supplier but all logistics are handled internally.

Each system has its pros and cons. Internal management allows for maximum control over the program, quick turnaround times, structure availability, and more. External management takes advantage of the expertise of a display house and their connections in the industry. It also allows an exhibit manager with limited time to focus on strategic planning and program management. A combination provides for the best of both options, but requires excellent communications structures.

What would work best for your department? It depends primarily on the resources available. Here the three options are explained with factors to consider for each approach.

Services for External Properties Management

In Chapter 3 you covered many of the dynamics of the exhibit supplier/client relationship when the new exhibit is built. Here we will see some of those dynamics as they relate to servicing the exhibit and your show program. The level of services among exhibit suppliers varies dramatically, but the key to this type of properties management is communications and trust. Full-service exhibit suppliers are necessary for this arrangement, and if you are beginning a relationship or looking for a supplier, look to Chapter 3 for guidelines on finding the level of services you need.

Here is a list of services that are available through some exhibit suppliers in the country. Expect to pay for these services either in the price of a new exhibit structure, or as you use them. Keep in mind that this is not a complete list of services that exhibit suppliers offer, only those services relating to properties management.

Local Properties Warehousing. Many exhibit suppliers have warehouse facilities and store client's properties for them between shows.

National Properties Warehousing. The largest exhibit houses in the country have offices in or near most major convention cities in the U.S. Their warehousing network allows you to store exhibit properties in various locations to accommodate your show schedule. For example if your office is in L.A. and you have a show in Chicago one month and in New York the following month, the exhibit can be shipped on to New York after the first show and stored in their warehouse, rather than returned to L.A.

Properties Inventory. This service varies from written inventory list to sophisticated computer inventories. One company received a complete notebook from their exhibit supplier with itemized computer inventory print-outs, drawings to illustrate exhibit properties components in the inventory, a graphics catalog, and worksheets for ordering components of their custom system exhibit when they planned for shows. This is not the kind of service that comes with a standard exhibit purchase. This came with an investment in a custom exhibit that totaled $300,000.

But if you are counting on your exhibit supplier to warehouse and inventory properties, expect an organized and regularly updated inventory, and a system for ordering properties for shows.

Exhibit Preparation. With warehousing and inventory must come exhibit preparation. The supplier will pull the appropriate structure out of inventory, assure that it is in good repair, and prepare it for shipment to each show.

Exhibit Preview. You will also have to count on the supplier to set up the structure for pre-show viewing.

Transportation. Many exhibit houses offer to arrange transportation services to shows. You pay a mark-up for their services, but they will schedule your exhibit pick-ups and deliveries and be responsible for assuring that it arrives at the show on time.

Installation/Dismantle Services. Your exhibit supplier can also schedule installation/dismantle for you. Some suppliers have their own team of installation supervisors and others contract this service out.

Properties Maintenance. When exhibits return from shows and the supplier checks them back into inventory, each component is viewed for surface or structural damage that needs repair. These needs are flagged and brought to your attention, for your decision on whether or not to make the repairs before storing the exhibit.

Selecting this option for properties management means turning over a great deal of control to an outside vendor. Trust is important here, but so are checks and balances. If you are considering this option, review the following guidelines. If you are currently using this system of properties management, use these guidelines as a check to assure it continues to be the most efficient for you.

Guidelines for External Properties Management

- Request that *one* person manage your program and be responsible for all functions the exhibit supplier offers.
- Be sure that you can contact the account executive managing your program 24 hours a day.
- Meet and request access to *all* other individuals involved with your program.
- Know where your exhibit is stored. Walk through the warehouse to be sure it is neat, that the climate is adequate, and your exhibit is stored safely.
- Plan your annual show schedule with your account executives as far in advance as possible.
- Define your communications requirements. How often do you want updates on show progress? What decisions can the A/E make without consulting you and for what decisions *must* they consult you?
- Establish advance notice guidelines for making changes. After what point in the process will it begin to cost you more to make changes in your plans? After what point will it be impossible to make changes?
- Know the suppliers they work with (for example, transportation or installation companies) and be comfortable with their reputation.
- Request regular inventory status reports.
- Assure that insurance coverage is adequate.
- Feel comfortable with the entire company, not just your account executive. If you are turning over properties management to them, the nitty-gritty details of your program will be handled by people other than the account executive. Being comfortable with that support is essential.

If your exhibit supplier is taking responsibilities for properties management, use their services as much as possible. The primary advantage to this arrangement is that it frees you up from logistics management and allows you to focus more on program management.

When Combining Internal and External Management Improves Efficiencies

This arrangement can take on a variety of forms, but most typically the exhibits are designed and built by an exhibit supplier and then warehoused and managed internally. There are a couple of situations where this can be most efficient. If your company is located a good distance from your exhibit supplier, it can be a logistical hassle to keep the structures at their facility. If you handle many shows, and do a lot of staging prior to each show, allowing participating divisions to view the structure and provide input, it is, again, logistically easier to accommodate that on-site.

A combination of internal and external management gives you more control over the process. It also requires more of your time (or that of your staff) to manage the process. If you are considering bringing more of the properties management functions inside, you will need at least one person dedicated to it full-time. It also requires that you or they have some design sense and can create your own design drawings and set-up plans for each show. Here are some guidelines for this type of properties management.

Guidelines for Combination Internal/External Properties Management

- Have at least one person with no other responsibilities than to manage exhibit properties. Depending on the size and scope of your program it may require more than one dedicated person. That person will probably not be the exhibit manager, whose primary responsibility should be coordinating the entire exhibit program, but someone who only handles logistics of properties management.

- Be sure that your warehouse is large enough to accommodate your existing structure and future growth. Also include a large staging area where exhibits can be set up and previewed prior to shipping them to shows.

- Be sure you have the necessary equipment in the warehouse, such as speed racks for storage, special carpet racks if you purchase your own carpet, storage crates for structure, forklift trucks, loading docks, etc.

- Make sure the loading dock is accessible to large trucks. Don't make them have to back down alleys or around tight corners to get in.

- Climate control will be important especially if you are storing graphics. Extreme heat, cold, and humidity can destroy graphics and warp structures.

- Proximity to sales and marketing offices is important if you plan to invite groups in to preview the structure before the shows. Of course you will want it close to your own office as well.

- Work with your company's insurance provider to assure that your properties are protected while they are in storage as well as in transit and at the shows. Also check on liability insurance for workers in the warehouse and visitors to the facility.

- Assure that the necessary fire protection equipment such as sprinklers, fire extinguishers, and fire escapes are installed in the warehouse.

- Set up a system for visual inspection of properties when they arrive at the warehouse after a show. Check the need for repairs and make them as soon as possible. Don't check in properties and then plan a visual check before they go out again. Exhibit requests can be very short notice and there often isn't time to make major repairs prior to shipping the structure out.

- Plan to handle your own refurbishing. You will need someone skilled in carpentry to handle touch-ups and minor refurbishing needs. Otherwise you will have a difficult time keeping the structure in good repair or will find yourself sending it out far too frequently to realize the advantages of internal management.

- Create a good inventory system. It does not have to be computerized, but organize and code crates, list contents, and create a system for check-in/check-out exhibit properties.

- Create a visual inventory system. Consider using a catalog of photos of exhibit properties and graphics, organized by your inventory codes, to help in planning exhibits with divisions. One exhibitor organized his graphics in poster displays like the ones you see in gift and record stores. He could flip through the hinged displays to easily view and select graphics with divisional reps for whom he was planning the display.

- Plan for installation/dismantle supervision. You or your staff can supervise installation at shows, or you can contract this out to an installation company.

- Have a good transportation provider. Here again you will be managing transportation yourself and a reliable and responsible supplier will be essential. One exhibitor said he knew he could trust his transportation supplier when the driver noticed that essential parts of a shipment hadn't been included, and reminded him about it.

- Keep up a positive relationship with your exhibit supplier because you will probably go back to them occasionally for major refurbish jobs, graphics production, additions to your structure, and design help for planning larger shows. Establish in advance how you will be billed for these occasional services.

The advantages here are greater control, accessibility, and flexibility, at the price of more time invested in the process. Also, the more you handle internally, the more you are relying on your own people for expertise in this management area. It will be important to watch for opportunities to learn about new ideas, new methods, new structures, new design techniques, and other management tools yourself, since you will not have an ongoing relationship with an exhibit supplier who might provide ideas and expertise in some of those areas.

Advantages and Risks of Internal Properties Management

A few companies find it most economical and efficient to handle all aspects of the exhibit structures internally, including designing and building the exhibit structure, handling all show logistics, managing the properties, and managing product display inventories.

Those who manage exhibits internally swear by the economies and efficiencies of the system. They know their inventories so well, turn-around time is next to nothing. Pieces can be built on-site in a snap without having to go through the time-consuming process of design approval, purchase orders, estimates, etc.

But this solution has its shortcomings too. Interestingly, some exhibit managers in this situation felt it was necessary to go outside for design help because they couldn't spend time keeping up with design trends and after awhile all of their designs began to look alike. Incestuous design, it was labeled.

Setting up an internal exhibit department is no small job. To give you an idea of the basics required, Paul McNutt, technical trade show exhibitry manager for Hewlett Packard's computer product sector, offers some advice on points to consider based on his ten years of experience managing an internal exhibit department.

ADVICE FROM THE EXPERTS: Internal Exhibit Properties Management: Three Essential Components

In his first year as exhibitry manager at Hewlett Packard, Paul McNutt built his first trade show exhibit with plywood and door hinges. Nine years later he purchased a custom exhibit system designed so that all parts are interchangeable with capabilities of filling booth spaces from 100 up to 7,000 sq. ft. in backwall, island, or peninsula configurations with over 80 product displays and five formal presentation areas.

He inventoried all exhibit components on a CAD system, and designs structures for all shows on that computer. His next step is to use the CAD system to generate three-dimensional perspective drawings (like photographs) of each exhibit designed. These CAD renderings serve several functions: to help demo coordinators visualize their environment; help set-up people view the final exhibit assembled; and provide upper management with a true view of the structure designed for a show plan they are asked to approve.

All exhibits and graphics, as well as packing, transportation, exhibit layout, and on-site installation, are the responsibility of his department. Over the years he has come up with a host of efficiency techniques, such as specially designed crates to speed up the packing and unpacking process, custom power distribution boxes for the enormous power needs for their systems (including junction boxes to split power lines for varying voltage needs of their products), graphics cataloging and inventory, exhibit design and construction, even pre-show previews and orientations for management and exhibit staff.

Here he discusses three essential components required for managing properties internally.

"1. **A person to run it.** This seems obvious but it is important that a person with the right balance of experience and skills manage the operations. The most important skill here is a good design sense and strong design background. The exhibits *must* look good and function efficiently. Everything else—carpentry, graphics, etc.—can be contracted out. But the process of designing the exhibit requires so much interplay between participating groups in the company that it needs to be handled by the person managing the operation.

That person must also be *client-oriented.* This means that they understand their role as a service provider, and that the divisions within the company who use those services are their clients. Two of the primary advantages of managing properties internally are cost savings and turnaround time. To keep those advantages strong, the operations manager must be extremely responsive, and constantly working to meet their client's needs in the most economical and efficient way possible.

That person must also be good at finding resources and pulling them together to get the job done. In our most recent year our two-person department produced 40 shows for our group. That includes everything from designing the structure to supervising set-up. There were many times when we called in outside suppliers to extend and support the services we offer the divisions. I regularly job out graphics production because I just don't want to deal with the OSHA regulations of operating a silk screen facility, for example. The person who manages the operations needs strong communications and people management skills.

(One resource I use regularly is 800 phone number information listings. If I am using a material and need to order more, I just need the name of the manufacturer and I can call the 800 information line, get the phone number, and order direct.)

The person will also need an understanding of carpentry skills or an assistant with those skills. While you can hire a local finish carpenter to come in and help with major construction, having someone on the spot for refurbs and side projects is helpful.

> **NOTE:** If you do hire a local finish carpenter to work in your facility, require written documentation that they have their own workman's compensation coverage, or you could be creating a liability for your company. Also, your selection of materials and construction for

the exhibit must adhere to applicable building fire codes for exhibit halls. Two-level exhibits often require engineering stamps.

Finally, the person managing the operation must be dedicated to it full-time—but not in a myopic sense. There are a lot of duties that are ancillary but connected to trade show participation that this person can handle. For example, depending on their skills base they could also contribute to public relations efforts, graphics design for other programs, pre-show orientations for exhibit staffers, product inventories and shipping for field demonstrations, trade show A-V production, to name just a few. If your program is not large enough to warrant a person dedicated just to that function, consider how their skills, and the department, could be put to use in other areas of the company.

2. **Place.** Again this seems obvious, but you need one central facility where all of the operations are managed. That means show planning, exhibit design, construction, inventory, packaging, and shipping must all be handled out of the same location. We use a 20,000-square-foot warehouse space separate from production and manufacturing facilities.

If you are building exhibits, plan to have a shop area where they can be constructed, and set up (ours is about 2,000 sq. ft., although we've built exhibits in a two-car garage). Consider ceiling heights and open floor space to provide for set-up as the structure is built.

The minimum equipment you will need are a table saw (that can cut to the center of a $4' \times 8'$ piece of plywood), a radial arm saw, drills and routers, and hand tools. Over the years we have acquired tools such as a surface planer, a lathe, and other pieces that we have purchased used as we saw opportunities. These pieces are not essential, but they do expand your construction possibilities.

Consider raw materials storage as well. We can get most of our materials on a "just in time" basis so we don't have to dedicate a lot of space to raw materials. But do have some shelves and space to accommodate $4' \times 8'$ sheets of plywood, plexiglas, and other materials that you use regularly. In the warehouse we have an office and design area where records are filed and the formal exhibit designs are produced. (We're of the cocktail napkin school of design so most of the design process can be taking place anywhere, but our CAD system and drafting board are set up in the office space.) We also have a carpentry shop, an electrical supplies area, a crate storage area, graphics inventory area, and a staging area where each exhibit can be completely set up for a preview before it is sent to a show. In a separate room there is space for an extensive product inventory (about 2,000 pieces) dedicated to trade show displays.

If you are planning on using warehouse space in your plan, consider that you may be tying up a loading dock for six to seven hours on any given day to load shipments, which could infuriate your shipping people. When the facility is separate you needn't worry about that.

With the facility, as with the people, don't be myopic about its potential. To get maximum return on your company's investment in the warehouse space consider additional uses for the facility. Are there other groups within the company who have a need for space with whom you could share some of the costs or which would help to justify the expense?

3. **A good network of suppliers.** I use outside vendors for silk screening, painting, typesetting, other graphics production, some sign building, some carpentry work, electrical, exhibit transportation, and other miscellaneous projects. Finding good suppliers and managing that network well is another essential ingredient of internal properties management.

There are two learning curves to consider with outside vendors. The first is that of the person managing the operations. He or she will need to know enough about the process of each service to guide and supervise vendors. The second learning curve is that of your vendors. The key to making the vendor network most useful is educating them about how trade show work is different than any other type of work they probably do.

Carpenters are a good example. If you are working with a carpenter who typically builds houses, deadlines are not particularly rigid for them. If the house doesn't get built by the scheduled deadline, there is always tomorrow, but trade show dates don't move.

They have to be continually reminded that there is no tomorrow in trade show work; that deadlines are rigid, not flexible, and why. They also might need to be educated about the transitory nature of show exhibits. Here again if they build houses, everything is constructed for permanence. With exhibits, construction must allow for easy installation and dismantle, and materials should be as lightweight and compact as possible to keep shipping costs to a minimum.

Sign companies are another example. They are used to doing outdoor and stationary work. Your signs will be transitory, and many will be viewed at closer ranges thus requiring more attention to clean details.

Managing exhibit properties internally is a bit controversial because of the overhead and resources a company devotes to the task. But in my experience I have seen the efficiencies and economies of this program demonstrated repeatedly. *Including the overhead* of warehousing space, and personnel, we have consistently realized savings of up to 50% on our structures and services as compared to costs we would incur for similar products and services through an exhibit supplier.

Admittedly, part of our economies are realized because we are located in an area where warehousing space is very reasonably priced. If you are located in Los Angeles or New York where space is more expensive, and you have to rent warehouse space, your overhead costs might be prohibitive. But compare what you pay per square foot or cubic foot of storage space at your display house with what you would pay for warehouse space.

Efficiencies are also realized regularly. Here's an example of how responsive we can be with the internal department. We had staged a new exhibit so that staffers responsible for demonstrating products could practice their demonstrations. One staffer said she felt uncomfortable demonstrating to groups who were craning their necks to see and asked if she could get a small platform to stand on. Before the next presentation was concluded we had a platform constructed that she could try.

We have more involvement in the process from design through to construction. There is no imaginary line drawn that defines when the design is finished and the construction begins. We are able to have more input and control in the construction process, and update and improve designs as we go. The advantage here is more flexibility in the process.

Also, during construction we don't have to deal with the process of making "change orders" when change requests come in from divisions, which significantly speeds up production time. We can often fill properties requests within 24 hours if we have to.

Another advantage of managing properties internally, which is difficult to quantify, is the inside knowledge we have of the corporate culture. For example, we have the internal connections to cross-check choices and decisions. We know these people and have access to them that would take years for an exhibit house to develop. This alone can contribute a great deal to both economies and efficiencies in a variety of ways.

Of course, internal properties management has its drawbacks as well. The toughest battle, which I have fought continually for the past seven years, is educating management about what we do. I find that I must continually justify our existence. I always have real cost comparisons available to discuss savings realized from this system. But the most difficult factor is that they just don't understand trade shows enough to see many of the efficiencies built into the system that are realized through time and experience. Your success here will depend on the attitudes of your managers and your ability to educate them as to the value of your department's contribution.

If you are located in a warehouse that is separate from the main facility, that physical isolation can be a drawback, too. You have to work much harder at keeping communications lines open with the rest of the group, with upper management, and with your clients in the company.

A second drawback which has been voiced by others in my position, is the limitations on our design capabilities. I recently had a new structure designed and constructed by an exhibit supplier because I felt that our designs were not as innovative as they could be. But we had just the minimum built and continue to supplement that with structures that we can build here in our facility. I find that I need to draw constantly on resources in the industry such as publications, seminars, and other exhibitors, to keep learning about prospects for making the program more innovative, more efficient.

We also have found that at times our learning curve can be expensive. When we work with outside vendors, getting them up to speed on our requirements can take additional time. But in talking with other exhibitors we have found that this can be true, perhaps to a lesser degree, even when working with exhibit suppliers.

Finally, exhibit suppliers often have a breadth and depth of experience in their firms that it takes years for a few people in an internal exhibits department to gain. If you are bringing someone new in to manage the department, you will be miles ahead by hiring someone who has already developed that experience.

Many exhibitors who are considering establishing internal exhibits departments voice a concern about problems they might encounter during exhibit installation at union convention centers if their exhibit is not built by union workers. In my experience, I never used a union-built exhibit during the first ten years I spent in this job and have never experienced any of the problems generally rumored to be associated with their use in union halls.

In summary, if you are considering bringing the properties management function inside, be sure you have the people (with the right experience), the facilities, and an available network of vendors. There are pros and cons to be considered, and they will change based on your corporate situation. It's not the best solution for all companies, but for us it has helped to realize a host of economies and efficiencies."

Exhibit 15-6   Properties Management: Pros and Cons

Pros	Cons

External Properties Management

Pros	Cons
• Expand resources and expertise without hiring additional staff. • More knowledge of industry and suppliers from exhibit supplier. • Free up exhibit manager's time for program management. • Innovation in design and construction techniques. • Resource for industry expertise in other areas such as marketing services.	• Less control over the structures. • Additional investment for services provided by exhibit supplier. • Less knowledge of your structure. • Less access to structures. • Less flexibility in timing. • Less involvement from other company managers (sales and marketing previews are more difficult).

Combination External/Internal Properties Management

Pros	Cons
• Good balance of control and expertise. • Quick turnaround on exhibit orders. • Can get design assistance when required. • Easy access to properties. • Provides for more participation from company managers. • Know your structure better.	• More taxing on resources of the exhibit department. • Greater overhead costs and liability considerations. • Can be isolated from industry knowledge and design trends. • More time invested working with suppliers.

Internal Properties Management

Pros	Cons
• Most control over properties. • Most knowledge of structures and graphics inventories. • Virtually no outside management costs. • Immediate access to structures. • Economies. • Efficiencies and quick turnaround	• Learning curve for managing program. • Requires ongoing PR to sell the program's benefits to management. • Manager must become expert in more areas. • Union considerations for exhibit construction/ installation.

To help you evaluate pros and cons of these alternatives more quickly, the chart in Exhibit 15-6 lists a synopsis of these factors.

In summary, you have a variety of choices on the types of exhibit properties available to you and the way in which the function is managed. Implementing the best system (especially if you are making major changes) will most likely require ongoing support of upper management. In the next chapter you will see some ideas and techniques for gaining that support regularly. The exhibits department can be one of the most visible in the company. You will see how to promote and take advantage of that visibility.

16

Building Management Support

If you had to isolate one factor that can most dramatically affect an exhibit manager's success and the growth of their department, it would have to be management support. Exhibit managers who enjoy control over their program and facilitate growth and change are willing to muddle through the corporate politics to make it happen. They, in fact, are masters at building support for their program among peers and managers.

In this chapter you will learn how to identify your key sources of support, their perspectives and hot buttons, resources and strategies for building an ongoing support network. Here you will see how to:

1. GET MANAGERS TO LISTEN: Identify your objectives, your support network, and work from their perspective.
2. GET MANAGERS CONVINCED: Compile your information and resources.
3. GET MANAGERS INVOLVED: Give them hands-on experience to facilitate understanding.

HOW TO GET MANAGEMENT'S EAR: THREE QUESTIONS TO ANSWER

A Trade Show Bureau Report indicates that "at firms with more than $400 million in sales, 51.4% of the top executives consider trade shows to be very important, while 16.7% consider trade shows to be unimportant." In firms with less than $50 million in sales, "71% of top executives are believed to consider trade shows very important, and only 4% consider trade shows to be unimportant."(1) As you can see, the larger your company, chances are the greater your challenge in building support for the trade show program. For some, the task may begin at the most fundamental level: getting people to listen. Others may find a skeptical ear, but an ear no less, and need to work at convincing people. Whatever the task, begin with the following three considerations.

The first question: **Why** do I want them to listen?

Unless you have very specific objectives for what you want to accomplish in building management support, your time will be undirected and essentially wasted. Your objectives will change as the program changes. Make it a continued practice to re-evaluate what needs to be accomplished in the effort to build management support.

The second question: **Who** needs to listen?

"Management" can be a fairly nebulous term. Identify exactly who you want to influence. This too will change, depending on your objectives and the type of impact managers have on your program. And think beyond just financial impact. Sales staff cooperation, product input, PR support . . . all can make or break a show plan.

The third question: **What** are their concerns and biases?

The entire strategy must be planned from the recipient's point of view. Your objectives are important, but most important is selecting the type of information and the presentation style that will be most convincing to your audience. The primary concerns of most managers are profit and performance. How does that translate for each individual on your list?

Let's begin at the beginning by exploring the first question.

Seven Objectives for Building Management Support

Determining your objectives requires some reflective thought. Begin by identifying areas in your program that are targeted for growth or improvement. Some of those areas will not need additional support from management in order to get them implemented (for example getting better service from your suppliers, or creating an inventory of exhibit components or graphics). But you will easily identify those areas where goals simply cannot be accomplished without support. (Getting longer lead times for a decision to participate in a show, or products to be displayed, for example.) The following list identifies a variety of goals for building management support. Check off any that are appropriate to your program and add your own as ideas surface.

This is a brainstorming exercise. Consider everything here that comes to mind. You will sort and organize later.

- ☐ **Budget Approval.** Do you have to present a budget for each show and have it approved? Or do you get an annual budget approved? Are you fighting for budget allocation with other media? In that case it will be extremely important to justify the value of show results vs. those of other media. Or are you looking for approval for a very specific budget item: staff training, for example? That strategy is completely different and more focused.

☐ **Cooperation from Salespeople.** Do you need to guarantee better quality staffers, a better attitude among your staffers, more staffers? Are you having trouble getting sales managers to take their best exhibit salespeople out of the field for your show? Do you feel as if you must beg, borrow, or steal for an exhibit staff?

☐ **Longer Lead Times.** Are your budgets skyrocketing because product divisions don't decide on what they are sending to the show until the last minute, and you pay for overnight airfreight? Do you get criticized for having a poor booth space in the show, but know it was only because you couldn't get a decision to participate until after the space selection deadline? Getting longer lead times from participating parties is a worthy goal and can significantly improve your entire show effort (and reduce your sleepless nights).

☐ **Show Plan Approval.** It is interesting how most people who have nothing to do with trade show participation become experts in the field when it comes time to review and approve show plans. If this is a goal, it will be important to identify here the decision-maker and key influencers.

☐ **New Exhibit Structure Approval.** This often becomes an education game. Many managers are simply floored by the cost of new exhibits because they don't understand exactly what goes into the design and construction. If you have a very cost-conscious manager, they may want to go for the low-ball bid. If you have a very image-conscious manager, they may readily select the structure that looks the best. Any strategy for approval of this type must include clear definition of the objectives for the structure and then a mechanism for evaluating which design best meets those objectives.

☐ **More Authority Credibility.** Authority, of course, is earned. But it is a worthy goal because once you begin building authority and credibility, people begin coming to you for advice and solutions.

☐ **Participation.** Perhaps you need to get managers more involved in your program. Would you like them to participate in pre-show meetings, booth duty, post-show follow-up? Then it will be important to convince them of why it is worth their time.

☐ **Others?** Now, what else has come to mind?

Once you have listed all possible goals for obtaining management support, prioritize them. Think about what will be most useful for your program this year. Think also about those that are most realistic. Doubling the budget allocations may be most useful, but might not be most realistic.

Deciding on where to start requires a balance of useful and realistic considerations. For example, getting a negative sales manager to cooperate in taking good salespeople out of the field to staff the exhibit may be most important and least realistic, but worth the extra effort required to make it happen. Keep that list of goals handy for the next exercise.

Six Critical Team Players

The next task in building management support is identifying exactly who you want on the team. It is important here to consider all of the decision-makers who can affect and even influence *all components* of your trade show program. For example, it might not occur to you that an engineering manager would influence your show program, until you are working to get input on new product introductions. The people you identify will vary based on the size of your company, the reach of your program, and your goals for building management support.

- **President/CEO.** At many small and mid-size companies, the president and/or CEO have quite a bit to say about the trade show program. In fact, they can suddenly appear out of nowhere and offer input that will change a strategy midstream. Or, their approval of a program or strategy can pave the way for acceptance throughout the organization.

- **Vice Presidents.** At mid-size companies, vice presidents can often have a great deal of influence at operational levels of the company. Do you need to go as high as the vice president of marketing, sales, operations, R&D? Maybe. If you can't get cooperation at middle management levels, their input may be helpful. Conversely, even if you do have a great deal of cooperation from middle managers, a negative attitude on the VP's part could sabotage that cooperation. Don't leave these people out of the picture.

- **Divisional Managers.** If you operate as a service arm in your organization and divisional managers make decisions about show participation and strategies, their success actually depends on your ability to respond to their needs (whether they realize it or not). If they don't give you the input, time, and support you need to do the job, it will be frustrating on both levels. By contrast, you can also provide not just support but expertise and direction to these folks to help them improve their results at shows . . . if they appreciate your abilities, and let you.

- **Product Managers.** These people can have the same control and influence as divisional managers depending on how the company is structured. But there's an additional significant influence they can have on your program. They provide the products for display and their cooperation in timing and communications is essential. If for no other reason, just hearing about activities and status on products is a good reason to keep open lines of communication with these folks.

☐ **Sales Managers.** A nemesis for many exhibit managers. If you rely on these people to provide staffers, their support should be a priority for you. They can make your life miserable. But if they believe in trade shows, and see the value in leads and/or sales generated by them, they can also be your most ardent supporter.

☐ **Advertising Managers.** What is their role in trade show participation? Is this person your boss? Then they will probably be juggling show allocations with those of other media. Even if their department is separate from yours, their input will be important as you create strategies for show participation to be consistent with communications messages in the advertising area.

☐ **Others?** Who else will you consider? _____

Issues and Attitudes You May Encounter

Finally, before embarking on your plan, consider the people you have identified more carefully. One trick to gaining support identified by exhibit managers who have succeeded at it is speaking management's language. Don't spend time telling them that you need more money for installation because drayage prices have increased and you won't be shipping your exhibit in crates. Instead connect budget increases of the past with increases in results to justify getting more money.

The following list includes just a few factors that may influence the thinking of your managers, and must in turn influence the strategy behind your efforts.

- **Management Mindset.** Most managers are primarily concerned with profits and performance. Interpret your points to illustrate how your plans will help them to save money or increase results. Sales managers are often especially concerned about the time their salespeople spend out of the field to participate in shows. Yet they don't often consider the efficiencies with which new prospects can be identified at shows versus in the field.

- **Goals and Objectives.** What are *their* goals and objectives for the year? Interpret for them, whenever possible, how your program will contribute to their goals.

- **Knowledge.** How much do they actually know about trade shows? Are they familiar with commonly used industry statistics proving the value of trade shows in generating new business? Or do they see trade shows as primarily a public relations event? Do they know the scope of your trade show program and how it contributes to long-range corporate objectives and short-term sales/marketing goals?

- **Attitudes.** Clearly define their attitudes about shows. Do they think shows are a waste of time and money? Why? Has anyone ever shown them results from shows? Are they marginally convinced of the value of shows but could easily lean one way or the other depending on who they talked to last? Even if they are staunch supporters of trade shows, be sure you know why. You may be talking dollars and cents to someone who thinks that trade shows are the greatest source for maintaining an image or educating an audience.

- **Past History.** Did this person have any experience with trade shows in a former life? Has he or she ever staffed a trade show exhibit, been responsible for a trade show program, measured trade show results? Was his or her past experiences primarily positive or negative? Get those cobwebs and skeletons out of the closet early instead of discovering them during the question/answer session in an executive briefing.

- **What Do They Want?** What would they like to get out of trade show participation? Do they want them to make their program/products look good? Do they want qualified sales leads? Do they want return on investment? Do they want to be the biggest, best, most important company in the industry? Do they personally want exposure and visibility within the industry? Do they want to know what the competition is up to? Do they need to be able to justify any approvals up the management hierarchy? Do they know the possibilities of what shows can do for them or their programs?

- **What Would It Take?** Don't be afraid to ask key participants what it would take for them to buy-in to the program.

Identifying How Management Attitudes Influence Your Goals

Now that the major issues have been identified, they need to be synthesized. First, list all of your goals on a sheet of paper in order of priority. Decide what to work on first, who to consider in the project, and what knowledge and techniques will be most useful and efficient toward convincing those people. The diagram in Exhibit 16-1 illustrates one way to synthesize these thoughts.

Select the goal with the top priority and write it down in the center of a sheet of paper and draw a circle around it. Then identify the people you want to include in areas around the circle, leaving enough room to write below each person. Connect the people to the goal with straight lines. Then beneath each person list two columns: on the left identify key factors you know about this person, and on the right identify information that will be useful in gaining their support.

Use colors to identify key issues. Circle in green those people who are positive influencers. Use red for those people who are negative, and yellow for those who are neutral. Color-code information areas. Highlight in yellow all of those that are cost-related, in blue all those that are results-oriented, etc. Thus, the color with the most representation will be

Exhibit 16-1

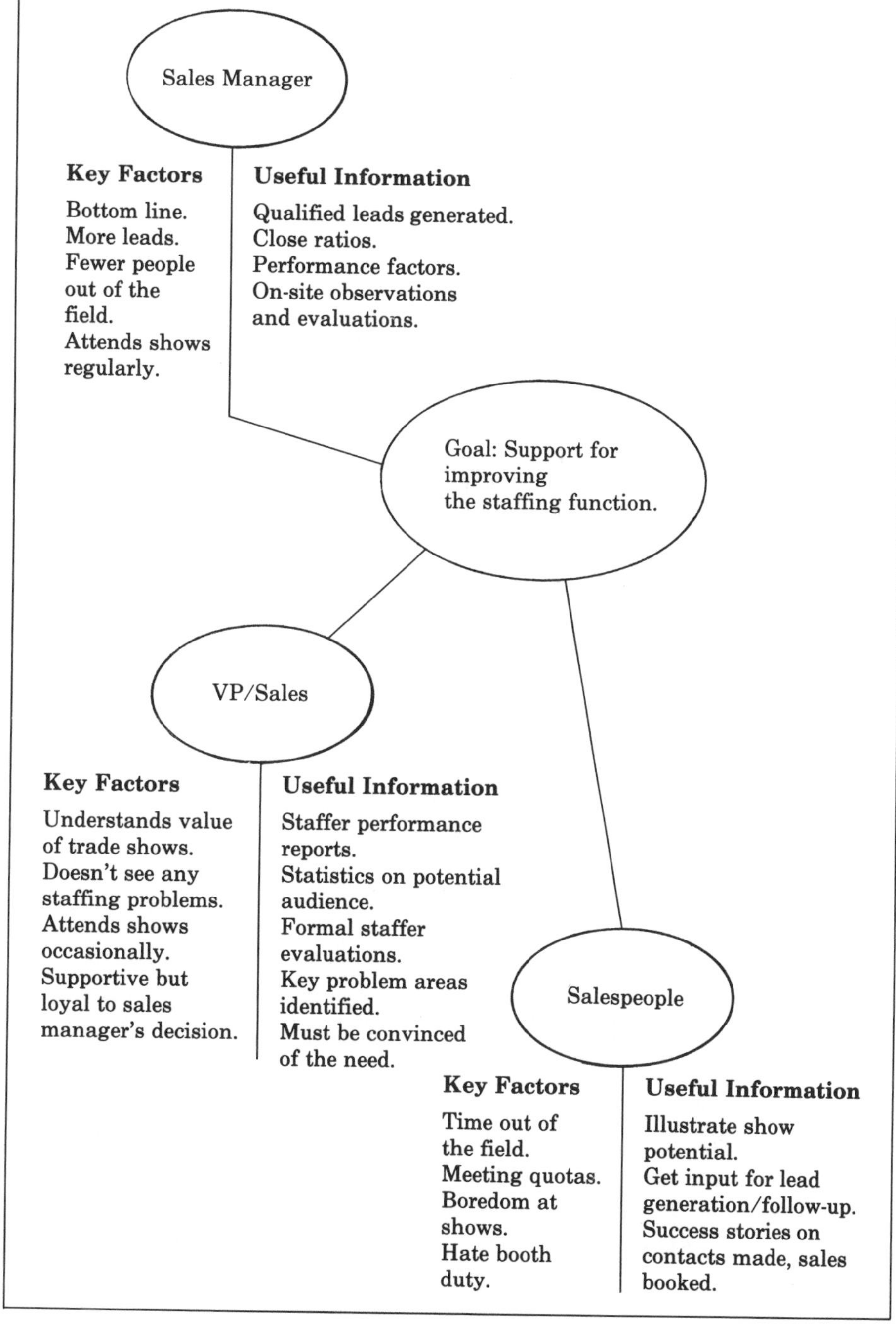

(Sales Manager)

Key Factors

Bottom line.
More leads.
Fewer people
out of the
field.
Attends shows
regularly.

Useful Information

Qualified leads generated.
Close ratios.
Performance factors.
On-site observations
and evaluations.

(Goal: Support for improving the staffing function.)

(VP/Sales)

Key Factors

Understands value
of trade shows.
Doesn't see any
staffing problems.
Attends shows
occasionally.
Supportive but
loyal to sales
manager's decision.

Useful Information

Staffer performance
reports.
Statistics on potential
audience.
Formal staffer
evaluations.
Key problem areas
identified.
Must be convinced
of the need.

(Salespeople)

Key Factors

Time out of
the field.
Meeting quotas.
Boredom at
shows.
Hate booth
duty.

Useful Information

Illustrate show
potential.
Get input for lead
generation/follow-up.
Success stories on
contacts made, sales
booked.

a primary theme in any communications or presentations you have with this group of people.

Exhibit 16-1 is an example of this kind of chart drawn for the objective of improving the staffing function.

If you have gone through this exercise and feel you need more information to build a solid case for these individuals, the next section identifies a variety of sources for this information.

HOW TO STRENGTHEN YOUR POSITION WITH MANAGEMENT

Once you have identified the key people involved and their concerns and hot buttons, the next step is formulating the strategy. What type of story do you want to tell, what type of information do you need in order to tell it, and how do you plan to do it? The sources for information fall into two categories: external and internal.

External Sources of Trade Show Information

A primary source for statistics that support the value of trade shows is The Trade Show Bureau. Their address is listed in the Appendix. Below is a sample list of the types of information available there. Actual statistics are not included here because in many cases the research is conducted annually or every few years and the statistics quickly become obsolete. If you think any of these examples would be useful to your strategy, call the Trade Show Bureau to inquire about the most recent statistics.

- Average budget allocations. Averages on how much companies spend on trade show participation.
- Show budgets as a percent of advertising and sales promotion. This is available by size of companies represented.
- Reasons for participating. Results from a survey on the primary reasons companies give for participating in trade shows.
- Departmental responsibility for shows. Where the trade show function lies within organizations.
- Management perceptions about trade shows. What percentage find them useful based on company sizes.
- Number of calls required to close a sale. This report compares the number of calls required to close sales from leads generated at trade shows vs. those to close an industrial sale.
- Buying plans of show audiences in recession years as opposed to non-recessionary years.
- Percentage of show visitors contacted by a sales representative in the 12 months prior to the show.

- Average cost to make a trade show contact as compared to the average cost of a field sales call.
- Roles of management in show-related decision making.
- How exhibit budgets are spent. Average allocations divided by exhibit construction, show space, transportation, installation/dismantle, etc.

The Trade Show Bureau updates reports and generates new reports regularly. They are often printed in industry publications, and are also available from the Bureau. Collect this information and file it for use as needed.

Other external sources of information include newspaper and magazine articles about trade shows. Use case studies and advice from experts whenever possible to support your case. *Exhibitor Magazine* also publishes an annual exhibit managers salary survey.

Internal Sources of Information for the Management Presentation

If you have documentation of past show participations, you probably have a veritable library of information resources in your files somewhere. It's worth the time to dig it out and mine for those nuggets of gold that will support your cause. Here are a few examples of what you might be able to find and use.

Strategic Plan Summary. All managers who participate in making decisions that affect the exhibits program should receive summary copies of the strategic plan. You might want to also include it as a handout during any formal presentations.

Show Results. Lead tracking results, independent survey results, return-on-investment calculations . . . these all can be used to justify either repeat participation in a show, or to support a decision to drop a show. When preparing results for a presentation, report, or memo, always boil them down to their simplest interpretations. Rather than submitting full lead tracking reports, do a synopsis of the number of sales booked by product category. Translate the figures to charts, graphs, or other visual illustrations whenever possible. Get a handle on all past results for shows as well as current, so that you can make some comparisons should people inquire about it.

Competitive Analysis. Managers are typically interested in what the competition is doing. Any information collected on what your competitors are doing at shows could bolster your story. Be careful, though, not to position your ideas as "keeping up with the Jones'." If you are a leader in your industry, management will want to be ahead of anything competitors are doing.

Instead, approach it from the vantage point of having a knowledge base about what the competition is doing. In other words, having done your homework. Some exhibitors take photographs of competing exhibits, collect their literature, and ask staffers to report on demonstrations, presentations, and promotions conducted in their exhibits.

Potential Audience Statistics. These figures are especially useful if you are working on approval for show participation. In Chapter 1 you saw how to calculate your potential audience at a show. During a presentation it can be useful to review these calculations. It is surprising to watch the reactions to the concept because many managers who have little or no direct experience with trade shows have no idea they can be evaluated that objectively. Just by way of review, here are a few statistics you can often get from show managers that will help tell your story:

- Product interests of show attendees
- Geographic distribution of show attendees
- Job function or job titles of show attendees
- Buying plans of show attendees

In addition to those, if you purchase custom surveys you can cull a variety of statistics from survey reports. They will even recommend for you the number of staffers and amount of booth space required for optimum participation in a show. Sometimes third-party input can provide just the objective voice needed to support your case.

Success Stories. Keep a file of success stories from past shows including big sales that were made, unexpected contacts with key prospects that resulted in long-term business relationships, positive feedback from competitors, industry influencers (press, consultants, etc.), exhibit staffers, and/or company executives. Remember, some of the best information is typically communicated through casual conversation and word-of-mouth. If you get these stories in post-show evaluations, you are that much further ahead. But if not, don't let them slip away; write them down and use them.

Budget Histories. These could tell a variety of stories based on what you find. They will at the very least explain the history of show expenditures. Use them to illustrate the need for an increased budget, or to illustrate how the program has become more cost efficient (if that is the story they tell). If last-minute decisions, entries, or changes caused significant budget overruns, use this information to build a case for longer lead times. A working knowledge of what has been spent in the past will be useful should this be challenged during a presentation.

Cost Comparisons/Justifications. Depending on the level of knowledge your managers have about trade shows, it may be necessary to explain *why* some of the costs are as high as they are. For example, a controller might challenge spending $150,000 on a show, but understand more clearly when he or she sees the cost breakdowns. Many people simply can't believe drayage charges until the calculations are explained to them. (Okay, and some still won't believe it.) Several industry publications are now printing costs when they publish case study articles about exhibit strategies. Use those as signposts of what other companies spend (especially those with exceptional programs).

Finally, your job of finding just the right information when you need it will be infinitely easier if you organize everything in a system that is easy for you to use. Put key statistics, quotes, and reference articles on index cards or in a computer file, organized by subject (for example, "cost justification," "competitor activities," etc.). Or file clippings by subject in a binder.

Four Opportunities to Communicate with Management

Just as the information you communicate is selected based on both your subjects and your subject matter, so, too is the method you use to communicate and build that support. Some exhibits managers have found that after spending some time informally trying to educate managers, they have been invited to discuss the value of trade shows with entire groups of managers. Should you have this good fortune, you will be preparing a formal presentation.

But more typically the work is done informally, at budget approval meetings, in efforts to recruit products or staffers, and in casual discussions. The techniques you choose will depend, to a great extent, on your corporate culture and your relationships with the people you have targeted. For example, one exhibit manager swears by formal reports, another says in his company they are neither read nor respected. Choose your techniques from the list below, or any others that you think will work.

Formal Presentations. These are useful for educating a large group of people in a short period of time. While interaction is limited, it does allow for some feedback and dialogue. Try to avoid a long agenda where trade shows are one of many topics. Work for presentations where trade shows are the only topic discussed. Make a mental list of participants and identify the supporters and the challengers.

Remember, in this situation you have the most control over how your material is presented. Construct your presentation to get buy-in as you go along. Begin with points that will foster agreement and build to those that are more controversial. Also keep in mind that many of the people you talk to may have never seen your company's exhibit or visited a trade show that you organized. Use photos, drawings, video tape, anything you can to make the story come alive. The essence of trade shows that differentiates them from other media is the dynamics of human interaction. Don't leave it to the imagination.

The content of a formal presentation depends on your objectives. The worksheet in Exhibit 16-2 is designed to help you make decisions on the three key questions discussed previously. This will provide the background information necessary for preparing the presentation. Exhibits 16-3 and 16-4 provide sample outlines for the two most common objec-

---

Exhibit 16-2   Presentation Planning Worksheet

1. Presentation Objectives

   ☐ Budget approval   ☐ Show plan approval
   ☐ Cooperation/sales   ☐ New exhibit
   ☐ Longer lead times   approval
   ☐ Participation   ☐ Authority/credibility
   ☐ Other _____   ☐ Other _____
   ☐ _____   ☐ _____
                                        ☐ _____

2. Presentation Participants

   ☐ President/CEO   ☐ Product managers
   ☐ Vice presidents   ☐ Sales managers
   ☐ Divisional managers   ☐ Advertising
   ☐ Others _____   managers
   ☐ _____   ☐ Others _____
                                        ☐ _____

   ☐ Roster of participants attached

   Notes on participants: _____
   _____
   _____
   _____

3. Presentation Content

   ☐ Industry statistics: ☐ Competitive
                                           evaluations
   _____   ☐ Potential audience
   _____   statistics
   _____   ☐ Success stories
   _____   ☐ Budget histories
   ☐ Strategic plan   ☐ Cost comparisons
   ☐ Show results   ☐ Other _____
                                        ☐ _____

tives: general education about trade shows, and getting show participation approval.

Informal Presentations. For some of these you can prepare, and for others you will have to be ready at a moment's notice. You could find yourself in a trade-show-related discussion in the cafeteria, during a meeting with a completely different agenda, even in the hallway. Seize the opportunities as they come up.

If you do have time to prepare for an informal presentation (made during a planning meeting, budget meeting, new exhibit design approval) have an agenda for your own use, and some visual aids prepared. It won't necessarily be overheads and slides, but take along copies of reports or

---

Exhibit 16-3   Sample Presentation Outline:
General Education

I. The Role of Trade Shows

A. How companies use them

A general sampling of different ways companies use trade shows, such as finding new prospects, introducing new products, etc. with case studies and examples.

B. Why companies use them

Industry statistics can be helpful here to tell the story of efficiencies (how many contacts per hour, number of sales calls to close a sale at trade shows and in the field) and economies (the cost of a field sales call vs. a trade show contact, percent of qualified leads that yield sales).

II. The Role of Trade Shows in Our Company

A. Specific objectives for participating

B. Samples of show strategies with goals and results

C. How trade shows support and interface with other marketing efforts such as advertising

III. How Our Company Participates

A. The organization of the show function

B. The planning process

C. Investment and return on investment (totals, not by show)

IV. How You Can Participate

A. Significant contributions made by participants

B. Plans for future participation

Exhibit 16-4 Sample Presentation Outline:
Show Participation Approval

I. Objectives for Show Participation

A. *Long-range objectives, not short-term goals*
B. *How objectives contribute to corporate direction*

II. Past Participation and Results

A. *Shows that will be repeated, with justifications*

   i. goals
   ii. results
   iii. intangible factors: location, strategy, attendance, etc.

B. *Shows that will be dropped, with justifications*

   i. goals
   ii. results
   iii. intangible factors: location, strategy, attendance, etc.

III. New Shows Added

A. *Potential audience targeted*
B. *Contribution to long-range objectives*

IV. Budget and Show Schedule

A. *Listing of all shows*
B. *Budget allocations required*
C. *Primary and alternate sources for budgeting*

magazine articles you plan to reference, lead tracking reports, or photos or drawings of the exhibit.

While formal presentations are wonderful for communicating a key message to a large audience at one time, informal presentations will probably provide the best opportunities to present your case. By eliciting feedback, you can learn a great deal about attitudes and opinions that will help you steer clear of land mines. Like a sales call, the informal presentation also gives you the opportunity to entertain and overcome objections.

Some people are stronger at formal presentations and others at informal settings. Of course work with your strength when you have a choice.

Formal Reports. Reports are limited because there is no channel provided for feedback. But, if you work in a corporation where it is difficult to get five minutes with a manager face-to-face, a formal report outlining the problems in a specific area and your proposed solutions may be the only way to get the ball rolling. Keep a list of key managers who should receive post-show reports and any planning strategies that are prepared. If nothing else, sending reports provides visibility for your program, and keeps managers updated on those activities.

Ongoing Input. Once support is built (or begun) maintain it with ongoing communications. Photocopy articles and highlight key points to distribute to managers. One exhibitor did this and a vice president distributed one of the articles (in person at the pre-show meeting) to a group of nearly 100 salespeople assigned to booth duty.

If you contract for custom post-show surveys, they often include executive summaries that you can distribute to managers. Prepare your own post-show summary format to send to key managers after each show. Many managers are negative about trade shows simply because they don't understand the medium. Education is an ongoing process.

Any formal presentation is rife with human dynamics and your outline should reflect what you anticipate from the participants. Even the best laid plans must be flexible to adjust to input. By all means, practice your presentation, get feedback if possible—and, if you haven't done a great deal of presenting, invest in an instructional book on the subject.

SIX AREAS FOR MANAGEMENT INVOLVEMENT

Recently I talked with an exhibit manager who had just begun educating his new boss, a marketing director. He had invited him to a show during installation, put him to work in the exhibit, and then toured him around the show floor. I bumped into them later at a trade show industry convention. The marketing director was enthusiastically explaining how he had no idea of the complexities of getting a solid show program off the ground, what was involved in the logistics of getting the exhibit installed and staffed, etc., etc. The marketing director received an education in a single day that would have been impossible to provide through a raft of reports, presentations, and articles.

As with the other considerations for building management support, there are a variety of opportunities to get managers involved in your trade show program. Here are a few that exhibit managers have used successfully.

- **Solicit their input during the planning process.** This is especially helpful with sales managers when you are providing sales leads to their people for follow-up. Ask them for input to design the lead card, get involved in lead tracking, and get feedback on plans for staffer training. This is possible and should be done with any group participating in the show plan (engineering, R&D, advertising, etc.). Get executive or upper management input or feedback for the strategic plan.
- **Invite them to the show.** If managers are not already attending the show, invite them . . . *but with a purpose.* If you ask managers to participate be sure that you have a role there for them, or they tend to show up in the

exhibit and "hang around" because they aren't sure how they fit into the strategy. Talk to salespeople about scheduling meetings with key clients or prospects, see about getting executives to participate in the conference schedule, give them booth duty. The company presidents I have talked with who participate in booth duty the same way the staffers do (welcoming visitors, prospecting for new business) find it an unparalleled education and opportunity to get in touch with customers.

- **Invite them to an installation.** When you do, let them know it is sort of a dirt and sawdust environment and remind them to dress casually. Brief them on what you will be doing and what to expect. Then when you are there, put them to work (set this as a premise for the invitation). Anyone unfamiliar with the environment and left to be pushed around by forklifts and union workers would feel uncomfortable. But when you guide their experience, they will get a hands-on perspective of what your job is about.

- **Tour the show.** When managers do show up, take the opportunity to walk the show floor with them a bit, with an objective in mind. For example, one exhibit manager saw a need for a significant improvement in their exhibit structure, for which a manager couldn't see fit to approve a budget. A quick walk around the show floor to show him examples of other similar structures used by their competitors and illustrating the difference between their look and that of his own company convinced him.

- **Follow-up.** If you have management participation at a show, don't miss out on the opportunity to get their feedback. Follow-up with a phone conversation to get their input. Yes, you may come up against criticism, but they will have had a chance to discuss it with you and you will hear it firsthand instead of through the rumor mill.

- **Invite them to speak** at your pre-show meeting, to either open or close it, and request that they sit through the rest of it. If you do, provide some guidelines on their purpose and what you would like them to cover. For example, let them know you would like them to close with a motivational anecdote. Or that you would like them to open with a few statements about why trade shows are valuable to the company.

Building management support is not only a challenge but also can be a political hot potato; another reason exhibit managers are reluctant to embark on the endeavor. It is important to reflect on and understand the political dynamics and ramifications of what you are doing. It is also important not to let them scare you from moving forward.

The title of this chapter is very intentionally called Building Management Support because it is a process. The strongest pyramids were built one stone at a time. Make your stones the casual conversations, occasional meetings, and opportunities for participation. And they weren't built overnight. This is a dynamic effort. Roles change, jobs change, needs change. Consider it one of those unwritten job responsibilities in career management.

17

Managing Growth
in the Trade Show
Department

"In the new corporation, creativity and individuality are
organizational treasures."

—John Naisbitt/Patricia Aburdeen
Reinventing the Corporation

Do you want to grow your department? Whether you see exhibit management as a career, or a stepping-stone, you probably have a few good
reasons to facilitate growth in your department. If you are in it for the long
haul, and see exhibit management as a career, your own job satisfaction is
tied to the contribution you and your department are making to the
company. Growing the department, improving it, increasing that contribution, and taking responsibility for it will likely be not only your own
personal measure of success, but also the yardstick by which you are
judged in the company.

In his book, *Thriving on Chaos*, Tom Peters says, "The manager in
today's world doesn't get paid to be a 'steward of resources,' a favored
term not so many years ago. He or she gets paid for one and only one
thing—to make things better (incrementally and dramatically), to make
things different (incrementally and dramatically), to change things, to
act—today."(1)

John Naisbitt sheds a similar light on what is going to be expected of
employees in the decades to come. He says, "We are shifting the idea of the
model employee from one who carries out orders correctly to one who
takes responsibility and initiative, monitors his or her own work, and uses
managers and supervisors in their new roles of facilitators, teachers, and
consultants."(2)

If you see exhibit management as a stepping-stone, managing growth and change can be equally important. New management theories and structures are encouraging more flexibility and lateral moves among managers. But with increasing mobility comes increasing expectations to do more than maintain the status quo in whatever area you take on. You'll be evaluated based on growth and changes you make in your tenure at any given job.

Either way, career or stepping-stone, exhibit management can provide unparalleled opportunities for personal exposure for you within your company.

Said one director of corporate communications of her response to being assigned the exhibits function, "I was thrilled. I knew that this gave me instant access to virtually every division within the corporation. I needed them . . . engineering, sales, R&D . . and it gave me a reason to introduce myself and build relationships with those people. It also gave me something to offer. My theme was 'How can we help?' I took every opportunity to take on tasks that increased the scope of our offerings to the company. When you do that, staff and pay increases must follow. Talk about visibility. You can't beat it!"

The question, of course, is how. Managing change and growth is an important subject concerning middle managers and corporate executives alike. In this chapter you will see some basic concepts for managing growth and change, translated for the exhibits department. You will see how to:

1. ASSESS YOUR SITUATION. Determine activities and attitudes that are in place.
2. DEFINE YOUR VISIONS. Determine new contributions the trade show department can make in the corporation, and how to see the changes required to make those contributions.
3. MANAGE CHANGE AND GROW YOUR DEPARTMENT. Use the three phases of implementing change.
4. EVALUATE YOUR SKILLS. Understand the skills for implementing change and determine your strengths, weaknesses, and areas for personal and professional growth.

HOW TO ASSESS PROGRAM EFFICIENCY AND EFFECTIVENESS

What exists? Whether this is your first day as exhibit manager, or your tenth year, managing growth requires first identifying, clearly, what exists. This occurs in three phases. What exists in terms of efficiency*, how the

---

*In *Thriving on Chaos*, Tom Peters differentiates efficiency from effectiveness this way: "Activities of mastering routine are efficiency, activities of vision and judgment are effectiveness."(3)

department is run, what exists in terms of effectiveness, what kind of contribution the department is making, and what exists in terms of attitudes.

Locating Efficiency Problems

Begin by reviewing efficiency. That's easiest, and you can use the worksheet in Exhibit 17-1 to organize your thoughts. Think through each component of the exhibits program. If you are new to the job and aren't even sure of what those components are yet, ask around. There is a list in the worksheet to help you as well. Write down any additional components that are not included on the list.

Then identify whether you consider the function to be operating efficiently or not, and most importantly *why*. For example, if you think exhibit installation and dismantle isn't being handled as efficiently as it could be, identify, not why it's not efficient, but what makes you think that it's not efficient. In this instance it could be because you continually pay overtime rates that were not planned, or that the installation takes longer than you think it should.

Do the same for those functions you feel are running very efficiently. For example, if you are very pleased with the exhibit properties inventory, identify why. It might be because you have ample structure and graphics to meet all of your exhibiting needs. The why's are going to help you set some direction and envision future possibilities. There is a completed worksheet in Exhibit 17-2 for your reference.

If you have been managing the department for awhile you should be able to do the evaluating yourself. If you are new to the department, it will be essential to get feedback from someone who has been around and can help you evaluate these areas. Try to get feedback from a couple of sources, and dig deep enough to get actual situations that justify the "satisfactory" or "needs work" evaluation.

Another evaluation trick that managers recommend is reviewing your greatest successes, and worst failures over the past year. If you are new to the department, of course, this won't work. And it is a purely subjective evaluation. Most important, try to jot down on a sheet of paper the reasons for the success and failure (painful as the latter exercise might be, it will be your most valuable information). And evaluating success can be equally useful. When we train staffers from the same company several years in a row, it is common to see them ride on their laurels after an extremely successful show. They forget to evaluate what made it so successful, and to bring those techniques into the planning for future participation.

When reviewing success, be careful to hang onto the theory and not just repeat the technique. For example, if you determined a great deal of

Exhibit 17-1   Assessment Level I: Efficiency Evaluation
Checklist

Function	Satis-factory	Needs Work	Why

Exhibit 17-2 Assessment Level I: Efficiency Evaluation Checklist

Function	Satis-factory	Needs Work	Why
Planning	√		Realistic plans are prepared and used regularly
Exhibit structure		√	Salespeople say portable exhibits used for regional shows are broken
Exhibit graphics		√	Graphics do not represent market segments we've targeted
Transportation	√		Haven't missed deadlines/ good svs.
Install/ dismantle		√	Over budget last three shows
Promotions		√	Need to begin using
Presentations	√		Well-attended by visitors/ clear
Lead-generating		√	Lead card not requesting enough info
Lead follow-up	√		Timing is adequate
Lead-tracking		√	Non-existent
Measuring results		√	Need to work on ROI measurements
Communicating	√		Open lines of communication
Management support	√		Support and participate
Other			
Other			
Other			

your success from a show was due to a promotion you used, make a point to use promotions again, instead of saying, "Boy, that t-shirt giveaway from last year worked well, let's do the same thing again."

How to Evaluate Your Program's Effectiveness

The next level of assessment is how effective your program is. This takes a bit broader look at your department relative to its contribution to your company's growth objectives. Here, your own subjective evaluation will be a bit myopic to serve your purposes. It's important to get a read on what key groups perceive about the exhibits function as well.

Any changes you make are sure to involve a key group of people. Knowing their perception of how your department is running is a prerequisite to getting them involved in the change process. The objective for this evaluation is to determine whether your perception of the contributions trade shows make are similar to their perceptions. In many cases their perception will be much more limited than yours. For example, you might consider that trade shows provide a good deal of information on what the competition is doing in the industry. However, a sales manager may have no idea that you are creating reports on competitive activities.

The chart in Exhibit 17-3 provides a structure for making this assessment. To use it, list under the "My view" column all of the contributions

Exhibit 17-3 Level II Assessment Worksheet
Perceptions of Contributions Trade Shows Make

		Their Perceptions	
My Perceptions	*Sales*	*Mktng.*	*Upper Mgmnt.*
Generate sales leads	A	A	A
Educate the industry	A	A	A
Build/change image	A	A	A
Find new markets	A	D	U
Competitive analysis	D	A	U
Industry intelligence-gathering	U	U	U
Publicity opportunities	U	A	A

Key: A = agree
      D = disagree
      U = unaware

that you think trade shows make to corporate growth. Then identify under the "Their View" column the key groups whose perceptions you want to identify. For example, in our samples we've identified sales, marketing, and upper management as key groups. You may have several more, or entirely different groups. Then in each column indicate whether their perception Agrees (A) with yours, Disagrees (D) with yours, or they are Unaware (U) of the contribution.

For example, you might identify that one contribution trade shows make is to provide industry information from target markets. Your sales manager might disagree with that, and think that the only contribution trade shows make is to generate sales leads. Upper management might not agree or disagree with that, but might simply be unaware of that contribution.

To gather this information, you have three options:

1. Casual conversation: Watch for things people say in the course of conversation that indicates their perceptions. Use feedback and clarify to assure you are getting the right message.

2. Phone interview: Intentionally solicit feedback. Ask people what they think are the contributions trade show participation makes. Keep an open mind and encourage them to spend a minute thinking about it.

3. Conduct a formal survey. Write up a survey and distribute it to identified influencers. Continue requesting input until you get all of the completed surveys you need in order to make a balanced assessment.

Keep in mind that the purpose of this assessment is to evaluate *what exists* and perceptions of that. It is not to identify directions to take. That will come in the next section. You will use this evaluation to identify where some of your energies will be devoted when working to build a team that will implement changes.

How to Identify Attitudes Which Affect Your Program

Finally, it is essential to identify attitudes that exist about shows. It would be nice if you could see just one attitude, but chances are you will find a whole range of attitudes among people involved in trade shows.

Evaluating attitudes deals with the broadest group of people who are involved in shows at your company. This will encompass everyone from the product people who provide display products, to technicians who install them, warehouse people who check exhibit inventories and arrange shipping (if this is handled internally), to exhibit staffers, and also includes all levels of management.

Learning about attitudes requires only listening. All conversations with any of these people offer an opportunity to identify attitudes.

Although you want to identify specific attitudes, you are looking for a fairly broad grouping here. Try to generally categorize attitudes into positive, negative, and neutral, and identify where those attitudes reside (for example a majority of exhibit staffers consider trade shows punishment).

The goal in assessing attitudes is to uncover the *reason* for the attitude. You can then implement incremental changes targeted at those concerns. For example, should you discover that exhibit staffers consider trade shows punishment, find out why. If it is because they have to take time away from their accounts, yet maintain monthly quotas, consider techniques you can use that will make trade shows more rewarding for them (incentive programs, bonuses linked to show results, etc.).

"The chief job of the leader," says Tom Peters "at all levels, is to oversee the dismantling of dysfunctional old truths and to prepare people and organizations to deal with—to love, to develop affection for—change per se, as innovations are proposed, tested, rejected, modified, and adopted."(4) Corporations are rife with "dysfunctional old truths" about trade shows. Here are a few to watch for.

Five Dysfunctional Old Truths About Trade Shows

"You never really know what you get from shows." Many managers who come from the "old school" of trade shows as a glad-handing event claim that results from shows can't be measured because you don't actually write orders there. The reality, though, is that companies who use trade shows most successfully measure their results regularly using computer programs, lead-tracking systems, and independent research.

"We only go because we'd be conspicuous by our absence." People swear by the fact that if you drop out of a show the rumor mill will start to confirm that you are going out of business. When Apple Computer dropped out of the industry's leading show to focus their resources on other more targeted efforts, there was a lot of discussion about it in the industry, but it certainly wasn't in anticipation of their going out of business. Participating in a trade show can be a pretty expensive way to avoid rumors.

"Our salespeople don't need trade show training. They already know how to sell." The result is people ill-equipped to work in a unique environment hold back the company from reaching their potential at shows. Companies who provide solid skills-based training for their salespeople prior to shows often double the number of sales leads generated there.

"Trade shows are a waste of time." This one typically comes from the man or woman who spent the entire show sitting on a chair in the back of their booth space smoking, chatting with other staffers, or even reading the newspapers. What is at the root of this attitude, though, is a lack of knowledge about what *can* be accomplished and what *has been* accomplished by other companies (sometimes by your competitors) when people understand how to use the medium efficiently.

"I love to go to trade shows. The parties are great!" Right answer, wrong reason. It is typical for people to view trade shows as "a week out of the office," a chance to take the family to Disney Land, or to invest time in finding the hottest hospitality event. Hmmmmm. . . . .

And this just scratches the surface. Uncover as many of these attitudes as you can. Remember, at this stage you are not the marauding crusader. This is not the time to shoot down those attitudes that raise the hair on your neck. Just listen, stay open, don't be judgmental. But make notes. This will provide direction for work on changing attitudes as you begin to implement changes.

The chart in Exhibit 17-4 illustrates one way you can begin to organize information gathered about attitudes. It identifies the continuum you will find from positive, to neutral, to negative. Divide a sheet of paper into three columns with those headings. Write down comments under each heading that they reflect. It might be useful to identify the source of the attitude, but it is not essential. You are working to uncover the reasons for those attitudes.

In this exercise it's not only important to uncover the negative, but also to focus on the positive. Don't get bogged down by negative attitudes. Instead, look for places you can build upon the positive attitudes. Remember, your changes will be incremental.

Doing the three levels of assessment take you right up to the point of understanding where you are. It might not feel as though you've gotten very far, but actually you have covered many miles in the journey. You've also reached a major turning point where you are ready to think about where you want to go.

THE ROLE OF VISION IN THE GROWTH OF YOUR DEPARTMENT

> "We believe the first ingredient in reinventing the corporation
> is a powerful vision—a whole new sense of where a company
> is going and how to get there."
>
> —*Reinventing the Corporation*

It's difficult to put the right verb in front of "vision." Is a vision for growth something you define, create, clarify, or something that simply springs full

Exhibit 17-4   Level III Assessment Attitudes
About Trade Shows

Positive	Neutral	Negative

blown from your mind while you are driving down a desert road? It is really the process of envisioning where you think the department needs to be at points in the future. As one exhibit manager aptly described it . . . evolution, not revolution.

Creating or defining a vision is an ideas business. It requires creative thinking. But the basis for most creative thinking is knowledge, so it first requires formal and informal learning. The discipline of architecture is very tradition-oriented, because architects believe that all new concepts are generated from ideas that have gone before. It is impossible to be a great architect without studying the great architects of history and the contributions they have made. While ours isn't quite as lofty a discipline, the idea here is the same. Learn as much as you can about what has been done, and what is being done.

Think big. It's hard to get excited about small, myopic visions. For example, you might see trade show participation as the primary vehicle within your corporation for staying in touch with the marketplace. Within that idea, you could consider how that will be accomplished through salespeople, using the medium for market research, and the importance of presenting the most positive, complete, and appropriate corporate story at each show in which you participate. You could create a theme for your department. . . "Trade Shows Keep Us in Touch."

If your corporation is very marketing-based, you might see trade shows as primarily positioning tools. Here everything from exhibit design, to products selected, to the attitudes and appearance of salespeople in the exhibit, and even show evaluations and research will be designed to align a product's position in the market and stimulate growth through market penetration. A theme here might be "Trade Shows Pave the Way" by softening the market, educating large numbers of people in a short amount of time, providing opportunities for new product introductions, publicity events, and other positioning efforts.

Think in terms of corporate objectives. Go back to your strategic plan for show participation and review the corporate mission statement. Align your ideas for growth with the corporate mission as much as possible.

Keep it dynamic. A vision provides long-term direction, but be careful not to fall into the trap of casting it in stone. Rather than coming up with one crystal clear picture of where you think the department should be in the next five years, you will probably see possibilities evolve. You may have one idea for the future, and change and adapt it as you go along. Then you'll find that the department has gone farther than you even expected it would.

Corporate changes, marketplace dynamics, personnel changes . . . all offer opportunities for growth. In his book, *The Renewal Factor*, Robert Waterman describes this concept as "informed opportunism,"(5) the delicate balance between planning and following a plan, yet staying flexible enough to take advantage of unexpected opportunities.

Interpret the vision. As you are thinking through a vision, consider at each point how this will be interpreted into components of your program. To do this, you can use all three levels of assessment from the previous section. As an example, we'll use the idea of trade shows as opportunities to stay in touch with the marketplace.

First, go back to your assessment of efficiency of the program (level I) and identify those components that contribute to making this idea a strong reality. (You might want to circle each one on your list.) In our example, planning, lead-generating, follow-up, and tracking and measuring results are going to be primary components that contribute to the success of this idea. This helps to set priorities about what to work on.

Next consider your level II assessment: perceptions of how trade shows contribute. Was this one of your perceptions? Was it a perception of key influencers in your program? This helps you to determine the amount of educating and promoting required just to introduce the concept. If it is an accepted view by everyone, your job will be easy. If it is not recognized by anyone involved, this will be a key place to begin.

Finally consider your level III assessment: attitudes. Think about how existing attitudes will need to be addressed and changed in order to accomplish your long-range objectives.

Consider also the level of influence contributed by people with varying attitudes. If one person has an extremely negative attitude but you are finding they are being quickly outnumbered and less influential, you may not have to focus a great deal of energy bringing them around to your way of thinking. Yet if an entire group of people has a negative attitude that is beginning to spread throughout other groups, this will have to be addressed. Attitudes are the underpinnings that can make the difference between an idea turning into reality, or just receiving lip service.

Contributions Trade Shows Can Make to Corporate Growth

There are a variety of tools for thinking about ideas for your program: Input from other exhibitors, observations at trade shows you attend, industry publications, disciplines outside the trade show industry. The following list of contributions trade shows can make is just a few ideas to get you started. You will, undoubtedly, come up with your own list.

1. Generate qualified sales leads for market penetration.
2. Identify market trends.

3. Analyze competitive strategies

4. Educate an industry about new concepts or practices you introduce through new products.

5. Market-test new products, ideas, concepts.

6. Educate dealers, distributors on products, and selling strategies.

7. Generate publicity for new products through trade, business, local, and national press.

8. Build, change, direct, and improve the company's image.

9. Build, change, direct, and improve product images.

10. Position products in niche markets.

11. Provide industry exposure for corporate executives.

As you envision improvements for the role trade shows play in your company, keep in mind the fact that it isn't something you do once and then it's complete. This type of creative thinking, problem-solving, and change is ongoing. If you are new to a department you might find that your first year is spent just trouble-shooting, understanding how things operate, and how to get them functioning efficiently. Thinking on a more creative level might be put on the back burner for awhile. But don't give up and don't pessimistically discard ideas for improvements. Instead, watch for opportunities to implement them.

HOW YOUR CORPORATE CULTURE INFLUENCES CHANGE STRATEGIES

For years I have heard many exhibit managers complain about the authority/responsibility gap that prevents them from achieving all that they could. The problem goes something like this. Exhibit managers have a great deal of responsibility for making a program run efficiently: managing large budgets, multiple properties, groups of suppliers, and presenting the company's image in its best light in a host of industries. Yet along with the responsibility they are not given the authority (in other words the power of managing people who report to them) to get the job done correctly.

Sound familiar? In companies that are organized on a hierarchical management structure this is often the case. The salespeople didn't report to the exhibit manager so it was impossible to get them to do what he wanted. The product managers didn't report to the exhibit manager so it was impossible to get them to have products ready on time. Getting efficiency down was a challenge under this structure. Implementing changes to improve effectiveness? Well, you just couldn't see it from here.

But management structures are changing. What is interesting about the most recent theories of corporate management is the recognition that even with authoritative power, you can't always get people to do what you want them to. People must be able to believe in and buy-in to a new concept enough to overcome the fear of risk and change that often keeps them from participating wholeheartedly in changes.

Managing by team-building is a concept with increasing popularity. Management experts talk about cutting through corporate politics to facilitate change. Here, exhibit managers who are experienced at running their department effectively could teach a lesson or two. Team-building among management peers, cutting through corporate politics, breaking down resistance to change . . . all are techniques the exhibit manager must use regularly to make any improvements in their program. The good news is now there is a lot of information out there to help you succeed at the challenge.

Understanding Your Corporate Culture

In managing change, it helps to start by knowing what you are up against. What is your corporate culture regarding change? Are you in a corporation with the "if it ain't broke don't fix it" mindset? And don't just settle on what you are hearing from the CEO or executive team. Their vision for the corporation may be far ahead of the actual reality. What are you hearing from middle management? From line employees?

One CEO of a family-owned business recently took over the business from his father. The business had grown almost miraculously under his father's direction with virtually no competition. He succeeded by finding an untapped niche, filling it, and networking through a rather small industry to create an untarnished reputation for quality.

By the time the son took over, competition was heating up, the industry was changing dramatically from market forces, and the old way was no longer effective. But, in trying to implement changes to manage a more mature business in a maturing marketplace, he faced ongoing challenges from loyal employees who had helped his father build the company.

This mindset is fairly typical as management changes hands from the old guard to the new generation.

You may have the good fortune of working in a company where change is an accepted and encouraged part of the corporate culture. Be careful not to rely on the corporate culture too heavily and assume that any changes you propose will be accepted just for the sake of change.

Change, or even the hint of change, carries with it these potentially harmful, supercharged characteristics:

- **Risk.** If I buy into this it might fail, and failure could be a threat to my job and my security.

- **Need to Know.** Most of us become comfortable with a way of doing things. Changing that might involve skills or knowledge that we either have a low level of comfort with or don't know at all.

  For example, when companies try to introduce computerized lead-gathering at shows, it often receives a mixed reception. One wise exhibit manager anticipated that there were people on the sales force who had never used a computer and were as intimidated by the keyboard as you and I might be by CAT scan equipment. They resisted the change. The exhibit manager offered two options for lead-gathering—computer or manual.

- **Uncertainty.** It's human nature. We are comfortable with things we know, uncomfortable with the unknown. When we conduct pre-show training sessions for our clients, there is a recognizable difference in attitude and comfort level among those staffers who know what to expect in the meeting because they have been informed through memos and announcements, and those who have no idea what to expect. This also affects people's ability to participate fully in a change. If they are uncertain about what to expect, they are also uncertain about what is expected of them. In other words "fear of the unknown."

It will certainly come as no surprise to you, then, that simply instituting change doesn't make it so. You know it's true because you've seen it. But the remaining question is how to effectively manage change in the small, detailed steps that bring it to success. The following are a few very basic guidelines. This is just the briefest of introductions as change relates to the exhibit department. Following that, in part IV you will have a chance to evaluate your own ability to manage change, and areas where you can grow in that skill. If you really want to succeed . . . study the experts in managing change.

The Role of Leadership in Affecting Change

When people begin teasing you about your soapbox, you know you've made good headway in supporting your cause. Begin by clearly defining for yourself exactly where you are going. That includes your long-range vision, and the step you are about to embark on toward that change.

Then take every reasonable opportunity to talk about, preach about, discuss, debate, and support your cause. Look for opportunities to promote and discuss it in the company newsletter, in meetings, in casual conversation. Create a theme or tag line that clearly identifies your mission, and use it whenever possible. Post it in your office space, put it on your personal stationery, or end memos and notes with it.

This, in and of itself, is not going to facilitate the change. But it is going to let everyone know, very clearly, where you are going. In turn, it will help you identify who wants to go along, and who would prefer to stay at home.

Three Steps Toward Implementing Change Effectively

At this juncture, you begin telling people, not only where you are going, but how you plan to get there. In his book *Innovating to Compete*, Richard E. Walton identifies a three-step process for innovation within corporations.(6) The concepts have been loosely adapted here as they relate to exhibit management. The three steps are explained here with a chart in Exhibit 17-5 to illustrate in an example how they can be planned.

Exhibit 17-5   Change task: Implementing pre-show promotion campaigns

Agreement on need	Trial solutions	Implementation
Budget for show advertising and promotions comes from the divisions. Buy-in from the divisional managers is essential. The trade show department coordinates logistics so it will be important to convince staff of the value of the extra time investment involved.	The new divisional manager in the unbreakables group used promotions fairly regularly in her former job. Her division might be a good place to launch a trial. Being new, she might be reluctant to break from corporate status quo. Will have to check on her attitude. Keep trial low-budget and simple as a "pilot" for future projects.	Plan word-of-mouth promotion of success in unbreakables group. See about a blurb in company newsletter. Watch for indications from other divisions of their interest in the concept. Document successes. Plan to report on these successes to all influencers, from divisional management to corporate when appropriate. Facilitate ongoing feedback.

Step #1: Agreement on the Need

The first phase of implementing change is getting agreement for the need for change in this area. Identify all influencers of the process. Campaign, educate, and get agreement from as many influencers as possible on the need to implement this change. Be as specific as possible about what will be involved, how resources will be found to implement the change, and who will be responsible for implementation tasks.

Step #2: Trial Solutions

Make the change in small steps. Instead of implementing a new lead-gathering system for all shows, try it at one or two shows and get feedback on the process. Refine and improve based on feedback and try it at a few more shows. These trials not only help you create a better solution, but they also reduce risk for all participants involved.

Step #3: Broad Implementation

Use successes from the trial solutions to sell the change on a broad basis. The trials should also provide information to identify the direction you plan to take very clearly, step-by-step. At this point you will be able to define tasks and responsibilities required for the change, information, and knowledge that will need to be disseminated, and strategies for making the change a success. All of this will aid in overcoming resistance.

Let's say, by way of example, that your vision for the trade show department was that it would provide opportunities to align product positions in selected marketplaces and contribute to growth through market penetration. You've identified that pre-show promotion provides an opportunity to contribute to product positioning by increasing "mind-share" (getting your message to the audience early, and getting your exhibit on the visitor's must see list). Pre-show promotion then would be an area that you target for incremental change.

The Value of Building a Network

As you experience success in the implementation of new ideas, you will also begin to build a "following" of people within the company who become believers. Stay in touch with those folks. Use their testimonials when you can. Watch for ways that you can be helpful to them in their endeavors. Like the director of corporate communications who loved trade shows because of the visibility it allowed her, take the opportunity to stay in touch with as many people in as many different areas of the company as you can.

Managing change doesn't necessarily follow as tidy a process as you've seen here. You will most likely find that you have several implementation tasks going at several stages in the process all at once. You won't always be moving full steam ahead either. It might be a three steps forward, two steps back type of endeavor. You might be in the middle of the trial phase on a task and discover that wasn't the right direction at all, and something new arose to take you in a new direction altogether.

There are always a host of factors that are completely outside our control, among them corporate mergers, downsizing, restructuring (one exhibit manager's company had been through so many reorganizations they had their own buzzwords; "We're going through another reorg," he told me), new players, budget cuts, increased demands (one exhibit manager told me his management asked him to improve performance over the previous year's show with less booth space and less money). The rapid pace with which we experience change today will force you to continually evaluate, reconsider, and update. But, even the most flexible plan for growth allows you to affect and direct change, rather than allowing it to direct you.

MANAGING YOUR CAREER GROWTH

The time-driven nature of trade shows forces a "tyranny of the urgent" style of management. When we deal with deadlines regularly, there is a tendency to focus only on the issue at hand, or the next five deadlines to be met. We become driven by tasks with little time to step back and evaluate, plan, even think about change. We find ourselves left with even less time to assess our own professional growth. To be effective managers of change, that will need to be the first item on the agenda.

Identify Your Attitude Toward Change

Begin by taking inventory of your own attitudes about change. Do you welcome change? Have you implemented changes successfully in the past? Or have you had negative experiences with change that make you apprehensive about taking on a leadership role in this area? Whether you find yourself enthusiastic or nervous, take a conscious inventory of your knowledge and skills related to managing change. Knowledge refers to how much you know about the concept of managing change (theories, techniques, current practices). Skills refer to your ability to do the job (leadership skills, communications skills, etc.).

"In a world that is constantly changing, there is no one subject
or set of subjects that will serve you for the foreseeable
future, let alone for the rest of your life. The most important
skill to acquire now is learning how to learn."

—Reinventing the Corporation

Where to Get the Knowledge You Need

If the concept of managing change is new to you, the time invested to learn more about the process will pay big dividends. There are many books available on the subject which can be found in most bookstores and libraries. If you can get the books on audio tape you can use drive time or plane time to get a quick synopsis of ideas.

For more breadth of information consider seminars on exhibits management. In the trade show industry there are two major conferences that offer educational seminars: TS2, the International Exhibitors Association Annual Conference, and The Exhibitor Show, produced by *Exhibitor Magazine*, along with one- and two-day seminars offered by educational companies. For more information on either of those, check the resource listings in the Appendix.

A Personal Skills Inventory

As you become more familiar with the concept of managing growth and change, you will be able to identify some of the skills required. The chart in Exhibit 17-6 provides a skills inventory to help you evaluate your strengths and weaknesses in this management discipline. For each area indicate whether you think the skill is a strength, weakness, or an unknown for you. An unknown would be a skill that you have not yet had an opportunity to test. Keep in mind that nobody is skilled in all of these areas. The idea is to improve areas in which you are weak, build on the strong areas, and, when possible, balance your weak areas with skills of team members, staff, and suppliers.

All of the skills identified here contribute significantly to the process of managing growth and change in your department. It means spending time up front to find out exactly what exists: efficiency, effectiveness, and attitudes. It requires learning so that you can draw from a broad perspective when defining a vision for the future of your department. And it requires a host of people skills—team-building, listening, communicating—to get the cooperation of different groups of people who will facilitate and contribute to the process of growth and change.

Do you consider yourself a leader? You may not be the charismatic

Exhibit 17-6 Skills Inventory			
Skill Category	**Strength**	**Weakness**	**Unknown**
Leadership Skills			
Envision change	☐	☐	☐
Support an idea	☐	☐	☐
Handle criticism	☐	☐	☐
Planning	☐	☐	☐
Evaluation	☐	☐	☐
Teambuilding Skills			
Delegate	☐	☐	☐
Share a vision	☐	☐	☐
Conflict resolution	☐	☐	☐
Problem-solving	☐	☐	☐
Role-clarification	☐	☐	☐
Facilitate cooperation	☐	☐	☐
Facilitate group process	☐	☐	☐
Communication Skills			
Active listening	☐	☐	☐
Eliciting feedback	☐	☐	☐
Writing	☐	☐	☐
Formal presentation skills	☐	☐	☐
Informal presentation skills	☐	☐	☐
Follow-up	☐	☐	☐

type who speaks the word and leagues follow. Most of us aren't. But you most likely can adopt and adapt the skills to become a changemaker in the exhibit department. In the final chapter you will see how one exhibit manager drew on a diverse background of professional experience to facilitate growth, efficiency, and effectiveness in the exhibit department of a major Fortune 500 company. The techniques he used are common-sense, down-to-earth, people management ideas. As he likes to put it, in his four years in the department, he facilitated "evolution, not revolution."

18

Managing Growth:
A Case Study

"You can look at the guidelines written for your job and know what you *must* do. That's the minimum. Or you can look at the next level, of rules that say what you *can't* do. There's a lot in between. Do you stop at "you shall" or do you go all the way to "you shan't?""

Case studies are enormously useful for shedding the cold, hard light of reality on theories. This story about Ed Roberts' experience as Convention and Exhibits Manager for Caterpillar, Inc. does just that for the theories recommended in Chapter 17.

J. Edward Roberts spent 30 years at Caterpillar, Inc. where he held a wide variety of positions, ranging from sales training through advertising manager, to manager of Convention and Exhibits. Ed has worked closely with the Caterpillar dealer network and has served as dealer promotions representative. One highlight of Ed's career has been his participation in the news-making Caterpillar 94,000-square foot exhibit at the 1988 Con-Expo which was featured in many sales and marketing publications.

Ed claims much of his knowledge about managing growth and change was gained through his experience in the Navy, learning to plan amphibious operations. The basic guidelines, he'll tell you, are the same: know where you are going, know how to get there, and know how to motivate people to get the job done.

But he is quick to acknowledge that in his experience at Caterpillar, it was rarely a straight line from point A to point B. His reasons will most likely sound familiar. He didn't work in a vacuum, or with absolute control, but had to implement changes in a way that would bring the changemakers—the people responsible for supporting the work and getting the job done—along with him.

"If I had absolute control, it [change] would progress 1-2-3. But I didn't have absolute control—so I had to go here, then there, then there, then I made it to the same place, but I had brought others along with me."

He also knows that sometimes you set out for point B and find it nearly impossible to get there. But for him, that didn't diminish the value of the process. In this case study of Ed's experience at Caterpillar, you will see his vision for Caterpillar's Convention and Exhibits section, how he interpreted that into specific needs for growth and improvement, and his successes (and quite a few attempts that were not completely successful) at managing the changes in his four years at the job.

He describes the process as evolution not revolution, "I had to keep in mind at all times that marketing is a fluid state. I couldn't sit there and say definitely what was going to happen in the next 12 or 18 months. But I could have a pretty good idea, and then keep an open mind and adjust in order to do the best we could."

"Planning for growth and change isn't something you do once. It is something you do constantly, looking for opportunities to grow and identifying them as you go along."

GAINING PERSPECTIVE THROUGH PROGRAM ASSESSMENT

Ed's vision for the section grew out of his knowledge of some of the company history (he'd been with Caterpillar for 30 years), along with the corporate reorganization that put him in the position of managing conventions and exhibits. First, a bit of background.

In the glory days from the 50s to the 70s Caterpillar took orders faster than they could produce equipment. Often, their plants ran at 110% capacity and they didn't need to use trade shows for prospecting. As a result, trade shows were viewed at Caterpillar (as they were by many corporations during that time) as a chance to see old friends, maintain the company image, and support the industry.

But two dramatic shifts at Caterpillar changed that. They moved into new, smaller, more diverse products, and actually doubled their product line. That, combined with the depression in the construction industry of 1985, forced a number of companies in that industry toward some changes. Now, they needed to prospect.

At the same time, the way that the exhibits function was handled at Caterpillar also changed dramatically. In the past, the Show and Exhibit section for machine sales had one supervisor, and five staff people, to handle shows for three of seven Caterpillar division subsidiaries. The other division subsidiaries operated autonomously and handled their show participation from within their own organizations with a part-time or full-time person responsible for the function.

As part of an effort to group "like" activities together, the offerings of the Show and Exhibit group were expanded to act as a service group for the trade show participation of all divisions, and their name was changed to the Convention and Exhibits section. Once they decided to attend a show, each division could go to the Convention and Exhibits group for logistical support. Convention and Exhibits would plan and organize Caterpillar's participation in the show, design and build the exhibit, facilitate product displays, assure appropriate graphics were selected or created, handle transportation, installation/dismantle, and return shipment of the exhibit.

For some divisions (about half) shows were carried in the budget of the Convention and Exhibits section. For others, participation came out of their own divisional budgets.

That created two primary challenges for Ed as he was asked to manage this new group. First, was overcoming the glad-handing image that the group had in the past. "This was extremely important because if managers perceived shows as merely entertainment functions, when their budgets were cut, they certainly had a difficult time justifying that expenditure for 'entertainment.'" (Interestingly, the name of the group was changed from Shows and Exhibits to Convention and Exhibits because "Shows" had become synonymous with "Parties.")

Moving Forward: A New Vision for the Program

The second challenge involved getting division managers to trust his group enough to solicit their help, and trust their guidance and participation. This formed the vision for growth and change: To turn the new Convention and Exhibit section (and the perception of the section among divisional managers) into a sales support group that facilitated prospecting for new business efficiently, effectively, and economically.

To put this information in perspective, we have to first review how the Convention and Exhibits section was structured. Ed, as the section manager, worked with the divisions to set a course for all show participation. He also helped to facilitate organization and direction for multi-division shows.

In the section, five Convention and Exhibits reps, who reported to Ed, managed the logistics of show participation. They were each assigned a group of shows for which they were responsible for getting the exhibit designed, constructed, shipped, installed, dismantled, and returned to inventory in their warehouse.

One of the great successes of the group at large, was that in the course of four years they, as a team, were able to double the number of shows they handled for divisions without increasing the number of reps in the section. Were they just overworked? No, they accomplished this by facilitating efficiencies in their operation.

From Vision to Action: Defining the Needs

If you recall, the Level I assessment chart from Chapter 17 is designed to identify areas within the exhibits program that need improved efficiencies. Although Ed did not use this chart, nor did he uncover the needs all in a single flash of inspiration, the chart will be completed here to identify how it would be used in this situation. Ed's chart would look something like the one in Exhibit 18-1.

From these general needs, new and even more specific needs evolved. For example, one of the points on the chart is building management support to get divisional managers to trust the exhibits section more and request their services more. Ed identified that in order to do that, the convention and exhibit section had to be ready and able to meet all of those requests, which led to rethinking and reorganization of their exhibit properties and graphics.

By making the very specific operations more efficient, they were able to be more responsive to needs, which was a key component to building trust. The following list summarizes the needs identified. In section II you will get an in-depth look at Ed's approach to making the changes required to meet those identified needs.

- Goal-setting: Since show goals drove the entire logistics planning function, they had to be set 18-24 months in advance. That required Ed to motivate the divisions to plan ahead. You will see how he facilitated that change.

- Budgeting: This is closely connected to goal-setting. An entirely new procedure for planning show budgets had to be implemented. It required negotiating across management lines.

- Educating management: Managers at a variety of levels within the divisions and in the Convention and Exhibits group were included in education strategies. While no formal program for education was designed, a very specific strategy was carried out.

- Increasing support to divisions: Part of getting the divisions to trust them was being efficient enough to handle anything that came their way, and to do it well. Structure and departmental staff management was a key here.

- Improving staffer performance: When the role of trade shows changes dramatically, and exhibit staffers are not informed, that gap can be deadly.

Exhibit 18-1 Efficiency Evaluation Checklist

Function	Satis-factory	Needs Work	Why
Goal-setting		√	Not planning far enough in advance to realize cost and logistics efficiencies.
Budgeting		√	Not budgeting by objective; planning budgets based on what was set previous year. Realizing cost overruns regularly.
Management support		√	Need to change perception of the role of trade shows at many levels. Want to build trust from divisional managers to use Convention and Exhibits section more.
Staff performance		√	Staff working the exhibit need to be informed of the new role of trade shows and to identify how they will contribute to the success of show participation more directly.
Measuring results		√	Measurement of results is random when existent at all. Need to implement more standard and objective forms of measurement to demonstrate effective contributions of show participation.

Here, Ed outlines his program for informing staffers throughout a variety of divisions, and a few lessons learned along the way.

- Measuring results: Here Ed knew the gap between the ideal and reality. He aimed at one level, landed significantly below it, but saw a great deal of value in working towards the ideal.

SIX STRATEGIES FOR IMPLEMENTING CHANGE

"The great challenge was finding out a way to get it done within the system. The best way to facilitate change is to get people to experience the advantages so that they are more willing to support them."

Strategy #1: Facilitating Change in Goal-Setting Procedures

Goal-setting and budgeting went together because goal-setting drove the budgeting process. Therefore, to make any changes in one required facilitating changes in the other.

One of the first things Ed identified was that goal-setting was going to have to begin much further in advance than it had. Divisional marketing managers were responsible for planning the strategy for show participation. The function of the Convention and Exhibits section was simply to implement that strategy. It would have been easy to complain about the fact that information didn't come in early enough to do an efficient job. Instead, Ed went to the divisional managers and worked to change the procedure. It was one of those efforts that landed clearly between the "you shall" and "you shan't."

He began in March for the following year. Since each division decided on which shows they would attend, the first step was to send a list to divisional marketing managers of *all* possible shows that he thought the corporation would be interested in for the following year. By show, he listed the divisions that he thought would be interested in participating with a "here's what I think you should take a look at" implication. The theme here, stated implicitly and directly, was "we're going to all get together on this."

He followed that with a form requesting some planning on the part of the divisional managers. The signal here: "It's time to get serious about this," He asked divisional managers to identify, for each show in which they planned to participate, their:

- Objectives for the show
- Goals for show participation
- Products and services they planned to display
- Plans for staffing assignments

Giving them about six to eight weeks to work on these, he then planned to meet with the top marketing person in each group in May to walk through the planning process and to discuss their plans. The quality of input varied among divisions, but with the advanced worksheet, Ed found that a good majority had at least taken time to think through the four elements he identified. And some would come to the meeting with their strategies planned and written out.

Conversely, some people just couldn't see the value in spending time on this planning. But Ed says that having the corporate culture behind him helped a great deal. Caterpillar is very strong on management by objectives. So, there was no startling change of philosophy to get this done. It was just a matter of executing the philosophy that existed—which became the challenge.

However, goal-setting procedures were essential because they gave order to every other component of the process. Then the reps in the Convention and Exhibits section could be planning and designing the show by objective, not by the most recent idea called in.

Strategy #2: Facilitating Change in Budgeting Procedures

Budgeting procedures rode right on the coattails of goal-setting. What Ed discovered upon joining the group was that many divisions were randomly setting total show budgets based only on what they had spent the previous year. One result of this was a great deal of budget overruns, because time had not been taken to establish exact participation costs.

Also, managers were uncomfortable with the exhibit function when they were presented with voluminous budgets for which there were no justifications. With random budgeting comes random budget cuts: "Just cut 10% out of that budget." They didn't realize that cutting 10% out of a budget might mean cutting a division's ability to participate in a specific show and promote to an identified target market. No one had spelled that out for them. Thus, with the changes, budgeting became a useful resource for educating management about shows. That will be discussed in the next section.

To alleviate this problem, Ed moved to zero-based budgeting procedures. First, goals for show participation were outlined. Then requirements for meeting those goals were identified (for example the products displayed, the amount of booth space required, the amount of existing structure and graphics that could be used along with what would have to be produced, etc.). Finally, once the requirements were established, a cost was identified for each item and *then* total show budget *estimates* were calculated. Whether the budget came out of his group, or from the division, Ed took responsibility to create budget estimates for them.

With goals set and resource needs identified, he estimated costs for the division's "wish list" for each show they wanted to attend. Then the negotiations began. When the budgets came out of the divisions, they would inevitably plan for a more ambitious project than their own budget warranted. This procedure helped them to identify the potential overruns early on. By bringing this back to the division, Ed got them involved in the decision-making process. They could find ways to swing the budget (look for other resources for the money, cost-share with other divisions, go to their own management for a budget increase approval) or make their own decisions about where to cut.

> "The disadvantages to creative financing of shows within divisions is that you can lose the ability to say, 'How much did we really spend on that show?' The costs can get scattered all over the place and then you don't know the reality."

Ed is adamant that the corporation ought to have a good idea of what they are spending and know whether it's worthwhile. Some of that control gets lost in the creative budgeting strategies that are nearly inevitable in a process like this one.

Even when the budget comes out of Ed's group, there are occasions where the division's ideas are too ambitious and they must negotiate changes. Here, too, there are times when they will find the money in their own budget to support a program they feel is worthwhile. Again, Ed is faced with not knowing the actual costs of the show. "That's one of those gaps between theory and practice that I could never close," he said.

But the actual process of reviewing the budget became one of the best opportunities for educating management and building support.

Strategy #3: Educating Management

Educating management about the potential for trade show participation is one of the most far-reaching and significant changes that had to be made in the program. He was coming out of an era when "shows" and "parties" were synonymous words. While there was no single strategy for implementing this change, Ed identified a variety of techniques that helped to make forward strides in this area.

Using the Existing System. Monthly reports were a system ingrained in Caterpillar procedures. Those monthly reports were circulated throughout all marketing areas, including international marketing. Ed recognized the channel for telling people about show participation. More specifically, he identified the products that had been displayed at shows that month, the leads generated, and the sales booked. From one show, he was able to track eight product sales back to the show within two months. He had a very strong supporter in that product's division.

> "Monthly reports were one of the major ways of promoting show results to get out of the 'fun and games' arena and into identifying some major benefits of participating."

Eating Lunch. Lunch in the cafeteria became one of Ed's favorite opportunities to talk about the programs. "There is so much opportunity there to sit down with reps from different divisions or departments and talk about what you are doing," he commented. "In this situation you need to have successes to discuss, literally on the tip of your tongue. This doesn't happen overnight," he says. "You have to use every opportunity available."

Briefings. When new department heads came in they often asked for briefings by all groups to update them on departmental activities. More than a briefing, Ed saw here the opportunity to sell a key manager on the most recent examples of the value of show participation. He often found an opportunity to sit down with various managers two or three times a year at their request to discuss shows.

Understanding Priorities. If you are looking for opportunities to discuss trade shows with management, wait until it's a high-priority area on their agenda; before a show while you are planning for participation, or after a show to discuss what happened. A key opportunity is during the budgeting process.

One way to facilitate this is to get the divisional managers involved in selling programs to their own management. One group for a major show had planned in some extras that would blow the budget. Ed forced that group to go to their management and give him the opportunity to say whether or not that could be done. That prior time, he says, can and should be used to pre-condition all of the people involved about what to expect and why. By forcing the group to get approval, they had to stick their necks out a little bit and have more ownership in the process. And the more people you can get to help sell the program, the easier it will be.

He operated the same way himself when proposing budgets to his managers. He always broke it down by the groups that were served. He found that managers might look at one huge lump sum and then look at you as if you were out of your mind. But when you review the expenses group by group, you are doing a significant education job. Then you can ask them to participate with you in determining where cuts they are demanding should be made. For example, one group might be promoting to two different key markets at these two shows. By cutting out one of the shows we prevent them from promoting to one of the markets. Ask him or her, "Which market do you think they should not promote to?" The reality of budget cutting hits them.

> "Now management has to start looking, not simply at dollars, but at what activity would be cut out of the process. Of course the effect of this depends on the type of boss you have. They might just say, 'I know it's important, but this is all of the money you are going to get, so see what you can do with it.' Even when that's the case, at least they are aware of the choices you were forced to make. And it identifies for the people you are serving that you've tried."

Exhibit Reviews. Prior to every show, the Convention and Exhibits section rep set up the exhibit in Caterpillar's exhibits warehouse, and invited divisional managers down for a preview. This facilitated their input and feedback on the exhibit and product displays *before* they arrived (or even left) for the show.

It also opened channels of communication between management and reps. "At this point the divisional management becomes a part of the process, " Ed explained. "Many times when they see the exhibit it is the first time they really think about it. Most people aren't visualizers and don't know the exhibitry enough to be able to visualize. Doing this about two months in advance increases the level of involvement significantly."

Educating management provided an ongoing challenge in the program. But the objective at all times was to let them know that participation was not random and without forethought, but based on pre-set objectives with expectations for specific results.

> "It makes it a lot easier for upper management to accept what you are trying to do when it looks like common sense and not something that came out of the blue."

Strategy #4: Increasing Support to Divisions

To grow from being able to support 30 shows a year to 60 shows a year, the Convention and Exhibits group facilitated a host of efficiency-related changes. This required that those reps, many of whom had been used to handling shows a certain way, had to be willing or motivated to participate in the changes.

Most significant among them was going from using exclusively custom-designed exhibitry, to employing a system structure. This may seem like a fairly insignificant change, but actually represented a major shift away from procedures they were used to and comfortable with. It also required a shift in attitude about the perceived image represented by system structures.

Ed began to see some benefits of merging system structures with the custom pieces they had in inventory to expand the number of shows they could support. The steps he followed in facilitating this change provide an example.

Introducing the New Idea

Before, the reps were very committed to producing something special for divisions and their show participation, which typically meant a custom-built structure. Part of their mindset was that using a system structure was only going halfway. It wasn't the very best they could offer. Ed tried to explain how the blend of custom and system components would allow them to do a lot more for the divisions for the same amount of money. That the blend could take them a long way.

Then, when they resisted he didn't make a mandate from on high. Since the exhibit system had already been purchased for a large show, he simply found opportunities to use the system materials himself. He was planning for a show where he knew a particular custom structure would work perfectly. But a rep came in with a late show request that required the same structure. He told the rep to go ahead and use the custom structure, and then created a copy of it with the system components for his own use. For just a bit more money they had two exhibits to accomplish both tasks. Then, he says, it wasn't long before they started seeing how it would make their job a whole lot easier, and it looked just as good.

Then they started using them a little at a time to build structures themselves. The reps started coming up with their own ideas of where the system structure could be used.

But the structure management wasn't the only area where Ed used techniques to build morale among the reps in his group. Here are a few more:

Help Without Telling. Rather than educate from behind his desk, Ed went out with every rep in the department to at least one show a year. That, he says, is where they really work. He had to see them in their environment to evaluate how they were doing and offer direction.

For example, he could see that the reps were frustrated by Caterpillar's purchasing policies because they often had to purchase services on-site when it's impossible to follow company procedures and fill out a purchase order to request a check. Ed observed that problem at shows and worked with the purchasing department to get enough freedom for the reps to do their job, while allowing purchasing the accountability they needed.

Give Them Freedom and Express Their Value. Assigning show schedules was a good example of the balance between managing the effort, and yet giving the reps freedom and autonomy in their jobs. Rather than just randomly assign shows to reps Ed got them involved in the process. They each took a schedule of shows and indicated their preferences on a basis of 1-10 (1 being their preference, 10 shows they absolutely don't want, and 5 indicating it didn't make a difference).

Says Ed "I had one rep who loved to go to New York City when the Gucci sales were on and hated farm shows. I had another who loved farm shows and would only go to New York if he was the last man on the list who could do the job. It makes their jobs just a little bit easier if they can have some choice and control over where they go. They became part of the process of assigning shows, but they weren't telling me which shows they were and weren't going to handle. They hadn't taken complete control, but they had input and significant levels of control."

The goal of each step in the change and motivating process was to increase support for the divisions.

"The more we solved their problems, the more they relied on us and the more willing they were to take our advice."

Strategy #5: Facilitating Improvements in Staffer Performance

If getting management support and motivating reps was the key to success in program management, then managing the exhibit staffers was the key to succeeding out there on the show floor where it counted. Divisional sales managers selected the people who would be staffing the exhibit, many of whom came out of the old school of trade shows. A major effort had to be made here to educate staffers generally about the change in strategy for trade show participation, and to train them in selling skills and strategy specifically for the shows they were assigned to attend.

To facilitate this education process Ed worked with Diane Weintraub, President of Communique Exhibitor Education, Inc., to produce an educational program that every division could use to facilitate the training process.

The program included self-study materials and a video tape that staffers could use to prepare for small regional shows where there would be no Convention and Exhibits section representative. It included meeting leader's materials for the section reps to lead pre-show meetings when they would be on-site. It included a miniature staffer's guide that synopsized the new philosophy and purpose for trade show participation which every staffer would receive prior to show participation.

The materials went a long way toward educating the staffers, but hindsight being what it is, Ed has since realized a major flaw in his strategy. He planned to rely on his Convention and Exhibits representatives to conduct the pre-show meeting, at the show site, the day before the show, for all division representatives assigned to booth duty. He discovered that the strategy was correct, but the choice of facilitators was not.

The department reps had neither the skills, time, nor authority, to execute the pre-show meetings effectively, at every show. First, they were asked to be presenters, or meeting leaders, and had rarely had experience with that medium before. Second, they were often extremely busy just before the show assuring that the exhibit properties and products were up and running in time. Finally, they were offering directives about show participation to staffers over whom they had no authority.

Another key factor (and in many companies this is the toughest task) Ed realized that you also have to get the people who are going to work the show to acknowledge that they need to know something. Their attitude is often "I worked the show last year, why do I need to know something this year?"

In retrospect, Ed can see that the desire, expectation, and requirements for pre-show meetings had to come from within each division's management. When divisional managers see the need and buy into the concept of preparing the staff for peak performance at a show, then the rest of the team comes along. When management doesn't take the reins, the staffers' efforts are scattered and less directed.

> "Until management starts to ask for accountability from their people, they won't put as much emphasis on preparing for shows."

If you evaluate this function from the perspective of managing change, the area that was misdirected here was identifying the people involved in making the change happen. Ed had determined that the Convention and Exhibits reps could make the change happen. Actually, facilitating this change was dependent on the divisional managers' appreciation of the need and cooperation. That is part of the learning and changing process. You don't always hit the target right-on the first time. But the more often you can, the more effective you will be and that's where planning and creating your strategy for implementing change helps.

Finally, some changes will simply be too big to implement right away. For Ed, this was true in the area of measuring results.

Strategy #6: Measuring Results

Ed had a very clear vision of the lead-tracking function that, when put in place, would provide all of the information necessary to measure results and realistically demonstrate the value of show participation. In his "wish list" system, their dealers would receive leads immediately following the show. Four months later, his section would simultaneously contact the dealer and the prospects. They would learn from the dealer what had happened with the leads, and sales that resulted. They would also find out from the prospects if anyone from Caterpillar had contacted them, if they purchased products they had seen at the show, and whether they had purchased them from Caterpillar or from a competing company.

This process was to be repeated at eight months for those prospects who reported they hadn't purchased yet but still planned to, and for those who hadn't responded at the four-months survey. At ten months, a synopsis of the show was to be prepared, and the file closed.

All of this information would be cataloged on a computer and reports generated regularly. If he could do that and make some comparisons, he could determine clearly, the value of shows. It would help to overcome the attitude of the salespeople that on leads they closed, they knew about it before the show anyway, and on leads they lost that there really wasn't any value there in the first place. That, he knew, provided the best solid information from the show.

Unfortunately, this was one area where he hadn't been able to justify the investment to get the system approved and up and running. It was another theory vs. reality factor. In theory he knew what needed to be implemented. In reality, he often had to choose between supporting show participation for a division and implementing the system.

"It's kind of a catch-22," he explained. "You could say that we shouldn't be participating in the show anyway if we don't have that kind of justification and procedures for measuring what we are getting out of them. But it doesn't make sense to invest in a tool to measure shows at the expense of participating in them."

In retrospect, Ed can see that this is an essential item that should get departmental budget approval above and beyond show participation. His choice, however, in allocating resources, was to first become a department built on the reputation of supporting the divisions. He gave priority to tasks that would facilitate that kind of support. The reality was that to do so he compromised on his evaluation methods. But he didn't give up all together.

Ed found alternatives that would allow him to evaluate show performance less expensively. He regularly contracted with an independent show audience research firm for post-show surveys that measured specific components of their performance. He varied the studies to illustrate not only show success, but more specific areas for show improvement.

For example, for two shows he used a stop frame film that illustrated very clearly traffic flow in the exhibit, how visitors entered, flowed through the space, and most importantly how they were greeted (or ignored) by staffers. This type of evaluation helped to pave the way for changes to improve staffer performance.

But reflecting on the experience Ed saw a great deal of value in going through the process of trying to put a lead-tracking program in place.

> "When you have to compromise, as I did with the lead-tracking system, if you have considered a plan and done some work to incorporate it, at least you have made a conscious choice about where to put your resources. You are not excluding it out of ignorance.
>
> "And at least you have gone through the mental process, so that you can continue to watch for opportunities to get the funding or whatever its implementation takes. That exercise alone illustrates how serious it is. You've gained part of the ground even if you haven't gone all the way."

These days, with his work in the Convention and Exhibits section behind him for the most part, Ed can see that while he was there his vision about what could be accomplished expanded significantly. Being immersed in the trade show industry, attending conferences, reading, learning from other exhibit managers and industry professionals, broadened his understanding of the process.

He has a larger vision now, but along with it he sees greater obstacles. Trade shows, he theorizes, are just one part of the big marketing picture. Managers should see each component—advertising, direct mail, PR, trade shows—in perspective and develop a program by which you can determine for each specific function or goal, which media would best accomplish it. Sometimes trade shows aren't the best place to put your resources. But each medium is rarely viewed in comparison to other media relative to its ability to accomplish specific marketing communications goals.

And this "vision" raises its own host of political concerns. He has observed, not just at Caterpillar but in most companies, that managers tend to stick with their own areas and not look beyond. It would take very strong leadership on the part of upper level management to get the job done. It would take someone who could invest the time to research and illustrate benefits of working within a new system over staying with the existing system.

Finally, he sees that since there is no perfect system, managers will continually change the structure to eliminate the existing problems, only to face a new set of problems.

He predicts that someday a manager will determine that more efficiencies can be realized when divisions have autonomous control over the trade show function within that group, and a reorganization will put the old structure back in place. That's not necessarily wrong. It's essential to strive for what will work best today. Changes are inevitable. Managing them is the challenge.

APPENDIX: Resources for Show Information

Show Directories and Listings

Exhibitor Magazine
745 Marquette Bank Building
Rochester, MN 55901
507/289-6556

Trade Shows and Exhibits Schedule
Successful Meetings Magazine
633 Third Avenue
New York, NY 10017
212/986-4800

Trade Show Week Data Book
12233 West Olympic Blvd.
Suite 236
Los Angeles, CA 90064
213/826-5696

Trade Show Week Newsletter
12233 West Olympic Blvd.
Suite 236
Los Angeles, CA 90064
213/826-5696

Trade Show and Professional Exhibits Directory
Gale Research
Book Tower
Department 77746
Detroit, MI 48227-0748
313/961-2242

Research and Statistics

B.R. Blackmarr & Assoc.
2515 McKinney Ave. LB17
Dallas, TX 75201
214/922-9030

Exhibit Surveys, Inc.
7 Hendrickson Ave.
Red Bank, NJ 07701
201/741-3170

The Trade Show Bureau
1660 Lincoln St.
Suite 2080
Denver, CO 80264
303/860-7626

Associations, Educational Forums, and Educational Materials

Health Care Exhibitors Association
Suite 500-D
5775 Peachtree-Dunwoody Rd.
Atlanta, GA 30324
404/252-3663

International Exhibitors Association
5103-B Backlick Road
Annandale, VA 22003-6085
703/941-3725

National Association of Exposition Managers
719 Indiana Ave., Suite 300
Indianapolis, IN 46202
317/638-6236

Exhibitor Show
Hall/Erickson, Inc.
150 Burlington Avenue
Clarendon Hills, IL 60514
312/850-7779

Communique Exhibitor Education, Inc.
995 N. Collier Blvd.
Marco Island, FL 33937
813/394-3333

Skyline Displays, Inc.
12345 Portland Avenue South
Burnsville, MN 55337-2982
612/894-3240

Publications

Exhibitor Magazine
745 Marquette Bank Building
Rochester, MN 55904
507/289-6556

Trade Show and Exhibits Manager
1150 Yale St., Suite 12
Santa Monica, CA 90403
213/828-1309

Trade Show Week
12233 West Olympic Blvd.
Suite 236
Los Angeles, CA 90064
213/826-5696

Footnotes to Chapters

Chapter 1
Footnotes

1. Below, Patrick, J., et al. *The Executive Guide to Strategic Planning*, Jossey Bass Publishers, San Francisco, 1988, pp. 9–12.
2. This calculation was created by Exhibit Surveys, Inc., founder Richard K. Swandby, and is considered an industry standard today.
3. Trade Show Bureau Research Report #21. "Audience Characteristics - Regional and National Trade Shows, May 1984.

Chapter 2
Footnotes

1. The original research and creation of these calculations was done by Richard K. Swandby, President of Exhibit Surveys, Inc., Red Bank, New Jersey.
2. Ibid.
3. Trade Show Bureau Study #27. "The Effect of Advertising on Booth Traffic," conducted for the IFT Food Expo by Exhibit Surveys, Inc., in October 1985.

    Note that the magazine selected for the study *Food Technology* is read regularly by roughly 70% of the show attendees which is an unusually high show audience readership. Typically it would be necessary to advertise in more than one publication to get the breadth of audience coverage.
4. From Exhibit Surveys research.
5. The research and Cost per Visitor Reached figures are calculated on a regular basis by Exhibit Surveys, Inc., Red Bank, New Jersey.
6. From the "Trade Show Exhibit Cost Analysis," conducted by Exhibit Surveys, Inc. for The Trade Show Bureau, 1987.

Chapter 3
Footnotes

1. Swandby, R.K. "Tracking Exhibit Performance." *Exhibitor Magazine*. Vol. 2, No. 5, 1983.
2. For more detailed information on exhibit graphics, see the following articles in *Exhibitor Magazine*.

    McMillan, Charlie. "The Basics of Graphics Techniques—Parts one and two." *Exhibitor Magazine*. January 1989 and February 1989.

3. For more information on readability of exhibit graphics see the following article in *Exhibitor Magazine.*

   McMillan, Charlie. "Exhibit Ergonomics." *Exhibitor Magazine,* Vol. 4, No. 15, August 1, 1985.

4. Knight, Lee. "The Rise of Exhibit Systems." *Exhibitor Magazine,* Vol. 6, No. 5, May 1987.

5. Knight, Lee. *Annual Buyer's Guide to Exhibits.* Exhibitor Publications, Inc. Annual

6. "How is the Exhibit Dollar Spent?" *Trade Show Bureau Research Report #2030.* November 1986.

Chapter 4
Footnotes

1. For more information on using billboards see the following article:

   "Marlow, Paula. "Using Billboards for Big Impact," *Exhibitor Magazine,* Sept. 1988, p. 34.

2. Christman, Christine. "Direct Response Exhibit Marketing," *Exhibitor Magazine,* January, 1987, p. 31.

3. NAEM Labor Guide. National Association of Exposition Managers, 1986.

4. This information is reprinted with permission from *The Checklist for Evaluating Exhibit Staffers* published by Communique Exhibitor Education, Inc.

Chapter 5
Footnotes

1. For more information on shipping options see the following article in *Exhibitor Magazine:* Chretien, Jim and Carol. "Exhibit Shipping: Six Options." *Exhibitor Magazine,* Vol. 3, No. 13, July 15, 1984.

2. Chretien, Jim and Carol. "Pros and Cons of Crating." *Exhibitor Magazine,* Vol. 3, No. 19, October 15, 1984.

3. For a detailed explanation of how shipping rates are calculated, see: Chretien, Jim and Carol. "Primer on Shipping Rates." *Exhibitor Magazine,* Vol. 3, No. 20, November 1, 1984.

4. Christman, Christine. "Literature vs. No Literature," *Exhibitor Magazine,* August, 1983.

Chapter 6
Footnotes

1. The United Press International Style Book is available from United Press International, 220 E. 42nd. St., New York, NY 10017.

2. Christman, Christine. "Product Space: One Less Random Decision," *Exhibitor Magazine.* Vol. 4, No. 10.

3. The information here is taken from the following article, used with permission: Weintraub, Diane K. "Who Should Staff Your Booth?" *Exhibitor Magazine.* Vol. 7, No. 1. January, 1988, pp. 37–38.

Chapter 7
Footnotes

1. Trade Show Bureau Research Report #2050. "Exhibitors—Their Trade Show Practices," July 1988.
2. Knight, Lee and Gade, Chris. "The Rise of Exhibit Systems," *Exhibitor Magazine.* May 1987, p. 24.
3. Knight, Lee. *Illustrated Buyer's Guide to Exhibits.* Exhibitor Publications, Inc., 1986.

   For further reading on selecting portable exhibits, see the following *Exhibitor Magazine* article: Chaffee, Hal, "Tips on Purchasing a Portable Display," *The Exhibitor Magazine,* Feb. 1988.

Chapter 8
Footnotes

1. Neumann, Michelle, "Staging Techniques: The Key to Better Work Flow," *Exhibitor Magazine.* Vol. 5, No. 2, 1986, pp. 13–14.
2. The Trade Show Bureau, Study Number 3. "The Trade Show Audience," April, 1979.

Chapter 9
Footnotes

1. Trade Show Bureau Research Report #2050, "Exhibitors, Their Trade Show Practices," July, 1988.

Chapter 10
Footnotes

1. James, Frank. "Trade Show Quarterback." *The Chicago Tribune.* September 24, 1989, pp. 1 and 8.
2. Christman, Chris. "Working with Unions," *Exhibitor Magazine.* January, 1987.
3. National Association of Exposition Managers. "The NAEM Labor Guide." February, 1986.
4. Kern, Gayle. "11 Steps to a Successful Variance." *Exhibitor Magazine.* November, 1983.
5. Neumann, Michelle. "Making Black & White Sense Out of Blueprints." *Exhibitor Magazine,* November, 1984.
6. Christman, Chris. "Working with Unions."
7. *Ibid.*
8. *Ibid.* Reprinted with permission.

Chapter 11
Footnotes

1. Trade Show Bureau Research Report #2010, "Exhibit Management Practices," July, 1986.
2. Knight, Lee. "Six Ways to Cut Exhibit Costs," *Exhibitor Magazine,* Vol. 1, #10, 1982.

Chapter 12
Footnotes

1. Virga, Patricia H., Ph.D. *The NMA Handbook of Management.* Prentice Hall, Englewood Cliffs, NJ, 1987, pp. 36–37.
2. Trade Show Bureau Study #2050, "Exhibitors—Their Trade Show Practices," July 1988.
3. *Ibid.*
4. *Ibid.*

Chapter 14
Footnotes

1. Kern, Gayle. "Sandoz Swat Team," *Exhibitor Magazine,* October, 1985.
2. Trade Show Bureau Research Report #4000, "Exhibit Personnel, A Behavioral Study."
3. Trade Show Bureau Research Report #2050, "Exhibitors—Their Trade Show Practices," July, 1988.

Chapter 15
Footnotes

1. Culbertson, Lize. "Triad's Portable Option to a Custom Exhibit," *Exhibitor Magazine,* August 1988.

Chapter 16
Footnotes

1. Trade Show Bureau Research Report #2040. "The Exhibit Management Function—Perceptions of Exhibit Management and Marketing Executives," November, 1986.

Chapter 17
Footnotes

1. Peters, Tom. *Thriving on Chaos,* Harper & Row, New York, 1987, p. 566.
2. Aburdeen, Patricia and Naisbitt, John. *Reinventing the Corporation,* Warner Books, New York, 1985, p. 83.
3. Peters, Tom. *Thriving on Chaos,* p. 484.
4. *Ibid.,* p. 468.
5. Waterman, Robert. *The Renewal Factor.* Bantam Books, New York, 1987, p. 6.
6. Walton, Richard. *Innovating to Compete,* Jossey-Bass Publishers, San Francisco, 1987, p. 224.

Index